THE SUMERIANS

THE SUMERIANS

THEIR HISTORY,

CULTURE,

AND CHARACTER

Samuel Noah Kramer

 THE UNIVERSITY OF CHICAGO PRESS

Chicago & London

THE UNIVERSITY OF CHICAGO PRESS, CHICAGO 60637
The University of Chicago Press, Ltd., London

ISBN: 0-226-45237-9 (clothbound); 0-226-45238-7 (paperbound)

Library of Congress Catalog Card Number: 63-11398

89 88 87 86 85   9 10 11 12

THE SUMERIANS

THEIR HISTORY,

CULTURE,

AND CHARACTER

Samuel Noah Kramer

 THE UNIVERSITY OF CHICAGO PRESS

Chicago & London

THE UNIVERSITY OF CHICAGO PRESS, CHICAGO 60637
The University of Chicago Press, Ltd., London

© 1963 by The University of Chicago. All rights reserved
Published 1963
Printed in the United States of America

ISBN: 0-226-45237-9 (clothbound); 0-226-45238-7 (paperbound)

Library of Congress Catalog Card Number: 63-11398

89 88 87 86 85   9 10 11 12

To the
UNIVERSITY OF PENNSYLVANIA
and its
UNIVERSITY MUSEUM

PREFACE

The year 1956 saw the publication of my book *From the Tablets of Sumer*, since revised, reprinted, and translated into numerous languages under the title *History Begins at Sumer*. It consisted of twenty-odd disparate essays united by a common theme—"firsts" in man's recorded history and culture. The book did not treat the political history of the Sumerian people or the nature of their social and economic institutions, nor did it give the reader any idea of the manner and method by which the Sumerians and their language were discovered and "resurrected." It is primarily to fill these gaps that the present book was conceived and composed.

The first chapter is introductory in character; it sketches briefly the archeological and scholarly efforts which led to the decipherment of the cuneiform script, with special reference to the Sumerians and their language, and does so in a way which, it is hoped, the interested layman can follow with understanding and insight.

The second chapter deals with the history of Sumer from the prehistoric days of the fifth millennium to the early second millennium B.C., when the Sumerians ceased to exist as a political entity. As far as I know, it presents the fullest and most detailed treatment of Sumer's political history available to date. Because of the fragmentary, elusive, and at times far from trustworthy character of the sources, not a few of the statements in this chapter are based on conjecture and surmise, and may turn out to be true only in part or even to be entirely false. To help the reader make his own judgments and decisions in the more crucial and doubtful cases, the various kinds of source material at the scholar's disposal are outlined and evaluated at the beginning of the chapter and their shortcomings, handicaps, and pitfalls pointed out.

The third chapter treats the social, economic, legal, and technological aspects of Sumerian city life. Sketchy as it is, because of the relative dearth and obscurity of the pertinent sources, it could hardly have been written at all were it not for the very recent contributions of Diakonoff, Falkenstein, and Civil, the three scholars who have done so much to illuminate one aspect or another of this area of research.

Chapters iv and v treat Sumerian religion and literature, the two areas of Sumerian culture to which I have devoted almost all my scholarly career. While they include, therefore, much that is found in my earlier publications, these chapters give a fuller and more comprehensive survey of the available material than has hitherto been possible, not to mention the numerous additions and corrections that are introduced in the cited translations.

Chapters vi and vii, concerned with Sumerian education and character, are my own "favorites," if an author can be permitted to have favorites. Here are two aspects of Sumerian culture of which practically nothing was known until quite recently, but which, as the two chapters show, can now be sketched and treated in considerable detail. In the chapter on education, for example, will be found four Sumerian essays dealing with school life, which were almost totally unknown only fifteen years ago. Chapter vii tries a comparatively new approach in Oriental studies: it attempts to isolate, analyze, and assess the inner motives and drives which helped to create—and destroy—Sumerian civilization.

Chapter viii sketches what may be termed the "legacy" of Sumer to the world and its culture. Beginning with a review of the give-and-take between the Sumerians and the other peoples of the ancient Near East, it continues with a summary of some of the more obvious facets of modern life which may go back to Sumerian roots. It concludes with a sketch of a number of theological, ethical, and literary ideas of the Sumerians which seem to have their parallels in the Bible—the book which played so large a role in Western culture—and which point to a far more intimate connection between the ancient Hebrews and Sumerians than has been suspected.

Finally, there are the Appendixes, especially prepared for those readers who prefer going to the original sources whenever possible; they include translations of a number of the more important documents utilized in the chapter on history, as well as several miscellaneous items which are of special interest to a book on Sumer and the Sumerians.

The work is dedicated to the University of Pennsylvania and its University Museum. This may seem rather unusual and unorthodox, but the fact is that were it not for these two institutions, this book could never have been written. Not only have the university administration and faculty encouraged my researches in every way, in spite of their rather remote and esoteric character, but the University Museum and its Babylonian Collection provided me with much of the original source material on which this book is based. Its dedication to these two institutions is therefore but a token of my deep and heartfelt gratitude to all the individuals connected with them who in one way or another were helpful to me and my Sumerological research throughout the years.

I also wish to express my thanks to the Department of Antiquities of the Republic of Turkey and to the Director of the Archaeological Museum in Istanbul for generously making it possible for me to utilize the Sumerian literary tablets in the Istanbul Museum of the Ancient Orient. To the two curators of the tablet collection of this museum, Muazzez Çiğ and Hatice Kizilyay, I am particularly grateful for their unsparing and ungrudging co-operation, which has been so fruitful for Sumerological research. I am also deeply indebted to the Directorate of Antiquities of the Republic of Iraq for its generous co-operation on numerous occasions. I owe a very special debt of gratitude to the Friedrich-Schiller University of Jena, in East Germany, which has made it possible for me to study the Sumerian literary tablets in the Hilprecht Collection, in co-operation with its assistant curator Inez Bernhardt. To Cyril J. Gadd, formerly of the British Museum, now professor emeritus of the School of Oriental and African Studies, I wish to express my thanks for generously putting at my disposal his copies of the Sumerian literary documents from Ur, to which he has devoted so much time and effort. Finally thanks are due to the Academy of Sciences of the U.S.S.R. and the Pushkin Museum for making possible the study and publication of a tablet inscribed with two Sumerian elegies.

To the American Council of Learned Societies, I give my heartfelt thanks for my first fellowship, which enabled me to go to Iraq in 1929–30. To the John Simon Guggenheim Memorial Foundation and the American Philosophical Society, I wish to stress, as I have in other writings, the very special debt I owe; they were "friends in need" during a crucial period in my scholarly career. And this is a fitting opportunity to mention my debt to William Foxwell Albright, who spoke warmly of my researches—still in their early stages—to the American Philosophical Society, although he and I had then never met. In recent years, the Bollingen Foundation has been most generous with a series of fellowships which have enabled me to obtain at least a minimum of scientific and clerical assistance. The Barth Foundation, too, was of some help in this respect; it provided a grant which enabled me to work for a time in the Hilprecht Collection of the Friedrich-Schiller University.

Let me close by expressing my thanks to my former assistant, Edmund Gordon, whose excellent researches in Sumerian wisdom literature were available to me before and during their publication, and to Miguel Civil, my former assistant, who made available to me his researches in Sumerian lexicography, medicine, and technology. Jane Heimerdinger, a research assistant in the University Museum, prepared the Index and helped in numerous ways in the preparation of the manuscript and its arrangement. And my very special thanks to Gertrude Silver, a nimble and knowing typist exemplifying the Sumerian proverb: "A scribe whose hand moves as fast as the mouth, that's a scribe for you."

CONTENTS

ILLUSTRATIONS

PLATES

xiii

FIGURES

THE SUMERIANS

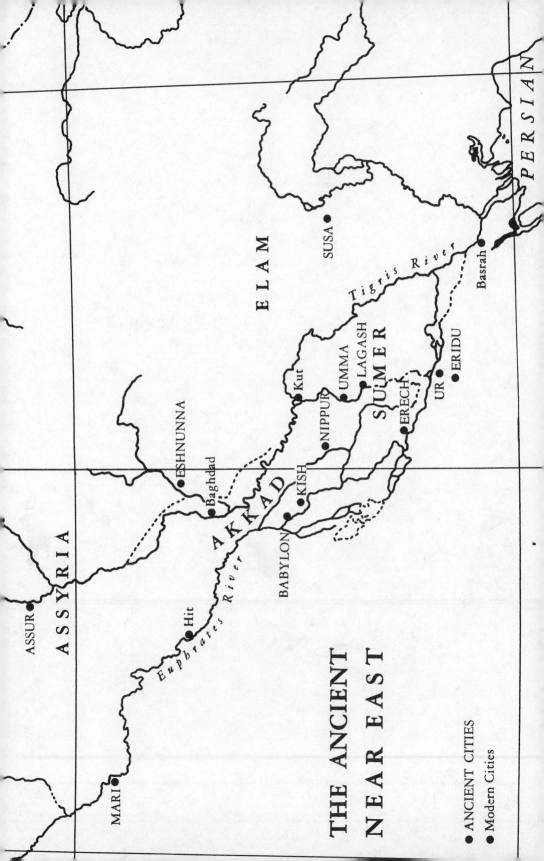

THE ANCIENT
NEAR EAST

● ANCIENT CITIES
● Modern Cities

PERSIAN

ELAM

SUSA ●

Tigris River

Basrah ●

UMMA ●
LAGASH ●
SUMER
ERIDU ●
ERECH ●
UR ●

Kut ●
NIPPUR ●

ESHNUNNA ●

Baghdad ●

AKKAD

KISH ●

BABYLON ●

ASSYRIA

ASSUR ●

Hit ●

Euphrates River

MARI ●

CHAPTER ONE

ARCHEOLOGY AND

DECIPHERMENT

Sumer, the land which came to be known in classical times as Babylonia, consists of the lower half of Mesopotamia, roughly identical with modern Iraq from north of Baghdad to the Persian Gulf. It has an area of approximately 10,000 square miles, somewhat larger than the state of Massachusetts. Its climate is extremely hot and dry, and its soil, left to itself, is arid, wind-swept, and unproductive. The land is flat and river-made, and therefore has no minerals whatever and almost no stone. Except for the huge reeds in the marshes, it had no trees for timber. Here, then, was a region with "the hand of God against it," an unpromising land seemingly doomed to poverty and desolation. But the people that inhabited it, the Sumerians, as they came to be known by the third millennium B.C., were endowed with an unusually creative intellect and a venturesome, resolute spirit. In spite of the land's natural drawbacks, they turned Sumer into a veritable Garden of Eden and developed what was probably the first high civilization in the history of man.

The people of Sumer had an unusual flair for technological invention. Even the earliest settlers had come upon the idea of irrigation, which made it possible for them to collect and channel the rich silt-laden overflow of the Tigris and Euphrates rivers and use it to water and fructify their fields and gardens. To make up for the dearth of minerals and stones, they learned to bake the river clay and mud, the supply of which was practically inexhaustible, into sickles, pots, plates, and jars. In lieu of the scarce building timber, they cut and dried the huge and plentiful marsh reeds, tied them into bundles or plaited them into mats, and with the

3

help of mud-plastering fashioned them into huts and byres. Later, the Sumerians invented the brick mold for shaping and baking the ubiquitous river clay and so had no more building-material problem. They devised such useful tools, skills, and techniques as the potter's wheel, the wagon wheel, the plow, the sailboat, the arch, the vault, the dome, casting in copper and bronze, riveting, brazing and soldering, sculpture in stone, engraving, and inlay. They originated a system of writing on clay, which was borrowed and used all over the Near East for some two thousand years. Almost all that we know of the early history of western Asia comes from the thousands of clay documents inscribed in the cuneiform script developed by the Sumerians and excavated by archeologists in the past hundred and twenty-five years.

The Sumerians were remarkable not only for their material progress and technological resourcefulness, but also for their ideas, ideals, and values. Clear-sighted, levelheaded, they took a pragmatic view of life and, within the limits of their intellectual resources, rarely confused fact with fancy, wish with fulfilment, or mystery with mystification. In the course of the centuries the Sumerian sages evolved a faith and creed which in a sense "gave unto the gods what was the gods'" and recognized and accepted as inevitable mortal limitations, especially helplessness in the face of death and divine wrath. On the material side they prized highly wealth and possessions, rich harvests, well-stocked granaries, folds and stalls filled with cattle, successful hunting in the plain, and good fishing in the sea. Spiritually and psychologically, they laid great stress on ambition and success, pre-eminence and prestige, honor and recognition. The Sumerian was deeply conscious of his personal rights and resented any encroachment on them, whether by his king, his superior, or his equal. No wonder that the Sumerians were the first to compile laws and law codes, to put everything down in "black and white" in order to avoid misunderstanding, misrepresentation, and arbitrariness.

While the Sumerians thus set a high value on the individual and his achievement, there was one overriding factor which fostered a strong spirit of co-operation among individuals and communities alike: the complete dependence of Sumer on irrigation for its well-being—indeed, for its very existence. Irrigation is a complicated process requiring communal effort and organization.

Canals had to be dug and kept in constant repair. The water had to be divided equitably among all concerned. To ensure this, a power stronger than the individual landowner or even the single community was mandatory: hence, the growth of governmental institutions and the rise of the Sumerian state. And since Sumer, because of the fertility of the irrigated soil, produced a vast surplus of grain but had practically no metals and very little stone and timber, the state was forced to obtain the material essential to its economy either through trade or military force. So that by the third millenium B.C., there is good reason to believe that Sumerian culture and civilization had penetrated, at least to some extent, as far east as India and as far west as the Mediterranean, as far south as ancient Ethiopia and as far north as the Caspian.

To be sure, all this was five thousand years ago and may seem of little relevance to the study of modern man and culture. But the fact is that the land of Sumer witnessed the origin of more than one significant feature of present-day civilization. Be he philosopher or teacher, historian or poet, lawyer or reformer, statesman or politician, architect or sculptor, it is likely that modern man will find his prototype and counterpart in ancient Sumer. Admittedly, the Sumerian origin of the modern offshoot can no longer be traced with directness or certainty: the ways of cultural diffusion are manifold, intricate, and complex, and its magic touch is subtle and evanescent. Even so, it is still apparent in a Mosaic law and a Solomonic proverb, in the tears of Job and a Jerusalem lament, in the sad tale of the dying man-god, in a Hesiodic cosmogony and a Hindu myth, in an Aesopic fable and a Euclidean theorem, in a zodiacal sign and a heraldic design, in the weight of a mina, the degree of an angle, the writing of a number. It is the history, social structure, religious ideas, educational practices, literary creations, and value motivations of the civilization created in ancient Sumer that will be briefly sketched in the following pages. First, however, a brief introductory review of the archeological "resurrection" of the Sumerians and their culture and of the decipherment of their script and language.

Remarkably enough, less than a century ago not only was nothing known of Sumerian culture; the very existence of a Sumerian people and language was unsuspected. The scholars and archeologists who some hundred years ago began excavating in Mesopotamia were looking not for Sumerians but for Assyrians; these were the people about whom they had considerable, though far from accurate, information from Greek and Hebrew sources. In the case of the Sumerians, however, there was no recognizable trace of the land, or its people and language, in the entire available Biblical, classical, and postclassical literature (or at least so it was thought; see pages 297–99 for the possibility that Sumer is mentioned in the Bible under a slightly variant form). The very name Sumer had been erased from the mind and memory of man for more than two thousand years. The discovery of the Sumerians and their language was quite unlooked for and came quite unexpectedly, and this rather irrelevant detail led to controversies which were responsible to some degree for the rather slow and troubled progress of Sumerological research.

The decipherment of Sumerian actually came about through the decipherment of Semitic Akkadian, known in earlier days as Assyrian or Babylonian, which, like Sumerian, is written in cuneiform script. And for Akkadian in turn, the key was found in Old Persian, an Indo-European tongue spoken by the Persians and Medes who ruled Iran during much of the first millennium B.C.; for some of the rulers of the Persian Achaemenid dynasty—the name goes back to Achaemenes, the founder of the dynasty who lived about 700 B.C.—found it politic to have their cuneiform inscriptions written in three languages: Persian, their own mother tongue; Elamite, an agglutinative language spoken by the natives of western Iran whom they conquered and subjugated; and Akkadian, the Semitic tongue spoken by the Babylonians and Assyrians. This group of trilingual cuneiform inscriptions, which was roughly the counterpart of the Egyptian Rosetta stone, did not come from Iraq but from Iran, although it is Iraq that is the home of cuneiform writing. And this brings us to the story of the explorations and excavations leading to the decipherment of the cuneiform script and the rediscovery of the Mesopotamian civilizations. It will here be sketched only briefly—it has been told repeatedly and in detail during the past decades (see Bibliography for specific works)—in order to give the reader at least a glimpse into the picture as a whole and at the same time to make a reverent and grateful bow to those long dead explorers, excavators, and armchair savants who unknowingly and unwittingly, and each in his own way, helped to make the writing of a book on the Sumerians possible.

The resurrection of the Assyrian, Babylonian, and Sumerian peoples, long buried under their desolate mounds, or tells, is an eloquent and magnificent achievement of nineteenth-century scholarship and humanism. To be sure there were isolated reports of ancient Mesopotamian ruins in the preceding centuries. In fact, as early as the twelfth century a rabbi of Tudela, in the kingdom of Navarre, by the name of Benjamin son of Jonah visited the Jews of Mosul and correctly identified the ruins in the vicinity of that city as those of ancient Nineveh, although his account was not published until the sixteenth century. On the other hand, the identification of Babylon was not made until 1616, when the Roman Pietro della Valle visited the mounds in the neighborhood of modern Hilla. This sharp-eyed traveler not only gave a remarkable description of the ruins of Babylon, but also brought back to Europe inscribed bricks that he had found there and at the mound now called by the Arabs Tal al Muqayyar, "the mound of pitch," which covers the ruins of ancient Ur; and thus it was that the first examples of cuneiform writing came to Europe.

Throughout the rest of the seventeenth and most of the eighteenth centuries numerous travelers, each with a different idea as to the identification of the various localities and ruins, journeyed to Mesopotamia, all trying to fit what they saw into the Biblical frame of reference. Between 1761 and 1767, there took place one of the most valuable of these expeditions, that of Carsten Niebuhr, a Danish mathematician who, besides copying at Persepolis the inscriptions which led to the decipherment of cuneiform, was the first to give his contemporaries a concrete idea of the ruins of Nineveh with the help of sketches and drawings. A few years later the French botanist A. Michaux sold to the Bibliothèque Nationale in Paris a boundary stone found near Ctesiphon, south of Baghdad, which proved to be the first really valuable inscription to come to Europe. Some absurd translations were made of this simple inscription, which actually contains the usual curse against anyone disturbing the boundary marker; one of these, for example, ran as follows: "The army of heaven will water us with vinegar in order to lavish on us the right remedies to effect our healing."

About this same time Abbé Beauchamp, vicar-general at Baghdad and correspondent of the Academy of Science, was making careful and accurate observations of what he saw around him, particularly in the ruins of Babylon; in fact, he actually made the first known archeological excavation in Mesopotamia, employing a few native workmen under the leadership of a master mason, in connection with a sculpture now generally known as the "Lion of Babylon," which can still be seen there by today's tourist. He was the first to describe parts of the Ishtar Gate, a beautiful replica of which can now be seen in the Near Eastern Section of the Berlin Museum; he also mentions finding solid cylinders covered with minute writings that he felt resembled the inscriptions from Persepolis. The memoirs of his travels, published in 1790, were translated almost immediately into English and German and created quite a sensation in the scholarly world.

One of the consequences of the spark kindled by Abbé Beauchamp was that the East India Company in London authorized their agents in Baghdad to do some archeological prospecting and reconnoitering. And so in 1811, we find Claudius James Rich, a resident for the East India Company in Baghdad, examining and mapping the ruins of Babylon and even excavating briefly, parts of them. Some nine years later, Rich turned up at Mosul, where he sketched and investigated the great mounds of ancient Nineveh. He collected many inscribed tablets, bricks, boundary stones, and cylinders, among them the famous Nebuchadnezzar and Sennacherib cylinders, carefully copied by his secretary Carl Bellino and sent to the epigrapher Grotefend for decipherment. Rich's collection formed the nucleus for the vast assemblage of Mesopotamian antiquities now in the British Museum.

Rich died in 1821 at the age of thirty-four, but his two memoirs on the ruins of Babylon with their typographical and inscriptional material lived on and may be said to mark the birth of Assyriology and the related cuneiform studies. He was followed by Robert Ker Porter who made accurate artistic reproductions of a number of Mesopotamian ruins, as well as a plan of the entire area of the ruins of Babylon. In 1828 Robert Mignan excavated briefly in the ruins of Babylon, where Rich had dug in 1811; he employed as many as thirty men and cleared an area of twelve square feet to a depth of twenty feet; he was the first to excavate an inscribed cylinder. Finally, in the eighteen-thirties, two Englishmen, J. Baillie Fraser and William F. Ainsworth, visited a number of sites in southern Mesopotamia; however, they had no inkling that these were part of ancient Sumer.

We now come to the large and more or less systematic excavations in Iraq which began in 1842 with that of Paul Emile Botta, the French consul at Mosul, and have continued, with numerous interruptions, to this day. The earlier of these excavations were conducted in northern Mesopotamia, in the land commonly known as Assyria, and the thousands of documents unearthed there were written in the Akkadian language. But this was not known at the time they were first excavated; all that could then be said was that the script resembled that of the third "class" of the trilingual inscriptions that were found in Iran, primarily at Persepolis and its environs. At Persepolis the ruins of a magnificent palace were still standing, with a large number of tall, beautiful columns still in place and sculptured monuments of various kinds scattered about. Surrounding the city were magnificently decorated tombs cut in the rocks. Many of the Persepolitan monuments were covered with a script which, by the end of the eighteenth century, had been recognized as similar to the inscriptions on the bricks from Babylon. Moreover, by the middle of the nineteenth century one of the inscriptions on the trilinguals had been deciphered and had provided a stock of proper names that could be used to decipher the third of the inscriptions, which in turn made it possible to read the "Assyrian" tablets being excavated in Iraq. In order to follow this process of decipherment of Akkadian, therefore, we must first have some idea of the decipherment of the first class of inscriptions on the Persepolitan trilingual and the nature of the information that it provided.

The ruins of Persepolis had become known to the European world in the sixteenth century when the itinerary of the Venetian ambassador to Persia, Geosofat Barbaros—in which he talks of them admiringly—was published in Venice in 1543. The writing on the monuments was first mentioned by Antonio de Goueca, the first ambassador of Spain and Portugal to Persia, in his book published in Lisbon in 1611, and described by him as being unlike that of the Persians, Arabs, Armenians, and Jews. His successor,

Don Garcia Silva Figueroa, in a book published in Antwerp in 1620, was the first to identify the ruins of Persepolis, using a description of Diodorus Siculus, as the palace of the Achaemenid ruler Darius. He, too, mentions the writing on the monuments, saying that it is unlike Chaldean, Hebrew, Arabic, and Greek, and describing it as long and triangular, shaped like a pyramid, and the characters as not differing from each other except in their position.

In a letter dated the twenty-first of October, 1621, Pietro della Valle stated that he had surveyed the ruins of Persepolis and even made a copy—though an incorrect one—of five of the characters on the inscriptions, and suggested that the inscriptions were to be read from left to right. In 1673, the young French artist André Daulier Deslandes published the first accurate engraving of the palace of Persepolis, but copied only three of the characters on the inscriptions and placed them in his engraving in a manner that tended to give the impression that the writing was merely decorative, a theory widely held during the eighteenth century. In 1677, Sir Thomas Herbert, an Englishman who had served the British ambassador to Persia some fifty years earlier, published a rather poor copy of what was apparently a three-line passage, which turned out to be a composite of lines from entirely different inscriptions. His characterization of the script is not without historical interest: "The characters are of a strange and unusual shape; neither like Letters nor Hieroglyphicks; yea so far from our deciphering them that we could not so much as make any positive judgment whether they were words or Characters; albeit I rather incline to the first, and that they comprehended words or syllables, as in Brachyography or Shortwriting we familiarly practice."

In 1693, there was published a copy of a two-line inscription from Persepolis consisting of twenty characters, which had been made by Samuel Flower, an agent of the East India Company. This was taken to be a genuine inscription, although it actually consisted of twenty-three separate signs selected from various inscriptions, an error which caused no little confusion and frustration to those attempting to decipher the script. In 1700, the script first received its appellation "cuneiform," which has stuck to it ever since, from Thomas Hyde, who wrote a book on the history of the religion of the Old Persians in which he reproduced Flower's inscription and described the characters as "cuneiform"; sadly enough he did not believe the signs were intended to convey meaningful speech, but rather to serve as decorations and ornaments.

The first complete inscription from Persepolis was not published until 1711, the author being Jean Chardin, a naturalized English citizen who had visited Persepolis three times during his youth. Three years later quite accurate copies of three trilingual inscriptions were published by Carneille Lebrun. But it was the Dane Carsten Niebuhr who paved the way for the decipherment of the Persian inscriptions. In 1778, he published careful and accurate copies of three trilingual inscriptions from Persepolis; he showed that they were written from left to right, that each of the three inscriptions contained three different types of cuneiform writing, which he labeled "Class I," "Class II," and "Class III," and finally that "Class I" represented an alphabetic method of writing, since it contained only forty-two signs according to his tabulation. Unfortunately, he was of the opinion that the three classes of script did not represent three different languages, but were used to write the same language in three different forms. In 1798 Friedrich Munter, another Dane, made the all-important observation that Niebuhr's Class I was an alphabetic script, while Classes II and III were respectively syllabic and ideographic; and that each class represented a different language as well as a different form of writing.

Thus the groundwork for the decipherment was now at hand: there were accurate copies of a number of inscriptions each of which contained three different types of cuneiform script representing three different languages; moreover, the first of the three classes in each inscription was correctly recognized to be alphabetical in character. But the decipherment itself took well-nigh half a century, and would probably have been impossible altogether had it not been for two scholars who made significant if unwitting contributions to the process by publishing studies which, though not concerned at all with the Persepolis cuneiform inscriptions, proved to be a fundamental aid to the decipherers. One of the scholars was the Frenchman A. H. Anquetil-Duperron, who spent much time in India collecting manuscripts of the

Avesta, the sacred book of Zoroastrianism, and learning how to read and interpret Old Persian, the language in which it was written. His relevant publications appeared in 1768 and 1771, and gave those attempting to decipher the Persepolis cuneiform inscriptions some idea of Old Persian, which proved most useful for the decipherment of Class I of the trilinguals once it had been postulated—because of its prominent position in the inscriptions— that it was Old Persian. The other scholar was A. I. Silvestre de Sacy, who in 1793 published a translation of the Pahlavi inscriptions found in the environs of Persepolis, which although dating centuries later than the Persepolis cuneiform inscriptions revealed a more or less stereotyped pattern that might be assumed to underlie the earlier monuments as well; this pattern was: X, great king, king of kings, king of . . . , son of Y, great king, king of kings. . . .

Turning back now to the actual decipherment of the Persepolis inscriptions, the first serious attempt was made by Oluf Gerhard Tychsen, who in studying the first class correctly identified four of the characters, recognized one of the frequently occurring signs as a word-divider—which made it possible to establish the beginning and end of each word—and made several other keen observations. But he erroneously assumed that the inscriptions dated from the Parthian dynasty, later by more than half a millennium than their true date, and his translations were pure guesswork and wrong throughout.

Tychsen published his results in 1798. In the same year, Friedrich Munter of Copenhagen submitted two papers to the Royal Danish Society of Sciences proving that the Persepolis documents belong to the Achaemenid dynasty, a fact that was of fundamental significance for the decipherment of the inscriptions. But Munter himself made no further progress in his decipherment efforts. It was Georg Friedrich Grotefend, a teacher of Greek in the Göttingen Gymnasium, who succeeded where the others had failed and achieved fame as the decipherer of the Persian cuneiform inscriptions, that is, the first of Niebuhr's three classes. He began by picking out those characters which occurred with greatest frequency and postulated that these were vowels. He took De Sacy's Pahlavi inscriptional pattern and with it found the spots where it seemed most likely that the names of the king who had the monument put up and of his father would occur, as well as such words as "king" and "son." He then manipulated the known names of the kings of the Achaemenid dynasty, primarily according to their length, into the proper spots, and used the relevant words in Anquetil-Duperron's studies of Old Persian to get at the readings for some of the other words on the inscriptions; he thus came up with the correct identification of ten of the signs and three proper names, and with a translation that contained numerous errors but nevertheless gave an adequate idea of its contents.

An extract of Grotefend's attempt at decipherment appeared in 1802, and three years later a fuller account was published. His efforts were lauded and approved by Tychsen, Munter, and especially by Rich, who kept on sending him copies of the cuneiform documents he had obtained in the ruins of Babylon and Nineveh. But Grotefend overstated his achievements, claiming that he had deciphered many more signs than was the case, and giving complete but unjustifiable transliterations and translations which could only evoke ridicule among some of his colleagues. However, Grotefend was on the right track with his decipherment, as was corroborated directly and indirectly in the course of the next several decades by the efforts of a number of scholars who kept on adding, subtracting, modifying: A. J. Saint-Martin, Rasmus Rask, Eugène Burnouf, and his close friend and collaborator, Christian Lassen, to name only the outstanding figures. But for a real insight into the Old Persian language and for the conclusive decipherment of all the characters, the Persepolis inscriptions were simply too short and did not supply a vocabulary large enough and meaningful enough for verification and control. This brings us to the dominant figure in early cuneiform studies, the brilliant, intuitive, and persevering Englishman, Henry Creswicke Rawlinson, and the remarkable fact that a group of inscriptions were deciphered independently by two men using practically identical criteria.

H. C. Rawlinson became interested in the cuneiform inscriptions scattered throughout Persia while in the service of the British army in Persia. He began to copy some of the trilinguals, especially the Mount Alvand inscription near Hamadan and the Behistun rock inscription about twenty miles from Kermanshah. The former consists of two short trilinguals, which he proceeded to copy in the year 1835; and without knowing anything of the work of Grotefend, De Sacy, Saint-Martin, Rask, Burnouf, and Lassen, he succeeded in reading them by following practically the same method which Grotefend and his followers had used. But he realized that in order to identify all the signs on these inscriptions and read them adequately, it would be necessary to have a large number of proper names on hand. And these he found in the Behistun rock inscription, engraved on a specially prepared surface of over twelve hundred square feet that was filled in part by a sculptured bas-relief and consisting of a trilingual running into hundreds of lines. Unfortunately, this monument was situated on the rock more than three hundred feet above the ground, and there was no means of ascent to it. Rawlinson, therefore, had to construct a scaffold to get to the inscription, and at times, in order to obtain as complete a copy as possible, had to be suspended by a rope dangling in front of the rock.

In 1835, Rawlinson began to copy the Persian columns of the Behistun trilinguals, which were five in number and contained 414 lines of text. He continued copying the inscription on and off over the years until in 1837 he had finished about 200 lines, or approximately half, and with the help of classical writers and medieval geographers managed to read a number of the several hundred place names that this inscription contained. By 1839 he had become acquainted with the work of his colleagues in Europe, and aided by the new information which they provided, he succeeded in translating the first two hundred lines of the Old Persian inscription of the Behistun trilingual. His ambition was to copy every bit of writing on the Behistun rock; but his military duties interrupted his efforts, and it was not until 1844 that he was able to resume his labor of love. In that year he returned to Behistun, finished the entire Old Persian inscription of 414 lines, and copied, as well, all of the 263 lines of the second, or Elamite, version, as it has now come to be known. In 1848 he sent off his manuscript, consisting of his copies, transliterations, translation, commentary, and notes, from Baghdad to the Royal Asiatic Society, and thus put the decipherment of the Old Persian inscriptions on an absolutely trustworthy foundation, a fact that was further confirmed when, in the very same year, the brilliant Irish linguist, Edward Hincks, published a paper that he had read two years earlier, in which he anticipated quite a number of significant observations made by Rawlinson independently. From here on, only minor changes, additions, and corrections could be made; especially noteworthy were those of Jules Oppert, a student of Lassen, in 1851. Hincks, Rawlinson, and Oppert—cuneiform's "holy triad"—not only put Old Persian on firm ground, but also launched Akkadian and Sumerian on the course to decipherment, and thus laid open the dusty pages of the clay "books" buried all over the ancient Near East.

And so we come back to the large systematic excavations in Mesopotamia and the decipherment of the Akkadian and Sumerian languages to which they led. In 1842 Paul Emile Botta was appointed French consul in Mosul. As soon as he arrived there he began excavations at Kuyunjik and Nebi Yunus, two mounds covering the ruins of Nineveh. These proved fruitless, and he turned his attention to Khorsabad, a short distance to the north of Kuyunjik, where he "struck it rich," archeologically speaking; for the Khorsabad ruins covered the palace of the mighty Sargon II, who ruled over Assyria in the first quarter of the eighth century B.C.—although this was unknown to the excavators, of course—and contained acres of Assyrian sculpture, friezes, and reliefs, many of which were covered with cuneiform inscriptions. Only three years later, the Englishman Austen Henry Layard began digging first at Nimrud, then at Nineveh, and again at Nimrud. In addition to the royal palaces covered with bas-reliefs, he found at Nineveh the library of King Ashurbanipal, the great grandson of Sargon II, which consisted of thousands of tablets and fragments inscribed with the lexical, religious, and literary works of the ancients. Thus by the middle of the nineteenth century, Europe had hundreds of cuneiform inscriptions, coming largely from Assyrian sites, which were crying for decipherment, as it were, but which presented difficulties and obstacles that seemed insurmountable at the time. And yet, primarily as a result of the genius and perseverance of Hincks, Rawlinson, and Oppert, it took no more than a decade or so for the decipherment to become an accomplished fact.

To be sure, the would-be decipherers did have one advantage. Long before Botta and Layard had begun their excavations, a limited number of inscriptions of one sort or another had found their way to Europe, especially from Babylonian ruins, and the writing on them had been recognized as resembling Niebuhr's third class on the Persepolis trilinguals. But unfortunately this third class, which could be reasonably assumed to be a translation of the first class, defied all efforts at decipherment. In the first place, the Persepolis inscriptions were far too brief for any insight into the language. Moreover, even a superficial analysis of the then extant Babylonian inscriptions revealed that they consisted of hundreds of signs, while the first class of the trilingual had only forty-two characters, which made it impossible to mark off the names or words that might be expected to be identical. Finally, within the Babylonian documents themselves the very same signs seemed to show considerable variation in shape and form. No wonder, then, that the first attempts at the decipherment of the Babylonian writing proved to be futile.

In 1847 came the first significant contribution; its author not unexpectedly was Edward Hincks. With the help of a copy of the relatively longer Old Persian version of the Behistun inscription, which contained a goodly number of proper names, he succeeded in reading correctly a number of vowels, syllables, and ideograms, as well as the first Babylonian word which was not a proper name, the pronoun *a-na-ku*—"I"— practically identical with its Hebrew counterpart. However, his major discovery, the one which proved crucial for the decipherment, did not come until 1850, and was based to some extent on the insight of Botta, who, not content with excavating alone, published in 1848 a study on the cuneiform signs that was extremely detailed. Botta did not try to read a single word, although he succeeded in getting at the meaning of several ideograms; his most fruitful contribution concerned the variants. After careful study and detailed documentation, he showed that there were quite a number of words which, though evidently identical in reading and meaning, were written in different ways. It was this minute study of variant writings which paved the way for Hincks's paper of 1850, in which at one stroke he was able to explain the seemingly incredible fact that the Babylonian script contained hundreds of signs, as well as give the reason for the existence of so many variants. The Babylonian-Assyrian (or as it is now called, Akkadian) script, stated Hincks, was not alphabetical, but both syllabic and ideographic, that is, the signs might represent syllables (of consonant plus vowel, vowel plus consonant, or consonant plus vowel plus consonant) which were combined in various ways to make a word, or each sign might express an entire word.

With this new insight into the Babylonian script, the decipherment could go on apace. But two major linguistic aids were still to come, both the result of the efforts and researches of the second of our triad, Rawlinson. In the year 1847, Rawlinson traveled once again from Baghdad to Behistun and at the risk of life and limb succeeded in making paper squeezes of the Babylonian version, which gave him a long text of 112 lines that could be deciphered and translated with the help of the already deciphered Old Persian text on the same monument. In the course of this work, moreover, he discovered the other all-important feature of Babylonian writing, "polyphony," that is, that one and the same sign could stand for more than one sound or "value." As a result, Rawlinson could now read about 150 signs correctly; he knew the reading and meaning of about two hundred words of the language, which was now definitely shown to be a Semitic tongue, and he was even able to give a grammatical sketch of it.

Rawlinson's remarkable studies were published in 1850 and 1851. In 1853, Hincks, with the help of Rawlinson's studies, succeeded in adding more than a hundred new values to the Babylonian signs, so that he could now identify close to 350 values or readings. But the principle of polyphony, which this identification involved, aroused doubt, suspicion, and antagonism among scholars, some of whom attacked the Hincks-Rawlinson translations as prejudiced and worthless; it was difficult to believe that the ancient people would devise a system of writing in which one and the same sign could have numerous values, since this, presumably, would so confuse the reader as to make it useless. At this crucial juncture, Jules Oppert, the third of the triumvirate, came to the rescue. In 1855 he gave a survey of the stage of decipherment reached at that point, showed the correctness of the Hincks-Rawlinson readings, and added a number of new signs that had more than one value. He was the first to make a thorough study of syllabaries prepared by the ancient scribes themselves, which were among the tablets excavated in the so-called Ashurbanipal library at Nineveh, and to utilize them extensively in his translation. His numerous treatises, text editions, and polemics helped to consolidate the new science, now generally becoming known as Assyriology—based on the fact that the earliest excavations were conducted in northern Iraq, the home of the Assyrian people —and to invest it with respect and high esteem.

The year 1857 was a fateful one for Assyriology, and it came through the ordeal with flying colors. It was a mathematician and inventor and not a professional Assyriologist who brought matters to a head. W. F. Fox Talbot, who did research on integral calculus and helped lay the foundations for present-day photography, was also an amateur Orientalist; he had studied the publications of Rawlinson and Hincks and had even published translations of a number of Assyrian texts. Having obtained a still unpublished copy of an inscription of the Assyrian king Tiglath-pileser I (1116–1076), he made a translation of it, and dispatched it sealed to the Royal Asiatic Society on March 17, 1857, suggesting that the society invite Hincks and Rawlinson to prepare independent translations of the same text and send them in sealed, so that the three independent translations might be compared. The society did so and also sent an invitation to Jules Oppert, who was then in London. All three accepted the invitation, and two months later the seals of the four envelopes containing the translations were broken by a specially appointed committee of five members of the Royal Asiatic Society. A report was issued stating among other things that the translations of Rawlinson and Hincks resembled each other most closely, that Talbot's renderings were rather vague and inexact, and that Oppert annotated his translations extensively and often differed from his English colleagues. All in all the verdict was favorable for Assyriology as then practiced; the similarities between the four translations were reasonably close and the validity of the decipherment vindicated.

Two years later, in 1859, Oppert published one of his most important scholarly works, *Déchiffrement des inscriptions cunéiformes;* it was so lucid, comprehensive, and authoritative a statement of Assyriology and its achievements to date that all opposition ceased. In the decades that followed scholars by the score, especially in France, England, and Germany, wrote articles, monographs, and books on all branches of the new discipline: language, history, religion, culture, and so on. Texts were copied and published by the thousands. Sign lists, glossaries, dictionaries, and grammars were compiled, and innumerable highly specialized articles on grammar, syntax, and etymology were written. And so the study of Assyrian, which was first called Babylonian and is now gradually becoming known as Akkadian—a term deriving from one used by the ancient Mesopotamians themselves—developed and matured, so that now in 1963, two separate, many-volumed dictionaries are in process of publication—one in English by the Oriental Institute of the University of Chicago, and the other in German under international auspices—a crowning achievement of more than a hundred years of cumulative scholarship.

Babylonian! Assyrian! Akkadian! But not a word yet about Sumer and Sumerians, and after all this is a book about the Sumerians. Unfortunately, up to the middle of the last century no one knew that a Sumerian people and language had ever existed. And so we must retrace our path a bit in order to follow the step-by-step developments that led to the rather surprising and unexpected realization that a people named Sumerians had once inhabited Mesopotamia. In 1850 Hincks read a paper before the British Association for the Advancement of Science in which he expressed some doubts concerning the general assumption that it was the Semitic inhabitants of Assyria and Babylonia who had invented the cuneiform system of writing, which they utilized. In the Semitic languages the stable element is the consonant, while the vowel is extremely variable. It seemed unnatural, therefore, that the Semites should invent a syllabic system of orthography in which the vowel seemed to be as unchanging as the consonant. The distinction between soft and hard palatals and dentals is a significant feature of the Semitic languages, but the cuneiform syllabary did not seem to express this distinction adequately. Then, too, if the Semites had invented the cuneiform script, it should be possible to trace the syllabic values of the signs to Semitic words. But this was rarely the case; the great majority of the syllabic values for the cuneiform signs seemed to go back to words or elements for which no Semitic equivalent could be found. Hincks thus began to suspect that the cuneiform system of writing was invented by some non-Semitic people who had preceded the Semites in Babylonia.

So much for Hincks and his suspicions. Two years later, in 1852, according to a note published by Hincks, we learn that Rawlinson, after studying the syllabaries excavated at Kuyunjik, had come to the conclusion that they were bilingual and that the Semitic Babylonian words in them explained corresponding words in an entirely new and hitherto unknown language, which he designated "Akkadian" and which he considered to be "Scythian or Turanian." Here, then, we learn for the first time of the possibility that there had existed a non-Semitic people and a non-Semitic language in Mesopotamia. In 1853, Rawlinson himself delivered a lecture before the Royal Asiatic Society in which he stated that there were unilingual cuneiform inscriptions on bricks and tablets from sites in southern Babylonia that were written in the "Scythian" language. And in a lecture before the same society two years later, he discussed in some detail the Kuyunjik bilingual syllabaries, which "were nothing more or less than comparative alphabets, grammars, and vocabularies of the Assyrian and Scythic dialects. The Babylonian Scyths, whose ethnic name is Akkad, may be assumed to have invented cuneiform writing." It was these Akkadians, Rawlinson continued, who "built the primitive temples and capitals of Babylonia, worshipping the same gods, and inhabiting the same seats as the Semitic successors; but they appear to have a different nomenclature, both mythological and geographical." As for the language of these Babylonian Scyths, the Kuyunjik tablets, said Rawlinson, "furnish volumes of comparative examples and interlineary translations." As a result of his study of this new "primitive" language from the bilinguals, he concludes that "it is doubtful if any close linguistic affinities are to be traced between the primitive tongue and any available dialect of modern times. The pronominal system approaches nearer to the Mongol and Manchu type than to any other branch of the Turanian family, but there is little or no resemblance of vocabulary." In short, Rawlinson had definitely discovered the Sumerians and their language, except that he designated them quite erroneously first as Babylonian Scyths and then as Akkadians, the very term now used for the Semites of the land.

The correct naming of the non-Semitic people who invented the cuneiform script we owe to the genius of Jules Oppert, whose contributions to all facets of Assyriology, and especially to the study of the syllabaries, were so outstanding. On January 17, 1869, Oppert delivered a lecture before the ethnographic and historical section of the French Society of Numismatics and Archeology in which he declared that these people and their language should be called Sumerian, basing his conclusions on the title "King of Sumer and Akkad" found in the inscriptions of some of the early rulers; for, he argued quite correctly, it was the name Akkad that applied to the Semitic people of Assyria and Babylonia, while the name Sumer referred to the non-Semitic inhabitants. Oppert even went on to say in this lecture that an analysis of the structure of the Sumerian language had led him to conclude that it had close affinities with Turkish, Finnish, and Hungarian—a brilliant insight into the structure of a language which only twenty years earlier had been non-existent as far as world scholarship was concerned.

The designation "Sumerian" was not followed immediately by the majority of cuneiform scholars, and the term "Akkadian" continued to be used for several decades. In fact, there was one famous Orientalist, Joseph Halévy, who, in spite of all the evidence to the contrary, denied the very existence of both the Sumerian people and language. Beginning with the 1870's and for more than three decades thereafter, he published article after article insisting that no people other than the Semites had ever been in possession of Babylonia, and that the so-called Sumerian language was merely an artificial invention of the Semites themselves devised for hieratic and esoteric purposes. For a very brief period he was even supported by several eminent Assyriologists. But all that is now only a matter of historical curiosity; for not long after Oppert's perspicacious conclusions about the non-Semitic people of Babylonia and their language, two excavations were begun in southern Babylonia which put the Sumerians on the map, as it were, with the discovery of statues and steles which revealed their physical features, and innumerable tablets and inscriptions significant for their political history, religion, economy, and literature.

The first significant excavation on a Sumerian site was begun in 1877 at Telloh, the ruins of ancient Lagash, by the French under the direction of Ernest de Sarzec. Between the years 1877 and 1900, De Sarzec conducted eleven campaigns and succeeded in excavating numerous statues, primarily of Gudea, steles—the Stele of the Vultures is one of the more important of these—the Gudea cylinders, and thousands of tablets, many of which dated to the dynasty of Ur-Nanshe. In 1884 the publication of Léon Heuzey's magnificent volume, *Découvertes en Chaldée par Ernest de Sarzec,* was begun, with the collaboration of two outstanding epigraphists, Arthur Amiaud and François Thureau-Dangin. The French continued to dig intermittently at Lagash: from 1903 to 1909 under the direction of Gaston Cros, from 1929 to 1931 under Henri de Genouillac, and from 1931 to 1933 under André Parrot. All in all the French conducted twenty campaigns in Lagash; and the results are summarized briefly in André Parrot's most valuable reference book, *Tello* (1948), which also gives a complete and detailed bibliography of all publications relating in one way or another to these excavations.

The second major excavation on a Sumerian site was that conducted by the University of Pennsylvania, the first American expedition to excavate in Mesopotamia. All through the eighties of the nineteenth century discussions had been going on in American university circles about the feasibility of sending an American expedition to Iraq, where both the British and French had been making such extraordinary archeological finds. It was not until 1887, however, that John P. Peters, professor of Hebrew at the University of Pennsylvania, succeeded in obtaining moral and financial support from various individuals in and about the university for the purpose of equipping and maintaining an excavating expedition in Iraq. Nippur, one of the largest and most important mounds in Iraq, was chosen, and four campaigns, long and grueling, were conducted there between the years 1889 and 1900 first under the direction of Peters, then under J. H. Haynes (originally the photographer of the expedition), and finally under the noted Assyriologist, H. V. Hilprecht, who had also been an epigraphist in the first campaign.

The hardships and handicaps were severe and discouraging. One young archeologist died in the field, and there was hardly a year in which one or another of the members of the expeditions did not suffer from serious illness. In spite of the obstacles, however, the excavating continued, and the expedition achieved magnificent, and in some respects unparalleled, results, at least in the inscriptional field. The Nippur expedition succeeded in excavating some thirty thousand tablets and fragments in the course of its four campaigns, the larger number of which are inscribed in the Sumerian language and range over more than two millenniums, from the second half of the third to the last centuries of the first millennium B.C. Publication of some of this material began as early as 1893 in accordance with a farsighted and long-range plan conceived by Hilprecht in which numerous scholars were to participate in addition to himself. Not all of the volumes that were planned have seen the light of day; like most grandiose plans, unforeseen obstacles and difficulties arose which prevented its complete execution. But quite a number of volumes have appeared, and these have proved to be of the greatest value to cuneiform scholars. This brings us back to Sumerology and its progress in the period following the days of its three great pioneers, Hincks, Rawlinson, and Oppert.

Up to the time of the excavations at Lagash and Nippur, practically all the source material for the study of the Sumerians and their language consisted of the bilingual syllabaries and interlinears excavated in the Ashurbanipal library in the ruins of Nineveh, which were being published in various sections of the five superb folio volumes entitled *Cuneiform Inscriptions of Western Asia*, edited by Rawlinson. But this material dates from the seventh century B.C., more than a millennium after the disappearance of the Sumerian people as a political entity and of the Sumerian language as a living tongue. To be sure, there were some inscriptions from Sumerian sites available in Europe, but these consisted primarily of a small group of bricks, tablets, and cylinders from the Sumerian and post-Sumerian periods which had found their way into the British Museum and from which little significant data could be gleaned. The excavation at Lagash and Nippur put at the disposition of scholars thousands of unilingual Sumerian inscriptions, which they could now try to translate and interpret with the help of whatever grammatical rules and lexical data had been obtained from the Kuyunjik bilingual syllabaries and interlinears. The vast majority of the inscriptions from Lagash and Nippur were administrative, economic, and legal in character, consisting of inventories of all types and sizes, promissory notes and receipts, deeds of sales, marriage contracts, wills, and

court decisions, and thus from them some idea could at last be
had of the Sumerian social and economic structure. These documents also contained hundreds of names of persons, deities, and
places which were of some value for learning about Sumerian
religion. Even more important were the hundreds of votive inscriptions on statue, stele, cone, and tablet which were of fundamental value for the study of Sumerian political history. Especially
from Nippur came numerous lexical and grammatical texts, the
Sumerian forerunners of the later Kuyunjik bilinguals, and these
proved to be invaluable for the study of the Sumerian language.
Finally, in Nippur there were found thousands of tablets and
fragments inscribed with Sumerian literary works; and although
these remained rather unintelligible for many a decade after their
discovery, Hilprecht, who handled and catalogued many of them,
realized their significance for the history of religion and literature.
It is not too much to state that it was as a direct result of the
Lagash and Nippur excavations that François Thureau-Dangin
could publish in 1905 his epoch-making *Les Inscriptions de Sumer
et Akkad* and Arno Poebel his equally epoch-making *Grundzüge
der sumerischen Grammatik* in 1923.

To be sure, both these scholars built on the efforts and contributions of their predecessors and contemporaries; there is no
other way for the progress of productive scholarship. To name
only some of the more outstanding figures: the Englishman A. H.
Sayce, who in 1871 edited the first unilingual Sumerian document,
a Shulgi inscription of twelve lines, and sketched in a detailed
philological commentary a number of important characteristics
of the Sumerian language; François Lenormant and his monumental *Etudes accadiennes* (begun in 1873); Paul Haupt, who
copied a large number of Sumerian bilinguals and unilinguals in
the British Museum and who made some notable contributions
to Sumerian grammar and lexicography; R. E. Brunnow, who
compiled a list of Sumerian signs and readings and an exhaustive
glossary of Sumerian words from the bilinguals known in his day
which proved of fundamental importance to all lexicographers
from the time it was first published, 1905–7, to the present, although it took a number of supplementary glossaries prepared
by other scholars to keep it up to date; J. D. Prince, who published
the first important Sumerian lexicon in 1905; and Friedrich

Delitzsch, who compiled both a Sumerian grammar and a Sumerian glossary based on word roots rather than signs and their readings.

But it was Thureau-Dangin's *Les Inscriptions de Sumer et Akkad* of 1905—appearing only two years later in a German translation under the title *Die sumerischen und akkadischen Königsinschriften*—which proved a milestone in the progress of Sumerian studies. It is a superb compendium of straightforward translation and tersely worded notes revealing a masterful distillation of the accumulated Sumerological knowledge of that day, not a little of which could be traced to Thureau-Dangin's own original contributions; after some five decades of cuneiform scholarship, it is still far from superseded, and in some respects never will be. And Poebel's *Grundzüge der sumerischen Grammatik* did for Sumerian grammar what Thureau-Dangin's book did for political history and religion. Based on painstakingly thorough and minutely detailed studies of the Sumerian inscriptions—both bilingual and unilingual and from all periods from the "classical" language of the third millennium B.C. to the late "book" Sumerian of the first millennium B.C. (the translations of inscriptions 1 through 35 in the Appendix are based primarily on several of these studies)—Poebel's *Grundzüge* set down with compelling logic the fundamental principles and rules of Sumerian grammar, illustrating them pertinently and, wherever possible, profusely. Subsequent grammatical studies prepared by Poebel himself as well as by other scholars, especially Adam Falkenstein and Thorkild Jacobsen, have resulted in a number of additions and corrections, and future studies will no doubt result in further modification of some of the grammatical details sketched in the *Grundzüge;* but by and large, Poebel's work has stood the test of time, and in spite of the current passion for changes in terminology and nomenclature, profound and otherwise, it will long remain the cornerstone of all constructive Sumerian grammatical efforts.

Poebel's grammar, however, is not organized pedagogically but logically and cannot be readily used by novices who would like to learn Sumerian on their own. A little book that is quite useful in this respect is C. J. Gadd's *A Sumerian Reading Book;* it was first published in 1924, however, and a revised and up-to-date version is urgently needed. Another useful grammar, pedagogically speaking, is Anton Deimel's *Shumerische Grammatik* (second edition, 1939), although it suffers no little from a rather superficial treatment of the problems involved in the translation of Sumerian texts. In the field of lexicography, the same author's *Shumerisches Lexikon,* based largely on the compilations by Brunnow and others, is indispensable to the scholar, although it has to be used with considerable critical caution and discrimination. The most far-reaching and fundamental lexicographical works now in the process of preparation are the *Materialien zum sumerischen Lexikon: Vokabulare und Formularbücher* of Benno Landsberger, the dean of Assyriologists. Eight volumes consisting of the most up-to-date compilations of the later syllabaries, vocabularies, and lexical bilinguals, as well as their earlier Sumerian forerunners, have already appeared under the auspices of the Pontifical Biblical Institute in Rome, an institution to which all cuneiformists owe a debt of profound gratitude for the Sumerological studies it has fostered over the past fifty years.

Let us now leave Sumerian linguistic research and return to archeology in order to sketch briefly the results of some of the more important excavations on Sumerian sites, which had begun so auspiciously with Lagash and Nippur. In 1902–3, a German expedition under the direction of Robert Koldewey worked at Fara, ancient Shuruppak, the home city of the flood-hero Ziusudra, and unearthed a large number of administrative, economic, and lexical texts dating from the twenty-fifth century B.C.—older, therefore, than the inscriptions of the Ur-Nanshe dynasty found at Lagash. The economic texts included sales of houses and fields, which indicated that private ownership existed in Sumer, a feature of Sumerian life that has long been a matter of controversy among Orientalists. The Fara lexical texts, too, were of rather extraordinary importance for the history of civilization, since they pointed to the existence of Sumerian schools as far back as the twenty-fifth century B.C. and perhaps even earlier. The excavators also unearthed a number of private and public buildings and tombs, numerous vases of stone, metal, and terra cotta, and many cylinder seals. In 1930, a University of Pennsylvania expedition under the direction of Erik Schmidt returned to Fara, but the new finds did not differ materially from those made almost thirty years earlier. It was my good fortune—young and inexperienced as I was—to be the epigraphist of this expedition. Most of the Fara tablets have been studied and published by Anton Deimel and the French Sumerologist R. Jestin.

In 1903, an expedition of the University of Chicago conducted by E. J. Banks excavated at Bismaya, the site of Lugalannemundu's capital Adab. Here, too, there was discovered quite a number of archaic tablets resembling those of Fara in form and content. Banks also unearthed the remains of several temples and palaces, numerous votive inscriptions, and a statue bearing the name Lugaldalu that dates from about 2400 B.C. The major publication resulting from this expedition is an Oriental Institute volume of texts copied by D. D. Luckenbill, which is of particular value for the history of Sargonic and pre-Sargonic Sumer.

From 1912 to 1914, a French expedition under the direction of the eminent cuneiformist Henri de Genouillac carried on excavations at Kish, the first city to which kingship had descended after the Flood. The First World War put an end to these excavations, but in 1923, an Anglo-American expedition returned to Kish under the direction of another eminent cuneiformist, Stephen Langdon, and worked there for ten consecutive seasons. They unearthed several monumental buildings, ziggurats, and cemeteries and a large number of tablets. A number of publications have been issued both by the Field Museum on the archeological material and by Oxford University on the epigraphic material. A small contingent of this Kish expedition also worked briefly in nearby Jemdet Nasr, a mound covering the ruins of a town whose ancient name is still unknown. This relatively minor excavation at a rather small site was fortunate enough to uncover several hundred tablets and fragments inscribed with semipictographic signs which dated back to about 2800 B.C. and were thus the earliest Sumerian inscriptions of any sizable quantity known at the time.[1] These tablets, copied and published by Stephen Langdon, marked a milestone in Sumerian epigraphic studies.

We now come to a place called Warka by modern Arabs, Uruk by the ancient Sumerians and Akkadians, and Erech in the Bible, where at this very day a most systematic and scientific excavation is being conducted, one that has proved fundamental for what

[1] See p. 229 for a description of the earlier Erech pictographic tablets.

might be termed the "stratigraphic" study of Sumerian history and culture. Systematic excavations were first begun there by a German expedition under the direction of Julius Jordan. Following the inevitable interruption caused by the First World War, the expedition returned in 1928 and continued its excavations until stopped by the Second World War in 1939. Throughout the years the expedition has had on its staff a number of outstanding epigraphists, including Adam Falkenstein, who has been a prolific and outstanding contributor to Sumerian studies over the past three decades. It is the Erech expedition that created a kind of relative dating for all Sumerian finds by sinking a large test-pit through some twenty meters of stratified occupation down to virgin soil and carefully studying and typing the finds of the numerous levels and periods, beginning with the very first settlers and ending with the middle of the third millennium B.C. It laid bare Sumer's earliest monumental buildings known at the time, dating from about 3000 B.C. Among its innumerable smaller finds, there was an alabaster vase, close to a meter in height, that was decorated with cultic scenes highly revealing for early Sumerian rite and ritual; there was also a life-sized marble head of a woman dating from about 2800 B.C., which indicates that early Sumerian sculpture in the round had reached unsuspected creative heights. In one of the early monumental temples more than a thousand pictographic tablets were unearthed, which made it possible to trace the cuneiform system of writing back to its earliest stages; many of these tablets were published in a superb volume prepared with great care and after much study by Adam Falkenstein. In 1954, the German expedition returned to Erech under a new director, H. Lenzen, and is carrying on its careful and methodical excavations, which will no doubt make Erech—the city of Sumer's great heroes—the keystone of Mesopotamian archeology in all its aspects: architecture, art, history, religion, and epigraphy.

From Biblical Erech we turn to Biblical Ur, or Urim as it was known to the Sumerians, the city which was excavated from 1922 to 1934 with skill, care, and imagination by the late Sir Leonard Woolley. Woolley has described his discoveries at Ur time and again, both for the scholar and for the layman—we need mention here only his latest work, *Excavations at Ur* (1954). Through his writings its royal tombs, ziggurat, and "Flood-pit" have almost become household words. Less well-known, but equally significant, contributions have been made by the epigraphists on the expedition, C. J. Gadd, Leon Legrain, and E. Burrows, who have copied, studied, and published a large part of the written documents discovered at Ur—documents which have shed new light on the history, economy, culture not only of Ur, but of Sumer as a whole.

Close to Ur, some four miles to the north, lies a small low mound known as al-Ubaid which, in spite of its size, has played a large role in Mesopotamian archeology. First explored by H. R. Hall of the British Museum in 1919, and later excavated methodically by Leonard Woolley, it was found to be in part a prehistoric mound containing evidence of the earliest immigrants into the land. These people, who have come to be known as Ubaidians, produced and used a special type of monochrome painted ware and tools of flint and obsidian, which were later found in the lowest layers of several Mesopotamian sites. Woolley also laid bare at this site a small temple to the goddess Ninhursag which, in addition to providing us with a vivid picture of what one of the smaller provincial temples looked like in the middle of the third millennium, proved beyond all doubt that the so-called First Dynasty of Ur, which scholars had tended to look upon as legendary, actually did exist; this discovery thus helped to reorient the prevalent overly skeptical attitude to the all-important King List, which in turn gave a clearer insight into Sumerian political history.

In the extreme northeast of Sumer east of the Tigris and somewhat off the beaten path, Sumerologically speaking, lay a series of mounds which attracted the attention of Henri Frankfort, one of the world's great archeologists, a perceptive art historian and philosophically oriented scholar whose untimely death was an irretrievable loss to Oriental studies. Between the years 1930 and 1936 he conducted careful and methodical excavations at the tells Asmar, Khafaje, and Agrab and unearthed temples, palaces, and private houses, tablets, cylinder seals, and a most exciting series of sculptures in the round, some of which reach back to about 2700 B.C.—only a century or so later than the famous head from Erech. Among Frankfort's fellow-workers were Pinhas Delougaz, an archeologist of long experience who is now director of the

Museum of the Oriental Institute; Seton Lloyd, who became advisor to the Iraqi Directorate of Antiquities and who has probably participated in the excavation of more Sumerian sites than any other living archeologist; and Thorkild Jacobsen, the rare scholar who is at home both in archeology and in epigraphy. The results of these excavations are appearing in a series of magnificent Oriental Institute publications that are outstanding for their detailed and profusely illustrated treatment of architecture as well as of artifacts and inscriptions.

From 1933 to 1956, interrupted only by the Second World War, a Louvre expedition under the direction of André Parrot, the archeologist who in a sense closed the book on Lagash, excavated at Mari, a city situated on the middle Euphrates considerably to the west of what is usually considered Sumer proper; and the results were both extraordinary and unexpected. Here is a city whose inhabitants were probably Semites from very early times—to date practically all the inscriptions discovered at Mari have been in Akkadian—and yet, culturally speaking, it can hardly be differentiated from a Sumerian city—the same types of temples, a ziggurat, sculpture, inlay, and even a statuette of a singer inscribed with the good Sumerian name Ur-Nanshe, the very name borne by the founder of the earliest known Lagash dynasty. The leading epigraphist with the Louvre expedition was the Belgian cuneiformist Georges Dossin, who, with Parrot, is jointly editing a most important series of volumes on the Mari inscriptional material in which a number of French and Belgian scholars are participating. With Lagash and Mari to their credit, the French are again taking top rank in Mesopotamian archeology and scholarship.

During the war years, when foreign expeditions were neither practical nor possible, the Iraqi Directorate of Antiquities, which has grown from small beginnings to a fine department of archeologists, epigraphists, registrars, and restorers, and which is keeping Mesopotamian archeology on a scientific keel, branched out on its own and made three excavations that are of particular relevance and importance to Sumerian studies. In a tell called Uqair, the ruins of a town whose ancient name is still unknown, an expedition under the direction of Fuad Safar unearthed in the years 1940 and 1941 the first known Sumerian painted temple, with colored frescoes covering the inside walls and the altar. It also laid bare some Ubaid houses as well as a number of archaic tablets. In tell Harmal, a small mound some six miles due east of Baghdad, Taha Baqir, then director of the Iraq Museum, conducted excavations from 1945 to 1949 and, to the surprise of scholars the world over, uncovered more than two thousand tablets, among which were some excellently preserved lexical and mathematical "textbooks," and a temple. And down at the southern tip of Sumer, in ancient Eridu (the seat of Enki, the Sumerian god of wisdom), Fuad Safar conducted excavations in the years 1946–49, uncovering the earliest Ubaid pottery, an Ubaid cemetery, and two palaces from the middle of the third millennium B.C. Enki's temple was followed down to its very first building phase, of about 4000 B.C. Sad to say, not a single tablet was discovered in Eridu; a strange state of affairs indeed for a city whose tutelary deity is the god of wisdom.

Following the war years, there have been only two major foreign expeditions excavating in Sumer: the Germans have returned to Erech; and the Americans, primarily as a result of Thorkild Jacobsen's efforts, have returned to Nippur and in alternate seasons have cleared the Enlil temple, unearthed over a thousand tablets and fragments (about five hundred of which are literary), and begun to lay bare a temple to the goddess Inanna. But the future of Sumerian excavations in Iraq lies in the hands of the Iraqis themselves, and there is every reason to hope that the Iraqi scholars and archeologists will not abandon or neglect their forefathers of the distant past who did so much not only for Iraq but for man the world over.

So much for the bird's-eye view of decipherment and archeology relevant to Sumer and the Sumerians. Before turning to the history of Sumer, the subject of our next chapter, however, the reader should have at least an inkling of one of the more vexing problems besetting the Near Eastern archeologist and historian—the problem of chronology. Nor has this problem been solved by the carbon-14 method of dating; because of purely physical and mechanical factors the results of this method have often proved to be ambiguous and misleading, not to mention the fact that in the case of Lower Mesopotamia, the margin of error allowed is too large for comfort.

In general, the dates assigned in the past to Sumerian rulers and monuments were far too high. To some extent this was due to the very understandable inclination on the part of archeologists to claim high antiquity for their particular discoveries. But in the main it was due to the available source material and in particular, to the several dynastic lists compiled by the ancient Sumerian and Babylonian scribes themselves;[2] for these frequently treated as consecutive dynasties of rulers which are now known from other documents to have been contemporaneous in whole or in part. While there is still no unanimity of opinion, the Sumerian dates have now been lowered very considerably from those found in earlier histories and handbooks, in some cases by as much as half a millennium.

The two key dates for Sumerian chronology are the end of the Third Dynasty of Ur, when the Sumerians lost their predominant political position in Mesopotamia, and the beginning of the reign of Hammurabi of Babylon, when to all intents and purposes the Sumerians ceased to exist as a political, ethnic, and linguistic entity. The latter date, it is now generally agreed, is approximately 1750 B.C., plus or minus fifty years. For the time span between this date and the end of the Third Dynasty of Ur, there is enough inscriptional material available to show by dead reckoning that it was approximately 195 years in length; the end of the Third Dynasty of Ur may therefore be placed at 1945 B.C., plus or minus fifty years. From this date backward, there are enough historical inscriptions, date-formulas, and synchronisms of various sorts to carry us back to approximately 2500 B.C. and a ruler by the name of Mesilim. Beyond this, all dating depends entirely on archeological, stratigraphic, and epigraphic inferences and surmises of one sort or another and the results of carbon-14 tests, which, as already said, have not proved to be as decisive and conclusive as had been anticipated.

[2] For one of the most important of these, the so-called Sumerian King List, see pp. 328–31.

CHAPTER TWO

HISTORY:

Heroes, Kings, and Ensi*'s*

Now that we have clarified, at least to some extent, the method and procedures by which the modern archeologist and scholar has resurrected the long dead Sumerians and reconstructed their long forgotten culture, we are ready to turn to the history of Sumer, to those political, military, and sociological events that brought about Sumer's rise and fall. But not quite ready! There is one disturbing aspect of the problem of reconstructing Sumerian history of which the reader must be forewarned: the tenuous, elusive, meager, and partial character of the pertinent source material. From around 4500 B.C., when the first settlements were established in Sumer, to about 1750 B.C., when the Sumerians ceased to exist as a people, is a stretch of close to three thousand years, and the reader might well ask where we get our historical information and how trustworthy it is.

Let us start with the dark, negative, and unpromising side of the picture—the fact that the Sumerians themselves wrote no history in the generally accepted sense of the word, that is, in terms of unfolding processes and underlying principles. The Sumerian academicians and men of letters possessed neither the essential intellectual tools of definition and generalization nor the evolutionary approach fundamental to historical evaluation and interpretation. Limited by the world view current in their day and accepted as axiomatic truth—that cultural phenomena and historical events came ready-made, "full grown . . . full blown," on the world scene, since they were planned and brought about by

33

the all-powerful gods—it probably never occurred to even the most thoughtful and learned of the Sumerian sages that Sumer had once been desolate marshland with but few scattered settlements and had only gradually come to be a bustling, thriving, and complex community after many generations of struggle and toil in which human will and determination, man-laid plans and experiments, and man-made discoveries and inventions played a predominant role. Intellectually immobilized by this sterile and static attitude to the history of man, the Sumerian man of letters could at best become an archivist rather than a historian, a chronicler and analyst rather than an interpreter and expositor of historical truths.

Even the archive-chronicle type of history, however, had to be first invented by someone, somewhere, to fill some need deemed to be significant for one reason or another. In the case of the Sumerians it came into being not as a result of an intrinsic interest in recording incidents and events for their own sake, but because of the religious conviction that the kings and rulers of the city-states, usually known as *ensi*'s, could ensure long lives for themselves as well as the well-being and prosperity of their subjects by building, repairing, and furnishing the temples that were presumably the dwelling places of their gods. Before the invention of writing, these royal and princely building activities, although accompanied no doubt by impressive rites and symbolic rituals, remained unrecorded for posterity. Once the cuneiform system of writing had been developed from its earlier pictographic state, however, it must have occurred to one or another of the temple priests and scribes to put down in writing the ruler's building activities and votive offerings and thus record them for all to see and remember unto distant days. There and then—and to judge from our present data this thought first took root in the second quarter of the third millennium B.C.—written history may be said to have originated.

To be sure, the first building and votive inscriptions consisted of very brief dedications of little historical value. But gradually, the scribes became more confident, original, and communicative; and by the twenty-fourth century B.C., we find such relatively intricate and diversified historical accounts as the treaty between Lagash and Umma inscribed on the Stele of the Vultures, Eanna-

tum's military summaries, Entemena's account of the perennial
civil war between Lagash and Umma, the precious Urukagina
records of man's first social reforms based on a sense of freedom,
equality, and justice, Lugalzaggesi's lyric glorification and exaltation of the peace and prosperity, the happiness and security,
which prevailed during his reign in Sumer. The writing material
utilized by our ancient "historians" was quite varied and diversified: stone and clay tablets, bricks, stones, and door sockets, bowls
and vases, clay nails and cones, mortars and maceheads, steles and
plaques, statues and statuettes of stone and metal. All in all these
votive and dedicatory inscriptions add up to nearly a thousand,
although unfortunately the contents of the great majority of them
are only too brief and laconic. In any case, it is this group of inscriptions, contemporaneous more or less with the events that they
record, that has proved to be a prime source for the political
history of Sumer, partial and problematical as it is. In fact, it is
not at all unlikely that the ancient Sumerian historians themselves
made frequent use of these sources to help them in the preparation
of their own literary and historical documents.

Another basic and important contemporary historical source
derives, rather unexpectedly, from economic and administrative
documents and consists of what are usually known as date-formulas. The dealings and transactions recorded in these documents
had to be fixed in time for practical purposes, and from as early
as about 2500 B.C., the more inventive scribes began to devise
usable dating schemes. Fortunately for us, they did not choose to
date them simply by numbers of years from some generally accepted starting point, such as the beginning of a new reign or
dynasty, but rather, after some experimenting, settled upon the
procedure of naming the years by outstanding religious and political events. This method of dating provides us with historical
information of primary value. To identify the years dating their
archives more precisely, the scribes also compiled lists of all the
year-names current in a given reign or succession of reigns, and
these ancient lists enable the modern scholar to arrange the
events recorded in the date-formulas in their proper chronological
order.

Based, no doubt, to a large extent on these date-formulas and
date lists, is one of the most valuable Sumerian historical docu-

ments, the so-called King List, which records the names of most of the kings of Sumer and the lengths of their reigns from what, for the Sumerians, was the beginning of history—the time in the distant past when "kingship (first) descended from heaven"—up to and including part of the Isin dynasty, which began its rule about 1950 B.C. To be sure, this unique document is actually a mixture of fact and fancy, and it is often difficult to decide when the one begins and other ends. Its author seemed to work under the delusion that all of the dynasties he lists followed each other in strict succession, when in fact most of them, if not all, were contemporaneous to a greater or lesser extent. Moreover, he attributes reigns of legendary and incredible length to many of the rulers of the earlier dynasties, and so comes up with a total of close to a quarter of a million years for the eight kings before the Flood and a total of more than twenty-five thousand years for the first two dynasties after the Flood. In spite of all its defects and shortcomings, however, the King List, if used with discrimination and understanding, provides us with a historical framework of inestimable value.[1]

Another highly revealing historical source consists of what might be termed "royal correspondence," the letters that went back and forth between the rulers and their officials. These first appear as early as the twenty-fourth century B.C., but the group of letters which is of special historical significance is that of the rulers of the Third Dynasty of Ur. These letters reveal the motives, temptations, rivalries, and intrigues which went on behind the scenes and give a lively, if at times far from enchanting, human touch to the rather curt and lifeless votive inscriptions and date-formulas. Interestingly enough, these royal letters did not come down to us in their original form, but in copies prepared by the professors and students of the Sumerian academies, or *edubba's*, several centuries later—a clear indication of the value and importance attached to them even in ancient days.[2]

A prosaic, inventory-like historiographic document that may turn out to be of extraordinary significance for early Sumerian history and chronology is the so-called Tummal inscription, a unique compilation concerned primarily with the restoration of

[1] For a translation of the King List, see Appendix E.

[2] For translations of five of these letters, see Appendix F.

the Tummal, the shrine of the goddess Ninlil in Nippur, and secondarily with the building of the various sections of Enlil's temple in the same city. Part of this text has been known for almost half a century, but its missing beginning lines have only recently become available, and it is the contents of this hitherto unknown portion of the text that has turned out to be of surprising and unexpected historical value.[3]

There are also two highly poetic compositions which may be termed historiographic, at least to some slight extent. Both center about one of the most catastrophic events in Sumer's history: the humiliating and disastrous invasion of the country by the ruthless and barbaric nomadic hordes from the mountains to the east. In the first, and longer, of the two, which may be entitled "The Curse of Agade," a Sumerian poet and sage explains the catastrophe as the result of the impious and sacrilegious acts of Naram-Sin, the fourth ruler of the Dynasty of Akkad. The second poem records the glorious victory of Utuhegal, a king of Erech, over Tirigan, the last of the Gutian kings, and the happy return of the kingship to Sumer.[4]

Nine Sumerian epic tales, ranging in length from a little over one hundred to more than six hundred lines, are now known wholly or in part, and five of these are of no little importance, especially for the very early periods of Sumerian history, for which there are practically no contemporary written documents extant. Four of the five concern the heroic figures Enmerkar and Lugalbanda, and their contents are noteworthy for the light they shed on the close interrelationship between Sumer and an otherwise unknown and still unlocated city-state in northern Iran named Aratta. The fifth of the historiographic epic tales, "Gilgamesh and Agga of Kish," is of very special significance for the history of political institutions; it not only helps to illuminate the obscure period of Sumerian history in which the early struggle between the Sumerian city-states took place, but also records the convening of man's first political assembly, a "bicameral congress," which met over forty-five hundred years ago to decide on the agonizing question of war or peace.[5]

[3] For full details, see pp. 46–49.

[4] For a translation of this poem, see pp. 325–26.

[5] For a translation of the poem, see pp. 186–90.

One rather disappointing literary genre, from the point of view of political history, is the "lamentation," a type of poetic composition which bemoaned the sorry plight of Sumer and its cities in times of misfortune and defeat. The earliest known prototype of the lamentation, which does provide us with a bit of important historical information, is found inscribed on a clay tablet from Lagash; it describes in some detail the terrible destruction Lagash suffered at the hands of its relentless enemy Umma.[6] But the later, and much longer, compositions, such as "The Lamentation over Ur" and "The Lamentation over Nippur," restrict themselves primarily to the harrowing depiction of the destruction of the Sumerian cities and the suffering of their inhabitants and pay little heed to the historical events which brought about this melancholy state of events.

Finally, a modicum of historical information may be gleaned even from such literary genres as myths, hymns, and "wisdom" literature. None of these are at all historically oriented, but here and there they may disclose, unintentionally and incidentally, a bit of historical information not otherwise known. Thus, for example, it is from the royal hymns that we learn that Sumer's most dreaded enemy, the Gutians, were still troublesome and formidable in the days of the Third Dynasty of Ur in spite of Utuhegal's vaunted victory. Or we may learn from a myth something about Sumer's relations with the rest of the world; or a proverb may mention the name of a ruler for one reason or another.

But votive inscriptions and date-formulas, royal epistles and lists of rulers and dynasties, epic songs of victory and bitter laments of defeat—all these hardly add up to history as we like to think of it. Moreover, for approximately the first two millenniums of Sumer's existence we have practically no written historical documents at all, and the votive inscriptions which we have from the later periods come from only a few Sumerian sites and therefore tend to give a one-sided picture of the events they record. As for the poetic compositions, and especially the epic tales, these contain at best but a kernel of historical truth, and the modern scholar usually finds himself hopelessly frustrated in his efforts to separate the wheat from the chaff, the real from the imagined, and thus isolate the historically significant residue.

---

[6] For a translation of this document, see pp. 322–23.

All the present-day Sumerologist can do is to analyze and interpret his fragmentary, obscure, and elusive data, and attempt to reconstruct at least a few of the outstanding political events and historical developments in accordance with his own reason, understanding, insight, and discernment—all of which necessarily leads to a more subjective and biased treatment than is desirable or perhaps even permissible. Under these circumstances, there is bound to be considerable difference of views even among the specialists in the field. The sketch of Sumerian history here presented suffers no doubt from the author's particular prejudices, conceits, and shortcomings; but this is the best he can do with the data available in the year 1963, and if his errors of commission as well as omission are many and dire, may the future generations and the Sumerian gods take account of the mitigating circumstances and judge him with mercy and compassion. In telling what little he knows, or thinks he knows, about Sumerian history, he is only following the dictate of the ancient Sumerian proverb: "He who knows, why should he keep it hidden?"

Sumer, or rather the land which came to be known as Sumer during the third millennium B.C., was probably first settled sometime between 4500 and 4000 B.C.—at least this was the consensus of Near Eastern archeologists until quite recently. This figure was obtained by starting with 2500 B.C., an approximate and reasonably assured date obtained by dead reckoning with the help of written documents. To this was added from fifteen hundred to two thousand years, a time span large enough to account for the stratigraphic accumulation of all the earlier cultural remains down to virgin soil, that is, right down to the beginning of human habitation in Sumer. At that time, it was generally assumed, Sumer was a vast swampy marsh broken up here and there by low islands of alluvial land built up by the gradual deposit of silt carried by the Tigris, Euphrates, and Karun rivers. Before that, most of Sumer was presumably covered by the waters of the Persian Gulf, which extended much farther than they do today, and human habitation was therefore impossible.

All this was accepted theory in archeological circles until 1952, when the two geologists Lees and Falcon published a paper which carried revolutionary implications for the date of Sumer's first settlement. In this study, entitled "The Geographical History of the Mesopotamian Plains,"[7] they adduced geological evidence to show that Sumer had been above water long before 4500–4000 B.C., and it was not at all impossible, therefore, that man had settled there considerably earlier than had been generally assumed. The reason traces of these earliest settlements in Sumer have not as yet been unearthed, it was argued, may be because the land has been sinking slowly at the same time that the water table has been rising. The very lowest level of cultural remains in Sumer may, therefore, now be under water and may never have been reached by archeologists, since they would have been misled by the higher water level into believing they had touched virgin soil. If that should prove to be true, Sumer's oldest cultural remains are still buried and untapped, and the date of Sumer's very first settlements may have to be pushed back a millennium or so.

Be that as it may, it is reasonably certain that the first settlers in Sumer were not the Sumerians. The pertinent evidence derives not from archeological or anthropological sources, which are rather ambiguous and inconclusive on this matter, but from linguistics. The name of Sumer's two life-giving rivers, the Tigris and Euphrates, or *idiglat* and *buranun* as they read in cuneiform, are not Sumerian words. Nor are the names of Sumer's most important urban centers—Eridu, Ur, Larsa, Isin, Adab, Kullab, Lagash, Nippur, Kish—words which have a satisfactory Sumerian etymology. Both the rivers and the cities, or rather the villages which later became cities, must have been named by a people that did not speak the Sumerian language, just as, for example, such names as Mississippi, Connecticut, Massachusetts, and Dakota indicate that the first inhabitants of the United States did not speak the English language.

The name of these pre-Sumerian settlers of Sumer is of course unknown. They lived long before writing was invented and left no telltale records. Nor can we identify them from the Sumerian documents of a later day, although it is barely possible that at least some of them were known in the third millennium as Subarians. But this we do know with a fair degree of certainty: they were the first important civilizing force in ancient Sumer, its first farmers, cultivators, cattle raisers, and fishermen; its first

[7] *Geographical Journal,* CXVIII, 24–39.

weavers, leatherworkers, carpenters, smiths, potters, and masons. Once again it was linguistic analysis that provided the proof. In a paper published in 1944 in a journal sponsored by the University of Ankara,[8] Benno Landsberger, one of the keenest minds in cuneiform research, analyzed a number of culturally significant "Sumerian" words—that is, words known from Sumerian documents of the third millennium b.c. and therefore generally assumed to be Sumerian—and showed that there is good reason to believe that they are not Sumerian at all. All of these words consisted of two or more syllables—in Sumerian, the majority of roots are monosyllabic—and in general showed the same pattern as the words for Tigris, Euphrates, and the non-Sumerian city names; Landsberger concluded that they must therefore belong to the language spoken by the same pre-Sumerian people that had named Sumer's two rivers and most of its cities. Among these words were those for farmer (*engar*), herdsman (*udul*), and fisherman (*shuhadak*), plow (*apin*) and furrow (*apsin*), palm (*nimbar*) and date (*sulumb*), metalworker (*tibira*) and smith (*simug*), carpenter (*nangar*) and basketmaker (*addub*), weaver (*ishbar*) and leatherworker (*ashgab*), potter (*pahar*), mason (*shidim*), and perhaps even merchant (*damgar*), a word which has almost universally been taken to be a Semitic hallmark. It therefore follows that the basic agricultural techniques and industrial skills were first introduced in Sumer not by the Sumerians but by their nameless predecessors. Landsberger called this people Proto-Euphrateans, a somewhat awkward name which is nevertheless both appropriate and useful from the linguistic point of view.

In archeology, the Proto-Euphrateans are known as the Ubaid people, that is, the people responsible for the cultural remains first unearthed in the tell known as al-Ubaid not far from Ur and later in the very lowest levels of a number of tells throughout ancient Sumer. These remains consisted of stone implements, such as hoes, adzes, querns, pounders, and knives, and of clay artifacts, such as sickles, bricks, loom weights, spindle whorls, figurines, as well as a distinctive and characteristic type of painted pottery. As already gathered from the linguistic evidence, therefore, the Proto-Euphrateans, or Ubaidians, were enterprising agriculturists who founded a number of villages and towns throughout the land

[8] *Dil ve Tarih-Coğrafya Dergisi,* I/5, II/3, III, 2 (1943–45).

and developed a rural economy of considerable wealth and stability.

The Ubaidians, however, did not long remain the sole and dominant power in ancient Sumer. Immediately to the west of Sumer lies the Syrian desert and the Arabian peninsula, the home of the Semitic nomads from time immemorial. As the Ubaidian settlers thrived and prospered, some of these Semitic hordes began to infiltrate their settlements both as peaceful immigrants and as warlike conquerors. To be sure, we have as yet no direct and conclusive evidence for this crucial inference. In the first place, however, it can be postulated a priori from what is known of the later history of Sumer. Again and again over the millenniums the barbaric Semitic nomads infiltrated and conquered the settled centers of Sumer, and there is no reason to assume that this did not happen in the fourth millennium B.C. as well. Then again, even the oldest Sumerian inscriptions contain a number of Semitic loanwords, and the Sumerian pantheon contains not a few deities which are of Semitic origin—some of these borrowings may reach back to very early days. Finally, the first dynasty of Sumer whose existence can be historically attested at least to some extent, the so-called First Dynasty of Kish, which according to the ancients themselves followed immediately upon the subsidence of the Flood, begins with a whole group of rulers bearing Semitic names. None of this evidence is really conclusive, but all in all it seems not unreasonable to conjecture that the Semites followed the Proto-Euphrateans into Sumer and that as a result of the cross-fertilization of their two cultures, there came into being the first relatively high civilization in Sumer, one in which the Semitic element was probably predominant.

Be that as it may, it is highly probable that the Sumerians themselves did not arrive in Sumer until sometime in the second half of the fourth millennium B.C. Just where their original home was is still quite uncertain. To judge from a cycle of epic tales revolving about Enmerkar and Lugalbanda, the early Sumerian rulers seem to have had an unusually close and intimate relationship with a city-state known as Aratta, probably situated somewhere in the region of the Caspian Sea. The Sumerian language is an agglutinative tongue, reminiscent to some extent of the Ural-Altaic languages, and this fact may also point to the same general area as Aratta. But wherever the Sumerians came from, and whatever type of culture they brought with them, this is certain: their arrival led to an extraordinarily fruitful fusion, both ethnic and cultural, with the native population and brought about a creative spurt fraught with no little significance for the history of civilization. In the course of the centuries that followed, Sumer reached new heights of political power and economic wealth, and witnessed some of its most significant achievements in the arts and crafts, in monumental architecture, in religious and ethical thought, and in oral myth, epic, and hymn. Above all, the Sumerians, whose language gradually became the prevailing speech of the land, devised a system of writing, developed it into an effective tool of communication, and took the first steps toward the introduction of formal education.

The first ruler of Sumer whose deeds are recorded, if only in the briefest kind of statement, is a king by the name of Etana of Kish, who may have come to the throne quite early in the third millennium B.C. In the King List he is described as "he who stabilized all the lands." On the assumption that this statement, found in a document dated a millennium or so later than the reign of Etana, embodies a trustworthy tradition, it may be inferred that he held sway not only over Sumer, but over some of the neighboring lands as well—in short, that he may have been man's first known empire-builder. That Etana was a notable and outstanding figure in the early history of Sumer is shown by the purely legendary note in the very same King List that he was "a man who ascended to heaven" and by a Semitic Akkadian poem current early in the second millennium B.C. that centers about this same mythical motif. According to this legend, for which a Sumerian prototype may well turn up some future day, Etana was a pious, god-fearing king who had practiced the divine cult faithfully and assiduously, but was cursed with childlessness and thus had no one to carry on his name. His fervent desire, therefore, was to obtain "the plant of birth," which, however, was located in heaven far from mortal reach. In order to get to heaven, Etana procured the aid of an eagle whom he had rescued from a pit where it had been cast by a serpent whose friendship it had betrayed and whose young it had devoured. This legend was quite popular among the seal-cutters, to judge from a number of seals depicting a mortal climbing heavenward on the wings of an eagle. To be sure, Etana did not stay put in heaven, for according to a recently translated funeral dirge on a tablet in the Pushkin Museum as well as to the long-known seventh tablet of the Akkadian Epic of Gilgamesh, we find Etana residing in the nether world whither all mortals, no matter how great their achievements—except, of course, the Flood-hero Ziusudra—must finally descend. But all these legendary traditions only help to demonstrate that Etana had been a powerful and impressive figure whose life and deeds had caught the imagination of the ancient bards and poets.

Etana, according to the King List, is followed by seven rulers, several of whom, to judge from their names, were Semites rather than Sumerians. The eighth was the king Enmebaraggesi, about whom we do have some historical, or at least saga-like, information from both the King List and other late Sumerian literary works. Moreover, only very recently, a precious three-word contemporary inscription was discovered on a small fragment of an alabaster vase by a young Sumerologist working in Baghdad, which proves beyond doubt that he was not at all a mythical king, but one of real flesh and blood.[9] By the time Enmebaraggesi came to the throne of Kish, another Sumerian city-state, far to the south of Kish, had come to the fore and was challenging Kish's supremacy; for not long after the reign of Etana, it would seem that a king by the name of Meskiaggasher, described in the King List as "the son of Utu (the Sumerian sun-god)," founded an ambitious and powerful dynasty in the city of Erech, which in his days was still known by the older name Eanna, "House of An (the heaven-god)." To judge from a rather ambiguous and obscure note attached to his name in the King List, which reads, "He entered the seas (and) ascended the mountains," he may have tried to extend his sway over the lands all around Sumer and far beyond. Be that as it may, his son Enmerkar, who, according to the King List, followed him on the throne, but who in the epic poems is given the epithet "son of Utu"—the same as that given to his father in the King List—was certainly one of the outstanding figures of early Sumer. According to the King List, he built the

[9] See D. O. Edzard in *Zeitschrift für Assyriologie,* LIII (1959), 9–26.

city of Erech; and according to the epic tales, he led a campaign against Aratta, somewhere in the neighborhood of the Caspian Sea, and subjugated it to Erech.

One of Enmerkar's heroic heralds and companions-in-arms in his struggle with Aratta was Lugalbanda, who succeeded Enmerkar to the throne of Erech. Since he is the major protagonist of at least two epic tales, he too must have been a venerable and impressive ruler; and it is not surprising to find that by 2400 B.C., and perhaps even earlier, he had been deified by the Sumerian theologians and given a place in the Sumerian pantheon. Unfortunately, neither the King List nor the epic tales give any information about his political and military achievements, except that he accompanied Enmerkar on his Aratta campaign.

Lugalbanda, according to the King List, is followed by Dumuzi, a ruler who became the major figure in a Sumerian "holy-marriage rite" and "dying-god" myth which left a deep impression on the ancient world. In fact, the women of Jerusalem, to the horror of the prophet Ezekiel, were still lamenting his death in the sixth century B.C. (Ezekiel 8:14). One of the months of the Jewish calendar bears his name to this day, and the fasting and lamentation which mark its seventeenth day no doubt hark back to the Sumerian days of the distant past. Just why Dumuzi was singled out by the later Sumerian theologians as the protagonist of this particular rite and myth is still unknown. It must have been due at least in large part to the deep impression Dumuzi made during his lifetime both as man and ruler, but as yet there is no historical data whatever to corroborate this view.

Dumuzi is followed, according to the King List, by Gilgamesh, a ruler whose deeds won him such wide renown that he became the supreme hero of Sumerian myth and legend. Poems extolling Gilgamesh and his deeds were written and rewritten throughout the centuries, not only in Sumerian, but in most of the other more important languages of western Asia. Gilgamesh became the hero par excellence of the ancient world—an adventurous, brave, but tragic figure symbolizing man's vain but endless drive for fame, glory, and immortality—to such an extent that he has sometimes been taken by modern scholars to be a legendary figure rather than a real man and ruler. We still have no contemporary records of him, although there is some hope that the excavations now being conducted in Erech may uncover some sooner or later. In 1955, however, there came to light the initial ten lines of a long-known Tummal inscription which put an entirely new light on Gilgamesh and his times. In fact, this passage, brief as it is, helps to clarify the political situation in those early days of Sumerian history in so significant and unexpected a fashion that it is advisable to go into the matter in some detail.

According to the King List, the first three Sumerian dynasties after the Flood were those of Kish, Erech, and Ur, in that order. But from Sumerian epic and hymnal lore it had been known for some time that the last two kings of the Kish dynasty, Enmebaraggesi (of whom, as was noted earlier, we now have a contemporary inscription) and his son Agga, were contemporaries of Gilgamesh, the fifth ruler of Erech, with whom they carried on a bitter struggle for supremacy over Sumer.[10] It was therefore generally accepted among cuneiformists that the First Dynasty of Kish and the First Dynasty of Erech overlapped to a large extent. As for the First Dynasty of Ur, from which we now have several contemporary inscriptions, its founder, Mesannepadda, was taken by practically all scholars to have lived considerably later than Gilgamesh of Erech, the suggested span of time between these two rulers varying from as little as forty to as many as four hundred years. It therefore came somewhat as a shock to realize, as a result of the new evidence based on a hitherto unknown passage of no more than ten lines, that Mesannepadda was actually an older contemporary of Gilgamesh—that even Mesannepadda's son, Meskiagnunna, was a contemporary of Gilgamesh—and that it was Mesannepadda of Ur who brought the First Dynasty of Kish to an end, not Gilgamesh or for that matter any other ruler of the First Dynasty of Erech, in spite of the statement in the King List reading, "Kish was smitten with weapons; its kingship was carried to Eanna."

The document on which this new evidence is based is the thirty-four-line historiographic text mentioned earlier, known as the Tummal Inscription, Tummal being the name of a district in Nippur consecrated to the goddess Ninlil, which no doubt contained her most important shrine. Except for the first ten lines, the

[10] For accounts of this struggle, see the epic tale "Gilgamesh and Agga," pp. 186–90.

Tummal text has been known almost in its entirety since 1914, when Arno Poebel published two tablets inscribed with the composition in his book *Historical Texts*.[11] Beginning with line 11, this text runs as follows:

11 For a second time, the Tummal fell into ruin,[12]
12 Gilgamesh built the Numunburra of the House
      of Enlil.
13 Ur-lugal, the son of Gilgamesh,
14 Made the Tummal pre-eminent,
15 Brought Ninlil to the Tummal.
16 For the third time, the Tummal fell into ruin,
17 Nanna built the "Lofty Park" of the House of
      Enlil.
18 Meskiag-Nanna, the son of Nanna,
19 Made the Tummal pre-eminent,
20 Brought Ninlil to the Tummal.
21 For the fourth time, the Tummal fell into ruin,
22 Ur-Nammu built the Ekur.
23 Shulgi, the son of Ur-Nammu,
24 Made the Tummal pre-eminent,
25 Brought Ninlil to the Tummal.
26 For the fifth time, the Tummal fell into ruin,
27 From the year of Amar-Sin
28 Until (the year when) Ibbi-Sin, the king,
29 Enamgalanna as the *en* of Inanna of Erech
30 Selected,
31 Ninlil was brought to the Tummal.
32 According to the word of Lu-Inanna, the
      ashgab-gal of Enlil,
33 Ishbi-Erra built the Ekurraigigalla,
34 The storehouse of Enlil.

From this text, even with the initial passage missing, it was clear that its author, who lived in the time of Ishbi-Erra, the founder of the First Dynasty of Isin, intended to give a brief historical

[11] Vol. IV, No. 1, of "Publications of the Babylonian Section of the University Museum of the University of Pennsylvania."

[12] In the translations cited throughout this book, two dots stand for the omission of a word, three dots for the omission of two words, four dots for the omission of three or more words. Brackets enclose doubtful restorations; parentheses enclose words helpful for the meaning, but not in the original text. Sumerian words are italicized. Where no meaning is given, it is unknown.

résumé of the various buildings in the Enlil temple-complex at Nippur and in particular of the restorations of Ninlil's Tummal. Moreover, the rather striking stylistic pattern utilized by the author made it possible to deduce the general character of the contents of the missing five lines immediately preceding, though not the names of the individuals involved. Thus, since the available text began with the five-line passage:

> For a second time, the Tummal fell into ruin,
> Gilgamesh built the Numunburra of the House of Enlil.
> Ur-lugal, the son of Gilgamesh,
> Made the Tummal pre-eminent,
> Brought Ninlil to the Tummal.

it seemed reasonable to conclude that the preceding five-line passage had read:

> For the first time, the Tummal fell into ruin,
> X built the Y-building of the House of Enlil.
> Z, the son of X,
> Made the Tummal pre-eminent,
> Brought Ninlil to the Tummal.

As for the passage at the very beginning of the document, there was no way of inferring its contents, though it seemed only common sense to guess that this should have stated who it was that built the House of Enlil and the Tummal in the first place.

Fortunately, there is now no longer any need for guesses, inferences, or restorations; the entire missing ten-line passage is found on two tablets in the Hilprecht Collection of the Friedrich-Schiller University, which I first studied in the course of a ten-week stay in Jena in the autumn of 1955 and which Inez Bernhardt, the assistant curator of the Hilprecht Collection, has copied for a volume of literary texts which appeared in 1961. Both are fragmentary, but fortunately they supplement each other in such a way that not a single sign is missing from the initial ten-line passage of the document. Here is what these lines say:

> 1   Enmebaraggesi, the king,
> 2   In this very city (that is, Nippur) built the
>   House of Enlil.
> 3   Agga, the son of Enmebaraggesi,
> 4   Made the Tummal pre-eminent,

5 Brought Ninlil to the Tummal.
6 For the first time, the Tummal fell into ruin,
7 Mesannepadda built the Burshushua of the House
   of Enlil.
8 Meskiagnunna, the son of Mesannepadda,
9 Made the Tummal pre-eminent,
10 Brought Ninlil to the Tummal.

The text then goes on:

11 For the second time, the Tummal fell into ruin,
12 Gilgamesh, etc.

Here, then, unless we are to assume that the Tummal document
is historically untrustworthy, is proof positive that Mesannepadda
and even his son Meskiagnunna preceded Gilgamesh in the control of the city of Nippur. Since, however, they followed Agga,
who was himself a contemporary of Gilgamesh, according to the
Gilgamesh-Agga synchronism mentioned above, it is obvious that
they, too, were contemporaries of Gilgamesh. The historical
events stated and implied in the newly recovered Tummal passage
should therefore probably be reconstructed as follows.

In the struggle for power over Sumer as a whole, Mesannepadda,
the founder of the First Dynasty of Ur, wrested the control of
Nippur from Agga, the last ruler of the First Dynasty of Kish. In
fact, he probably attacked Kish itself and was directly responsible
for Agga's downfall, which would explain why Mesannepadda was
called "king of Kish" rather than "king of Ur" on his own seal inscription, since the title "king of Kish" carried time-honored
prestige. But Mesannepadda must have been an old man by the
time Nippur fell into his hands, and he therefore only had time
to build a new building in the Enlil temple-complex, the Burshushua. It was left to his son, Meskiagnunna, to restore the
Tummal for Ninlil. But then Meskiagnunna's control of Nippur
was brought to an end by Gilgamesh, who, when a young man,
had evidently had his own difficulties with Agga of Kish as well
as his father Enmebaraggesi. By this time, however, Gilgamesh
must also have been far along in years; in any case, it was not he
but his son, Ur-lugal, who restored the Tummal.

Since Mesannepadda, the founder of the First Dynasty of Ur,
was an older contemporary of Gilgamesh, who probably reigned

some time about 2600 B.C.—he had already been deified by about 2500 B.C.—the date of his reign is about a century or so earlier than scholars had usually assigned it on the available, but far from conclusive, epigraphic evidence. This raises, however, another chronological problem which cannot be resolved for the present, but should at least be borne in mind. In the course of excavating the renowned Royal Cemetery at Ur, there was uncovered a white shell cylinder seal inscribed with the words "Meskalamdug, king" and another cylinder seal inscribed with the words "Akalamdug, king of Ur." Neither of these rulers are mentioned in the King List, and so there is no way of knowing whether they preceded or followed Mesannepadda. The excavator, Sir Leonard Woolley, claims that since several seal impressions bearing the name of Mesannepadda were recovered from a mass of rubbish spread over the part of the Royal Cemetery in which the Meskalamdug and Akalamdug seals were found, these two kings must be earlier in date than Mesannepadda. This may turn out to be so; but there is considerable room for error when it comes to interpreting archeological and stratigraphic evidence, and the possibility that Mesannepadda preceded the other two rulers is not to be excluded.

The bitter three-cornered struggle for supremacy by the rulers of Kish, Erech, and Ur must have seriously weakened Sumer and impaired its military might. In any case, immediately following the First Dynasty of Ur, according to the King List, the kingship of Sumer was carried off to foreign parts, to the kingdom of Awan, an Elamitic city-state not far removed from Susa. Just how and when Sumer recovered from this blow is quite uncertain. The King List records that "Awan was smitten by weapons" and that its kingship "was carried off to Kish." But no inscriptions from the rulers of this dynasty, the Second Dynasty of Kish, have been recovered to date; and this, together with the fact that the Second Dynasty of Kish was followed by another Elamitic dynasty, that of the kingdom of Hamazi, would seem to indicate that the Sumerians had not yet recovered their former might. The dynasty of Hamazi, according to the King List, was followed by a Second Dynasty of Erech, for which no inscriptional material has as yet been discovered. It is following this dynasty that we come upon a ruler who may well have been the savior of Sumer. His name is Lugalannemundu, a king of Adab, to whom the King List attributes the incredibly long reign of ninety years. He has left behind him a document that indicates that he was a great conqueror and military leader who was in control of the entire Fertile Crescent, from the Mediterranean to the Zagros Mountains. To be sure, this inscription has come down to us only in the form of a copy dating from nearly a millennium later than the events that it records. But its contents are carefully, minutely, and convincingly detailed, and ring quite genuine and trustworthy.

Lugalannemundu, according to this document, is "king of the four quarters (of the universe)," a ruler "who made all the foreign lands pay steady tribute to him, who brought peace to (literally, 'made lie in the pastures') the peoples of all the lands, who built the temples of all the great gods, who restored Sumer (to its former glory), who exercised kingship over the entire world." The text then proceeds to name thirteen *ensi*'s, together with the city-states over which they wielded power, who banded together in rebellion against him and whom he defeated. It is not uninteresting to note that most of these *ensi*'s, even those ruling Elamite kingdoms, have Semitic names. Lugalannemundu next seized Gutium, whose people are known from later inscriptions to have been Sumer's most dreaded enemy, and a number of other lands—but unfortunately the text is very fragmentary at this point.

The main part of the document is devoted to the building in Adab of a temple named Enamzu, dedicated to the chief deity of the city, the mother-goddess Nintu; the temple was particularly noteworthy for its seven gates and seven doors, each of which had a special name, such as "Lofty Gate," "Great Gate," "Gate of (divine) Decrees," "Lofty Door," "Door of Refreshing Shade," and so on. When the temple was completed, our document continues, Lugalannemundu dedicated it to the goddess with sacrifices of "seven times seven" fatted oxen and fatted sheep, and the viziers, or *sukkalmah*'s, of "Cedar Mountain" land, Elam, Marhashi, Gutium, Subir, Martu, Sutium, and Eanna (the old name for the kingdom of Erech) came with sacrifices to the Adab temple in order to participate in the celebration. This rather extraordinary dedicatory inscription then closes with the exhortation that the goddess Nintu should grant long life to the *ensi*'s of these seven lands if they continue to bring offerings and sacrifices to the Enamzu of Adab.

Lugalannemundu, it is clear from this inscription, was therefore one of the more powerful and dynamic rulers of Sumer; to judge from the list and location of lands he controlled—"Cedar Mountain" Land, Elam, Marhashi, and Gutium in the east, Subir in the north, Martu in the west, and Sutium and Eanna in the center and south—he might well call himself a ruler of the "four quarters" of the universe. As for the date of his rule, it may go back to the twenty-sixth century B.C., that is, at least a half century or so before the rulers of Sumer whose dates can be closely calculated by dead reckoning with the help of the Lagash documents, for these rulers follow each other in close succession and leave no room for so powerful and dominant a figure as Lugalannemundu.

Starting with about 2500 and ending with about 2350 B.C., we have a whole series of dedicatory inscriptions which enable us to reconstruct a more or less continuous and unbroken history of Sumer—at least as far as the major figures and events are concerned. These derive primarily from Lagash, a city-state in the southeastern part of Sumer, which, for some as yet unknown reason, is not mentioned in the King List, but which played a very important role in the political history of Sumer between about 2450 and 2300 B.C. To be sure, Lagash was only one of the kingdoms that constituted the land of Sumer throughout this stretch of one hundred and fifty years; there were more than half a dozen others existing alongside each other, for example, Mari, Adab, Erech, Ur, Kish, and Akshak. But unfortunately, we know little of what actually transpired in them, since practically nothing but the names of the rulers have come down to us; only rarely is a document found that records a significant political and military event. From Lagash, on the other hand, we have several hundred dedicatory inscriptions, and while the great majority are laconic and repetitive, there are several that are of outstanding value for the history of this period. This means, of course, that we see the events through Lagashite eyes; but to judge from those cases which can be verified from other sources, the Lagashite historians seem to have respected the truth and recorded the facts as they actually took place, although the pious and religious character of the historical style they developed is sometimes obscure and confusing. It is, then, primarily from these Lagash inscriptions that the course of historical events about to be sketched can be reconstructed.

Not much later than about 2500 B.C., there came on the Sumerian scene a ruler named Mesilim, who took the title King of Kish and seemed to be in control of the entire land—his inscribed macehead was found in Lagash; several of his inscribed objects were found in Adab; and most important of all, he was the responsible arbitrator in a bitter boundary dispute between the kingdoms of Lagash and Umma. A generation or so following Mesilim's reign, 2450 B.C. or thereabouts, a man named Ur-Nanshe established himself as king of Lagash and founded a dynasty which was to endure for five generations. We do not know where Ur-Nanshe came from or how he rose to power—there is even a bare possibility that he was originally not a Sumerian but a Semite from a land known as Tidnum, to the west of Sumer. Be that as it may, he has left behind him some fifty inscriptions on tablets, plaques, door sockets, bricks, and nails, which record primarily the building of temples, digging of canals, and fashioning of divine statues.[13] One of the sentences occurring repeatedly in these inscriptions, however, carries political and economic implications of a rather startling character, although it is to be noted that the translation here offered is not yet fully assured. The statement reads, "The ships of Dilmun brought him (Ur-Nanshe) wood as a tribute from foreign lands," which implies that Ur-Nanshe was powerful enough to control a number of foreign lands beyond the Persian Gulf.[14] To date, however, there is no other evidence to verify so far-reaching a claim, and it may be advisable to let the matter rest as uncertain for the present.

One of Ur-Nanshe's sons, Akurgal, succeeded him on the throne of Lagash. Early in his reign he apparently ran into difficulties with the Ummaites, and his rule was of short duration. He was succeeded by his son Eannatum, whose military conquests made him the most powerful figure of his day, so much so that he dared assume, at least for a few brief years, the title King of Kish, which carried with it the claim to supremacy over all Sumer. He began his reign peacefully enough with the building and rebuilding of

[13] Three selected inscriptions may be found on pp. 308–9.

[14] For the location of Dilmun, see pp. 281–84.

those parts of his kingdom which must have been destroyed by the Ummaites in the days of Akurgal. But he later embarked on a series of victorious military enterprises conducted against Elam to the east, Umma to the north, Erech and Ur to the west, not to mention several cities whose location is still unknown. The immediate causes for these wars are unknown, except in the case of Umma. For an account of this struggle we have the rather detailed document prepared by one of the archivists of Eannatum's nephew Entemena, and from it we may reconstruct the background and drama of the conflict between Lagash and Umma and Eannatum's temporarily successful role in it as follows.

In the days when Mesilim was king of Kish and at least the nominal suzerain of Sumer, a border dispute arose between the cities of Lagash and Umma, both of which evidently acknowledged Mesilim as their overlord. The latter proceeded to arbitrate the controversy by measuring off a boundary line between the two cities in accordance with what was given out to be an oracle of Sataran, a deity in charge of settling complaints. Moreover, he erected an inscribed stele to mark the spot and prevent future disputes.

However, the decision, which was presumably accepted by both parties, seemed to favor Lagash over Umma. In any case, not long afterward Ush, an *ensi* of Umma, violated the terms of the decision—the time is not stated, but there are indications that this violation took place not long before Ur-Nanshe founded his dynasty at Lagash. Ush ripped out Mesilim's stele to indicate that he was not bound by its terms and then crossed the border and seized the northernmost territory belonging to Lagash, known as the Guedinna.

This land remained in the hands of the Ummaites until the days of Eannatum, the grandson of Ur-Nanshe, who attacked and defeated the Ummaites and made a new border treaty with Enakalle (then the *ensi* of Umma). He dug a ditch in line with the new boundary which would help ensure the fertility of the Guedinna, erected there for purposes of future record the old Mesilim stele, as well as several steles of his own, and constructed a number of buildings and shrines to several of the more important Sumerian deities. Moreover, to help minimize the possible source of future conflict between Umma and Lagash, he set aside a strip of fallow land on the Umma side of the boundary ditch as a kind of no-man's land. Finally, Eannatum, probably in an effort to alleviate the feelings of the Ummaites to some extent, since he was eager to expand his conquests in other directions, agreed to let them farm the fields lying in the Guedinna and even further south. But, he granted this only under the condition that they pay the Lagash rulers a share of the crops for the use of the land, thus assuring himself and his successors a considerable revenue.

Eannatum followed up his victories over Elam and the more southerly cities of Sumer, such as Umma, Erech, and Ur, with military triumphs over northern Sumer, which was under the control of the city of Kish and the neighboring Akshak. Kish, to be sure, seemed to have been weakened by a defeat at the hands of Enshakushanna, who described himself as *"en of Sumer"* and "king of the 'Land' "; and it was Zuzu, the king of Akshak, who led an invasion of the northern forces into Lagash. Eannatum routed the invading forces and pursued them "from the Anta-surra" (the northern boundary of Lagash) to Akshak itself, in-flicting heavy losses on them.

Eannatum was now at the acme of his power; he even felt powerful enough to take the title "King of Kish" with its implied claim of suzerainty over Sumer as a whole; or as the ancient author puts it, "To Eannatum, the *ensi* of Lagash . . . Inanna (the tutelary deity of Kish), because she loved him, gave the kingship of Kish in addition to the *ensi*-ship of Lagash." It was at this time, too, that he must have erected and dedicated the Stele of the Vultures commemorating his well-earned victories. It appears that a brief period of peace now followed for Sumer, and we find Eannatum taking time out to dig a new canal, which he named exultantly Lummagimdug, "Good (?)-like-Lumma," Lumma being Eannatum's Tidnum name, that is, presumably the name given him by the Semitic Martu people to the west of Sumer where Tidnum is known to have been located.

But before the canal was finished, before in fact he had time to line its walls with bricks, Eannatum was again at war. This time it was he who was on the defensive, just barely succeeding in holding his enemies at bay and staving off defeat. First the Elamites attacked him from the east, and though he threw them back to their homeland, he was unable to follow up his success and invade Elam itself. For by this time his old enemies from the north, Kish and Akshak, had invaded Lagash. No sooner did he drive them back from Lagash territory than the Elamites returned with new allies, to be followed once again by the troops of Kish and Akshak, supported this time by a new enemy, the kingdom of Mari, far to the west. In pitched battles fought at the Asuhur, Lagash's eastern boundary, and the Antasurra, its northern boundary, Eannatum won a decisive victory over his enemies. Once again there was a brief respite from wars, and Eannatum was in a position to renew his building activities, reinforcing the walls of the canal Lummagimdug and constructing a huge reservoir for its waters. But in spite of his victories and his proud epithet "Prostrater of all the Lands for Ningirsu," Eannatum seems to have come to an unfortunate end, for his successor was not one of his sons but his brother Enannatum. This points to the probability that he did not die a natural death but fell in a battle that must have been catastrophic for Lagash, a battle from which it never fully recovered.

Enannatum, upon succeeding his brother to the rule of Lagash, soon found himself in serious difficulties with the Ummaites, for despite their defeat at the hands of Eannatum, it took them less than a generation to recover their confidence, if not their former strength. In any case, Ur-Lumma, the son of the unfortunate Enakalle, repudiated the bitterly rankling agreement with Lagash and refused to pay Enannatum the revenue imposed upon Umma. Moreover, he proceeded to drain the boundary ditches, rip out and put to fire both Mesilim's and Eannatum's steles with their irritating inscriptions, and destroy the buildings and shrines which Eannatum had constructed along the boundary ditch to warn the Ummaites that they must not trespass on Lagash territory. He was now set to cross the border and enter the Guedinna. To further assure himself of victory, he sought and obtained the military aid of the "foreigners" to the north of Sumer.

The two forces met in the Gana-ugigga of the Guedinna, not far south of the border. The Ummaites and their allies were under the command of Ur-Lumma himself, while the Lagashites were led by Entemena, since his father Enannatum must have been quite an old man at the time. The Lagashites were victorious;

Ur-Lumma fled, hotly pursued by Entemena, and many of his troops were waylaid and killed.

But Entemena's victory proved to be ephemeral. Upon Ur-Lumma's defeat and probable death, a new enemy appeared on the scene: Il, the temple head of a city named Hallab, situated not far from Umma to the north. Il had evidently been shrewd enough to wait it out while Entemena and Ur-Lumma were struggling for a decision. But as soon as the battle was over, he attacked the victorious Entemena, met with initial success, and penetrated deep into Lagash territory. To be sure, he was unable to hold on to his gains south of the Umma-Lagash border; but he did succeed in making himself *ensi* of Umma.

Il now proceeded to show his contempt for the Lagash claims in almost the same manner as his predecessor, Ush. He deprived the boundary ditches of the water so essential to the irrigation of the nearby fields and farms and refused to pay all but a fraction of the revenue imposed upon Umma by the old Eannatum treaty. And when Entemena sent envoys to him demanding an explanation for his unfriendly acts, he answered by arrogantly claiming the entire Guedinna as his territory and domain.

The issue between Il and Entemena, however, was not decided by war. Instead, a compromise seems to have been forced upon them by a third party, probably once again the northern non-Sumerian ruler who claimed lordship over Sumer as a whole. By and large, the decision seems to have favored Lagash, since the old Mesilim-Eannatum line was retained as the fixed boundary between Umma and Lagash. On the other hand, nothing was said about compensation by the Ummaites for the revenue they had withheld; nor do they seem to have been held responsible any longer for ensuring the water supply of the Guedinna—this task was now left to the Lagashites themselves.[15]

Entemena was the last of the great *ensi*'s of the Ur-Nanshe dynasty; his son Enannatum II reigned only briefly and achieved but little, to judge from the fact that only one of his inscriptions has been recovered to date—a door socket dedicated to the restoration of Ningirsu's beer brewery. He was followed as *ensi* of Lagash by Enetarzi, who was probably a usurper; from the days

[15] For a translation of the document containing this information, see pp. 313–15.

of his rule we have a large number of administrative documents but no dedicatory inscriptions. However, a letter has been recovered that is addressed to Enetarzi by Luenna, the *sanga* (temple head) of Ninmar, reporting the defeat of a band of six hundred Elamites who had raided and plundered Lagash.[16]

Enetarzi is followed as *ensi* of Lagash by Lugalanda, who, like his predecessor, has left us only administrative documents and no dedicatory inscriptions; we therefore know practically nothing about his reign. Lugalanda is followed in turn by Urukagina who has become renowned not for his military exploits—in fact, he may have been man's first pacifist—but for his social and ethical reforms, the earliest in the recorded history of man. Unfortunately, his reign was brief and came to a sad end when Lugalzaggesi, an ambitious and military-minded *ensi* from neighboring Umma, burned, looted, and destroyed practically all the holy places of Lagash. These vicious deeds of Lugalzaggesi are carefully recorded in a rather remarkable document written by a Lagashite scribe and theologian no doubt at the behest of Urukagina, who—there is reason to believe—survived the catastrophe. The closing passage of this document reveals a faith in the justice of the gods on the part of Urukagina which, although quite touching, may well have brought about his undoing; it reads: "Because the Ummaite destroyed the bricks (?) of Lagash, he committed a sin against the god Ningirsu; he (Ningirsu) will cut off the hands lifted (?) against him. It is not the sin of Urukagina, the king of Girsu. May Nidaba the (personal) goddess of Lugalzaggesi, the *ensi* of Umma, make him (Lugalzaggesi) bear all (these) sins."[17] All of which leaves the impression that Urukagina had in fact offered no resistance to his aggressive fellow Sumerians from Umma, so confident was he in the justice of the gods and the retribution they would wreak on the evildoer—although just what good that would do the victim is not clear. In any case, Lugalzaggesi's career, which began with the conquest of Lagash and was for a time crowned with phenomenal success, came to an ignominious end.

Lugalzaggesi has left us one important inscription, the text of which was pieced together by Hermann Hilprecht more than half

---

[16] For a translation of the document, see Appendix F.

[17] For a translation of the entire document, see pp. 322–23.

a century ago from hundreds of vase fragments.[18] In it Lugalzaggesi describes himself proudly as "king of Erech (and) king of
the Land," as one who had made all the foreign lands subservient
to him, so that there was nothing but peace, happiness, and prosperity throughout his realm, which extended "from the Lower
Sea along the Tigris and Euphrates Rivers to the Upper Sea."
But, as was said earlier, all this did not long endure; after some
two decades of military successes and triumphs, he was brought
in a neck stock to the gate of Nippur to be reviled and spat upon
by all who passed by. His conqueror was a Semite named Sargon,
the founder of the powerful Dynasty of Akkad, which began,
consciously or not, the Semitization of Sumer that finally brought
about the end of the Sumerian people, at least as an identifiable
political and ethnic entity.

Sargon the Great, as he has come to be known to the modern
historian, was one of the most remarkable political figures of the
ancient Near East—a military leader of genius as well as an
imaginative administrator and builder with a sense of the historic
significance of his deeds and achievements. His influence made
itself felt in one way or another all over the ancient world from
Egypt to India. In later centuries Sargon became a legendary
figure around whom the poets and bards wove sagas and wonder
tales—which were in general, however, based on a kernel of truth.
Fortunately, in the case of Sargon we have no need to go to
these later chronicles and tales for our historical facts, since we
have his own inscriptions recording his more important military
conquests and achievements; for Sargon, as well as his two sons,
Rimush and Manishtushu, who succeeded him, commemorated
their victories by erecting in Enlil's temple at Nippur inscribed
statues of themselves and also steles depicting themselves and
their prostrated enemies. To be sure, except for an occasional
diorite fragment of an original, none of these statues and steles
has been recovered to date; even the new Nippur excavations
have proved disappointing in this respect, and it may be, of
course, that they were destroyed in ancient days. But luckily for
the modern historian, several centuries after they had been dedicated in the Enlil temple, an anonymous scholar and researcher
copied all the inscriptions on the statues and steles with the care

18 For a full translation of the inscription, see pp. 323–24.

and fidelity that would do honor to any modern archeologist and epigrapher, even noting whether the copied inscriptions came from the statue itself or from the pedestal with such phrases as "(this is) the inscription on the statue," or "(this is) the inscription on the pedestal," or "the pedestal is uninscribed." Just why he prepared these copies is altogether unknown; perhaps the temple and its monuments were in danger of being destroyed, and his purpose was to save them for posterity. If so, he succeeded almost better than he could possibly have anticipated; for his precious tablet was recovered almost in its entirety by the old Nippur expedition, and its contents have been made available to posterity by the two scholars Arno Poebel and Leon Legrain.

Sargon, though a Semite, began his career as a high official—the cupbearer, in fact—to a Sumerian king of Kish named Ur-Zababa. It was this ruler whom the ambitious Lugalzaggesi must have dethroned and perhaps killed when he embarked on his path of conquest following his destruction of Lagash. Sargon's first goal was to eliminate Lugalzaggesi from the political scene. To this end he made a surprise attack against Lugalzaggesi's capital, Erech, "smote it," and destroyed its walls. The Erech defenders seem to have fled the city, and after getting strong reinforcements —fifty *ensi*'s from the provinces came to their help, according to the inscription—took their stand against the pursuing Sargon. In a pitched battle, the latter routed the Erech forces. It was only then, it seems, that Lugalzaggesi, who must have been away from Erech on a distant campaign, came upon the scene with his army. This time, too, Sargon was victor, so overwhelmingly that he could bring Lugalzaggesi in chains, or rather in a neck stock, to the gates of Nippur.

Following Lugalzaggesi's capture, Sargon returned to the more southerly part of Sumer where Lugalzaggesi's *ensi*'s still had hopes of checking his progress. He first attacked Ur in the extreme southwest, then the region of Eninmar, which stretched from the city of Lagash to the shores of the Persian Gulf, where he washed his weapons, no doubt in a ritual ceremony commemorating his victories. On his way back from the sea, he attacked Umma, a Lugalzaggesi stronghold, and destroyed its walls, thus completing his conquest of southern Sumer. He now turned west and north and subjugated the lands Mari, Jarmuti, and Ibla up to the

"Cedar Forest" and the "Silver Mountain," that is, the Amanus and the Taurus ranges. We next find him campaigning east of Sumer, attacking Elam and neighboring Barahshi, and carrying off their possessions.

This brings us to the end of the Nippur copies of the inscriptions on Sargon's statues and steles, which, however, cover only a part of his reign. To judge from the much later legends and chronicles, Sargon's conquests continued to range far and wide; he may even have sent his armies to Egypt, Ethiopia, and India. To control so vast an empire, he stationed military garrisons at various key outposts. In Sumer itself, where rebellion was chronic, he appointed fellow Semites to the higher administrative posts and garrisoned the cities with all Akkadian troops. For himself and his huge court of officials and soldiers—he boasts that "5400 men ate bread daily before him"—he built the city of Agade, not far from Kish, the city where he had begun his phenomenal career as cupbearer of the reigning Ur-Zababa. In a brief span of time Agade became the most prosperous and resplendent of the cities of the ancient world; to it gifts and tributes were brought from the four corners of Sargon's realm, and at its quays ships docked from far-off Dilmun, Magan, and Meluhha (that is, perhaps, India, Egypt, and Ethiopia).[19] Most of Agade's citizens were no doubt Semites related to Sargon by ties of blood and language, and it is from the name Agade, or rather from its Biblical counterpart, Akkad (Genesis 10:10), that the word Akkadian has come to designate today the Mesopotamian Semites in general.

Sargon was followed by his son Rimush, who found his empire torn by revolts and rebellions. In bitter battles involving tens of thousands of troops, he conquered, or rather reconquered, the cities of Ur, Umma, Adab, Lagash, Der, and Kazallu, as well as the countries of Elam and Barahshi. He reigned, however, only nine years, and was followed by his "elder brother"—perhaps his twin—Manishtushu, who continued in the same military and political pattern. Moreover, like his father Sargon, he carried his victorious armies to far-distant lands, or at least so it might seem from a passage in one of his inscriptions which reads: "When he (Manishtushu) had crossed the Lower Sea (that is, the Persian Gulf) in ships, thirty-two kings gathered against him, but he

19 For the identification of these lands, see pp. 276–81.

defeated them and smote their cities and prostrated their lords and destroyed [the whole (?) countryside (?)] as far as the silver mines."

Manishtushu reigned fifteen years and was followed by his son Naram-Sin who raised Agade to new heights of power and glory, only to see it come to a bitter and tragic end. His military successes were numerous and prodigious: he defeated a powerful coalition of rebellious kings from Sumer and the surrounding lands; he conquered the region to the west as far as the Mediterranean Sea and the Taurus and Amanus ranges; he extended his dominion into Armenia and erected his statue of victory near modern Dierbakir; he fought the Lullubi in the northern Zagros ranges and commemorated his victory with a magnificent stele; he turned Elam into a partially Semitized vassal-state and constructed numerous buildings in Susa; he brought booty from Magan after defeating its king Manium, whom some scholars have identified with the renowned Menes of Egypt. No wonder that he felt himself powerful enough to add the epithet "king of the four quarters" to his titulary and that he was presumptuous enough to have himself deified as "the god of Agade."

But then came the fatal calamity which crushed Naram-Sin and the city of Agade and threatened to engulf all of Sumer—the demoralizing and destructive invasion of the Gutians, a ruthless barbaric horde from the mountains to the east. This we learn primarily from a historiographic poem which may be entitled "The Curse of Agade: The Ekur Avenged." It was composed by a Sumerian poet living several centuries after the Gutian catastrophe when Agade had long been abandoned to ruin and desolation. The document is memorable not only for its vivid description of Agade before and after its fall but as one of the earliest recorded attempts to interpret a historical event in the framework of a currently held world view. In searching for the causes behind the humiliating and disastrous Gutian invasion, the author comes upon what he thinks is undoubtedly the true answer and informs us of an outrage committed by Naram-Sin, unknown as yet from any other source. According to our author, Naram-Sin had sacked Nippur and committed all sorts of desecrating and defiling acts against Enlil's sanctuary, and Enlil had therefore turned to the Gutians and brought them down from their mountain abode to destroy Agade and avenge his beloved temple. Moreover, eight of the more important deities of the Sumerian pantheon, in order to soothe the spirit of their ruler Enlil, laid a curse upon Agade that it should remain forever desolate and uninhabited. And this, added the author at the end of his work, was indeed the case: Agade had remained desolate and uninhabited.

Our historiographer begins his work with an introduction contrasting the glory and power of Agade that marked its rise and the ruin and desolation that engulfed it after its fall. The first several lines of the composition read: "After, with frowning forehead, Enlil had put the people of Kish to death like the Bull of Heaven, and like a lofty ox had crushed the house of Erech into dust; after, in due time, Enlil had given to Sargon, the king of Agade, the lordship and kingship from the lands above to the lands below," then (to paraphrase some of the more intelligible passages) did the city of Agade become prosperous and powerful under the tender and constant guidance of its tutelary deity, Inanna. Its buildings were filled with gold, silver, copper, tin, and lapis lazuli; its old men and women gave wise counsel; its young children were full of joy; music and song resounded everywhere; all the surrounding lands lived in peace and security. Naram-Sin, moreover, made its shrines glorious and raised its walls mountain-high while its gates remained open. To it came the nomadic Martu, the people who "know not grain" from the west, bringing choice oxen and sheep; to it came Meluhhaites, "the people of the black land," bringing their exotic wares; to it came the Elamite and Subarian from the east and north carrying loads like "load-carrying asses"; to it came all the princes, chieftains, and sheiks of the plain bringing gifts monthly and on the New Year.

But then came the catastrophe; or as the author puts it: "The gates of Agade, how they lay prostrate; .... the holy Inanna leaves untouched their gifts; the Ulmash (Inanna's temple) is fear-ridden (since) she has gone from the city, left it; like a maid who forsakes her chamber, the holy Inanna has forsaken her Agade shrine; like a warrior with raised weapons she attacked the city in fierce battle, made it turn its breast to the enemy." And so in a very short time, "in not five days, not ten days," lordship and kingship departed from Agade; the gods turned against her, and

Agade lay desolate; Naram-Sin sulked by himself, dressed in sackcloth; his chariots and boats lay unused and neglected.

How did this come to be? Our author's version is that Naram-Sin, during the seven years in which his rule was firmly established, had acted contrary to Enlil's word: he had permitted his soldiers to attack and ravage the Ekur and its groves; he had demolished the buildings of the Ekur with copper axes and hatchets, so that "the house lay prostrate like a dead youth"—indeed, "all the lands lay prostrate." Moreover, at the gate called "Gate of No Grain-Cutting," he cut grain; "the 'Gate of Peace' he demolished with a pickax"; he desecrated the holy vessels and cut down the Ekur's groves; he ground up its gold, silver, and copper vessels into dust; and he loaded up all the possessions of the destroyed Nippur on boats docked right by Enlil's sanctuary and carried them off to Agade.

But no sooner had he done these things than "counsel left Agade" and "the good sense of Agade turned to folly." Then "Enlil, the raging flood which has no rival, because of his beloved house which has been attacked, what destruction wrought"; he lifted his eyes to the mountains and brought down the Gutians, "a people which brooks no controls"; "it covered the earth like the locust," so that none could escape its power. Communication, whether by land or sea, became impossible throughout Sumer. "The herald could not proceed on his journey; the sea-rider could not sail his boat . . . . ; brigands dwelt on the roads; the doors of the gates of the land turned to clay; all the surrounding lands were planning evil in their city walls." As a result, dire famine came upon Sumer. "The great fields and meadows produced no grain; the fisheries produced no fish; and the watered gardens produced neither honey nor wine." Because of the famine, prices were inflated to such an extent that one lamb brought only half a *sila* of oil, or half a *sila* of grain, or half a mina of wool (see Fig. 4, p. 107, for all measures).

With misery, want, death, and desolation thus threatening to overwhelm practically all "mankind fashioned by Enlil," eight of the more important deities of the Sumerian pantheon—namely, Sin, Enki, Inanna, Ninurta, Ishkur, Utu, Nusku, and Nidaba—decided that it was high time to soothe Enlil's rage. In a prayer to Enlil they vowed that Agade, the city which destroyed Nippur,

The surroundings of Nippur today—sand dunes and desolation. (Joint Nippur Expedition of the Oriental Institute and the American Schools for Oriental Research.)

The ziggurat at Eridu, the city of Enki (partly excavated). The remains of the temple can be seen at the foot of the ziggurat. (Photograph, Iraq Museum.)

Ur-Nanshe, king of Lagash, with his children and courtiers (limestone plaque). In the upper register, he is carrying a dirt-filled basket for building a temple; in the lower, he is celebrating its completion. (Louvre.)

Stele of the Vultures (limestone). Eannatum leading the Lagashites to battle. The inscription over the soldiers' heads records his victory over the Ummaites. (Louvre.)

Head of Ur-Nammu (*left*), enlarged from a copper statuette that was among the contents of the foundation box of Ur-Nammu from the Inanna temple at Nippur. (Joint Nippur Expedition of the Oriental Institute and the American Schools for Oriental Research.)

Gudea (*below*), *ensi* of Lagash (diorite). (University Museum.)

Hand copy of the map of the city of Nippur (*opposite page*). In the center is the name of the city (1). The buildings shown on the map are: the *Ekur* (2), Sumer's most renowned temple; the *Kiur* (3), a temple adjacent to the *Ekur*; the *Anniginna* (4), an enclosure of some sort; and far out on the outskirts of the city, the *Eshmah* (6), "Lofty Shrine." In the corner formed by the southeast and southwest walls is Nippur's "Central Park" (5), the *Kirishauru*. Forming the southwest boundary of the city is the Euphrates River (7). On the northwest, the city is bounded by the *Nunbirdu* canal (8). Flowing through the middle of the city in the *Idshauru*, "Central Canal" (9). There are three gates in the southwest wall (10, 11, 12); three in the southeast wall (13, 14, 15); but only one in the northwest wall (16). Finally, there is a moat running parallel to the northwest wall (17), and another parallel to the southeast wall (18). (Hilprecht Collection. Hand copy by Inez Bernhardt, assistant keeper of the Collection.)

Map of the city of Nippur (*above*) inscribed on a clay tablet dating from about 1500 B.C. The writing on the map gives the names of various buildings, rivers, and gates and is in Sumerian and Akkadian. (Hilprecht Collection, Friedrich-Schiller University, Jena.)

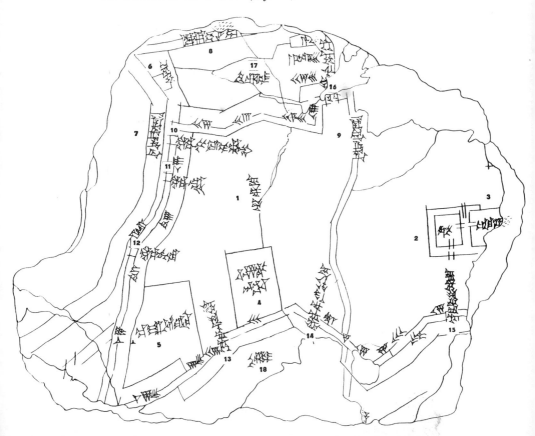

Stele of Ur-Nammu (limestone). The lower two registers depict the building of the temple. (University Museum.)

Reconstruction of the temple at Harmal (*ca.* 1900 B.C.). The temple consisted of an entrance vestibule, courtyard, antecella, and cella, all arranged with communicating doors on a single axis, so that the niche in the cella, on which may have rested the statue of the deity, was visible from the street when all doors were open. Life-sized terra-cotta lions guarded the doorways. (Reconstruction by Mohammed Ali Mustapha. Iraq Museum.)

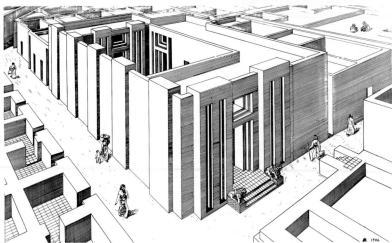

Medical tablet (*ca.* 2200 B.C.). Fifteen prescriptions are inscribed on this tablet. (University Museum.)

Head of a female statue found buried in the sanctuary floor of the VII level of the Inanna temple at Nippur (*ca.* 2500 B.C.). (Joint Nippur Expedition of the Oriental Institute and the American Schools of Oriental Research.)

Bearded statuette from Khafaje (*ca.* 2600 B.C.) (University Museum.)

would itself be destroyed like Nippur. And so these eight deities "turn their faces to the city, pronounce (a curse of) destruction upon Agade":

> City, you who dared assault the Ekur, who [defied] Enlil,
> Agade, you who dared assault the Ekur, who [defied] Enlil,
> May your groves be heaped up like dust, ...
> May your clay (bricks) return to their abyss,
> May they become clay (bricks) cursed by Enki,
> May your trees return to their forests,
> May they become trees cursed by Ninildu.
> Your slaughtered oxen—may you slaughter your wives instead,
> Your butchered sheep—may you butcher your children instead,
> Your poor—may they be forced to drown their precious (?) children, ... ,
> Agade, may your palace built with joyful heart, be turned into a depressing ruin . . . . ,
> Over the places where your rites and rituals were conducted,
> May the fox (who haunts) the ruined mounds, glide his tail . . . . ,
> May your canalboat towpaths grow nothing but weeds,
> May your chariot roads grow nothing but the "wailing plant,"
> Moreover, on your canalboat towpaths and landings,
> May no human being walk because of the wild goats, vermin (?), snakes, and mountain scorpions,
> May your plains where grew the heart-soothing plants,
> Grow nothing but the "reed of tears,"
> Agade, instead of your sweet-flowing water, may bitter water flow,
> Who says "I would dwell in that city" will not find a good dwelling place,
> Who says "I would lie down in Agade" will not find a good sleeping place.

And, our historian concludes, that is exactly what happened:

> Its canalboat towpaths grew nothing but weeds,
> Its chariot roads grew nothing but the "wailing plant,"
> Moreover, on its canalboat towpaths and landings,
> No human being walks because of the wild goats, vermin (?), snakes, and mountain scorpions,
> The plains where grew the heart-soothing plants, grew nothing but the "reed of tears,"

Agade, instead of its sweet-flowing water, there flowed bitter
water,
Who said "I would dwell in that city" found not a good
dwelling place,
Who said "I would lie down in Agade" found not a good
sleeping place.

The defeat of Naram-Sin at the hands of the Gutians brought
political confusion and anarchy to Sumer, although Naram-Sin's
son, Sharkalisharri, appears to have tried to undo some of the
mischief wrought by his father, to judge from several of his
dedicatory inscriptions in which he describes himself as "the
builder of the Ekur, the house of Enlil." But if so, he was too
late; he saw his dominion reduced to the city of Agade and its
immediate environs. He bears only the title "king of Agade" and
no longer dares use his father's proud epithet "king of the four
quarters." To be sure, in his date-formulas, he claims victories
over the Gutians, Elamites, and Amorites, but these were probably defensive battles fought to stave off the enemy from the
gates of Agade. All the indications are that it was the Gutian
rulers who were the dominant political element throughout the
seven or eight decades following the death of Naram-Sin; they
seem to have been in a position to appoint and remove the rulers
of the Sumerian cities almost at will. And for one reason or another—probably because they found the *ensi*'s of Lagash pliant
and co-operative—the Gutians seemed to favor Lagash, which for
almost half a century became the dominant city in southern
Sumer, controlling at times Ur, Umma, and perhaps even Erech.
In any case, toward the end of the "Gutian period" we find a
dynasty of *ensi*'s in Lagash which carried on the political and
religious policies of the great reformer Urukagina, giving "unto
Caesar the things which are Caesar's" in order to better serve the
gods.

The founder of this new Lagash dynasty of *ensi*'s was Ur-Bau,
who has left us several dedicatory inscriptions recording the
building of numerous temples in Lagash. He was also in control
of Ur; at least he was influential enough to have his daughter
installed as high priestess of Nanna, Ur's tutelary deity. Ur-Bau
had three sons-in-law, Gudea, Urgar, and Namhani (also written
Nammahni), each of whom became *ensi* of Lagash. Gudea's

rather immobile face and expressionless features have become
familiar to the modern student from the numerous statues of him
that have been recovered. Some of these carry long inscriptions
recording his religious activities in connection with the building
and rebuilding of Lagash's more important temples. From them
we learn that, in spite of Gutian domination, Gudea had trade
contacts with practically the entire "civilized" world of those days.
He obtained gold from Anatolia and Egypt, silver from the Taurus
range, cedars from the Amanus, copper from the Zagros, diorite
from Egypt, carnelian from Ethiopia, and timber from Dilmun.
Nor did he seem to find any difficulty in obtaining craftsmen from
Susa and Elam for the decoration of his temple. Gudea's two clay-
cylinders unearthed at Lagash more than seventy-five years ago
are inscribed with the longest known Sumerian literary work,
close to fourteen hundred lines of a narrative composition, ritualistic and hymnal, commemorating his rebuilding of Lagash's main
temple, the Eninnu. Gudea even reports one important military
victory—that over the state Anshan, Elam's neighbor to the south.
He also speaks of fashioning a number of cultic and symbolic
weapons such as the *sharur* and maces with fifty heads. This may
indicate considerable military activity on his part, although perhaps only as a vassal of the Gutians. Gudea, like his father-in-law
Ur-Bau, also controlled the city of Ur, where three of his inscriptions have been unearthed.

Gudea was followed by his son, Ur-Ningirsu, and his grandson,
Ugme, who between them ruled less than a decade. They were
succeeded, perhaps, by Urgar, another of Ur-Bau's sons-in-law,
whose rule, however, was ephemeral. There then followed the
third of Ur-Bau's sons-in-law, Namhani, who was probably *ensi* of
Umma as well as of Lagash. That Namhani co-operated with the
Gutians, and might thus be termed a traitor to Sumer, is quite certain, for he dates one of his inscriptions to the days when "Yarlagan was king of Gutium." But by this time a savior had arisen in
Sumer, Utuhegal of Erech, who succeeded in breaking the Gutian
yoke and in bringing back the kingship to Sumer. This is told
in a historiographic type of narrative poem composed either in
Utuhegal's own day or not long thereafter. Beginning with a bitter
denunciation of the Gutians, "the snake (and) scorpion of the
mountain," for their vicious attacks on Sumer, it describes vividly

Utuhegal's victorious campaign against the Gutian king Tirigan, who was taken prisoner and brought fettered and blindfolded before Utuhegal to "set his foot upon his neck."[20]

But in spite of his resounding victory, Utuhegal did not long hold power over Sumer; the indications are that after some seven years of rule, the throne was usurped by Ur-Nammu, one of his more ambitious governors, who succeeded in founding the last important Sumerian dynasty, commonly known as the Third Dynasty of Ur. Ur-Nammu, who reigned for sixteen years, proved to be a capable military leader, a great builder, and an outstanding administrator; he promulgated the first law code in man's recorded history.

Ur-Nammu began his reign by attacking and killing Namhani, a son-in-law of Ur-Bau of Lagash, who had evidently been encroaching on Ur's territory, no doubt with the help of his Gutian overlords. Having made himself master of Ur and Lagash, he then proceeded to establish his authority throughout Sumer; his inscriptions have been found in Erech, Nippur, Adab, and Larsa as well as in Ur. He may even have succeeded in extending his control over some of the lands bordering Sumer, to judge from one of his date-formulae in which he boasts that "he made straight the highways from (the lands) below to (the lands) above."

Ur-Nammu, to judge from the statement that "he had been abandoned in the battlefield like a crushed vessel,"[21] probably died in battle with the Gutians, who, in spite of Utuhegal's vaunted victory, continued to trouble Sumer throughout the period of the Third Dynasty of Ur. He was succeeded by his son, Shulgi, who ruled forty-eight years and ushered in a period of relative peace and prosperity for Sumer. Shulgi extended his rule over Elam and Anshan to the east and also over the nomadic peoples of the Zagros ranges. He was even in control of Ashur and Irbil in Subarian territory to the far north of Sumer. That he had considerable trouble in pacifying and subjugating the Subarians, however, is shown by a letter which one of his high officials, Aradmu by name, dispatched to him from somewhere in Subir. Aradmu had been commissioned by Shulgi "to keep in good condition the expedition roads to the land of Subir," to

[20] For a translation of this document, see pp. 325–26.
[21] See pp. 130–31.

stabilize the borders of the country, "to make known the ways of
the country," and "to counsel the wise of the assembly against (?)
the foul (?) seed (?)," the latter term probably being a derogatory epithet for some unnamed Subarian leader who refused to
submit to Shulgi's authority. But Aradmu found the situation
quite hopeless; the "foul seed" seemed to be rich and powerful,
and he so terrified and demoralized Aradmu that the latter could
only clamor for help from Shulgi. We also have Shulgi's answer
to this letter in which Shulgi suspects Aradmu of treachery and
makes use of both threats and cajolery in an effort to keep
Aradmu from joining up with the Subarian rebels.

Shulgi, as has been pointed out recently,[22] may have tried to
follow consciously in the footsteps of Naram-Sin, the fourth ruler
of the Semitic dynasty of Akkad. Like the latter, he took the
title "king of the four quarters" and had himself deified during
his lifetime. His queen was an energetic and active Semitic lady
named Abisimti, who survived Shulgi and continued as dowager
queen under Shulgi's three successors, two of whom at least—
Shu-Sin and Ibbi-Sin—bore Semitic names. But though Shulgi
thus seems to have been Semitically oriented, he was a great lover
of Sumerian literature and culture and a prime patron of the
Sumerian school, the *edubba* (see chapter vi). In his hymns he
boasts of the learning and erudition that he himself obtained in
the *edubba* in the days of his youth, and he claims to have mastered its curriculum and become a skillful scribe.

Shulgi was followed by his son Amar-Sin, who ruled only nine
years but succeeded in retaining control over Sumer and its
provinces, including far-off Ashur to the north. His brother
Shu-Sin, who succeeded him, also ruled nine years. It is in the
course of his reign that we hear for the first time of a serious
incursion of Sumer by a Semitic people known as the Amorites
from the Syrian and Arabian desert. Shu-Sin found it necessary
to build a huge fortified wall to keep these barbaric nomads at
bay, although with little success. In the early years of the reign
of Ibbi-Sin, the fifth and last of the Ur-Nammu dynasty, the
Amorites made major inroads, and their attacks together with
those of the Elamites to the east compelled Ibbi-Sin to build large

[22] Edmond Sollberger, "Sur la Chronologie des Rois d'Ur," *Archiv für Orientforschung*, XVII, 17–18.

walls and fortifications about his capital, Ur, as well as Sumer's religious center, Nippur.

Ibbi-Sin succeeded in holding on as ruler of Sumer for twenty-four years. But throughout his reign his situation was insecure and even pathetic; much of the time he was confined to the city of Ur itself, which often suffered hunger and famine. As a result of the incursions of the Amorites and the attacks of the Elamites, his empire tottered and crumbled, and the governors of all the more important cities of Sumer found it advisable to abandon their king and to fend for themselves. We learn of this piteous state of affairs primarily from Ibbi-Sin's correspondence with his provincial governors, which provides a graphic picture of the rather confused and pathetic Ibbi-Sin and of his scheming, ambitious, and double-dealing functionaries.

The text of three letters belonging to this royal correspondence is now available. The first contains a report sent to Ibbi-Sin by Ishbi-Erra on the results of a grain-buying expedition with which Ibbi-Sin had charged him; the letter sheds considerable light on the incursions of the Amorites into western Sumer as well as on the difficulties the Elamites were making for Ibbi-Sin. Ishbi-Erra begins his report with the statement that he succeeded in buying seventy-two thousand *gur* of grain at the normal price of one shekel per *gur;* but having heard that the hostile Amorites had entered Sumer and "seized the great fortresses one after the other," he had brought the grain not to Ur the capital but to Isin. If the king would now send him six hundred boats of one hundred twenty *gur* each, he continues, he will deliver the grain to the various cities of Sumer; however, he should be put in charge "of the places where the boats are to be moored." The letter closes with a plea to Ibbi-Sin not to give in to the Elamites—presumably, they were actually laying siege to Ur and its environs—for he had enough grain to satisfy the hunger of the "palace and its cities" for fifteen years. In any case, he pleads, the king must put him in charge of both Nippur and Isin.

That Ibbi-Sin had great confidence in Ishbi-Erra and actually did entrust Nippur and Isin to him we learn from his letter of reply, which although still unpublished has recently been summarized by Thorkild Jacobsen.[23] Unfortunately for Ibbi-Sin, Ishbi-

23 *Journal for Cuneiform Studies*, VII, 41.

Erra turned out to be as disloyal as he was capable and competent; he was successful not only in defending Isin and Nippur but in usurping his master's throne as well. This we learn, of course, not from Ishbi-Erra's correspondence with Ibbi-Sin but from a letter written to the latter by Puzur-Numushda, a governor of the city Kazallu, and Ibbi-Sin's reply.

According to Puzur-Numushda's letter, Ishbi-Erra had become firmly established as the ruler of Isin, which he had turned into his royal residence; he had, moreover, subdued Nippur and extended his sway all along the Tigris and Euphrates from Hamazi in the north and east to the Persian Gulf. He had taken prisoner those of Ibbi-Sin's governors who had remained loyal and returned to office those who presumably had been dismissed by Ibbi-Sin because of their disloyalty. Ibbi-Sin's pathetic impotence and pitiable vacillation are revealed in his answer to Puzur-Numushda. Although he realized full well that the latter was on the point of betraying him—he had actually failed to march to the help of Ibbi-Sin's loyal governors although a select body of troops had been put at his disposal for that purpose—he could do nothing more than plead with him to stay loyal, with the dubious assurances that somehow Ishbi-Erra, "who is not of Sumerian seed," would fail in his ambition to become master of Sumer and that the Elamites would be defeated, for "Enlil has stirred up the Amorites out of their land, and they will strike down the Elamites and capture Ishbi-Erra"—the very Amorites, incredibly enough, who had been plaguing Sumer from the days of Shu-Sin, Ibbi-Sin's predecessor.

With the growth of Ishbi-Erra's independence and power, Sumer found itself under the rule of two kings—Ibbi-Sin, whose dominion was limited to his capital, Ur, and Ishbi-Erra, who controlled most of the other cities of Sumer from his capital, Isin. In the twenty-fifth year of Ibbi-Sin's reign, however, the Elamites finally captured Ur and carried off Ibbi-Sin a prisoner, leaving a garrison in control of the city. Several years later Ishbi-Erra attacked this garrison and drove it out of Ur, thus becoming king of all Sumer, with Isin as his capital.

Ishbi-Erra founded a dynasty in Isin which endured for over two centuries, although its later rulers were not his direct descendants. Theoretically, Isin laid claim to the suzerainty of all

Sumer and Akkad. Actually, however, the land was breaking into
a number of city-states under separate rulers, and there was no
longer a centralized empire. For close to a century, it is true, Isin
remained the most powerful of these states; it controlled Ur, the
old imperial capital, and Nippur, which continued as Sumer's
spiritual and intellectual center throughout this period. The
fourth ruler of the Isin dynasty, Ishme-Dagan, boasts in the
hymns of restoring Nippur to its former glory; prior to his reign,
it seems to have suffered a severe attack at the hands of an enemy,
perhaps the Assyrians from the north. His son and successor,
Lipit-Ishtar, claimed control over the major deities of Sumer and
took the proud title "king of Sumer and Akkad." Early in his
reign he promulgated a new Sumerian law code, which was the
model of the renowned code of Hammurabi, although the latter
is written in the Akkadian, not the Sumerian, tongue.

But in the third year of Lipit-Ishtar's reign, an ambitious and
dynamic ruler named Gungunum came to the throne of Larsa, a
city southeast of Isin, and began to build up the political strength
of the city with a series of military successes in the region of Elam
and Anshan. Only a few years later we find this same Gungunum
in control of Ur, the old imperial capital that had meant much
for Isin's prestige and power. To be sure, it was a "friendly"
occupation—Ur was threatened by a new invasion of the Amorites
—but from then on Isin ceased to be a significant political force,
although it held on to some of its former claims for another century or more. It was finally attacked and seized by Rim-Sin, the
last ruler of Larsa, who attached so much importance to this conquest that he dated all documents throughout the last thirty years
of his reign by this event.

But Rim-Sin, himself, was unable to exploit his victory. To the
north, in the previously unimportant city of Babylon, an outstanding Semitic ruler named Hammurabi came to prominence. After
some three decades of a rather troubled rule, he attacked and
defeated Rim-Sin of Larsa, as well as the kings of Elam, Mari,
and Eshnunna, and thus, about 1750 B.C., became the ruler of a
united kingdom reaching from the Persian Gulf to the Habur
River. With Hammurabi the history of Sumer comes to an end,
and the history of Babylonia, a Semitic state built on a Sumerian
foundation, begins.

CHAPTER THREE

SOCIETY:

The

Sumerian City

Sumerian civilization was essentially urban in character, although it rested on an agricultural rather than an industrial base. The land Sumer, in the third millennium B.C., consisted of a dozen or so city-states, each having a large and usually walled city surrounded by suburban villages and hamlets. The outstanding feature of each city was the main temple situated on a high terrace, which gradually developed into a massive staged tower, a ziggurat, Sumer's most characteristic contribution to religious architecture. The temple usually consisted of a rectangular central shrine, or cella, surrounded on its long sides by a number of rooms for the use of the priests. In the cella there was a niche for the god's statue, fronted by an offering table made of mud brick. The temple was built largely of mud bricks, and since this material is unattractive in texture and color, the Sumerian architects beautified the walls by means of regularly spaced buttresses and recesses. They also introduced the mud-brick column and half-column, which they covered with patterns of zigzags, lozenges, and triangles by inserting thousands of painted clay cones into the thick mud plaster. Sometimes the inner walls of the shrine were painted with frescoes of human and animal figures as well as a varied assortment of geometrical motifs.[1]

The temple was the largest, tallest, and most important building in the city, in accordance with the theory accepted by the Sumerian religious leaders and going back no doubt to very early

[1] For additional details about temple architecture, see pp. 135–37.

times that the entire city belonged to its main god, to whom it had been assigned on the day the world was created. In practice, however, the temple corporation owned only some of the land, which it rented out to sharecroppers; the remainder was the private property of individual citizens. In early days political power lay in the hands of these free citizens and a city-governor known as *ensi*, who was no more than a peer among peers. In case of decisions vital to the city as a whole, these free citizens met in a bicameral assembly consisting of an upper house of "elders" and a lower house of "men." As the struggle between the city-states grew more violent and bitter, and as the pressures from the barbaric peoples to the east and west of Sumer increased, military leadership became a pressing need, and the king, or as he is known in Sumerian, the "big man," came to hold a superior place. At first he was probably selected and appointed by the assembly at a critical moment for a specific military task. But gradually kingship with all its privileges and prerogatives became a hereditary institution and was considered the very hallmark of civilization. The kings established a regular army, with the chariot—the ancient "tank"—as the main offensive weapon and a heavily armored infantry which attacked in phalanx formation. Sumer's victories and conquests were due largely to this superiority in military weapons, tactics, organization, and leadership. In the course of time, therefore, the palace began to rival the temple in wealth and influence.

But priests, princes, and soldiers constituted after all only a small fraction of the city's population. The great majority were farmers and cattle breeders, boatmen and fishermen, merchants and scribes, doctors and architects, masons and carpenters, smiths, jewelers, and potters. There were of course a number of rich and powerful families who owned large estates; but even the poor managed to own farms and gardens, houses, and cattle. The more industrious of the artisans and craftsmen sold their handmade products in the free town market, receiving payment either in kind or in "money," which was normally a disk or ring of silver of standard weight. Traveling merchants carried on a thriving trade from city to city and with surrounding states by land and sea, and not a few of these merchants were probably private individuals rather than temple or palace representatives.

The view that the Sumerian economy was relatively free and that private property was the rule rather than the exception runs counter to the claim of a number of Oriental scholars that the Sumerian city-state was a totalitarian theocracy dominated by the temple, which owned all the land and was in absolute control of the entire economy. The fact that the overwhelming majority of tablets from pre-Sargonic Sumer, that is, the Sumer of about 2400 B.C., are inventory documents from the temples of Lagash, which deal solely with temple land and personnel, has led scholars to the unjustified conclusion that all the land of Lagash—and presumably, of the other city-states—was temple property. It is also true, however, that there are quite a number of documents from Lagash as well as from other sites which indicate quite clearly that the citizens of the city-states could buy and sell their fields and houses, not to mention all kinds of movable property. Thus, for example, several documents from about 2500 B.C. have been unearthed in Fara and Bismaya that record real estate sales by private individuals, and they are no doubt but a small fraction of those still under ground. From Lagash comes a stone tablet recording a sale of land to Enhegal, a king of Lagash and a predecessor of Ur-Nanshe, which shows that even a king could not merely confiscate property whenever he wished but had to pay for it. Another stone document has been found in which one Lummatur, a son of Enannatum I, purchases land from various individuals and families. In the Urukagina reform text we find that even the poor and lowly own houses, gardens, and fishery ponds. But the idea of a temple theocracy in absolute control of the city had taken hold in the minds of several key scholars, and in order to uproot it, a thorough re-study of the hundreds of available economic documents, especially those from Lagash, was an urgent necessity. This has now been achieved by I. M. Diakanoff, a Russian scholar who has devoted much time and labor to the task and whose detailed study appeared in 1959.[2] Following, then, is a sketch of the economic structure of the Sumerian city-state based primarily on Diakanoff's illuminating analysis.

The fundamental error which led to the assumption that the

[2] Diakanoff, *Sumer: Society and State in Ancient Mesopotamia* (Moscow, 1959; in Russian with English résumé).

temple of each city-state owned all its land was made by the late Anton Deimel, a highly productive scholar who devoted many years to the study of the Lagash documents and contributed significantly to cuneiform studies as a whole. By adding together all the parcels of land mentioned in them, he estimated that the total area of the temple estates in Lagash was between two and three hundred square kilometers, a quite justifiable figure, which, if anything, is too low. But he then goes on to make the assumption that this was the total area of the city-state of Lagash, a claim that is quite unwarranted by the data. In studying more carefully all the available Lagash documents, Diakanoff estimates that the territory of Lagash probably comprised some three thousand square kilometers of which about two thousand consisted of naturally irrigated land. The total area of the temple estates, even if Deimel's estimate were doubled—as there is some reason to believe it should be—would comprise a considerable fraction of the territory of the city-state, but only a fraction. This temple land, which could not be bought, sold, or alienated in any way, was divided into three categories: (1) *nigenna*—land that was reserved for the maintenance of the temple; (2) *kurra*—land allotted to the farmers working the *nigenna* land and also to artisans and some of the administrative personnel of the temple in payment for their services (this land could not be inherited and could be exchanged or taken away altogether by the temple administration whenever it decided to do so for one reason or another); and (3) *urulal*—land allotted in exchange for a share of the crop to different individuals, but especially to personnel of the temple to supplement their income.

As for the land which did not belong to the temple and which comprised by far the larger part of the territory of the city-state, the documents show that much of it was owned by the "nobility," that is, the ruling princes and their families and palace administrators as well as the more important priests. These noble families often possessed huge estates measuring hundreds of acres, much of which they obtained by purchase from the less fortunate citizens. The labor on these estates was performed by clients or dependents, whose status resembled that of the dependents of the temple, who were clients of the more prosperous temple officials and administrators. The rest of the land—that is, the land not owned by the temple or the nobility—belonged to the ordinary citizens of the community, probably more than half of the population. These free citizens or commoners were organized in large patriarchal families and also in patriarchal clans and town communities/The hereditary land in the possession of the patriarchal families from the earliest days could be alienated and sold, but only by some member or members of the family—not necessarily the head—who acted as the chosen representative of the family community. Ordinarily, other members of the family participated in the transaction as witnesses, thus indicating their agreement and consent; these witnesses received a payment, just as the sellers themselves did, although it was usually more or less nominal. In many cases unpaid witnesses on the side of the buyer were also recorded, and sometimes representatives of the government took part in the transactions.

All in all, as a result of Diakanoff's detailed and imaginative investigations, we get a picture of the socioeconomic structure of the Sumerian city-state that is quite different from that currently in vogue among Oriental scholars. We see that the population consisted of four categories: nobles, commoners, clients, and slaves. The nobility owned large estates, partly as private individuals, partly in the form of family possessions, which were worked by free clients or dependents as well as slaves. It was the nobility, too, which controlled the temple land, although this land gradually came under the domination of the ruler and later even became his property. The upper house of the assembly, or "town meeting," probably consisted of the members of the nobility.

The commoner owned his own plot of land in the city-state, but as a member of a family rather than as an individual; it was the commoners who probably constituted the lower house of the assembly.

The clients consisted of three categories: (1) the well-to-do dependents of the temple, such as the temple administrators and more important craftsmen; (2) the great mass of the temple personnel; and (3) the dependents of the nobility. Most of the clients in the first two categories got small plots of temple land (but only as temporary possessions), although some got rations of food and wool. The clients of the nobles, who worked their estates, were no doubt also paid in accordance with similar arrangements.

Slavery was a recognized institution, and temples, palaces, and rich estates owned slaves and exploited them for their own benefit. Many slaves were prisoners of war, although not necessarily foreigners since they could be fellow Sumerians from a neighboring city defeated in battle. Sumerian slaves were recruited in other ways. Freemen might be reduced to slavery as a punishment for certain offenses. Parents could sell their children as slaves in time of need, or a man might turn over his entire family to creditors in payment of a debt, although for no longer than three years. The slave was the property of his master like any other chattel. He could be branded and flogged and was severely punished if he attempted to escape. On the other hand, it was to his master's advantage that his slave stay strong and healthy, and slaves were therefore usually well treated. They even had certain legal rights: they could engage in business, borrow money, and buy their freedom. If a slave, male or female, married a free person, the children were free. The sale price of a slave varied with the market and the individual involved; an average price for a grown man was twenty shekels, which was at times less than the price for an ass.

The basic unit of Sumerian society was, as with us, the family, whose members were knit closely together by love, respect, and mutual obligations. Marriage was arranged by the parents, and the betrothal was legally recognized as soon as the groom presented a bridal gift to the father. The betrothal was often consummated with a contract inscribed on a tablet. While marriage was thus reduced to a practical arrangement, there is some evidence to show that surreptitious premarital love-making was not altogether unknown. A woman in Sumer had certain important legal rights: she could hold property, engage in business, and qualify as a witness. But her husband could divorce her on relatively light grounds, and if she had no children, he could marry a second wife. Children were under the absolute authority of their parents, who could disinherit them or even sell them into slavery. But in the normal course of events they were dearly loved and cherished and at the parents' death inherited all their property. Adopted children were not uncommon, and they, too, were treated with utmost care and consideration.

As can be gathered from what has already been said about social and economic organization, written law played a large role in the Sumerian city. Beginning about 2700 B.C., we find actual deeds of sales, including sales of fields, houses, and slaves. From about 2350 B.C., during the reign of Urukagina of Lagash, we have one of the most precious and revealing documents in the history of man and his perennial and unrelenting struggle for freedom from tyranny and oppression. This document records a sweeping reform of a whole series of prevalent abuses, most of which could be traced to a ubiquitous and obnoxious bureaucracy consisting of the ruler and his palace coterie; at the same time it provides a grim and ominous picture of man's cruelty toward man on all levels—social, economic, political, and psychological. Reading between its lines, we also get a glimpse of a bitter struggle for power between the temple and the palace—the "church" and the "state" —with the citizens of Lagash taking the side of the temple. Finally, it is in this document that we find the word "freedom" used for the first time in man's recorded history; the word is *amargi*, which, as has recently been pointed out by Adam Falkenstein, means literally "return to the mother." However, we still do not know why this figure of speech came to be used for "freedom."

Of the events which led to the corrupt, lawless, and oppressive state of affairs in Lagash as depicted in the Urukagina reform document, there is not a trace in the text itself. But we may surmise that they were the direct result of the political and economic forces unloosed by the drive for power which characterized the ruling dynasty founded by Ur-Nanshe around 2500 B.C. Smitten with grandiose ambitions for themselves and their state, some of the rulers resorted to imperialistic wars and bloody conquests. In a few cases they met with considerable success, and for a brief period, one of them, Eannatum, extended the sway of Lagash over Sumer as a whole and even over several of the neighboring states. The earlier victories proved ephemeral, however, and in less than a century Lagash was reduced to its earlier boundaries and former status. By the time Urukagina came to power, Lagash had been so weakened that it was a ready prey for its unrelenting enemy to the north, the city-state of Umma.

It was in the course of these cruel wars and their tragic after-maths that the citizens of Lagash found themselves deprived of their political and economic freedom; for in order to raise armies and supply them with arms and equipment, the rulers found it necessary to infringe on the personal rights of the individual citizen, to tax his wealth and property to the limit, and to appropriate, as well, property belonging to the temple. Under the impact of war, they met with little opposition. And once introduced, the palace coterie showed itself most unwilling to relinquish the domestic controls, even in times of peace, for they had proved highly profitable. Indeed, our ancient bureaucrats had devised a variety of sources of revenue and income, taxes and imposts, which in some ways might well be the envy of their modern counterparts. Citizens were thrown in jail on the slightest pretext: for debt, non-payment of taxes, or trumped-up charges of theft and murder.

But let the historian who lived in Lagash more than forty-two hundred years ago, and who was therefore a contemporary of the events he reports, tell it more or less in his own words. Three duplicating versions of his text, and there may well have been more, have been unearthed in Lagash indicating that Urukagina and his fellow reformers were proud, and not unjustifiably so, of the social and moral revolution that they had brought about.[3]

In the days preceding Urukagina, or as the author puts it rather pompously, "formerly, from days of yore, from (the day) the seed (of man) came forth," palace appointees practiced such abuses as seizing, presumably without right or warrant, property belonging to the citizens of Lagash—their donkeys, sheep, and fisheries. Other citizens were mulcted more or less indirectly of their goods and possessions by being compelled to have their rations measured out in the palace, much to their disadvantage, or to bring their sheep to the palace for shearing and to pay in "cold cash" for the service, at least in certain specified cases.

If a man divorced his wife, the *ensi* got five shekels, and his vizier got one shekel. If a perfumer made an oil preparation, the *ensi* got five shekels, the vizier got one shekel, and the *abgal*

[3] The reader will find a full and thoroughly revised translation of all three versions, based largely, but not altogether, on one of Arno Poebel's still unpublished manuscripts, on pp. 317–22.

(palace steward) got another shekel. As for the temple and its property, the *ensi* took it over as his own. To quote our ancient narrator literally: "The oxen of the gods plowed the *ensi*'s onion patches; the onion and cucumber patches of the *ensi* were located in the gods' best fields." In addition, the more important temple officials, particularly the *sanga*'s, were deprived in one way or another of many of their donkeys and oxen as well as of much of their grain and wearing apparel.

Even death brought no relief from levies and taxes. When a dead man was brought to the cemetery for burial (there were two grades of cemeteries—an ordinary one and another called "the reeds of Enki"), quite a number of officials and parasites made it their business to be on hand to relieve the bereaved family of quantities of barley, bread, and date wine, and various furnishings. From one end of the state to the other, our venerable reporter observes bitterly, "there were the tax collectors." No wonder, then, that the palace waxed fat and prosperous. Its lands and properties formed one vast, continuous estate. In the literal words of our Sumerian commentator: "The houses of the *ensi* and the fields of the *ensi*, the houses of the palace harem and the fields of the palace harem, the houses of the palace nursery and the fields of the palace nursery crowded each other side to side."

Also prevalent were other abuses seemingly not directly at-tributable to the palace bureaucracy but resulting no doubt from the general state of injustice, cynicism, and self-aggrandizement induced by its corrupt and oppressive actions: artisans and ap-prentices were reduced to abject poverty and had to beg for their food. Blind men—presumably, prisoners of war and slaves who had been blinded in order to prevent them from attempting to escape—were seized and put to watering the fields like animals and were given only enough food to keep them alive. The rich, "the big men" and the supervisors, were getting richer and richer at the expense of the less fortunate citizens, such as the *shub-lugal*'s (perhaps originally, "king's retainers"), by forcing them to sell their donkeys and houses at low prices and against their will. The indigent, the poor, the orphaned, and the widowed were mistreated and deprived in one way or another of what little they had by men of power and influence.

At this low point in the political and social affairs of Lagash, our Sumerian historian tells us, the new and god-fearing ruler, Urukagina, was chosen by Ningirsu, the tutelary deity of the city, out of the whole multitude of Lagash citizens and enjoined to re-establish the "divine laws" which had been abandoned and neglected by his predecessors. Urukagina held close to Ningirsu's words and carried out the god's commands to the full. He banned such practices as the seizure of donkeys, sheep, and fisheries belonging to the citizens, and the exaction of payment to the palace in one way or another for measuring their rations and shearing their sheep. When a man divorced his wife, neither the *ensi* nor his vizier got anything. When a perfumer made an oil preparation, neither the *ensi* nor the vizier nor the *abgal* got anything. When a dead man was brought to the cemetery for burial, the various officials received considerably less of the dead man's goods than formerly, in some cases a good deal less than half. As for the temple property that the *ensi* had appropriated for himself, he, Urukagina, returned it to the proper owners, the gods; in fact, it now seems that the temple administrators were put in charge of the palace of the *ensi* as well as the palaces of his wife and children. From one end of the land to the other, our contemporary historian observes, "there were no tax collectors."

But removing the ubiquitous bailiffs, tax collectors, and other parasitic officials was not Urukagina's only achievement. He also put a stop to the injustice and exploitation suffered by the poor at the hands of the rich and mighty. Permanent rations of food and drink were allotted to the craftsmen guilds, certain blind laborers and other workers, and also various *gala*-priests (probably temple singers). Artisans and apprentices no longer had to beg for their food. To prevent the supervisors and "big men" from taking advantage of less fortunate citizens, such as the *shub-lugal*'s, he promulgated two ordinances forbidding them to force their more lowly brethren to sell their donkeys or their houses against their will. He amnestied and set free the citizens of Lagash who had been imprisoned for debt or failure to pay taxes or on trumped-up (presumably) charges of theft or murder. As for the orphan and the widow, ready and helpless victims of the rich and powerful, "Urukagina made a covenant with the god Ningirsu that a man of power must not commit an injustice against them."

Finally, in one of the versions of the Urukagina document (see pages 321–22), we find a series of regulations which, if correctly translated and interpreted, should be of no little significance for the history of law; they indicate that great stress was laid by the Sumerian courts on the need of making manifest to all, by means of the written word, the guilt for which the accused was punished. Thus, the thief and the woman who marries two husbands must be stoned with stones on which their evil intent has been inscribed; and the woman who has sinned by saying something to a man which she should not have said (the text giving her words is unfortunately unintelligible) must have her teeth crushed with burnt bricks upon which, presumably, her guilty deed has been inscribed.

As is apparent from the Urukagina reform text, the promulgation of laws and legal regulations by the rulers of the Sumerian states was a common phenomenon by 2400 B.C. and probably even considerably earlier. It is not unreasonable to infer, therefore, that in the three centuries that followed, more than one official judge, or palace archivist, or professor of the *edubba* must have come upon the idea of writing down the current and past laws or precedents either for purposes of reference or teaching. But, as of today, no such compilations have been recovered for the period between the days of Urukagina and those of Ur-Nammu, the founder of the Third Dynasty of Ur, who began his reign about 2050 B.C.

The Ur-Nammu law code was originally inscribed no doubt on a stone stele, not unlike that on which the Akkadian law code of Hammurabi was inscribed some three centuries later. But what has been unearthed to date is not this original stele, nor even a contemporary copy of it, but a poorly preserved clay tablet prepared several hundred years later. This tablet was divided by the ancient scribe into eight columns, four on the obverse and four on the reverse. Each of the columns contained about forty-five small ruled spaces; fewer than half of these are now legible. The obverse contains a long prologue which is only partially intelligible because of the numerous breaks in the text. Briefly summarized, its contents may be reconstructed in part as follows.

After the world had been created and after the fate of the land Sumer and of the city Ur had been decided, An and Enlil, the two leading deities of the Sumerian pantheon, appointed the moon-god, Nanna, as the king of Ur. Then one day, Ur-Nammu was selected by the god as his earthly representative to rule over Sumer and Ur. The new king's first acts were concerned with the political and military safety of Ur and Sumer. In particular, he found it necessary to do battle with the bordering city-state of Lagash, which was expanding at Ur's expense. He defeated and put to death its ruler, Namhani, and then "with the power of Nanna, the king of the city," he re-established Ur's former boundaries.

Now came the time to turn to internal affairs and to institute social and moral reforms. He removed the chiselers and grafters, or as the code itself describes them, the "grabbers" of the citizens' oxen, sheep, and donkeys. He then established and regulated honest and unchangeable weights and measures. He saw to it that "the orphan did not fall a prey to the wealthy," "the widow did not fall a prey to the powerful," and "the man of one shekel did not fall a prey to the man of one mina (sixty shekels)." And, although the relevant passage is destroyed, this side of the tablet no doubt contained a statement to the effect that Ur-Nammu promulgated the laws which followed to insure justice in the land and to promote the welfare of its citizens.

The laws themselves probably began on the reverse of the tablet and are so badly damaged that only the contents of five of them can be restored with some degree of certainty. One of them deals with an accusation of witchcraft and involves a trial by the water ordeal; another treats of the return of a slave to his master. But it is the other three laws, fragmentary and difficult as their contents are, which are of very special importance for the history of man's social and spiritual growth; for they show that even before 2000 B.C., the law of "eye for eye" and "tooth for tooth" had already given way to the far more humane approach in which a money fine was substituted as a punishment. These three laws read as follows:

If a man has cut off with an . . -instrument the foot of another man whose . . . . , he shall pay 10 shekels of sliver.

If a man has severed with a weapon the bones of another man whose . . . . , he shall pay 1 mina of silver.

If a man has cut off with a *geshpu*-instrument, the nose of another man, he shall pay ⅔ of a mina of silver.

As of today, no law codes have been uncovered from any of the other rulers of the Third Dynasty of Ur, the dynasty founded by Ur-Nammu. But for the thirty-eight-year period beginning with the thirty-second year of Shulgi, Ur-Nammu's son and successor, and ending with the third year of the tragic and pathetic Ibbi-Sin, we have a group of over three hundred court records which are highly revealing for the legal practices and court procedures of the Sumerian city-states as well as for their social and economic organization. To be sure, these records all stem from a time when the Sumerians were approaching the end of their history, but there is little doubt that they reflect to some degree the customs and modes of earlier days.

The great majority of these court archives were excavated in Lagash and have been copied, published, and partly translated by French scholars, especially Charles Virolleaud and Henri de Genouillac. In 1956, new transliterations and translations of all these court documents were published by Adam Falkenstein, together with a detailed commentary and discussion—thus adding another to his significant series of contributions to Sumerology. The following sketch of the legal procedures current in the Sumerian city-state is based almost entirely on Falkenstein's publication.

The court records are designated by the ancient scribes themselves as *ditilla*'s, a word which means literally "completed lawsuits." At least thirteen of these, however, are not lawsuits at all, but merely court notarizations of agreements or contracts involving marriage, divorce, support of a wife, gifts, sales, and the appointment of various individuals to temple offices. The remainder, which are all records of actual lawsuits, concern marriage contracts, divorces, inheritance, slaves, hiring of boats, claims of all sorts, pledges, and such miscellaneous items as pretrial investigations, subpoenas, theft, damage to property, and malfeasance in office.

Theoretically—at least by the time of the Third Dynasty of Ur—it was the king of the whole of Sumer who was responsible for law and justice, but in practice the administration of law was in the hands of the *ensi*'s, the local rulers of the various city-states. In the earlier court documents only the *ensi*'s name appears as a kind of official signature; later the *ensi*'s name appears together with the names of the judges who decided the case; and still later the names of the judges appear without the name of the *ensi*. However, in the inscription on the tablet containers, where these documents were stored and filed in chronological order, the name of the *ensi* is usually given along with those of the judges.

The temple, to judge from the available material, played practically no role in the administration of justice, except as the place where oaths were administered. There is one instance, however, in which an individual is described as "the judge of the house of Nanna" (that is, the main temple at Ur), and this might indicate that there were special judges appointed by the temple for one reason or another.

The courts usually consisted of three or four judges, although in some cases only of one or two. There were no judges by profession; of the thirty-six men listed as judges in the documents, the majority were important temple administrators, sea merchants, couriers, scribes, constables, inspectors, augurs, prefects, archivists, city elders, and even *ensi*'s. There are, however, several individuals designated as "royal judges," and one of the documents ends with the words "the *ditilla* of the seven royal judges of Nippur," which points to the existence of a special court at Nippur, perhaps a kind of court of last appeal. Nothing is known of the methods or criteria governing the appointment of the judges, the length of their service, or how much, if any, remuneration they received.

Immediately preceding the names of the judges on the court archives, there usually appears the name of the *mashkim,* who seems to have been a kind of court clerk and bailiff who was charged with the preparation of the case for the court and with taking care of the details in the court procedure. More than one hundred *mashkim*'s are listed in the *ditilla*'s, and they all come from the same social stratum as the judges; the role of *mashkim,* therefore, was also not a regular and permanent profession. There is some indication that the *mashkim* was paid for his services; thus there is a statement in one of the documents which reads:

"1 shekel of silver and 1 lamb were (payment) for what the *mashkim* did."

In some of the *ditilla*'s, the names of the judges and *mashkim* are followed by a list of individuals described as witnesses of one type or another, who seem to represent not the litigants but the public at the court trials.

In a lawsuit, Sumerian court procedure was as follows: A suit was initiated by one of the parties or—if the state's interests were involved—by the state administration. The testimony brought before the court might consist of statements made by witnesses, usually under oath, or by one of the parties under oath; or it might be in the form of written documents or statements made by "experts" or important officials. The verdict was conditional and became operative only after an oath had been administered in the temple to the party of whom the court demanded it as proof of their claim. This oath was usually given to the witnesses—one or two in number—rather than to the litigants, except in cases where the testimony of the witnesses was denied by the litigant. No oath was necessary if a written document was available to one of the parties. At times the *mashkim* who had participated in an earlier court action relevant to the issue on hand took the oath. The verdict was usually expressed quite tersely with such phrases as "it (that is, the object or slave involved in the litigation) was confirmed as belonging to X (the winning party)," or "X (the winning party) has taken it (the object or slave) as his due," or even "Y (the losing party) must pay." Sometimes, but by no means always, the reason for the verdict was stated. Following the verdict, the document occasionally contained a clause of renunciation and abjuration.

Some two hundred years after Ur-Nammu, a ruler from the dynasty of Isin named Lipit-Ishtar promulgated a law code, which has been unearthed in the form of fragments of one large twenty-column tablet originally containing the entire text and four "excerpt" tablets used for school practice. Like the Akkadian code of Hammurabi, it consists of three sections: a prologue, the laws themselves, and an epilogue. The prologue begins with a statement put in the mouth of the king, Lipit-Ishtar, that after An and Enlil had given Nininsinna, the goddess who was the tutelary deity of Isin, the kingship of Sumer and Akkad, and after they had called him (Lipit-Ishtar), "to the princeship of the land" in order to bring "well-being to the Sumerians and the Akkadians," he promulgated a code of justice in Sumer and Akkad. He then cites some of his achievements in regard to the welfare of his subjects: he freed "the sons and daughters of Sumer and Akkad" from slavery which had been imposed upon them and re-established a number of equitable family practices. The end of the prologue is unfortunately destroyed.

As for the laws themselves, the available text permits the restoration wholly or in part of some thirty-eight, practically all of which belong to the second half of the code, the first half being almost entirely destroyed. The subject matter treated in these laws includes the hiring of boats; real estate, particularly orchards; slaves and perhaps servants; defaulting of taxes; inheritance and marriage; rental of oxen. Immediately after the last of the laws comes the epilogue, which is only partially intelligible because of the numerous breaks in the text. It begins with a reiteration by Lipit-Ishtar that he established justice in the land and that he brought well-being to its people. He then states that he set up "this stele"—the code was, therefore, as might have been expected, inscribed on a stele of which the tablets were copies— and proceeds to pronounce a blessing on those who will not damage it in any way and a curse against those who will.[4]

Turning from the socioeconomic structure of the Sumerian city to its more material aspects, we might start by trying to estimate the size of its population. This can hardly be done, however, with any reasonable degree of exactness since there was no official census; at least no traces of any have as yet been found. For Lagash, Diakanoff (see above, page 75), after studying the rather incomplete and indirect data provided by the economic texts, estimates a free population of about 100,000. And for Ur, at about 2000 B.C., when it was the capital of Sumer for the third time, C. L. Woolley, in his recent article, "The Urbanization of Society,"[5] estimates a population of some 360,000 souls. His figure is based on tenuous comparisons and dubious assumptions, and it

---

[4] For the full text of the Lipit-Ishtar code, see Appendix H.

[5] *Journal of World History*, IV (1957), 246–47.

might be wise to cut it by about half, which would still give Ur a population of close to 200,000.

Except for the *temenos*, the sacred area of the city with its main temples and ziggurat, the Sumerian city was hardly an attractive site. To quote Woolley, "If the residential quarters excavated at Ur give, as presumably they do, a fair sample of the city as a whole, we see something that has grown out of the conditions of the primitive village, not laid out on any system of town-planning. The unpaved streets were narrow and winding, some-times mere blind alleys leading to houses hidden away in the middle of a great block of haphazard buildings; large houses and small are tumbled together, a few of them flat-roofed tenements one storey high, most of them two storeys, and a few, apparently of three. Lanes sheltered by awnings and lined with open booths correspond to the bazaars of the modern Middle Eastern town."

Nevertheless, to judge from passages in the "Lamentation over the Destruction of Ur" (see below, pages 142–44) it had its at-tractions: "lofty gates" and avenues for promenading as well as boulevards where feasts were celebrated. And from "A Scribe and His Perverse Son" and "Love Finds a Way" (see below, pages 243–46 and 250–52), we learn that the city had a public square which was not devoid of appeal to the young and the pleasure-seeking.

The average Sumerian house was a small one-story, mud-brick structure consisting of several rooms usually grouped around an open court. The well-to-do Sumerian, on the other hand, probably lived in a two-story house of about a dozen rooms, built of brick and plastered and whitewashed both inside and out. The ground floor of the two-story house consisted of a reception room, kitchen, lavatory, servants' quarters, and sometimes even a private chapel. For furniture there were low tables, high-backed chairs, and beds with wooden frames. Household vessels were made of clay, stone, copper, and bronze; there were also baskets and chests made of reeds and wood. Floors and walls were covered with reed mats, skin rugs, and woolen hangings. Below the house there was often a family mausoleum where the family dead were buried, although there also seem to have been special cemeteries for the dead out-side the cities.

The economic life of the Sumerian city depended primarily on the highly developed skills of farmers and husbandmen, artisans and craftsmen. The Sumerians developed no theoretical "science"; we know of no general laws of a scientific character formulated by their men of learning. Sumerian thinkers classified the natural world into the following categories: domestic animals, wild animals (from elephant to insect), birds (including some flying insects), fishes, trees, plants, vegetables, and stones. Lists of all possible items in these categories were compiled as textbooks for use in the *edubba;* these lists consist, however, of nothing but names, although the teachers no doubt added explanations—lectures, as it were—for the benefit of the students. This is apparent to some extent from the literary texts in which the "shepherd-bird," for example, is described in these words:

> The "shepherd-bird" says ri-di-ik, ri-di-ik,
> The "shepherd-bird" (has) a variegated neck like
>   the *dar*-bird,
> He has a crest upon his head.

Or the *mur*-fish—probably the skate or ray—is described as:

> The head, a hoe, the teeth, a comb,
> Its bones, a tall fir tree,
> Its stomach, the water-skin of Dumuzi,
> Its slender tail, the whip of the fishermen,
> Its scaleless skin needs no processing . . . . ,
> The sting serves as a nail.

Or the contrast between the cat's patience and the directness of the mongoose is noted in these words:

> A cat—for its thoughts,
> A mongoose—for its actions.

Astronomy, which in the last half of the first millennium B.C. became one of the highest scientific attainments of the Sumerians' cultural heirs, the Babylonians, was practically unknown in ancient Sumer; at least as of today we have only a list of about twenty-five stars and nothing more from Sumer. Observation of the heavenly bodies must have been practiced in Sumer for calendrical purposes if for no other reasons, but if the results of these observations were ever recorded, they are not preserved. Astrology, however, must have had considerable vogue to judge from Gudea's dream (see below, page 138) in which the goddess Nidaba appeared, studying a clay tablet on which the starry heaven was depicted, thus indicating that Gudea was to build the Eninnu temple in accordance with the "holy stars."

The Sumerians divided the year into two seasons: *emesh,* "summer," beginning in February-March, and *enten,* "winter," beginning in September-October. The new year was probably supposed to fall sometime in April-May. The months were strictly lunar; they began with the evening of the new moon and were 29 or 30 days in length. The names of the months, which were often derived from agricultural activities or from feasts in honor of certain deities, varied from city to city. To take care of the difference in length between the lunar and solar years, an intercalary month was introduced at regular intervals. The day began with sunset and was twelve double-hours in length. The night was divided into three watches of four hours each. Time was measured by a water clock, or clepsydra, shaped like a cylinder or prism; the shadow clock or rod clock was also probably known.

The Sumerian system of numeration was sexagesimal in character, but not strictly so since it makes use of the factor 10 as well as 6 thus: 1, 10, 60, 600, 3600, 36,000, etc. From the point of view of writing, there were actually two systems of numeration; the one used normally, which has special signs for each order of units (see Fig. 1, page 92), and the "learned" system, the only one used in the mathematical texts, which is purely sexagesimal and positional, like our decimal system. Thus, while according to the decimal system, the number written 439, for example, stands for $(4 \times 10^2) + (3 \times 10) + 9$, in the sexagesimal system, the same number would stand for $(4 \times 60^2) + (3 \times 60) + 9$, or 14,589. The zero was unknown to the Sumerians, and the absolute value of the units was not indicated in the writing, so that a number written

$$\text{𝍸𝍸 ≪𝍸𝍸 ≪≪𝍸𝍸}$$

which we may transcribe as 4, 23, 36, can be read either $(4 \times 60^2) + (23 \times 60) + 36 = 15,816$, or as $(4 \times 60^3) + (23 \times 60^2) + (36 \times 60) = 948,960$, etc.; or it can be read as $(4 \times 60) + 23 + (36/60) = 236\%$, or as $4 + (23/60) + (36/3600) = (59/4150)$, etc. Like our decimal system, therefore, the sexagesimal system

Old	Late	Value	Old	Late	Value
D	𐎟	1	D DO	𐏑	600
D D	𐎟𐎟	2	○	◇	3600
D D D	𐎟𐎟𐎟	3	◎	◈	36000
D D D D	𐎟𐎟 𐎟𐎟	4	FRACTIONS		
D D D D D	𐎟𐎟𐎟 𐎟𐎟	5			⅙
○	⟨	10			½
D	𐎟	60			⅔

Examples:

$$\text{D} \begin{smallmatrix}DD\\DD\end{smallmatrix} \text{O} \begin{smallmatrix}DDD\\DD\end{smallmatrix} = 600 + 60 \times 4 + 10 + 5 = 855$$

$$= 36000 \times 2 + 3600 \times 4 + 600 \times 3$$
$$+ 10 \times 5 + 6 + \tfrac{2}{3} = 88256\tfrac{2}{3}.$$

A sign 𐎟 (l á = minus) is used in the following way:

$$\text{⟨𐎟} = 10 - 1 = 9, \quad \text{⟨⟨𐎟𐎟𐎟} = 20 - 3 = 17.$$

The fractions can also be expressed by: i g i − n − g á l.
i g i − 4 − g á l = ¼,   i g i − 5 − g á l = ⅕,   etc.

Fig. 1.—*Sumerian Numerical Signs*

permits a flexibility in number writing which is highly favorable to the development of mathematics.

The mathematical school texts which have come down to us are of two types: tables and problems. The former include tabulations of reciprocals, multiplications, squares and square roots, cubes and cube roots, the sums of squares and cubes needed for the numerical solution of certain types of equations, exponential functions, coefficients giving numbers for practical computation (like the approximate value of $\sqrt{2}$), and numerous metrological calculations giving areas of rectangles, circles, etc. The problem texts deal with Pythagorean numbers, cubic roots, equations, and such practical matters as excavating or enlarging canals, counting bricks, and so on. As of today, almost all problem texts are Akkadian, although they must go back in large part to Sumerian prototypes since nearly all the technical terms used are Sumerian. (Fig. 2, page 94, reproduces a Sumerian tablet of about 2500 B.C., excavated at Fara, which contains a table for calculating the surface of square-shaped fields.)

Until quite recently practically nothing was known of Sumerian medicine, although there were hundreds of Akkadian medical texts from the first millennium B.C. utilizing all kinds of Sumerian medical words and phrases. Even today we have only two Sumerian medical tablets, and one of these is a small piece containing only one prescription. The other, however, is a tablet 3¾ × 6¼ inches in size, inscribed with fifteen prescriptions, which is of no little importance for the history of medicine. To judge from the careful, large, and elegant script, the tablet was inscribed some time in the last quarter of the third millennium B.C. and contains, therefore, what is by all odds the oldest pharmacopoeia known to man. Although the tablet was excavated some sixty to seventy years ago, it did not become known to the scholarly world until 1940. Since then several translations of the text, which is replete with linguistic difficulties because of the technical phraseology, have been published, the last and most trustworthy being that prepared by Miguel Civil, then research associate in the University Museum of the University of Pennsylvania.[6]

[6] *Revue d'Assyriologie*, LIV (1960), 59–72. See also *Ciba Journal*, No. 12, pp. 1–7.

$$600 \text{ sag gar-du} \times 600 \text{ sá} = 1080 \times 3 + 180 \times 2 \qquad = 3600 \text{ iku}$$

$$(60 \times 9)(60 \times 9) = 1080 \times 2 + 180 \times 4 + 18 \times 2 = 2916 \text{ iku}$$

$$(60 \times 8)(60 \times 8) = 1080 \times 2 + 180 \times 8 \qquad = 2304 \text{ iku}$$

$$(60 \times 7)(60 \times 7) = 1080 + 180 \times 3 + 18 \times 8 \qquad = 1764 \text{ iku}$$

$$(60 \times 6)(60 \times 6) = 1080 + 180 + 18 \times 2 \qquad = 1269 \text{ iku}$$

$$(60 \times 5)(60 \times 5) = 180 \times 5 \qquad = 900 \text{ iku}$$

$$(60 \times 4)(60 \times 4) = 180 \times 3 + 18 \times 2 \qquad = 576 \text{ iku}$$

$$(60 \times 3)(60 \times 3) = 180 + 18 \times 8 \qquad = 324 \text{ iku}$$

$$(60 \times 2)(60 \times 2) = 18 \times 8 \qquad = 144 \text{ iku}$$

etc.

This table is intended to help in the computation of the area of square fields. The first column (left) gives the length of the side (s a g) measured in g a r - d u (1 g a r - d u = 6 yards approx.). The second column (middle) gives the length of the other side, stating that it is equal (s á) to the first side. The third column (right) gives the area measured in iku (1 i k u = 100 g a r - d u²). Thus to obtain the area in g a r - d u², multiply the results given in the third column by 100.

Note that a special set of number signs is used in surface measurements:

○ = 1080 i k u   ✿ = 180 i k u   ○ = 18 i k u

Fig. 2.—*Mathematical Text from Fara (after A. Deimel, "Schultexte aus Fara," No. 82)*

The document contains 145 lines, or rather, cases. The first 21 lines are so badly damaged that it is impossible to get a clear idea of the contents. A priori, and on analogy with the cuneiform medical documents of the first millennium B.C., it was hoped that they might contain a statement such as "if a man suffers from," followed by the name of this or that illness. But the relatively few signs and phrases that are preserved, such as "root of a . . . . plant" (cases 1 and 2), "head of . . . ." (cases 3 and 5), "wool" (cases 9 and 10), and "salt" (case 15), do not point in this direction.

The prescriptions themselves, fifteen in all, begin with line 22 (near the bottom of the first column of the tablet). They may be divided into three classes in accordance with the manner in which the remedies were applied. The first class consists of eight prescriptions in which the application is in the form of a poultice. In general their content runs as follows: first a list of the simples to be utilized in each prescription; then the direction to pulverize them and mix them with a liquid in order to form a paste which is to be fastened as a poultice to the sick part of the body after the latter has been rubbed with oil, an action performed either for its intrinsic therapeutic value or to keep the paste from clinging to the skin. Here are literal translations of the last five of these poultice prescriptions (the first three are too fragmentary for translation).

Prescription No. 4. Pulverize the *anadishsha*-plant, the branches of the "thorn"-plant (probably the *Prosopis stephaniana*), the seeds of the *duashbur* (perhaps the *Atriplex halimus* L.), (and) . . . . (names of at least two simples destroyed); . . . . pour water-diluted beer over it (the mass of pulverized simples); rub (the sick spot) with vegetable oil, (and) fasten (the paste formed by pouring the liquid over the pulverized simples) as a poultice.

Prescription No. 5. Pulverize river mud (and) . . . . ; knead it with water; rub with crude oil, (and) fasten as a poultice.

Prescription No. 6. Pulverize pears (?) (and) "manna," pour the lees of beer over it; rub with vegetable oil, (and) fasten as a poultice.

Prescription No. 7. Pulverize the lees of the dried vine, pine tree, and plum tree; pour beer over it, rub with oil, (and) fasten as a poultice.

Prescription No. 8. Pulverize the roots of the . . . -tree, ... , and dried river bitumen; pour beer over it; rub with oil, (and) fasten as a poultice.

The second group of prescriptions, three in number, consists of remedies which are to be taken internally. The first is somewhat complicated and involves the use of beer and river bitumen oil:

Prescription No. 9. Pour strong beer over the resin of . . . . -plant; heat over a fire; put this liquid in river bitumen oil, (and) let the (sick) man drink.

In the remaining two, the process is identical; the instructions are to pulverize two or three simples and dissolve them in beer for the sick man to drink:

Prescription No. 10. Pulverize pears (?) (and) the roots of the "manna"-plant; put (the pulverized simples) in beer, (and) let the (sick) man drink.

Prescription No. 11. Pulverize the seeds of the *nignagar*-vegetable, myrrh (?), (and) thyme; put in beer, (and) let the (sick) man drink.

The third set of prescriptions is introduced by a difficult and enigmatic passage which reads: "Arrange (?) the rushes over the hands and feet of the (sick) man." It is by no means clear at present what this operation refers to and why it was placed at this particular point. In spite of its obscurity, the line is of paramount importance since it gives at least an inkling of the ailing parts of the body to be treated.

The prescriptions themselves follow this introductory statement. They are four in number, and their components are more complex and less homogeneous than those of the preceding eleven. In the first three, the operations prescribed consist primarily of washing the ailing organ with a specially prepared solution and then immediately covering (?) it with a substance which, in two cases, seems to be burnt ashes. The fourth and last prescription, whose initial lines are destroyed, seems to contain only the names of a series of simples followed immediately by the covering (?) operation, and it is not impossible, therefore, that the writer had inadvertently omitted at least one intervening operation. Following is a translation of the last four prescriptions:

Prescription No. 12. Sift and knead together—all in one—turtle shell, the sprouting (?) *naga*-plant (a plant used to obtain soda and other alkalies), salt, (and) mustard; wash (the sick spot) with quality beer (and) hot water; scrub (the sick spot) with all of it (the kneaded mixture); after scrubbing, rub with vegetable oil (and) cover (?) with pulverized fir.

Prescription No. 13. Pour water over a dried and pulverized water snake, the *amamashumkaspal*-plant, the roots of the "thorn"-plant, pulverized *naga,* powdered fir turpentine, (and) the feces of the *garib* (?)-bat; heat (the infusion), (and) wash (the sick spot) with this liquid; after washing with the liquid, rub with vegetable oil (and) cover with *shaki.*

Prescription No. 14. Pour water over the dried (and) pulverized hair of the inner lining (?) of a cow, branches of the "thorn"-plant, the "star"-plant, the roots of the "sea"-tree, dried figs, (and) *ib*-salt; heat (and) wash with this liquid; after washing with the liquid, cover (?) with the ashes (?) of rushes.

Prescription No. 15. . . . . (a number of signs destroyed) which you have extracted from the willow, the dregs (?) of the *girbi*-vase, the lees of wine, the *nigmi*-plant, the *arina*-plant—roots and trunk—(and) cover (?) with ashes (?).

As our document shows, the Sumerian physician, not unlike his modern counterpart, went to botanical, zoölogical, and mineralogical sources for his materia medica. His favorite minerals were sodium chloride (salt), river bitumen, and crude oil. From the animal kingdom he utilized wool, milk, turtle shell, and water snake. But most of his medicinals came from the botanical world, from plants such as thyme, mustard, plum tree, pears, figs, willow, *Atriplex halimus* L., *Prosopis stephaniana,* "manna"-plant, fir, and pine, and from processed products such as beer, wine, and vegetable oil.

Our ancient document, it is well worth noting, is entirely free from the magic spells and incantations which are a regular feature of the cuneiform medical texts of later days; not a single deity or demon is mentioned in the text. The physician who wrote this document, therefore, seems to have practiced his medicine along empirico-rational lines. To be sure, it is hardly likely that he resorted to consciously planned experimentation and verification. Nevertheless, it would seem reasonable to assume that the treatments he prescribed had considerable therapeutic value, since his professional reputation was at stake, and it is not inconceivable that they might prove of some practical value to modern medical research.

Sad to say, our ancient pharmacopoeia does not provide us with any clear idea of the diseases or maladies for which the prescriptions are intended. The introduction preceding the prescriptions, which takes up most of the first column of the tablet, is badly damaged; in any case, to judge from the few preserved signs, it did not contain names of diseases. In the badly broken first prescription we find the Sumerian words for "back" and "buttocks," but in a fragmentary, unintelligible passage. Introducing the third set of prescriptions is a passage mentioning hands and feet, but in this case, too, the context is obscure and enigmatic. We do not even know whether each prescription was intended for a specific malady or whether several were intended for the same malady. It is not impossible, however, that these details, and many others, were explained orally to the reader of the tablet, which brings us to the purpose of the document and the motives which prompted its compilation and inscription.

The ancient physician who prepared our pharmacopoeia, it is worth stressing, was not just a narrow practitioner of his profession but an educated and cultured humanist. To learn to write correctly and elegantly the complex cuneiform syllabary, with its hundreds of signs and thousands of readings, he had to spend much of his youth in the Sumerian school, or *edubba*, where he studied and absorbed whatever scientific and literary knowledge was current in his day. The "textbooks" consisted primarily of compilations of words, phrases, paragraphs, extracts, and whole compositions prepared by the *ummia*'s, or professors, of the academy, which the student had to copy and recopy until he knew them by heart. These compilations, which were concise, terse, and unadorned, were no doubt accompanied by oral explanations, or lectures. Our ancient pharmacopoeia may well have been a compilation of this sort prepared by a practicing physician who was a "lecturer" on medicine in the academy. If this supposition should prove to be correct, our Sumerian document could not inaptly be described as a page from the oldest known textbook in the history of medicine.

The content of the second medical tablet was published as early as 1935, but was treated as a business document and remained unrecognized until 1960, when Michel Civil, as a result of his work on the larger tablet discussed above, identified it and translated it as follows:

Having crushed turtle shell and . . . , and having anointed the opening (of the sick organ, perhaps) with oil, you shall rub (with the crushed shell) the man lying prone (?). After rubbing with the crushed shell you shall rub (again) with fine beer; after rubbing with fine beer, you shall wash with water; after washing with water, you shall fill (the sick spot) with crushed fir wood. It is (a prescription) for someone afflicted by a disease in the *tun* and the *nu*.

The *tun* and the *nu* are probably two still unidentified parts of the sexual organs, and the treatment may therefore have been intended for some type of venereal disease. As the reader will note, the treatment described in this tablet is very similar to Prescription No. 12 in the larger medical document discussed above.

The medical doctor is known in Sumerian as the *a-zu*, the literal translation of which may be the "water-knower." The first physician on record is a practitioner named Lulu; the words "Lulu, the doctor" are found on a tablet excavated at Ur by the late Sir Leonard Woolley, which dates from as early as about 2700 B.C. The doctor must have had a relatively high social status to judge from the fact that one of the Lagash physicians by the name of Urlugaledinna, whose cylinder seal and stone votive inscription have been preserved, held an important position under Ur-Ningirsu, the son of Gudea. There were also veterinarians known as "the doctor of the oxen" or "the doctor of the donkeys"; but they are only mentioned in the lexical texts, and nothing else is known about them as yet from Sumerian times.

In the field of art, the Sumerians were particularly noted for their skill in sculpture. The earliest sculptors tended to be abstract and impressionistic. Their temple statues show great emotional and spiritual intensity rather than skill in modeling. This came gradually, however, and the later sculptors were technically superior, although their images lost in inspiration and vigor. Sumerian sculptors were quite skillful in carving figures on steles and plaques and even on vases and bowls. It is from this sculpture that we learn a good deal about Sumerian appearance and dress.

The men either were clean shaven or wore long beards and long hair parted in the middle. The most common form of dress was a kind of flounced skirt, over which long cloaks of felt were sometimes worn. Later the chiton, or long skirt, took the place of the flounced skirt. Covering the skirt was a big fringed shawl, which was carried over the left shoulder, leaving the right arm free. Women often wore dresses which looked like long tufted shawls, covering them from head to foot and leaving only the right shoulder bare. Their hair was usually parted in the middle and braided into a heavy pigtail, which was then wound around the head. They often wore elaborate headdresses consisting of hair ribbons, beads, and pendants.

Music, both instrumental and vocal, played a large role in Sumerian life, and some of the musicians were important figures in the temples and court. Beautifully constructed harps and lyres were excavated in the royal tombs of Ur. Percussive instruments, such as the drum and tambourine, were also common, as were pipes of reed and metal. Poetry and song flourished in the Sumerian schools. Most of the recovered works are hymns to gods and kings for use in the temple and palace; but there is every reason to believe that music, song, and dance were a major source of entertainment in the home and market place.[7]

One of the most original contributions of the Sumerians to the arts was the cylinder seal, a small cylinder of stone engraved with a design that became clear and meaningful when rolled over a clay tablet or the clay sealing of a jar. The cylinder seal became a sort of Mesopotamian trade-mark, although its use penetrated Anatolia, Egypt, Cyprus, and Greece. The Sumerian artists were highly ingenious in devising suitable designs, especially when the seal was first invented. The earliest cylinder seals are carefully incised gems depicting rows of animals or fairy-tale creatures and monsters and such scenes as the king on the battlefield and the shepherd defending his cattle against wild beasts. Later the designs became more decorative and formalized. Finally one design became predominant, almost to the exclusion of all others: the presentation scene in which a worshipper is presented to a god by his "good angel."

[7] See, for example, "Love Finds a Way," pp. 250–52.

In spite of the fact that Sumer was destitute of metal and stone and poor in timber, the craftsmen of Sumer were among the most highly skilled in the ancient world, although it is not improbable that, at least originally, many of them came from foreign parts to practice their skills in connection with the construction of temples. We get a rather vivid and illuminating glimpse of the Sumerian artisans and craftsmen at work from a large tablet excavated at Ur by Leonard Woolley, in which two supervisors of the temple workshops, or ateliers, give a résumé of the work completed during the twelfth year of the reign of Ibbi-Sin, who ruled about 1975 B.C. Eight ateliers are listed in this tablet: the "houses" of the "chisel-worker," or sculptor, the jeweler, the lapidary, the carpenter, the smith, the leatherworker, the fuller, and the basket maker.

First in the list is the chisel-worker, whose job was to sculpt the figurines and other small objects of ivory and rare wood. In the year with which we are concerned, twenty-one pounds of ivory were worked into such objects as figurines, both male and female, small birds, boxes, and rings.

The jeweler worked largely in gold and silver, although he also set semiprecious stones such as lapis lazuli, carnelian, and topaz. He did excellent foundry work with three and four-piece molds, and hammered metal sheets over a wooden core, finishing them with *repoussé* or stamping. He knew how to fasten pieces of gold and silver with pins or rivets as well as by soldering and was expert in making use of filigree work and granulation. The lapidaries—in our tablet—worked only on semiprecious stones for the jeweler, but they could also, no doubt, prepare stones for building.

Carpenters were always quite numerous in Sumer, for in spite of the dearth of wood, it was utilized on a large scale for making all kinds of furniture as well as boats, wagons, and chariots. In the atelier recorded in our tablet, the carpenters built a dais of ivory weighing no less than forty pounds, not to mention objects made of oak, fir, ebony, and willow. Other woods used by the carpenter, not mentioned in our tablet, are cedar, mulberry, tamarisk, and plane. The most common tree found in Sumer, the

Early Pictographs	Archaic Cuneiform Signs	Graphic Representations or Reconstructions	Objects
			Plow
			Sledge
			Boat (with Sails?)
	not continued		Boat
			Chisel
			Ax
	not continued		Saw
			War Mace

FIG. 3.—*Tools, Implements, and Vehicles as Represented in the Early Pictographs.*

palm, was little used by the carpenters since its wood is of poor quality. To make up to some extent for the difficulty of obtaining wood, old furniture was constantly reused. Thus in the atelier described in the Ibbi-Sin tablet, three old table tops and four fir boxes were reused to make one table, two beds, and one small box. In the year recorded on the tablet, the carpenters mainly made chairs of various types, tables, beds, and boxes. Among the tools used by the Sumerian carpenter were the saw, chisel, hammer, and drill bit.

The list of metals used in the foundry of the smith recorded in our tablet includes almost all those known at the time: gold, silver, tin, lead, copper, bronze, and a metal called *sugan* (perhaps antimony) utilized in small quantities as an alloy. Copperworking was highly developed as early as the beginning of the third millennium B.C.; not only was copper casting well known, but also such other techniques as hammering, annealing, filigree, and granulation. The smith, or metallurgist, had at his disposal a special type of bellows which could be worked by hand or foot to raise the temperature of his furnace to a degree of heat that would melt copper. Wood and reeds were used as kindling, and it took two pounds of wood and three "reed bundles"—or six reed bundles if no wood was used—to melt half a pound of copper. The more common products made of copper and bronze were tools such as hoes, axes, chisels, knives, and saws; arms such as lance points and arrowheads, swords, daggers, and harpoons; vessels and containers; nails, pins, rings, and mirrors.

The leatherworker in our tablet received during the year a large number of skins of bulls, calves, pigs, and especially sheep. From the skin and leather quite a number of objects were manufactured: water-skins, bags, harnesses and saddles, tires for chariot wheels, slings, and above all, shoes and sandals. For tanning purposes, the leatherworker utilized alkalies, sumac, and other still unidentifiable substances. Fat was used to make the skins supple and impermeable. The leatherworker mentioned in our Ur tablet made use of flour to finish off certain special skins and also "powder of gold" to decorate some of the manufactured pieces.

The fuller of our tablet seems to have had only a small shop, and little is said about him. The last of the artisans is the basket maker. He received quantities of reeds, a very important commodity in Sumer, and bitumen in order to manufacture baskets and boats.

The textile industry, not mentioned in our Ur tablet, was probably the largest in the land and the most important from the point of view of commerce. Many thousands of tons of wool were worked annually in Ur alone. Tremendous flocks of goats, sheep, and lambs were raised to obtain wool. The "shearing" was done by plucking. A spindle was used to spin the wool, and the weaving was done on both horizontal and vertical looms; usually, these two operations were performed by a team of three women, who would take as many as eight days to prepare a piece of material 3½ × 4 meters. The woven cloth was then turned over to the fullers, who soaked it in an alkaline solution in large vats and then trampled it by walking over it with their feet. Although wool was by all odds the most common textile used for cloth, flax was also cultivated, and linen garments seem to have been used especially by certain priests and holy men.

Materials and goods were transported in Sumer by man and beast or with the help of such implements as sledges, wagons, chariots, and boats. The sledges were probably used especially to carry very heavy loads, such as large blocks of rocks. The wagons were both four-wheeled and two-wheeled and were usually drawn by oxen. The chariots were rather heavy, small in size, and drawn by onagers. Transportation by boat was quite feasible and economical, and one boat of a little over five register tons could haul as heavy a load as a hundred minas. There were also very large boats constructed of wood in special shipyards, and these were no doubt used for long sea voyages to such lands as Meluhha and Dilmun. The common boat in use was the one known today in Iraq as the *guffa* and in ancient times as "the turnip"; it was made of reeds, covered with skin, and shaped like a basket. The sailboat, too, was probably known in ancient Sumer, to judge from the model of a boat found in Eridu. Oars and punting poles were in common use from earliest times. Along the river banks, however, the boats were often pulled by men or oxen.

Some of the more far-reaching technological achievements of the Sumerians were connected with irrigation and agriculture. The construction of an intricate system of canals, dikes, weirs,

and reservoirs demanded no little engineering skill and knowledge. Surveys and plans had to be prepared which involved the
use of leveling instruments, measuring rods, drawing, and mapping. Farming, too, had become a methodical and complicated
technique requiring foresight, diligence, and skill. It is not surprising, therefore, to find that the Sumerian pedagogues had compiled a "farmers' almanac" that consisted of a series of instructions
to guide a farmer throughout his yearly agricultural activities
beginning with the inundation of the fields in May-June and
ending with the winnowing and cleaning of the freshly harvested
crop in the following April-May. The text of this document, which
consists of 107 lines of instructions preceded by a one-line introduction and followed by a three-line colophon, has been pieced
together from more than a dozen tablets and fragments, of which
one of the most important is a still unpublished piece excavated
at Ur by the late Leonard Woolley more than a quarter-century
ago. This fragment has now been copied by C. J. Gadd, formerly
a Keeper in the British Museum and now professor emeritus of
the University of London, who has generously made it available
for the better restoration of the text as a whole. The translation
of the text is quite difficult and hazardous, in particular because
of its technical terminology, and the present effort (which is given
in Appendix I) is to be taken as tentative and provisional; it was
prepared in collaboration with Thorkild Jacobsen and Benno
Landsberger of the Oriental Institute of the University of Chicago, and Miguel Civil, then of the University Museum of the
University of Pennsylvania. An extensive paraphrase of the text
follows.

Our farm manual is introduced with the following line: "In
days of yore a farmer instructed his son." The directions which
follow concern all the more important chores and labors that a
farmer must perform to ensure a successful crop. Since irrigation
was the prime essential for Sumer's parched soil, our ancient
mentor begins by advising that care must be taken that the in-
undating waters do not rise too high over the field. When the
waters subside, shod oxen are to be let loose to trample the wet
ground, thus stamping out the weeds and leveling the surface of
the field, which must then be dressed with small, light axes until
it is even. Since the hoofs of the oxen have left their mark on the

still wet ground, men with pickaxes must go all around the field and smooth it out, and the crevices made by the oxen must be worked over with a drag.

While the field is drying, the farmer is counseled to have his household prepare the essential tools; particular stress is laid on whips, goads, and other "disciplinary" instruments which serve to keep both laborers and beasts working strenuously and constantly. He is also advised to have an extra ox for the plow since this will pay off well in the long run—he will succeed in planting the rather large amount of three *gur* over one *bur* of ground.

Before actually beginning to till the ground, the farmer is told to have it thoroughly plowed up twice with two different deep-soil plows (the *shukin-* and *bardil*-plows), then harrowed and raked three times, and finally pulverized with hammers. During the performance of these labors, the farmer is urged to keep the workers under constant surveillance so that they may not slacken their efforts for one instant. On the other hand, he himself must show self-discipline and not demand from them the usual attendance upon his person.

The actual plowing and sowing can now begin; the two operations are carried on simultaneously by means of a seeder, that is, a plow with an attachment that carries the seed from a container through a narrow funnel down to the furrow. The farmer is instructed to plow eight furrows to each *garush* (a strip between six and seven meters long). He must see to it that the seed is placed at an even depth of two "fingers." If the seed fails to penetrate properly, he must change the share, "the tongue of the plow." There were several kinds of furrows, according to our ancient expert, but except where he talks of straight and diagonal furrows, the text is rather obscure on this point. Following the planting of the furrows, the field had to be cleared of all clods and ground elevations and depressions had to be leveled off so that the sprouting of the barley would not be impeded in any way.

"After the sprout had broken through the (surface of) the ground," the handbook continues, the farmer should say a prayer to Ninkilim, the goddess of field mice and vermin, lest they harm the growing grain; he should also scare off the flying birds. When the barley has grown sufficiently to fill the narrow bottoms of the furrows, it is time to water it; and when it "stands high as (the

1—Measures of Length

𒋗𒋛	š u - s i		"finger"
𒌑	k ù š	= 30 s u - s i	"cubit"
𒄀	g i	= 6 k ù š	"reed"
𒃼	g a r - (d u)	= 2 g i	
𒂠	è š	= 10 g a r - (d u)	"line"
𒁕𒈾	d a n n a	= 1800 g a r - (d u)	"league"

One k ù š is about 50 cm. or 20 inches.

2—Measures of Area

𒊬	s a r	= g a r - (d u)^2	"garden"
𒅆	i k u	= 100 s a r	"field"
𒁹	b ù r	= 18 i k u	
𒊹	š á r	= 1080 i k u	

One s a r corresponds to 35 square meters or 376 sq. ft.

3—Measures of Capacity

𒂊	g í n		
𒋓	s i l a₃	= 60 g i n	
𒄥	g u r	= 144 s i l a	
𒄥𒈗	g u r - l u g a l	= 300 s i l a	
𒄥	g.u r₇	= 3600 s i l a	

One s i l a₃ equals 0.850 liters (almost one-fifth of a gallon).

4—Measures of Weight

𒊺	š e		"grain"
𒂊	g í n	= 180 š e	"shekel"
𒈠𒈾	m a - n a	= 60 g í n	"mina"
𒄘	g ú	= 60 m a - n a	"talent"

One m a - n a corresponds to about 500 gr. (approximately 1 pound).

FIG. 4.—*Sumerian Measures and Their Equivalents (translations are given when known).*

straw of) a mat in the middle of a boat," it is time to water it a second time. He is to water it a third time when it is "royal" barley, that is, when it has reached its full height. Should he then notice a reddening of the wet grain, it is the dread *samana*-disease, which endangers the crops. If the barley is doing well, however, he is to water it a fourth time and thus obtain an extra yield of 10 per cent.

The time has now come for harvesting. The farmer is cautioned not to wait until the barley bends under its own weight but to cut it "in the day of its strength," that is, at just the right moment. Three men are to work as a team on the standing stalks of barley: a reaper, a binder, and a man who arranges the sheaves. There then follows a passage which, if correctly translated, is of no little ethical and Biblical significance: it exhorts the farmer to leave on the ground some of the fallen ears of barley for the "young" and the "gleaners" (see Leviticus 19:9–10 and Ruth 2:3 ff.), a charitable deed for which his god will show him lasting favor.

The threshing, which follows immediately upon the harvesting, is done in two stages. First, the mounds of barley are trampled down by wagons drawn back and forth over them for five consecutive days. Then a threshing sled, consisting of beams with teeth fastened with leather strips and held secure by bitumen, is used to "open the barley." Here follows another Biblical parallel, an exhortation that the oxen should be fed to satiety during the threshing when their mouths are watering, as it were, for the tempting, fresh-smelling barley (see Deuteronomy 25:4).

The time has now come for winnowing, which is to be performed by two "barley lifters." From here on, the text is not altogether clear, but we can gather that the winnowing process consisted of lifting the "dirty" mixture of barley and chaff as it came off the threshing floor on forks or shovels, thus freeing the barley from the straw and husks which, in a sense, contaminated it. The document closes with a three-line statement intended to impress the reader and student with the claim that the instructions which the farmer has given to his son are actually those of the god Ninurta, who, according to the Sumerian theologians, was the "trustworthy farmer of Enlil," the leading deity of the Sumerian pantheon.

The author of this unique agricultural document, in spite of its introductory lines, was not a farmer; farmers were probably illiterate and in any case would hardly have had the time or the desire to prepare an agricultural manual. It was undoubtedly composed by one of the professors, or *ummia*'s, of the Sumerian school, the *edubba*—his literary mannerisms are evident in not a few of its passages. The purpose of the composition was pedagogic; it was intended to teach the students of the *edubba*—especially the more advanced among them—all about the art and skill of successful farming. This is proved by the fact that the composition has been found inscribed on numerous duplicates and extracts, and needless to say, many more are probably still lying buried in the ruins of Sumer. We may conclude, therefore, that it was quite popular with both professor and student, and no wonder, since it probably helped the graduate of the *edubba* to get a good job and hold it, as we can see from a hitherto practically unknown essay which may be entitled "Colloquy between an *ugula* and a Scribe," which shows the *edubba*-graduate in the role of a successful and articulate manager of a large estate.

The cereals raised by the Sumerians were barley—by all odds the most important—wheat, millet, and emmer. Quite a number of vegetables were grown, including chick-peas, lentils, vetches, onions, garlic, lettuce, turnips, cress, leeks, mustard, and various kinds of cucumbers. The use of a belt of trees to protect the garden from the withering sun and desiccating winds was known to the Sumerians and was even made into a mythical theme (see pages 162–64). The most extensively used tool for gardening was the hoe, and there was a special type of harrow known as the "garden harrow."

The tree that played a predominant role in Sumerian economic life was the date palm, from which a sweet substance known as *lal*, or "honey," was extracted. Artificial fertilization of the female palm was known and practiced in Sumerian times. And from the early second millennium B.C., there are Sumerian lexicographical lists containing close to one hundred fifty words for the various kinds of palms and their different parts.

Animal husbandry, like agriculture, was fundamental to the Sumerian economy—it was the source of transportation, food, and clothing. The animal commonly used for transportation was the donkey; the horse was apparently known in late Sumerian days but was never used extensively. The most useful of the domesticated animals was undoubtedly the ox, the only draft animal that was more or less properly harnessed in those early days. It was used for plowing, pulling carts and sledges, and carrying heavy loads. Bulls, cows, and calves were invaluable for their meat and skin.

Some two hundred Sumerian words designating the various types and varieties of sheep have come down to us, although most of them cannot be identified as yet. From the economic point of view, the most important—in addition to the ordinary ones— were the fattened sheep, the fat-tailed sheep, and the mountain sheep, probably the mouflon. Goats and kids were also plentiful, and goat hair was used extensively for weaving carpets and large cratelike containers. Pigs were used for their fat and skin as well as their meat—pork was looked on with favor by the Sumerians— and there was a special swineherd as well as a swine butcher in charge of slaughtering and preparing the meat.

Animal husbandry was supplemented by hunting, and there are texts recording the deliveries of deer, wild boars, and gazelles. There was also the fowler, who caught birds with a whole arsenal of nets, and there are recorded deliveries of as many as fifty-four roasted birds. Fishing, too, was a very important food-producing industry, although to a much greater extent in earlier than in later Sumerian times to judge from the fact that over fifty different types of fish are mentioned in texts dating earlier than 2300 B.C. and only half a dozen or so after that. The net was the implement most commonly used for catching fish, although traps and fishing lines are also mentioned.

The most popular beverage among the Sumerians was beer, the drink that rejoiced the "hearts" and "lives" of both gods and men, not to mention its medicinal value. The brewing techniques are still rather obscure, and what is known has been admirably treated by Leo Oppenheim in his monograph "On Beer and Brewing Techniques in Ancient Mesopotamia."[8] The preparation of beer was closely related to the fabrication of cereal cakes from sprouted barley; it was this malting that gave a greater nutritional value to the grain that now had a large content of carbohydrates and protein. There was a special goddess in charge of beer prep-

[8] Supplement No. 10 to the *Journal of the American Oriental Society* (1950).

aration called Ninkasi, a name which seems to mean literally "the lady who fills the mouth." Although she was a goddess "born in sparkling-fresh water," it was beer that was her first love; and she is described in a hymn of glorification addressed to her by one of the devotees of the Inanna cult as the brewer of the gods who "bakes with lofty shovel the sprouted barley," who "mixes the *bappir*-malt with sweet aromatics," who "bakes the *bappir*-malt in the lofty kiln," and who "pours the fragrant beer in the *lahtan*-vessel which is like the Tigris and Euphrates joined." It is evident then that even beer had its divine and sublime qualities for the Sumerian poets and sages.

CHAPTER FOUR

RELIGION:

Theology, Rite, and Myth

In the course of the third millennium B.C. the Sumerians developed religious ideas and spiritual concepts which have left an indelible impress on the modern world, especially by way of Judaism, Christianity, and Mohammedanism. On the intellectual level Sumerian thinkers and sages, as a result of their speculations on the origin and nature of the universe and its *modus operandi*, evolved a cosmology and theology which carried such high conviction that they became the basic creed and dogma of much of the ancient Near East. On the practical and functional level, the Sumerian priests and holy men developed a colorful and variegated complex of rites, rituals, and ceremonies which served to please and placate the gods as well as provide an emotional valve for man's love of pageantry and spectacle. On the aesthetic plane, the illiterate Sumerian minstrels and bards, and their later heirs, the poets and scribes of the *edubba*, created what is by all odds the richest mythology of the ancient Near East, which cut the gods down to human size, but did so with understanding, reverence, and above all, originality and imagination.

Let us start with cosmogony and theology. Scientifically speaking, the Sumerian philosophers and thinkers had at their disposal only the most rudimentary and superficial ideas about the nature of the universe and its method of operation. In the eyes of the Sumerian teachers and sages, the major components of the universe (in the more narrow sense of the word) were heaven and earth; indeed, their term for universe was *an-ki*, a compound

112

word meaning "heaven-earth." The earth was a flat disk surmounted by a vast hollow space, completely enclosed by a solid surface in the shape of a vault. Just what this heavenly solid was thought to be is still uncertain; to judge from the fact that the Sumerian term for tin is "metal of heaven," it may have been tin. Between heaven and earth they recognized a substance which they called *lil*, a word whose approximate meaning is wind, air, breath, spirit; its most significant characteristics seem to be movement and expansion, and it therefore corresponds roughly to our "atmosphere." The sun, moon, planets, and stars were taken to be made of the same stuff as the atmosphere, but endowed, in addition, with the quality of luminosity. Surrounding the "heaven-earth" on all sides, as well as top and bottom, was the boundless sea in which the universe somehow remained fixed and immovable.

From these basic facts concerning the structure of the universe —facts which seemed to the Sumerian thinkers obvious and indisputable—they evolved a cosmogony to fit. First, they concluded, there was the primeval sea; the indications are that they looked upon the sea as a kind of first cause and prime mover, and they never asked themselves what preceded the sea in time and space. In this primeval sea was somehow engendered the universe (that is, "heaven-earth"), consisting of a vaulted heaven superimposed over a flat earth and united with it. Between them, however, came the moving and expanding "atmosphere" which separated heaven from earth. Out of this atmosphere were fashioned the luminous bodies, the moon, sun, planets, and stars. Following the separation of heaven and earth and the creation of the light-giving astral bodies, plant, animal, and human life came into existence.

Operating, directing, and supervising this universe, the Sumerian theologian assumed, was a pantheon consisting of a group of living beings, manlike in form but superhuman and immortal, who, though invisible to the mortal eye, guided and controlled the cosmos in accordance with well-laid plans and duly prescribed laws. The great realms of heaven, earth, sea, and air; the major astral bodies, sun, moon, and planets; such atmospheric forces as wind, storm, and tempest; and finally, on earth, such natural entities as river, mountain, and plain, such cultural entities as city and state, dike and ditch, field and farm, and even such implements as the pickax, brick mold, and plow—each was deemed to be under the charge of one or another anthropomorphic, but superhuman, being who guided its activities in accordance with established rules and regulations.

Behind this axiomatic assumption of the Sumerian theologian lay, no doubt, a logical if perhaps unarticulated inference, since he could hardly have seen any of the human-like beings with his own eyes. Our theologian probably took his cue from human society as he knew it and reasoned from the known to the unknown. He noted that lands and cities, palaces and temples, fields and farms—in short, all imaginable institutions and enterprises— are tended and supervised, guided and controlled by living human beings; without them lands and cities become desolate, temples and palaces crumble, fields and farms turn to desert and wilderness. Surely, therefore, the cosmos and all its manifold phenomena must also be tended and supervised, guided and controlled by living beings in human form. But the cosmos being far larger than the sum total of human habitations, and its organization being far more complex, these living beings must obviously be far stronger and much more effective than ordinary humans. Above all they must be immortal; otherwise the cosmos would turn to chaos upon their death, and the world would come to an end, alternatives which for obvious reasons did not recommend themselves to the Sumerian metaphysician. It was each of these invisible, anthropomorphic, and at the same time superhuman and immortal beings that the Sumerian designated by his word *dingir*, which we translate by the word "god."

How did this divine pantheon function? In the first place, it seemed reasonable to the Sumerian to assume that the deities constituting the pantheon were not all of the same importance or of equal rank. The god in charge of the pickax or brick mold could hardly be expected to compare with the deity in charge of the sun. Nor could the deity in charge of dikes and ditches be expected to equal in rank the deity in charge of the earth as a whole. Then, too, on analogy with the political organization of the human state, it was natural to assume that at the head of the pantheon was a deity recognized by all the others as their king and ruler. The Sumerian pantheon was therefore conceived as functioning as an assembly with a king at its head; the most important groups in this assembly consisted of seven gods who "decree the fates" and fifty deities known as "the great gods." But a more significant division set up by the Sumerian theologians within their pantheon is that between creative and non-creative deities, a notion arrived at as a result of their cosmological views. According to these views, the basic components of the cosmos are heaven and earth, sea and atmosphere; every other cosmic phenomenon exists only within one or another of these realms. Hence, it seemed reasonable to infer that the deities in control of heaven, earth, sea, and air were the creative gods and that one or another of these four deities created every other cosmic entity in accordance with plans originated by them.

As for the technique of creation attributed to these deities, our Sumerian philosophers developed a doctrine which became dogma throughout the Near East, the doctrine of the creative power of the divine word. All that the creating deity had to do, according to this doctrine, was to lay his plans, utter the word, and pronounce the name. This notion of the creative power of the divine word was probably also the result of an analogical inference based on observation of human society: if a human king could achieve almost all he wanted by command, by no more than what seemed to be the words of his mouth, how much more was possible for the immortal and superhuman deities in charge of the four realms of the universe. But perhaps this "easy" solution of the cosmological problems, in which thought and word alone are so important, is largely a reflection of the drive to escape into hopeful wish fulfilment characteristic of practically all humans in times of stress and misfortune.

Similarly, the Sumerian theologians adduced what was for them a satisfying metaphysical inference to explain what kept the cosmic entities and cultural phenomena, once created, operating continuously and harmoniously without conflict and confusion; this was the concept designated by the Sumerian word *me*, the exact meaning of which is still uncertain. In general, it would seem to denote a set of rules and regulations assigned to each cosmic entity and cultural phenomenon for the purpose of keeping it operating forever in accordance with the plans laid down by the deity creating it. In short, another superficial, but evi-

dently not altogether ineffective, answer to an insoluble cosmological problem which merely hid the fundamental difficulties from
view with the help of a layer of largely meaningless words.

Our primary source of information about the *me*'s is the myth
"Inanna and Enki: The Transfer of the Arts of Civilization from
Eridu to Erech" (see pages 160–62). The author of the poem divided civilization as he knew it into over one hundred elements,
each of which required a *me* to originate it and keep it going. He
lists the hundred-odd *me*'s four times in the myth; but in spite of
these repetitions, only some sixty-odd are at present intelligible,
and some of these are only bare words which, because of lack of
context, give but a hint of their real significance. Nevertheless,
enough remains to show the character and import of this first
recorded attempt at culture analysis, resulting in a considerable
list of what are now generally termed culture traits and complexes; as will be seen, these items consist of various institutions,
priestly offices, ritualistic paraphernalia, mental and emotional attitudes, as well as sundry beliefs and dogmas.

Here are the more intelligible portions of the list in the exact
order given by the ancient Sumerian writer:

(1) *en*-ship, (2) godship, (3) the exalted and enduring crown, (4)
the throne of kingship, (5) the exalted scepter, (6) the royal insignia,
(7) the exalted shrine, (8) shepherdship, (9) kingship, (10) lasting
ladyship, (11) (the priestly office) "divine lady," (12) (the priestly
office) *ishib*, (13) (the priestly office) *lumah*, (14) (the priestly office)
guda, (15) truth, (16) descent into the nether world, (17) ascent from
the nether world, (18) (the eunuch) *kurgarra*, (19) (the eunuch)
girbadara, (20) (the eunuch) *sagursag*, (21) the (battle) standard,
(22) the flood, (23) weapons (?), (24) sexual intercourse, (25)
prostitution, (26) law (?), (27) libel (?), (28) art, (29) the cult
chamber, (30) "hierodule of heaven," (31) (the musical instrument)
gusilim, (32) music, (33) eldership, (34) heroship, (35) power, (36)
enmity, (37) straightforwardness, (38) the destruction of cities, (39)
lamentation, (40) rejoicing of the heart, (41) falsehood, (42) art of
metalworking, (47) scribeship, (48) craft of the smith, (49) craft of
the leatherworker, (50) craft of the builder, (51) craft of the basket
weaver, (52) wisdom, (53) attention, (54) holy purification, (55)
fear, (56) terror, (57) strife, (58) peace, (59) weariness, (60) victory,
(61) counsel, (62) the troubled heart, (63) judgment, (64) decision,
(65) (the musical instrument) *lilis*, (66) (the musical instrument) *ub*,
(67) (the musical instrument) *mesi*, (68) (the musical instrument) *ala*.

The Sumerian gods, as illustrated graphically by the Sumerian myths, were entirely anthropomorphic; even the most powerful and most knowing among them were conceived as human in form, thought, and deed. Like man, they plan and act, eat and drink, marry and raise families, support large households, and are addicted to human passions and weaknesses. By and large they prefer truth and justice to falsehood and oppression, but their motives are by no means clear, and man is often at a loss to understand them. They were thought to live on the "mountain of heaven and earth, the place where the sun rose," at least, presumably, when their presence was not necessary in the particular cosmic entities over which they had charge. Just how they traveled is by no means certain from the available data, although we know that the moon-god traveled in a boat, the sun-god in a chariot, or, according to another version, on foot, and the storm-god on the clouds. Boats were frequently used. But the Sumerian thinkers seem not to have troubled themselves too much with such practical and realistic problems; and so we are not informed about the way in which the gods were supposed to arrive at their various temples and shrines in Sumer and in what fashion they actually performed such human activities as eating and drinking. The priests presumably saw only their statues, which they no doubt tended and handled with great care. But how the stone, wooden, and metal objects were to be conceived as having bone, muscle, and the breath of life—this kind of question—never occurred to them. Nor do the Sumerian thinkers seem to have been troubled by the inherent contradiction between immortality and anthropomorphism. Although the gods were believed to be immortal, they nevertheless had to have their sustenance; they could become sick to the point of death; they fought, wounded, and killed, and presumably could themselves be wounded and killed. No doubt our Sumerian sages developed numerous theological notions in a futile attempt to resolve the inconsistencies and contradictions inherent in a polytheistic system of religion. But to judge from the available material, they probably never wrote them down in systematic form, and we will therefore never learn much about them. In any case, it is hardly likely that they resolved many of the inconsistencies. What saved them from spiritual and intellectual frustration was no doubt the fact that many a question which, according to our way of thinking, should have troubled them, never came to their minds.

By the middle of the third millennium B.C. at the latest, we find that hundreds of deities, at least by name, existed among the Sumerians. We know the names of many of these, not merely from lists compiled in the schools but also from lists of sacrifices on tablets that have been unearthed over the past century and from such proper names as "X is a shepherd," "X has a great heart," "who is like X," "the servant of X," "the man of X," "the beloved X," "X has given me," etc., in which X represents the name of a deity. Many of these deities are secondary, that is, they are the wives, children, and servants thought up on the basis of the human pattern for the major deities. Others are perhaps names and epithets of well-known deities which we cannot at present identify. However, quite a large number of deities were actually worshipped throughout the year with sacrifices, adoration, and prayer. Of all these hundreds of deities the four most important were the heaven-god, An, the air-god, Enlil, the water-god, Enki, and the great mother-goddess, Ninhursag. They usually head the god lists and are often listed as performing significant acts together as a group; at divine meetings and banquets they were given the seats of honor.

There is good reason to believe that An, the heaven-god, was at one time conceived by the Sumerians to be the supreme ruler of the pantheon, although in our available sources reaching to about 2500 B.C. it is the air-god, Enlil, who seems to have taken his place as the leader of the pantheon. The city-state in which An had his main seat of worship was called Erech, a city which played a pre-eminent political role in the history of Sumer and where, not long before the Second World War, a German expedition uncovered hundreds of small clay tablets inscribed with semipictographic signs which date from about 3000 B.C., not long after writing was first invented. An continued to be worshipped in Sumer throughout the millenniums, but he gradually lost much of his prominence. He became a rather shadowy figure in the pantheon, and he is rarely mentioned in the hymns and myths of later days; by that time most of his powers had been conferred upon the god Enlil.

By far the most important deity in the Sumerian pantheon, one who played a dominant role throughout Sumer in rite, myth, and prayer, was the air-god, Enlil. The events leading up to his general acceptance as a leading deity of the Sumerian pantheon are unknown; but from the earliest intelligible records, Enlil is known as "the father of the gods," "the king of heaven and earth," "the king of all the lands." Kings and rulers boast that it is Enlil who has given them the kingship of the land, who has made the land prosperous for them, who gave them all the lands to conquer by his strength. It is Enlil who pronounces the king's name and gives him his scepter and looks upon him with a favorable eye.

From later myths and hymns we learn that Enlil was conceived to be a most beneficent deity who was responsible for the planning and creation of most productive features of the cosmos. He was the god who made the day come forth, who took pity on humans, who laid the plans which brought forth all seeds, plants, and trees from the earth; it was he who established plenty, abundance, and prosperity in the land. It was Enlil who fashioned the pickax and the plow as the prototypes of the agricultural implements to be used by man. I stress the beneficent features of Enlil's character in order to correct a misconception which has found its way into practically all handbooks and encyclopedias treating Sumerian religion and culture, the belief that Enlil was a violent and destructive storm deity whose word and deed practically always brought nothing but evil. As not infrequently happens, this misunderstanding is due largely to an archeological accident; for it happened that among the earliest Sumerian compositions published, there was an unusually large proportion of lamentation types in which, of necessity, Enlil had the unhappy duty of carrying out the destruction and misfortunes decreed by the gods for one reason or another. As a result he was stigmatized a fierce and destructive deity by earlier scholars, and he has never lived this down. Actually, when we analyze the hymns and myths —some of which have been published only in more recent days— we find Enlil glorified as a most friendly, fatherly deity who watches over the safety and well-being of all humans and particularly, of course, over the inhabitants of Sumer.

The deep veneration of the Sumerians for the god Enlil and his temple, the Ekur in Nippur, can be sensed in a hymn (whose text has only recently become available) which reads in part as follows:

> Enlil, whose command is far-reaching, whose word is holy,
> The lord whose pronouncement is unchangeable, who forever
>   decrees destinies,
> Whose lifted eye scans the lands,
> Whose lifted beam searches the heart of all the lands,
> Enlil who sits broadly on the white dais, on the lofty dais,
> Who perfects the decrees of power, lordship, and princeship,
> The earth-gods bow down in fear before him,
> The heaven-gods humble themselves before him . . . . .
>
> The city (Nippur), its appearance is fearsome and awesome,
> The unrighteous, evil oppressor,
> The . . . . , the informer,
> The arrogant, the agreement-violator,
> He does not tolerate their evil in the city,
> The great net . . . . ,
> He does not let the wicked and evildoer escape its meshes.
>
> Nippur—the shrine where dwells the father, the "great
>   mountain,"
> The dais of plenty, the Ekur which rises . . . ,
> The high mountain, the pure place . . . ,
> Its prince, the "great mountain," Father Enlil,
> Has established his seat on the dais of the Ekur, lofty shrine;
> The temple—its decrees like heaven cannot be overturned,
> Its pure rites like the earth cannot be shattered,
> Its decrees are like the decrees of the abyss, none can look
>   upon them,
> Its "heart" is like a distant shrine, unknown like heaven's
>   zenith . . . . ,
> Its words are prayers,
> Its utterances are supplication . . . . ,
> Its ritual is precious,
> Its feasts flow with fat and milk, are rich with abundance,
> Its storehouses bring happiness and rejoicing, ... ,
> Enlil's house, it is a mountain of plenty . . . . ;
> The Ekur, the lapis lazuli house, the lofty dwelling
>   place, awe-inspiring,
> Its awe and dread are next to heaven,

Its shadow is spread over all the lands,
Its loftiness reaches heaven's heart,
All the lords and princes conduct thither their holy
    gifts, offerings,
Utter there prayer, supplication, and petition.

Enlil, the shepherd upon whom you gaze (favorably),
Whom you have called and made high in the land, ... ,
Who prostrates the foreign lands wherever he steps forth,
Soothing libations from everywhere,
Sacrifices from heavy booty,
Has brought; in the storehouse,
In the lofty courtyards, he has directed his offerings;
Enlil, of the worthy shepherd, ... ,
Of the leading herdsman of all who have breath (the king),
Brought into being his princeship,
Placed the holy crown on his head . . . . .

Heaven—he is its princely one; earth—he is its great one,
The Anunnaki—he is their exalted god;
When, in his awesomeness, he decrees the fates,
No god dare look on him.
Only to his exalted vizier, the chamberlain Nusku,
The command, the word of his heart,
Did he make known, did he inform,
Did he commission to execute his all-embracing orders,
Did he entrust all the holy laws, all the holy decrees.

Without Enlil, the great mountain,
No cities would be built, no settlements founded,
No stalls would be built, no sheepfolds established,
No king would be raised, no high priest born,
No *mah*-priest, no high priestess, would be chosen by
    sheep-omen,
Workers would have neither controller nor supervisor . . .
The rivers—their flood waters would not bring overflow,
The fish of the sea would lay no eggs in the canebrake,
The birds of heaven would not build nests on the wide earth,
In heaven the drifting clouds would not yield their moisture,
Plants and herbs, the glory of the plain, would fail to grow,
In field and meadow the rich grain would fail to flower,
The trees planted in the mountain forest would not
    yield their fruit . . . . .

The third of the leading Sumerian deities was Enki, the god in charge of the abyss, or, in Sumerian, the *abzu*. Enki was the god of wisdom, and it was primarily he who organized the earth in accordance with the decisions of Enlil, who only made the general plans. The actual details and executions were left to Enki, the resourceful, skillful, handy, and wise. We learn much about Enki from the myth "Enki and the World Order: The Organization of the Earth and Its Cultural Processes" (see pages 171–73), which provides a detailed account of Enki's creative activities in instituting the natural and cultural phenomena essential to civilization. This myth serves as a vivid illustration of the Sumerians' superficial notions about nature and its mysteries. Nowhere is there an attempt to get at the fundamental origins of either the natural or cultural processes; all are ascribed to Enki's creative efforts usually by merely stating what amounts to "Enki did it." Where the creative technique is mentioned at all, it consists of the god's word and command, nothing more.

Fourth among the creating deities was the mother-goddess, Ninhursag, also known as Ninmah, "the exalted lady." In an earlier day this goddess was probably of even higher rank, and her name often preceded that of Enki when the four gods were listed together for one reason or another. Her name may originally have been Ki, "(mother) Earth," and she was probably taken to be the consort of An, "Heaven,"—An and Ki thus may have been conceived as the parents of all the gods. She was also known as Nintu, "the lady who gave birth." The early Sumerian rulers liked to describe themselves as "constantly nourished by Ninhursag with milk." She was regarded as the mother of all living things, the mother-goddess pre-eminent. In one of her myths, she plays an important role in the creation of man, and in another she starts a chain of divine births in Dilmun, the paradise of the gods, which leads up to the "forbidden fruit" motif.

In addition to these four leading deities, there were three important astral deities: the moon-god, Nanna, who is also known by the name of Sin, which is probably of Semitic origin; Nanna's son, the sun-god, Utu; and Nanna's daughter, the goddess Inanna, known to the Semites as Ishtar. It may be that it is this group of seven deities, An, Enlil, Enki, Ninhursag, Nanna-Sin, Utu, and Inanna that is referred to as the seven deities who "decree the fates." The fifty "great gods" are never named but seem to be identical with the Anunnaki, the children of An, at least with those of them who are not confined to the nether world. No doubt some of the numerous gods mentioned throughout this book belong to the Anunnaki, or at least to the fifty "great gods." There was also a group of gods designated as Igigi, though they seem to play a relatively minor role to judge from the fact that they are but rarely mentioned in the extant literary works.

Turning from god to man, we find that the Sumerian thinkers, in line with their world view, had no exaggerated confidence in man and his destiny. They were firmly convinced that man was fashioned of clay and created for one purpose only: to serve the gods by supplying them with food, drink, and shelter so that they might have full leisure for their divine activities. Man's life was beset with uncertainty and haunted by insecurity, since he did not know beforehand the destiny decreed him by the unpredictable gods. When he died, his emasculated spirit descended to the dark, dreary nether world where life was but a dismal and wretched reflection of its earthly counterpart.

One fundamental moral problem, a high favorite with Western philosophers, never troubled the Sumerian thinkers at all, namely, the delicate and rather slippery problem of free will. Convinced beyond all need for argument that man was created by the gods solely for their benefit and leisure, the Sumerians accepted their dependent status just as they accepted the divine decision that death was man's lot and that only the gods were immortal. All credit for the high moral qualities and ethical virtues that the Sumerians had evolved gradually and painfully over the centuries from their social and cultural experiences was attributed to the gods; it was the gods who planned it that way, and man was only following divine orders.

The Sumerians, according to their own records, cherished goodness and truth, law and order, justice and freedom, righteousness and straightforwardness, mercy and compassion, and naturally abhorred their opposites, evil and falsehood, lawlessness and disorder, injustice and oppression, sinfulness and perversity, cruelty and pitilessness. Kings and rulers, in particular, boast constantly of the fact that they have established law and order in the land, protected the weak from the strong and the poor from the rich,

and wiped out evil and violence. Urukagina, for example, proudly
records that he restored justice and freedom to the long-suffering
citizens of Lagash, did away with ubiquitous and oppressive
officials, put a stop to injustice and exploitation, and protected
the widow and the orphan. Less than four centuries later, Ur-
Nammu, the founder of the Third Dynasty of Ur, promulgated
his law code, which lists in its prologue some of his ethical
achievements: he did away with a number of prevalent bureau-
cratic abuses, regulated weights and measures to ensure honesty
in the market place, and saw to it that the widow, the orphan,
and the poor were protected from ill treatment and abuse. Some
two centuries later Lipit-Ishtar of Isin promulgated a new law
code in which he boasts that he was especially selected by the
great gods An and Enlil for "the princeship of the Land" in order
to establish justice in the Land, to banish complaints, to turn
back enmity and rebellion by force of arms, and to bring well-
being to the Sumerians and Akkadians. The hymns of quite a
number of Sumerian rulers abound in similar claims of high ethical and moral conduct.

The gods, of course, also preferred the ethical and moral to the
unethical and immoral, according to the Sumerian sages, and
practically all the major deities of the Sumerian pantheon are
extolled in their hymns as lovers of the good and the just, of truth
and righteousness. Indeed, there were several deities who had the
supervision of the moral order as their main function: for example,
the sun-god, Utu. Another deity, the Lagashite goddess named
Nanshe, also played a significant role in the sphere of man's
ethical and moral conduct. She is described in one of her hymns
as the goddess

> Who knows the orphan, who knows the widow,
> Knows the oppression of man over man, is the orphan's
>   mother,
> Nanshe, who cares for the widow,
> Who seeks out (?) justice (?) for the poorest (?).
> The queen brings the refugee to her lap,
> Finds shelter for the weak.

In another passage of this hymn, she is pictured as judging mankind on New Year's Day; by her side are Nidaba, the goddess of

writing and accounts, and her husband, Haia, as well as numerous witnesses. The evil human types who suffer her displeasure are

> (People) who walking in transgression reached out with
>   high hand, ... ,
> Who transgress the established norms, violate contracts,
> Who looked with favor on the places of evil, ... ,
> Who substituted a small weight for a large weight,
> Who substituted a small measure for a large measure,
> Who having eaten (something not belonging to him) did
>   not say "I have eaten it,"
> Who having drunk, did not say "I have drunk it," . . . . ,
> Who said "I would eat that which is forbidden,"
> Who said "I would drink that which is forbidden."

Nanshe's social conscience is further revealed in lines which read:

> To comfort the orphan, to make disappear the widow,
> To set up a place of destruction for the mighty,
> To turn over the mighty to the weak . . . . ,
> Nanshe searches the heart of the people.

Unfortunately, although the leading deities were assumed to be ethical and moral in their conduct, the fact remained that, in accordance with the world view of the Sumerians, they were also the ones who in the process of establishing civilization had planned evil and falsehood, violence and oppression—in short, all the immoral and unethical modes of human conduct. Thus, for example, among the list of *me*'s, the rules and regulations devised by the gods to make the cosmos run smoothly and effectively, there are not only those which regulate "truth," "peace," "goodness," and "justice," but also those which govern "falsehood," "strife," "lamentation," and "fear." Why, then, one might ask, did the gods find it necessary to plan and create sin and evil, suffering and misfortune, which were so pervasive that one Sumerian pessimist could say, "Never has a sinless child been born to his mother"? To judge from our available material, the Sumerian sages, if they asked the question at all, were prepared to admit their ignorance in this respect; the will of the gods and their motives were at times inscrutable. The proper course for a Sumerian Job to pursue was not to argue and complain in face of seemingly unjustifiable misfortune, but to plead and wail, lament and confess, his inevitable sins and failings.

But will the gods give heed to him, a lone and not very effective mortal, even if he prostrates and humbles himself in heartfelt prayer? Probably not, the Sumerian teachers would have answered. As they saw it, gods were like mortal rulers and no doubt had more important things to attend to; and so, as in the case of kings, man must have an intermediary to intercede in his behalf, one whom the gods would be willing to hear and favor. As a result, the Sumerian thinkers contrived and evolved the notion of a personal god, a kind of good angel to each particular individual and family head, his divine father who had begot him, as it were. It was to him, to his personal deity, that the individual sufferer bared his heart in prayer and supplication, and it was through him that he found his salvation.

We learn all this from a recently pieced-together poetic essay dealing with suffering and submission, a theme made famous in world literature and religious thought by the Biblical Book of Job. The Sumerian poem in no way compares with the latter in breadth of scope, depth of understanding, or beauty of expression. Its major significance lies in the fact that it represents man's first recorded attempt to deal with the age-old and yet very modern problem of human suffering—more than a thousand years before the composition of the Book of Job.

The main thesis of our poet is that in cases of suffering and adversity, no matter how seemingly unjustified, the victim has but one valid and effective recourse, which is to continually glorify his god and keep wailing and lamenting before him until he turns a favorable ear to his prayers. The god concerned is the sufferer's "personal" god, that is, the deity who, in accordance with the accepted Sumerian credo, acts as the man's representative and intercessor in the assembly of the gods. To prove his point, our author does not resort to philosophical speculation but to a practical application; he cites a case: Here is a man, unnamed to be sure, who had been wealthy, wise, and righteous, or at least seemingly so, and blest with both friends and kin. One day sickness and suffering overwhelmed him. Did he defy the divine order and blaspheme? Not at all. He came humbly before his god with tears and lamentation and poured out his heart in prayer and supplication. As a result, his god was highly pleased and moved to compassion; he gave heed to his prayer, delivered him from his misfortune, and turned his suffering to joy.

Structurally speaking, the poem may be tentatively divided into four sections. First comes a brief introductory exhortation, the first five lines of which read:

> Let man utter constantly the exaltedness of his god,
> Let the young man praise artlessly the words of his god,
> Let him who lives in the straightforward Land make moan,
> In the house of song (?) let him comfort (?) his friend
>   and companion,
> Let him soothe his heart.

The poet then introduces the unnamed individual who, upon being smitten with sickness and misfortune, addresses his god with tears and prayers. The sufferer's petition follows, constituting the major part of the poem. It begins with a description of the ill treatment accorded him by his fellow men—friend and foe alike; continues with a lament against his bitter fate, including a rhetorical request to his kin and to the professional singers to do likewise; and concludes with a confession of guilt and a direct plea for relief and deliverance.

> I am a man, a discerning one, yet who respects me
>   prospers not,
> My righteous word has been turned into a lie,
> The man of deceit has covered me with the South Wind,
>   I am forced to serve him,
> Who respects me not has shamed me before you.
>
> You have doled out to me suffering ever anew,
> I entered the house, heavy is the spirit,
> I, the man, went out to the streets, oppressed is the heart,
> With me, the valiant, my righteous shepherd has become
>   angry, has looked upon me inimically,
> My herdsman has sought out evil forces against me who
>   am not his enemy,
> My companion says not a true word to me,
> My friend gives the lie to my righteous word,
> The man of deceit has conspired against me,
> And you, my god, do not thwart him.
>   (Three lines omitted)
> I, the wise, why am I bound to the ignorant youths?

I, the discerning, why am I counted among the ignorant?
Food is all about, yet my food is hunger,
On the day shares were allotted to all, my allotted
   share was suffering.
                    (Ten lines omitted)
My god, [I would stand] before you,
Would speak to you . . . . , my word is a groan,
I would tell you about it, would bemoan the bitterness
   of my path,
[Would bewail] the confusion . . . . .
                    (Three lines omitted)
Lo, let not my mother who bore me cease my lament before
   you,
Let not my sister utter the happy song and chant,
Let her utter tearfully my misfortunes before you,
Let my wife voice mournfully my suffering,
Let the expert singer bemoan my bitter fate.

My god, the day shines bright over the land, for me
   the day is black,
The bright day, the good day has . . like the . . . ,
Tears, lament, anguish, and depression are lodged within me,
Suffering overwhelms me like one chosen for nothing
   but tears,
Evil fate holds me in its hand, carries off my breath of life,
Malignant sickness bathes my body.
                    (About 22 lines omitted)
My god, you who are my father who begot me, lift up my face,
Like an innocent cow, in pity . . . the groan,
How long will you neglect me, leave me unprotected?
Like an ox . . . . ,
Leave me without guidance?

They say—valiant sages—a word righteous and
   straightforward:
"Never has a sinless child been born to its mother,
 . . . . a sinless youth has not existed from of old."
                    (14 lines omitted)

So much for the man's prayers and supplication; the "happy ending" follows:

[The man]—his [god] harkened to [his bitter tears and
   weeping],

[The young man]—his lamentation and wailing soothed
 the heart of his god,
The righteous words, the pure words uttered by him,
 his god accepted,
The words which the young man prayerfully confessed,
Pleased (?) the . . . , the flesh (?) of his god, (and)
 his god withdrew his hand from the evil word,
 . . which oppresses the heart . . . . , he embraces,
The encompassing sickness-demon, which had spread wide
 its wings, he swept away,
The [disease] which had smitten him like a . . . . he
 dissipated,
The evil fate which had been decreed for him in accordance
 with his sentence he turned aside,
He turned the man's (?) suffering into joy.
Set by him the . . kindly . . spirit as a watch and guardian,
Gave him . . the genii of friendly mien,
(And so) [the man] utters constantly the exaltation
 of his god,
[The young man] brings forth . . . . , makes known . . . . .

But guardian angel or not, the fact is that man did die sooner
or later, and as far as the rather hard-eyed and realistic Sumerian
thinkers could see, he went to the world below never to return.
Needless to say, this was a source of anxiety and perplexity; the
problem of death and the nether world was beset with enigmas,
paradoxes, and dilemmas, and it is no wonder that the Sumerian
ideas pertaining to them were neither precise nor consistent, as
will be seen from the following analysis of the relevant material.

From the point of view of Sumerian cultural behavior, the royal
multiple-burial tombs excavated at Ur with such care and skill by
the late Sir Leonard Woolley were of epoch-making significance;
they indicate with reasonable certainty that the early rulers of
Sumer were customarily accompanied to the grave not only by
some of their most precious personal possessions but by a considerable human retinue as well. Needless to say, immediately
upon this rather startling discovery, the cuneiformists—and particularly the Sumerologists—began searching the documents for
inscriptional verification of one sort or another, but without
success. Moreover, in the past two decades, quite a number of
Sumerian myths, epic tales, hymns, lamentations, and historio-

graphic documents have become available, and it seemed not unreasonable to hope that one or another of these might shed light on the Sumerian burial customs relating to the royal tombs. But this hope also failed to materialize to any significant extent, which is not too surprising in view of the fact that the royal tombs date from about 2500 B.C., whereas the majority of our available literary documents were probably first composed about 2000 B.C.

As of today, the only Sumerian literary document which seems to confirm the archeological evidence that the ancient rulers were accompanied to their graves by a human retinue is a small tablet in the University Museum of the University of Pennsylvania inscribed with the last 42 lines of a Gilgamesh epic tale, probably the one tentatively entitled "The Death of Gilgamesh," of which only fragmentary remains are available at present. This text states in poetic phraseology that Gilgamesh presented gifts and offerings to the various deities of the nether world and to the important dead dwelling there for all who "lay with him" in his "purified palace" in Erech: his wife, son, concubine, musician, entertainer, chief valet, and household attendants. It is not unreasonable to assume that the poet pictured these gifts as presented by Gilgamesh after he and his retinue had died and descended to the nether world. If this interpretation should turn out to be correct, we would have literary corroboration for the multiple-burial type of royal tomb uncovered by Woolley, especially since, as we now know from the Tummal composition (see pages 46–49), Gilgamesh was a contemporary of Mesannepadda and therefore belongs roughly to the period represented by the tombs.

Another document which sheds no little light on the funerary practices relating to the royal dead is the six-column tablet in the University Museum inscribed with a unique Ur-Nammu composition belonging to a literary genre as yet unclassifiable. The first column, which is broken away entirely, may have contained a poetic description of Ur-Nammu's outstanding achievements in war and peace and of the unfortunate incidents leading to his death. The available text, which begins with the second column, seems to relate how Ur-Nammu, "who had been abandoned on the battlefield like a crushed vessel," was lying on his bier in his palace, mourned (probably) by his family and kin and by the people of Ur. We next find him in the nether world—as in the

case of Gilgamesh—presenting gifts to its "seven gods," slaughtering oxen and sheep to the important dead, and presenting weapons, leather bags, vessels, garments, ornaments, jewels, and other
paraphernalia to Nergal, Gilgamesh, Ereshkigal (?), Dumuzi,
Namtar, Hubishag, and Ningishzida—each in his own palace; he
also presented gifts to Dimpimekug and to the "scribe of the
nether world." How Ur-Nammu got to the nether world with all
these rich gifts and offerings is not stated by our poet, unless it
should turn out that the "chariots" mentioned in the very obscure
lines immediately preceding the "nether world passage" were
utilized for this purpose. In any case, Ur-Nammu finally arrived
at the spot which (probably) the priests of the nether world had
assigned to him. Here certain of the dead were turned over to
him, perhaps to be his attendants, and Gilgamesh, his beloved
brother, explained to him the rules and regulations of the nether
world.

But, our poem continues, "after seven days, ten days had
passed," "the wail of Sumer" reached Ur-Nammu. The walls of
Ur which he had left unfinished, his newly built palace which he
had left unpurified (?), his wife whom he could no longer turn
on his lap, his son whom he could no longer fondle (?) on his knee
—all these brought tears to his eyes, and he set up a long and
bitter lament. The burden of his outcry seems to be that although
he had served the gods well, they failed to stand by him in time
of need; now he was dead, and his wife and friends and supporters
were sated with tears and lamentation. The conclusion of the
composition is altogether unknown since the last column is completely destroyed.

As can be seen from the preceding tentative sketch of its contents, it is difficult to classify the literary genre to which the poem
belongs; it may be a kind of historiographic composition, similar
in some respects to the "Curse of Agade" (see pages 62–66), in
which a Sumerian poet gives vent to his feelings at the sad state
of affairs existing in Sumer immediately after the death of Ur-
Nammu. In any case, the Ur-Nammu document sheds considerable light on the life of the dead in the world below as pictured
by the Sumerian sages. We find once again the gods who had to
be placated as well as the important dead priests. The newly
arrived deceased person had a special place assigned to him and

was instructed in the laws of the nether world, at least if he was a king. Though dead, the deceased could in some unexplained manner be in sympathetic contact with the world above, could suffer anguish and humiliation, and could cry out against the undependable gods. Unlike "The Death of Gilgamesh" poem, however, no mention is made of a human retinue attending the king to the nether world; indeed, the wife and children are described as living in the world above. It would therefore seem safe to conclude that by the time of Ur-Nammu at least it was no longer customary to have the king accompanied to his grave by any of his family or attendants.

Turning from royalty to more ordinary mortals, we learn quite a number of hitherto unknown details about the Sumerian nether world from the two dirges on the Pushkin Museum tablet. On this tablet we read for the first time that the Sumerian thinkers held the view that the sun after setting continued its journey through the nether world at night, turning its night into day, and that the moon spent its "day of rest," that is, the last day of each month, in the nether world. We learn, too, that there was a judgment of the dead by the sun-god, Utu, and that the moon-god, Nanna, too, "decreed the fate" of the dead. In the nether world, according to the tablet, were to be found "bread-eating heroes (?)" and ". . -drinkers" who satisfy the thirst of the dead with fresh water. We learn, too, that the gods of the nether world can be called upon to utter prayers for the dead, that the personal god of the deceased and his city's god were invoked in his behalf, and that the welfare of the family of the deceased was by no means overlooked in the funerary prayers.

The Sumerian document which provides the most detailed information about the nether world and the life going on within its confines is the poem "Gilgamesh, Enkidu, and the Nether World." According to this composition, which characterizes the nether world euphemistically as the "Great Dwelling," there was an opening of some sort in Erech that led down to the world of the dead, through which such wooden objects as the *pukku* and the *mikku* could fall and into which a hand and foot could be placed. There was also a gate in Erech in front of which one could sit down and through which a mortal—at least if he was a hero like Enkidu—might descend to the nether world, although just how this descent took place is not made clear. There were certain taboos, however, which, according to the author of the poem, anyone wishing to descend to the nether world must beware of violating: he must not wear clean clothes, anoint himself with "good" oil, carry a weapon or staff, wear sandals, make a noise, or behave normally toward the members of his family. If he broke any of those taboos, he would be surrounded by the "stewards" and by the shades inhabiting the lower regions and would be held fast by "the outcry of the nether world." Once seized by this "outcry," it was impossible for a mortal to reascend to the earth, unless one or another of the gods intervened on his behalf. In the case of Enkidu, it was Enki who came to his rescue; he had Utu open the *ablal* of the nether world, and Enkidu reascended to the earth, seemingly "in the flesh" rather than as a ghost. According to the poem, a heartbreaking colloquy between Gilgamesh and Enkidu followed in which the latter is purported to have described the state of the dead, or rather of a few selected categories of the dead.

Turning from mortals, ordinary and extraordinary, to the immortal gods, it would seem that the nether world would be the last place to look for their "undying" presence. Nevertheless, we find quite a number of deities there, and while some seem to belong there, as it were, others were originally sky-gods condemned to the nether world by the Sumerian mythographers as a result of theological speculation and invention. As of today, however, only a few of the relevant myths have been recovered, and except for one, all concern the ambitious Inanna and her unfortunate spouse, Dumuzi (see pages 153–60). The one exception is the myth "Enlil and Ninlil: Birth of the Moon-God," which tells how Enlil himself, the most powerful of the Sumerian gods and the chief of the Sumerian pantheon, was banished to the nether world and followed thither by his wife, Ninlil. This myth is also significant as the sole source for the Sumerian belief that there was a "man-devouring" river which had to be crossed by the dead as well as a boatman who ferried the dead across to their destination, a belief prevalent throughout the ancient Near Eastern and Mediterranean world.

A highly revealing myth relating to death and the nether world is "Inanna's Descent to the Nether World," which is now available almost in its entirety. According to this poem, the nether world is a place to which one descends and from which one ascends—presumably through an opening or a gate situated in Erech, although this is nowhere explicitly stated. In the nether world there is a place described as a "lapis lazuli mountain," whose locked and bolted gates are guarded by gatekeepers under the supervision of Neti, their chief. The nether world is governed by divine regulations and rules, among which one of the most important seems to be that its denizens must be stark naked. Another rule, one that proved fatal to Dumuzi, was that no one once in the nether world, not even a deity, could reascend to the world above unless a substitute had been found to take his place. Thus, for example, it was to make sure that Inanna, who had been revived through the clever efforts of Enki, would provide a suitable surrogate to take her place that the seven *galla's* stuck by her side until she turned over Dumuzi to them.

All in all, therefore, we find that the Sumerian picture of death and the nether world was rather blurred and contradictory. In general the nether world was believed to be the huge cosmic space below the earth corresponding roughly to heaven, the huge cosmic space above the earth. The dead, or at least the souls of the dead, descended into it presumably from the grave, but there also seem to have been special openings and gates in Erech as well as, no doubt, in all the important city centers. There was a river which the dead had to cross by ferry, but where it was situated in relation to the earth or the nether world is not stated in the available myths. The nether world was ruled by Ereshkigal and Nergal, who had a special entourage of deities, including seven Anunnaki and numerous unfortunate sky-gods as well as a number of constable-like officials known as *galla's*. All of them, except the *galla's*, apparently needed food, clothing, weapons, vessels of various sorts, jewels, etc., just like the gods in the sky or mortals on earth. There was a palace with seven gates where Ereshkigal held court but it is uncertain where it was supposed to be located.

The dead seem to have been arranged in a hierarchy, like the living, and no doubt the highest seats were assigned to the dead kings and to high priestly officials who had to be taken care of with special sacrifices by such of the deceased as Gilgamesh and

Ur-Nammu. There were all kinds of rules and regulations in the nether world, and it was the deified Gilgamesh who saw to it that the denizens of the nether world conducted themselves properly. Although in general one has the feeling that the nether world was dark and dreary, this would seem to be true only of daytime; at night the sun brought light to it, and on the twenty-eighth day of the month the sun was joined by the moon. The deceased were not treated all alike; there was a judgment of the dead by the sun-god, Utu, and to a certain extent by the moon-god, Nanna, and if the judgment was favorable, the dead man's soul would presumably live in happiness and contentment and have all it desired. However, the indications are that the Sumerians had but little trust in hopes of a blissful life in the nether world even for the good and the deserving. By and large the Sumerians were convinced that life in the nether world was but a dismal, wretched reflection of life on earth.

While private devotion and personal piety were not unimportant, it was rite and ritual which, because of the world view of the Sumerians, played the predominant role in their religion. Since man was created for no other purpose than to serve the gods, it was obviously his major duty to perform and perfect this service in a manner pleasing and satisfactory to his masters. Why was Ziusudra saved from the destruction of the deluge? Because he had humbly and piously performed the daily rites for the gods. The rulers of Sumer did not weary of repeating that they had performed their cult duties in accordance with the prescribed rules and regulations.

The center of the cult was of course the temple. One of the very earliest temples was excavated in Eridu, the city of which Enki was the tutelary deity, at least in later days. Though it was a shrine of very simple shape measuring only about twelve feet by fifteen, it contained from the beginning two features that characterize the Sumerian temple throughout the millenniums: a niche for the god's emblem or statue and an offering table of mud brick in front of it. In the course of later rebuilding, this Eridu shrine was enlarged and improved. It then had a cella in the center surrounded by a number of subsidiary rooms, and the altar, faced by an offering table, was placed against one of the short walls; the dull mud-brick walls of the temple were ornamented with regularly placed buttresses and recesses, and the whole structure was built on a platform reached by a set of stairs leading up to its entrance on the long side of the building.

Farther to the north in Erech, there is a temple probably dedicated to the god An, and dating from about 3000 B.C., which is built by and large along the same lines as the Eridu temple, except that the platform is replaced by an artificial hill rising some forty feet above the plain. A stairway built against its northeastern face led to the summit where a small whitewashed shrine stood. A similar temple was unearthed at Uqair; and although the platform on which it was built was only fifteen feet high, it rose in two stages and may thus be taken to be the prototype of the ziggurat, the staged tower which became the hallmark of Mesopotamian temple architecture and which was intended to serve as connecting link, both real and symbolic, between the gods in heaven and the mortals on earth. The temple of Uqair is noteworthy for another architectural innovation, one which does not seem to have been followed in the other Sumerian temples: the inside walls were covered with frescoes consisting of color washes and painted ornament. The arrangement was as follows: First came a band of plain color, usually some shade of red, forming a dado over three feet high all about the room. Above this a band of geometrical ornament over a foot high was painted. The upper parts of the walls were then decorated with scenes of human and animal figures painted on a plain white ground.

Another architectural innovation was made in Erech when the builders of the Eanna temple developed a unique method of ornamenting the dreary-looking mud-brick walls and columns of the building by covering them with tens of thousands of small clay cones that had been dipped in different colors so that their tops were either red, black, or buff. These colored cones were inserted side by side in thick mud plaster in such a way that they formed polychrome triangles, lozenges, zigzags, and other geometrical designs.

The temples continued to follow the same general pattern throughout the third millennium B.C., although they tended to become larger and more complex. The forecourt became a permanent feature. The plan of the building might now be oval as well as rectangular in shape. A new and seemingly not very appropriate building material was introduced—the plano-convex brick, flat on one side and curved on the other. Foundations were now usually constructed of rough blocks of limestone.

By the time of the Third Dynasty of Ur, the temples in the larger cities had become vast building complexes. Thus the Nanna temple of the city of Ur, the Ekishnugal, consisted of an enclosure measuring about 400 × 200 yards which contained the ziggurat as well as a large number of shrines, storehouses, magazines, courtyards, and dwelling places for the temple personnel. The ziggurat, the outstanding feature, was a rectangular tower whose base was some 200 feet in length and 150 feet in width; its original height was about 70 feet. The whole was a solid mass of brickwork with a cover of crude mud bricks and an outer layer of burnt bricks set in bitumen. It rose in three irregular stages and was approached by three stairways consisting of a hundred steps each. On its top there was probably a small shrine built entirely of blue enameled bricks. The ziggurat stood on a high terrace surrounded by a double wall. Partly on this terrace and partly at its feet lay a large temple for the moon-god, Nanna, with a wide outer court surrounded by numerous store chambers and offices. Not far from it was another temple dedicated to both Nanna and his wife, Ningal; then came a building known as the *dublal*, which was used as a kind of court house, and finally the temple sacred to Ningal, known as the *giparku*.

The building and rebuilding of a temple was accompanied by numerous rites and diverse rituals, as is evidenced by that long and remarkable hymnal narrative poem inscribed on the two Gudea cylinders excavated in Lagash, which contain 54 columns and close to 1400 "spaces" of text. This document, which is practically the only literary work preserved from this period, was probably composed by one of the poets of the Eninnu temple at Lagash to commemorate its construction by the pious Gudea. His literary style is rather inflated, grandiloquent, and diffuse, and the picture he paints of the rites and rituals that accompanied the building of Eninnu seem to contain more fancy than fact. Even so, it is highly significant and informative, as the following sketch of its contents will show.

To hear the poet tell it, it all began soon after the fates were decreed and the city Lagash was blessed with the rich overflow of the Tigris. It was then that Ningirsu, the tutelary deity of Lagash, decided to have Gudea build his Eninnu for him in grand fashion. He therefore appeared to Gudea in a dream which reads like a pure *ad hoc* invention on the part of the poet, although he narrates the events as if they had actually taken place.

In the dream, Gudea saw a man of tremendous stature with a divine crown on his head, the wings of a lion-headed bird, and a "flood wave" as the lower part of his body; lions crouched to his right and left. This huge man commanded Gudea to build his temple, but he could not grasp the meaning of his words. Day broke—in the dream—and a woman appeared holding a gold stylus and studying a clay tablet on which the starry heaven was depicted. Then a "hero" appeared holding a tablet of lapis lazuli on which he drew a plan of a house; he also placed bricks in a brick mold which stood before Gudea together with a carrying basket. At the same time a specially bred male donkey was impatiently pawing the ground.

Since the meaning of the dream was not clear to him, Gudea decided to consult the goddess Nanshe, who interpreted dreams for the gods. But Nanshe lived in a district of Lagash called Nina, which could best be reached by canal. Gudea therefore journeyed to her by boat, making sure to stop at several important shrines along the way to offer sacrifices and prayers to their deities in order to obtain their support. Finally the boat arrived at the quay of Nina, and Gudea went with lifted head to the court of the temple where he made sacrifices, poured out libations, and offered prayers. He then told her his dream and she interpreted it for him point by point, thus:

The man of tremendous stature with a divine crown on his head, the wings of a lion-headed bird, a flood wave as the lower part of his body, and lions crouching to his right and left—that is her brother Ningirsu, who commanded him to build the temple Eninnu. The breaking of day over the horizon—that is Ningish-zida, Gudea's personal god, rising like the sun. The woman holding a gold stylus and studying a clay tablet on which the starry heaven was depicted—that is Nidaba (the goddess of writing and the patron deity of the *edubba*), who directs you to build the house in accordance with the "holy stars." The hero holding a tablet of lapis lazuli—that is the (architect) god Nindub drawing the temple plan. The carrying basket and brick mold in which "the brick of fate" was placed—these betoken the bricks for the Eninnu temple. The male donkey pawing the ground impatiently —that, of course, is Gudea himself, who is impatient to carry out his task.

Nanshe then proceeded to advise Gudea to construct a new and beautifully decorated war chariot for Ningirsu and to present it to him together with its span of male donkeys and the god's emblem and weapons, accompanied by the sound of drums. This done, Ningirsu, in another dream, gave him more detailed directions, blessed Lagash with abundance and overflow, and assured Gudea that his people would work most diligently to build the Eninnu with all kinds of wood and stone brought to him from different lands the world over.

Gudea rose from his sleep and, after making a sacrifice and finding its omen favorable, proceeded humbly to carry out Ningirsu's directions. He issued instructions to the people of his city, who responded enthusiastically and unitedly. He first purified the city morally and ethically: there were to be no complaints and accusations or punishments; the mother must not scold her child, nor must the child raise its voice against the mother; the slave was not to be punished for wrongdoing; the slave girl was not to be struck by her mistress for disrespect; all the unclean were banished from the city. Following another series of omens and oracles, sacrifices, ceremonies, and prayers, he proceeded valiantly to the task of building the Eninnu, which is then described by the poet in great, repetitive, and unfortunately, often obscure detail.

The poem inscribed on the first cylinder ends with the completion of the building of the Eninnu complex. The hymnal narrative then continues on the second cylinder, beginning with a prayer of Gudea to the Anunnaki, followed by his announcement to Ningirsu and his wife, Bau, that the temple has been completed and is ready for habitation. With the help of a number of deities, Gudea then cleansed the temple and prepared all food, libations, and incense to be used in the ceremony celebrating the entrance of the gods to their home. Once again Gudea cleansed the city, ethically and morally. He next proceeded to appoint a whole group of deities to care for the temple needs: a doorkeeper, a butler, two armorers, a messenger, a chamberlain, a coachman, a goatherd, two musicians, a grain inspector, a fisheries inspector, a gamekeeper, and a bailiff. These appointments are described in a style reminiscent of the description of the appointment of the various supervising deities by Enki in the myth "Enki and the World Order" (see pages 179–82). After Ningirsu and Bau had united in marital bliss, there followed a seven-day celebration crowned by a banquet for the great gods An, Enlil, and Ninmah. Following a blessing by Ningirsu, the poem closes with a paean of praise for the Eninnu and its god, Ningirsu.

Turning from this highly idealized picture of a temple and its cult to the actual day-by-day rites and rituals, we may take it for granted that in the temple of every major city daily sacrifices were offered, consisting of animal and vegetable foods, libations of water, wine, and beer, and the burning of incense. No doubt the ceremonies were much more spectacular and impressive on special feasts and holidays. There were numerous perennial festivals, judging from such month names as "The Month of the Eating of Barley of Ningirsu," "The Month of the Eating of the Gazelles," and "The Month of the Feast of Shulgi." Some of these feasts lasted several days and were celebrated with special sacrifices and processions. In addition, there were regular monthly feasts on the day of the new moon as well as on the seventh, fifteenth, and last day of each month.

The most important holiday of all was the New Year holiday, which was probably celebrated over several days with special feasts and celebrations. The most significant rite of the New Year was the *hieros-gamos*, or holy marriage, between the king, who represented the god Dumuzi, and one of the priestesses, who represented the goddess Inanna, to ensure effectively the fecundity and prosperity of Sumer and its people. Just how and when this rite originated is uncertain, although we may perhaps reconstruct the events as follows.

Early in the third millennium B.C., Dumuzi was a prominent ruler of the important Sumerian city-state of Erech, and his life and deeds made a deep impression upon his own and future generations. The tutelary deity of Erech was Inanna, a goddess who throughout Sumerian history was deemed to be the deity primarily responsible for sexual love, fertility, and procreation,

and the names of Dumuzi and Inanna no doubt became closely
intertwined in the early myth and ritual of Erech. Toward the
middle of the third millennium, however, when the Sumerians
were becoming more and more nationally minded and the theologians were in the process of systematizing and classifying the
Sumerian pantheon accordingly, a seemingly quite plausible and
not unattractive idea arose that the king of Sumer, no matter who
he was or from what city he originated, must become the husband
of the life-giving goddess of love, that is, Inanna of Erech, if he
was to ensure effectively the fecundity and prosperity of the land
and its people. After the initial idea had become accepted dogma,
it was carried out in ritual practice by the consummation of a
marriage ceremony, which was probably repeated every New
Year, between the king and a specially selected hierodule from
Inanna's temple in Erech. To lend importance and prestige to
both the credo and the rite, however, it was advisable to trace
them back to earlier times, and the honor of being the first mortal
ruler to have become the husband of Inanna, Erech's most revered
deity, not unnaturally fell to Dumuzi, the Erech ruler who over
the centuries had become a memorable figure in Sumerian legend
and lore.

Concerning the priests in charge of the cult, we know little
more than the names of their offices. The administrative head of
the temple was the *sanga,* and his duties were, no doubt, to keep
the temple buildings and finances in good order and to see to it
that the temple personnel carried out their duties efficiently. The
spiritual head of the temple was the *en,* who lived in a part of
the temple known as the *gipar.* The *en*'s, it seems, could be
women as well as men, depending upon the sex of the deity to
whom their services were dedicated. Thus in Erech's main temple,
the Eanna, of which the goddess Inanna became the main deity,
the *en* was a man; the heroes Enmerkar and Gilgamesh were
originally designated *en*'s, though they may also have been kings
and were certainly great military leaders. The *en* of the Ekishnugal in Ur, whose main deity was the moon-god, Nanna, was a
woman and usually the daughter of the reigning monarch of
Sumer. (We actually have the names of almost all, if not all, the
en's of the Ekishnugal from the days of Sargon the Great.)

Under the *en* were a number of priestly classes, including *guda, mah, ishib, gala,* and *nindingir,* of whose duties we know very little except that the *ishib* may have been in charge of libations and lustrations, and the *gala* may have been a kind of temple singer and poet. There were also a whole corps of singers and musicians and—especially in the temples dedicated to Inanna—large numbers of eunuchs (castrates) and hierodules. In addition to those involved in one way or another in the religious services, the temple personnel included many secular officials, workers, and slaves who helped conduct its various agricultural and economic enterprises, as is evidenced by the innumerable administrative documents excavated in the ancient Sumerian temples.

The destruction of a Sumerian temple was the most disastrous calamity that could befall a city and its people, as revealed by the bitter laments composed by distressed temple poets and bards. To cite only one example, here is a stanza from the "Lamentation over the Destruction of Ur," which paints a picture of the utter desolation that befell Ur and its temple, the Ekishnugal, after the Elamites had attacked it and carried off Ibbi-Sin, the last ruler of the Third Dynasty of Ur:

O queen, how has your heart led you on, how can you stay alive!
O Ningal, how has your heart led you on, how can you stay alive!
O righteous woman whose city has been destroyed, how now can
   you exist!
O Ningal, whose land has perished, how has your heart led you on!
After your city had been destroyed, how now can you exist!
After your house had been destroyed, how has your heart led
   you on!
Your city has become a strange city; how now can you exist!
Your house has become a house of tears, how has your heart
   led you on!
Your city which has been made into ruins—you are no
   longer its mistress,
Your righteous house which has been given over to the pickax—
   you no longer inhabit it,
Your people who have been led to slaughter—you are no
   longer their queen,
Your tears have become strange tears, your land weeps not,
Without "tears of supplication" it inhabits foreign lands,
Your land like one who has multiplied . . . shuts tight its mouth.

Your city has been made into ruins; how can you exist!
Your house has been laid bare; how has your heart led you on!
Ur, the shrine, has been given over to the wind; how now
    can you exist!
Its *guda*-priest no longer walks in well-being; how has your
    heart led you on!
Its *en* dwells not in the *gipar;* how now can you exist!
Its . . . who cherishes lustrations makes no lustrations for you,
Father Nanna, your *ishib*-priest has not perfected the holy
    vessels for you,
Your *mah* in the holy *giguna* dressed not in linen,
Your righteous *en* chosen . . . , in the Ekishnugal,
Proceeds not joyfully from the shrine to the *gipar,*
In the *ahu*, your house of feasts, they celebrated not the feasts;
On the *ub* and *ala* they played not for you that which brings
    joy to the heart, the *tigi*-music.
The black-headed people do not bathe themselves for your feast,
Like flax dirt has been decreed for them; their appearance
    has changed.
Your song has been turned into weeping, ... ,
Your *tigi*-music has been turned into lamentation . . . . .

Your ox has not been brought into its stable, its fat is
    not prepared for you,
Your sheep stays not in its fold, its milk is not presented to you,
Who used to bring your fat, no longer brings it to you from
    the stall, ...
Who used to bring your milk no longer brings it to you from
    the sheepfold, ...
The fisherman who used to bring you fish is overtaken by
    misfortune,
The bird hunters who used to bring you birds were carried off
    by the . . . , you can now barely exist,
Your river which had been made fit for the *magur*-boats—
    in its midst the . . . -plant grows,
On your road which had been prepared for the chariots, the
    mountain thorn grows.
O my queen, your city weeps before you as its mother;
Ur, like the child of a street which has been destroyed,
    searches for you,
The house, like a man who has lost everything, stretches out
    the hands to you,

Your brickwork of the righteous house, like a human being,
cries your "Where, pray?"

O my queen, you have departed from the house; you have
departed from the city.
How long, pray, will you stand aside in the city like an enemy?
O Mother Ningal, (how long) will you hurl challenges in the
city like an enemy?
Although you are a queen beloved of her city, your city . . .
you have abandoned;
[Although] you are a queen beloved of her people, your people
. . . you have abandoned.
O Mother Ningal, like an ox to your stable, like a sheep to
your fold!
Like an ox to your stable of former days, like a sheep to your fold!
Like a young child to your chamber, O maid, to your house!
May An, the king of the gods, utter your " 'tis enough."
May Enlil, the king of all the lands, decree your (favorable) fate.
May he return the city to its place for you; exercise its queenship!
May he return Ur to its place for you; exercise its queenship!

In turning now to Sumerian mythology, it is important to note
first of all that Sumerian myths have little if any connection with
rite and ritual in spite of the fact that the latter played so important a role in Sumerian religious practice. Practically all the
extant Sumerian myths are literary and etiological in character;
they are neither "rite spoken," as myth has often been erroneously
categorized, nor verbalized appendages to ritual acts. They revolve primarily about the creation and organization of the universe, the birth of the gods, their loves and hates, their spites and
intrigues, their blessings and curses, their acts of creation and
destruction. There is very little in them about the struggle for
power between the gods, and even when this does occur, it is
never depicted as a bitter, vindictive, and gory conflict.

Intellectually speaking, the Sumerian myths reveal a rather
mature and sophisticated approach to the gods and their divine
activities; behind them can be recognized considerable cosmological and theological reflection. By and large, however, the Sumerian mythographers were the direct heirs of the illiterate
minstrels and bards of earlier days, and their first aim was to
compose narrative poems about the gods that would be appealing,

inspiring, and entertaining. Their main literary tools were not logic and reason but imagination and fantasy. In telling their stories, they did not hesitate to invent motives and incidents patterned on human action that could not possibly have any basis in rational and speculative thought. Nor did they hesitate to adopt legendary and folkloristic motifs that had nothing to do with cosmological inquiry and inference.

As yet, no Sumerian myths have been recovered dealing directly and explicitly with the creation of the universe; what little is known about the Sumerian cosmogonic ideas has been inferred from laconic statements scattered throughout the literary documents. But we do have a number of myths concerned with the organization of the universe and its cultural processes, the creation of man, and the establishment of civilization. The major protagonists involved in these myths are relatively few in number: the air-god, Enlil, the water-god, Enki, the mother-goddess, Ninhursag (also known as Nintu and Ninmah), the god of the south wind, Ninurta, the moon-god, Nanna-Sin, the Bedu-god, Martu, and most frequently, the goddess Inanna, particularly in relation to her unlucky spouse, Dumuzi.

Enlil, as has already been noted earlier in this chapter, was the most important deity of the Sumerian pantheon, "the father of the gods," "the king of heaven and earth," "the king of all the lands." According to the myth "Enlil and the Creation of the Pickax," he was the god who separated heaven from earth, brought up "the seed of the land" from the earth, brought forth "whatever was needful," fashioned the pickax for agricultural and building purposes, and presented it to the "black-heads," that is, the Sumerians, or perhaps even mankind as a whole. According to the disputation "Summer and Winter," Enlil was the god who brought forth all trees and grains, produced abundance and prosperity in "the Land," and appointed "Winter" as the "Farmer of the Gods," in charge of the life-producing waters and of all that grows. The gods—even the most important among them—were all eager for his blessing. One myth relates how the water-god, Enki, after building his "sea-house" in Eridu, journeyed to Enlil's temple in Nippur in order to obtain his approval and benediction. When the moon-god, Nanna-Sin, the tutelary deity of Ur, wanted to make sure of the well-being and prosperity of his domain he journeyed to Nippur on a boat loaded with gifts and thus obtained Enlil's generous blessing.

Although Enlil was the chief of the Sumerian pantheon, his powers were by no means unlimited and absolute. One of the more human and tender of the Sumerian myths concerns Enlil's banishment to the nether world as a result of the following events:

When man had not yet been created and the city of Nippur was inhabited by gods alone, "its young man" was the god Enlil; "its young maid" was the goddess Ninlil; and "its old woman" was Ninlil's mother, Nunbarshegunu. One day, the latter, evidently having set her mind and heart on Ninlil's marriage to Enlil, instructs her daughter thus:

> In the pure stream, woman, bathe in the pure stream,
> Ninlil, walk along the bank of the stream Nunbirdu,
> The bright-eyed, the lord, the bright-eyed,
> The "great mountain," father Enlil, the bright-eyed,
>   will see you,
> The shepherd . . . who decrees the fates, the bright-eyed
>   will see you,
> Will forthwith embrace (?) you, kiss you.

Ninlil joyfully follows her mother's instructions:

> In the pure stream, the woman bathes, in the pure stream,
> Ninlil walks along the bank of the stream Nunbirdu,
> The bright-eyed, the lord, the bright-eyed,
> The "great mountain," father Enlil, the bright-eyed,
>   saw her,
> The shepherd . . . who decrees the fates, the bright-eyed
>   saw her.
>
> The lord speaks to her of intercourse (?), she is unwilling,
> Enlil speaks to her of intercourse (?), she is unwilling;
> "My vagina is too little, it knows not to copulate,
> My lips are too small, they know not to kiss". . . . .

Whereupon Enlil calls his vizier, Nusku, and tells him of his desire for the lovely Ninlil. Nusku brings up a boat, and Enlil rapes Ninlil while sailing on the stream and impregnates her with the moon-god, Sin. The gods are dismayed by this immoral deed, and although Enlil is their king, they seize him and banish him from the city to the nether world. The relevant passage, one of the few to shed some indirect light on the organization of the pantheon and its method of operation, reads as follows:

> Enlil walks about in the Kiur (Ninlil's private shrine),
> As Enlil walks about in the Kiur,
> The great gods, the fifty of them,
> The fate-decreeing gods, the seven of them,
> Seize Enlil in the Kiur (saying):
> "Enlil, immoral one, get you out of the city,
> Nunamnir (an epithet of Enlil), immoral one, get you
> out of the city."

And so Enlil, in accordance with the fate decreed by the gods, departs in the direction of the Sumerian Hades. Ninlil, however, now pregnant with child, refuses to remain behind and follows Enlil on his forced journey to the nether world. This disturbs Enlil, for it would seem that his son Sin, originally destined to be in charge of the largest luminous body, the moon, would have to dwell in the dark gloomy nether world instead of in the sky. To circumvent this, he seems to have devised the following rather complicated scheme. On the way to the nether world from Nippur, the traveler meets three individuals, minor deities no doubt: the gatekeeper in charge of the Nippur gates, the "man of the nether world river," and the ferryman, the Sumerian "Charon," who ferries the dead across to Hades. Enlil takes the form of each of these in turn—the first known example of divine metamorphosis—and impregnates Ninlil with three nether world deities as substitutes for their older brother Sin, who is thus free to ascend to heaven.

One of the more detailed and revealing of the Sumerian myths concerns the organization of the universe by Enki, the Sumerian water-god and god of wisdom; a new, complete translation of it will be found in chapter v ("Literature: The Sumerian Belles-Lettres"). Another Enki myth tells an intricate and as yet somewhat obscure tale involving the paradise-land Dilmun, perhaps to be identified in part with ancient India. Very briefly sketched, the plot of this Sumerian "paradise" myth, which treats of gods, not humans, runs as follows:

Dilmun is a land that is "pure," "clean," and "bright," a "land of the living" which knows neither sickness nor death. What is lacking, however, is the fresh water so essential to animal and

it life. The great Sumerian water-god, Enki, therefore orders
, the sun-god, to fill it with fresh water brought up from the
earth. Dilmun is thus turned into a divine garden, green with
fruit-laden fields and meadows.

In this paradise of the gods eight plants are made to sprout by
Ninhursag, the great mother-goddess of the Sumerians, perhaps
originally Mother Earth. She succeeds in bringing these plants
into being only after an intricate process involving three generations of goddesses, all conceived by the water-god and born—so
our poem repeatedly underlines—without the slightest pain or
travail. But probably because Enki wanted to taste them, his
messenger, the two-faced god Isimud, plucks these precious
plants one by one and gives them to his master, who proceeds
to eat them each in turn. Whereupon the angered Ninhursag
pronounces the curse of death upon him. Then, evidently to make
sure that she will not change her mind and relent, she disappears
from among the gods.

Enki's health begins to fail; eight of his organs become sick.
As Enki sinks fast, the great gods sit in the dust. Enlil, the air-god,
the king of the Sumerian gods, seems unable to cope with the
situation when a fox speaks up. If properly rewarded, he says to
Enlil, he, the fox, will bring Ninhursag back. As good as his word,
the fox succeeds in some way—the relevant passage is unfortunately destroyed—in having the mother-goddess return to the
gods and heal the dying water-god. She seats him by her vulva,
and after inquiring which eight organs of his body ache, she
brings into existence eight corresponding healing deities, and
Enki is brought back to life and health.

Although our myth deals with a divine, rather than a human,
paradise, it has numerous parallels with the Biblical paradise
story. In fact, there is some reason to believe that the very idea
of a paradise, a garden of the gods, originated with the Sumerians.
The Sumerian paradise is located, according to our poem, in
Dilmun, a land somewhere to the east of Sumer. It is in this
same Dilmun that the Babylonians, the Semitic people who conquered the Sumerians, later located their "land of the living,"
the home of their immortals. And there is good indication that
the Biblical paradise, too, which is described as a garden planted
eastward in Eden, from whose waters flow the four world rivers,

including the Tigris and Euphrates, may have originally been identical with Dilmun, the Sumerian paradise-land.

Again, the passage in our poem describing the watering of Dilmun by the sun-god with fresh water brought up from the earth is reminiscent of the Biblical passage: "But there went up a mist (?) from the earth, and watered the whole face of the ground" (Genesis 2:6). The birth of the goddesses without pain or travail illuminates the background of the curse against Eve that it shall be her lot to conceive and bear children in sorrow. And obviously enough, Enki's eating of the eight plants and the curse uttered against him for this misdeed recall the eating of the fruit of the tree of knowledge by Adam and Eve and the curses pronounced against each of them for this sinful action.

But perhaps the most interesting result of our comparative analysis of the Sumerian poem is the explanation which it provides for one of the most puzzling motifs in the Biblical paradise story, the famous passage describing the fashioning of Eve, "the mother of all living," from the rib of Adam—for why a rib? Why did the Hebrew storyteller find it more fitting to choose a rib rather than any other organ of the body for the fashioning of the woman whose name, Eve, according to the Biblical notion, means approximately "she who makes live." The reason becomes quite clear if we assume a Sumerian literary background, such as that represented by our Dilmun poem, to underly the Biblical paradise tale; for in our Sumerian poem, one of Enki's sick organs is the rib. Now the Sumerian word for "rib" is *ti* (pronounced tee); the goddess created for the healing of Enki's rib was therefore called in Sumerian Nin-ti, "the Lady of the rib." But the Sumerian word *ti* also means "to make live." The name Nin-ti may thus mean "the Lady who makes live" as well as "the Lady of the rib." In Sumerian literature, therefore, "the Lady of the rib" came to be identified with "the Lady who makes live" through what may be termed a play on words. It was this, one of the most ancient of literary puns, which was carried over and perpetuated in the Biblical paradise story, although there, of course, the pun loses its validity, since the Hebrew words for "rib" and "who makes live" have nothing in common.

There is another Enki-Ninhursag myth concerned with the creation of man from "clay that is over the abyss." The story

begins with a description of the difficulties of the gods in pro-
curing their bread, especially, as might have been expected, after
the female deities had come into being. The gods complain, but
Enki, who, as the Sumerian god of wisdom, might have been
expected to come to their aid, is lying asleep in the deep and fails
to hear them. Thereupon his mother, the primeval sea, "the
mother who gave birth to all the gods," brings the tears of the
gods before Enki, saying:

> O my son, rise from your bed, from your . . . work
>   what is wise,
> Fashion servants of the gods, may they produce their
>   doubles (?).

Enki gives the matter thought, leads forth the host of "good and
princely fashioners," and says to his mother, Nammu, the primeval
sea:

> O my mother, the creature whose name you uttered, it exists,
> Bind upon it the image (?) of the gods;
> Mix the heart of the clay that is over the abyss,
> The good and princely fashioners will thicken the clay,
> You, do you bring the limbs into existence;
> Ninmah (another name for Ninhursag) will work above you,
> The goddesses (of birth) . . . . will stand by you at
>   your fashioning;
> O my mother, decree its (the new-born's) fate,
> Ninmah will bind upon it the mold (?) of the gods,
> It is man . . . . .

The poem then turns from the creation of man as a whole to
the creation of certain imperfect human types in an obvious attempt to explain the existence of these abnormal beings. It tells
of a feast arranged by Enki for the gods probably to commemorate
man's creation. At this feast Enki and Ninmah drink much wine
and become somewhat exuberant. Ninmah takes some of the clay
which is over the abyss and fashions six different varieties of
abnormal individuals, while Enki decrees their fates and gives
them bread to eat. After Ninmah has created these six types of
man, Enki decides to create one of his own. The manner in
which he goes about it is not clear, but whatever it is, the resulting
creature is a failure; it is weak and feeble in body and spirit. Enki

is now anxious that Ninmah help this forlorn creature; he therefore addresses her as follows:

> Of him whom your hand has fashioned, I have
> decreed the fate,
> Have given him bread to eat;
> Do you decree the fate of him whom my hand
> has fashioned,
> Do you give him bread to eat.

Ninmah tries to be good to the creature but to no avail. She talks to him, but he fails to answer. She gives him bread to eat, but he does not reach out for it. He can neither sit nor stand nor bend his knees. Following a long but as yet unintelligible conversation between Enki and Ninmah, the latter utters a curse against Enki because of the sick, lifeless creature that he produced, a curse which Enki seems to accept as his due.

Concerning Ninurta, the god of the stormy south wind, there is a myth with a dragon-slaying motif. Following a brief hymnal passage to the god, the plot begins with an address to Ninurta by Sharur, his personified weapon. For some unstated reason, Sharur had set his mind against Asag, the demon of sickness and disease, whose abode is in the *kur*, or nether world. In a speech, which is full of phrases extolling the heroic qualities and deeds of Ninurta, he urges him to attack and destroy the monster. Ninurta sets out to do as bidden. At first, however, he seems to have met more than his match, and he "flees like a bird." Once again the Sharur addresses him with reassuring and encouraging words. Ninurta now attacks the Asag fiercely with all the weapons at his command, and the demon is destroyed.

With the destruction of the Asag, however, a serious calamity overtook Sumer. The primeval waters of the Kur rose to the surface, and as a result of their violence, no fresh waters could reach the fields and gardens. The gods of Sumer who "carried its pickax and basket," that is, who had charge of irrigating Sumer and preparing it for cultivation, were desperate. The Tigris did not rise; it had no "good" water in its channel.

> Famine was severe, nothing was produced,
> At the small rivers, there was no "washing of the hands,"
> The waters rose not high,
> The fields are not watered,

There was no digging of (irrigation) ditches,
In all the lands there was no vegetation,
Only weeds grew.

Thereupon the lord put his lofty mind to it,
Ninurta, the son of Enlil, brought great things into being.

Ninurta set up a pile of stones over the Kur and heaped them up like a great wall in front of Sumer. These stones held back "the mighty waters," and as a result, the waters of the Kur could rise no longer to the surface of the earth. As for the waters which had already flooded the land, Ninurta gathered them and led them into the Tigris, which was now able to water the fields with its overflow.

What had been scattered, he gathered,
What of the Kur had been scattered,
He guided and hurled into the Tigris,
The high waters it pours over the fields.
Behold, now, everything on earth,
Rejoiced afar at Ninurta, the king of the land,
The fields produced abundant grain,
The vineyard and orchard bore their fruit,
The harvest was heaped up in granaries and hills,
The lord made mourning to disappear from the land,
He made happy the spirit of the gods.

Hearing of her son's great and heroic deeds, his mother, Ninmah, is taken with pity for him; she becomes so restless that she is unable to sleep in her bedchamber. She therefore addresses Ninurta from afar with a prayer for permission to visit him and gaze upon him. Ninurta looks at her with the "eye of life," saying:

O Lady, because you would come to the Kur,
O Ninmah, because for my sake you would enter the
    inimical land,
Because you have no fear of the terror of the battle
    surrounding me,
Therefore, of the hill which I, the hero, have heaped up,
Let its name be Hursag (mountain) and you be its queen.

Ninurta then blesses the Hursag that it may produce all kinds of herbs, wine and honey, various kinds of trees, gold, silver, and bronze, and cattle, sheep, and all "four-legged creatures." Following this blessing, he turns to the stones, cursing those which had been his enemies in his battle with the Asag-demon and blessing those which had been his friends.

Not a few of the Sumerian myths revolve about the ambitious, aggressive, and demanding goddess of love, Inanna—the Akkadian Ishtar—and her husband, the shepherd-god, Dumuzi—the Biblical Tammuz. The wooing of the goddess by Dumuzi is told in two versions. In the first he contends for her favor with the farmer-god, Enkimdu, and is successful only after a good deal of quarrelsome argument leading to threats of violence. In the other, Dumuzi seems to find ready and immediate acceptance as Inanna's lover and husband. But little does he dream that his marriage to Inanna will end in his perdition and that he will be literally dragged down to Hell. This story is told in one of the best preserved Sumerian myths, "Inanna's Descent to the Nether World," which has been published and revised three times in the course of the past twenty-five years, and is about to be revised a fourth time with the help of several hitherto unknown tablets and fragments. Briefly sketched, this myth tells the following tale.

Inanna, "Queen of Heaven," the ambitious goddess of love and war whom the shepherd Dumuzi had wooed and won for a wife, decides to descend to the nether world in order to make herself its mistress and thus perhaps to raise the dead. She collects the appropriate divine laws and, having adorned herself with her queenly robes and jewels, is ready to enter the "land of no return."

The queen of the nether world is her older sister and bitter enemy, Ereshkigal, the Sumerian goddess of death and gloom. Fearing, not without reason, lest her sister put her to death in the domain she rules, Inanna instructs her vizier Ninshubur, who is always at her beck and call, that if after three days she has failed to return, he is to set up a lament for her by the ruins in the assembly hall of the gods. He is then to go to Nippur, the city of Enlil, the leading god of the Sumerian pantheon, and plead with him to save her and not let her be put to death in the nether world. If Enlil refuses, Ninshubur is to go to Ur, the city of the moon-god, Nanna, and repeat his plea. If Nanna, too, refuses, he is to go to Eridu, the city of Enki, the god of wisdom, who "knows the food of life," who "knows the water of life," and he will surely come to her rescue.

Inanna then descends to the nether world and approaches Ereshkigal's temple of lapis lazuli. At the gate she is met by the chief gatekeeper, who demands to know who she is and why she has come. Inanna concocts a false excuse for her visit, and the gatekeeper, on instructions from his mistress, leads her through the seven gates of the nether world. As she passes through one gate after another, her garments and jewels are removed piece by piece in spite of her protests. Finally, after passing through the last gate, she is brought stark naked and on bended knees before Ereshkigal and the Anunnaki, the seven dreaded judges of the nether world. They fasten upon her their eyes of death, and she is turned into a corpse, which is then hung from a stake.

Three days and three nights pass. On the fourth day, Ninshubur, seeing that his mistress has not returned, proceeds to make the rounds of the gods in accordance with her instructions. As Inanna had surmised, both Enlil and Nanna refuse all help. Enki, however, devises a plan to restore her to life. He fashions the *kurgarra* and the *kalaturra*, two sexless creatures, and entrusts to them the "food of life" and the "water of life," with which they are to proceed to the nether world where Ereshkigal, "the birth giving mother," lies sick "because of her children"; naked and uncovered, she keeps moaning, "woe my inside" and "woe my outside." They, the *kurgarra* and *kalaturra*, are to repeat her cry sympathetically and add, "From my 'inside' to your 'inside,' from my 'outside' to your 'outside.' " They will then be offered water of the rivers and grain of the fields as gifts, but, Enki warns, they must not accept them. Instead, they are to say, "Give us the corpse hanging from a nail," and to sprinkle upon it "the food of life" and "the water of life," which he had entrusted to them, and thus revive the dead Inanna. The *kurgarra* and *kalaturra* do exactly as Enki bid them, and Inanna revives.

Though Inanna is once again alive, her troubles are far from over, for it was an unbroken rule of the nether world that no one who had entered its gates might return to the world above unless he produced a substitute to take his place. Inanna could not be an exception to the rule. She was indeed permitted to reascend to the earth, but was accompanied by a number of heartless demons with instructions to bring her back to the lower regions if she failed to provide another deity to take her place. Surrounded by these ghoulish constables, Inanna first proceeds to visit the two Sumerian cities Umma and Bad-tibira. The protecting gods of these cities, Shara and Latarak, terrified at the sight of the unearthly arrivals, clothe themselves in sackcloth and grovel in the dust before Inanna. Inanna seems to be gratified by their humility, and when the demons threaten to carry them off to the nether world, she restrains the demons and thus saves the lives of the two gods.

Inanna and the demons, continuing their journey, arrive at Kullab, a district in the Sumerian city-state of Erech. The king of this city is the shepherd-god, Dumuzi, who, instead of bewailing the fact that his wife had descended to the nether world where she had suffered torture and death, has "put on a noble robe, sat high on a throne," that is, he was actually celebrating her misfortune. Enraged, Inanna looks down upon him with "the eye of death" and hands him over to the eager and unmerciful demons to be carried off to the nether world. Dumuzi turns pale and weeps. He lifts his hands to the sky and pleads with the sun-god, Utu, who is Inanna's brother and therefore his own brother-in-law. Dumuzi begs Utu to help him escape the demons by changing his hand into the hand of a snake and his foot into the foot of a snake.

But at that point in the story—in the middle of Dumuzi's prayer—the available tablets come to an end, and until recently the reader has been left hanging in mid-air. Now, however, we have the melancholy end: Dumuzi, in spite of three interventions by Utu, is carried off to die in the nether world as a substitute for his angered and embittered wife, Inanna. This we learn from a hitherto largely unknown poem which is not actually a part of the "Inanna's Descent to the Nether World" but is intimately related to it, and which, moreover, speaks of Dumuzi's changing into a gazelle rather than a snake. This new composition has been found inscribed on twenty-eight tablets and fragments dating from about 1750 B.C.; the full text has only recently been pieced together and translated, at least tentatively, although some of the pieces were published decades ago. In fact, the first of the pieces belonging to the myth was published as early as

1915 by Hugo Radau, but it contained only the last lines of the poem. In 1930, the French scholar, Henri de Genouillac, published two additional pieces which contained the initial fifty-five lines of the poem. But since the entire middle portion was still unknown, there was no way of knowing that the Radau and De Genouillac pieces belonged to the same poem. By 1953 six additional pieces of the poem, published and unpublished, became available, and Thorkild Jacobsen, of the Oriental Institute of the University of Chicago, was the first to give an idea of its plot and to translate several passages.[1] Since then, I have identified nineteen additional tablets and fragments, ten of which are in the Museum of the Ancient Orient in Istanbul (copies of these ten have been made by me and the curators of the tablet collection of the museum, Mmes Muazzez Çiğ and Hatice Kizilyay). As a result of all these new documents, it was possible, at long last, to restore the text of the poem almost in full and to prepare the tentative translation on which the following sketch of its content is based.

The myth, which may be entitled "The Death of Dumuzi," begins with an introductory passage in which the author sets the melancholy tone of the tale he is to tell. Dumuzi, the shepherd of Erech, has a premonition that his death is imminent and so goes forth to the plain with tearful eyes and bitter lament:

> His heart was filled with tears,
> He went forth to the plain,
> The shepherd—his heart was filled with tears,
> He went forth to the plain,
> Dumuzi—his heart was filled with tears,
> He went forth to the plain,
> He fastened his flute (?) about his neck,
> Gave utterance to a lament:

> Set up a lament, set up a lament,
> O plain, set up a lament!
> O plain, set up a lament, set up a wail (?)!
> Among the crabs of the river, set up a lament!
> Among the frogs of the river, set up a lament!

[1] Jacobsen and Kramer, "The Myth of Inanna and Bilulu," *Journal of Near Eastern Studies,* XII, 165–66; and Leo Oppenheim, "The Interpretation of Dreams in the Ancient Near East," *Transactions of the American Philosophical Society,* 1956, p. 246.

Let my mother utter words of (lament),
Let my mother, Sirtur, utter words of (lament).

Let my mother who has (?) not five breads (?)
   utter words of (lament) (?),
Let my mother who has (?) not ten breads (?)
   utter words of (lament),
On the day I die she will have none to care (?) for her,
On the plain, like my mother, let my eyes shed tears (?),
On the plain, like my little sister, let my eyes shed tears.

Dumuzi, the poem continues, then lies down to sleep and has an ominous and foreboding dream:

Among the buds (?) he lay down, among the buds (?)
   he lay down,
The shepherd—among the buds (?) he lay down,
As the shepherd lay down among the buds (?), he
   dreamt a dream,
He arose—it was a dream, he trembled (?)—it was a vision,
He rubbed his eyes with his hands, he was dazed.

The bewildered Dumuzi calls his sister, Geshtinanna, the divine poetess, singer, and interpreter of dreams, before him and tells her his portentous vision:

My dream, O my sister, my dream,
This is the heart of my dream!
Rushes rise up all about me, rushes sprout all about me,
One reed standing all alone bows its head for me,
Of the reeds standing in pairs, one is removed for me,
In the wooded grove, tall (?) trees rise fearsomely
   all about me,
Over my holy hearth, water is poured,
Of my holy churn—its stand (?) is removed,
The holy cup hanging from a peg, from the peg has fallen,
My shepherd's crook has vanished,
An owl holds a . . . . ,
A falcon holds a lamb in its claws,
My young goats drag their lapis beards in the dust.
My sheep of the fold paw the ground with their bent limbs,
The churn lies (shattered), no milk is poured,
The cup lies (shattered), Dumuzi lives no more,
The sheepfold is given over to the wind.

Geshtinanna, too, is deeply disturbed by her brother's dream:

> Oh, my brother, your dream is not favorable, which
> you tell me!
> Oh, Dumuzi, your dream is not favorable which you tell me!
> Rushes rise up all about you, rushes sprout all about you.
> (This means) outlaws will rise up to attack you.
> One reed standing all alone bows its head for you,
> (This means) your mother who bore you will lower her
> head for you,
> Of the reeds standing in pairs, one is removed,
> (This means) I and you—one of us will be removed . . . .

Geshtinanna proceeds to interpret, item by item, her brother's somber and foreboding dream, ending with a warning that the demons of the nether world, the *galla*'s, are closing in on him and that he must hide immediately. Dumuzi agrees and implores his sister not to tell the *galla*'s of his hiding place:

> My friend, I will hide among the plants,
> Tell no one my (hiding) place,
> I will hide among the small plants,
> Tell no one my (hiding) place.
> I will hide among the large plants,
> Tell no one my (hiding) place.
> I will hide among ditches of Arallu,
> Tell no one my (hiding) place.

To which Geshtinanna replies:

> If I tell your (hiding) place, may your dogs devour me,
> The black dogs, your dogs of "shepherdship,"
> The wild dogs, your dogs of "lordship,"
> May your dogs devour me.

And so the *galla*'s, the inhuman creatures who

> Eat no food, know not water,
> Eat not sprinkled flour,
> Drink not libated water,
> Accept no gifts that mollify,
> Sate not with pleasure the wife's bosom,
> Kiss not the children, the sweet . . . . ,

come searching for the hidden Dumuzi but cannot find him. They seize Geshtinanna and try to bribe her to tell them of Dumuzi's whereabouts, but she remains true to her word.

Dumuzi, however, returns to the city, probably because he fears that the demons will kill his sister. There the *galla*'s catch him, belabor him with blows, punches, and lashes, bind his hands and arms fast, and are ready to carry him off to the nether world. Whereupon Dumuzi turns to the sun-god, Utu, the brother of his wife, Inanna, with the prayer to turn him into a gazelle so that he can escape the *galla*'s and carry off his soul to a place known by the name of Shubirila (as yet unidentified), or as Dumuzi himself puts it:

> Utu, you are my wife's brother,
> I am your sister's husband,
> I am he who carries food for Eanna (Inanna's temple),
> In Erech I brought the marriage gifts,
> I kissed the holy lips (?),
> Caressed (?) the holy lap, the lap of Inanna—
> Turn my hands into the hands of a gazelle,
> Turn my feet into the feet of a gazelle,
> Let me escape my *galla*-demons,
> Let me carry off my soul to Shubirila . . . . .

The sun-god hearkened to Dumuzi's prayer; in the words of the poet:

> Utu took his tears as a gift,
> Like a man of mercy, he showed him mercy,
> He turned his hands into the hands of a gazelle,
> He turned his feet into the feet of a gazelle,
> He escaped his *galla*-demons,
> Carried off his soul to Shubirila . . . . .

Unfortunately, the pursuing demons catch up with him once again and beat and torture him as before. A second time, therefore, Dumuzi turns to Utu with the prayer to turn him into a gazelle; this time, he wishes to carry off his soul to the house of a goddess known as "Belili, the wise old lady." Utu answers his prayer, and Dumuzi arrives at the house of Belili, pleading:

> Wise lady, I am not a man, I am the husband of a goddess,
> Of the libated water, let me drink a little (?),
> Of the flour which has been sprinkled, let me eat a little (?).

He has barely had time to partake of food and drink when the *galla*'s appear and beat and torment him a third time. Again Utu turns him into a gazelle, and he escapes to the sheepfold of his ster, Geshtinanna. But all in vain; five of the *galla's* enter the sheepfold and strike Dumuzi on the cheek with a nail and a stick, and Dumuzi dies. Or, to quote the melancholy lines that end the poem:

> The first *galla* enters the sheepfold,
> He strikes Dumuzi on the cheek with a piercing (?) nail (?),
> The second one enters the sheepfold,
> He strikes Dumuzi on the cheek with the shepherd's crook,
> The third one enters the sheepfold,
> Of the holy churn, the stand (?) is removed,
> The fourth one enters the sheepfold,
> The cup hanging from a peg, from the peg falls,
> The fifth one enters the sheepfold,
> The holy churn lies (shattered), no milk is poured,
> The cup lies (shattered), Dumuzi lives no more
> The sheepfold is given to the wind.

Thus Dumuzi comes to a tragic end, a victim of Inanna's love and hate.

Not all the Inanna myths, however, concern Dumuzi. There is one, for example, which relates how the goddess, through trickery, obtained the divine laws, the *me*'s which govern mankind and his institutions. This myth is of considerable anthropological interest because its author found it desirable, in connection with the story, to give a full list of the *me*'s, and to divide civilization as he conceived it into over one hundred culture traits and complexes relating to man's political, religious, and social institutions, to the arts and crafts, to music and musical instruments, and to a varied assortment of intellectual, emotional, and social patterns of behavior (see page 116). Briefly sketched, the plot of this revealing myth runs as follows.

Inanna, queen of heaven, the tutelary goddess of Erech, is anxious to increase the welfare and prosperity of her city, to make it the center of Sumerian civilization, and thus to exalt her name and fame. She, therefore, decides to go to Eridu, the ancient seat of Sumerian culture, where Enki, the lord of wisdom, "who knows the very heart of the gods," dwells in his watery abyss, the Abzu; for Enki has under his charge all the divine decrees that are fundamental to civilization. If she can obtain them, by fair means or foul, and bring them to Erech, its glory and her own

Bull's Head made of lapis lazuli and gold. Detail from a lyre found in the Royal Cemetery at Ur (*ca.* 2500 B.C.). (University Museum.)

Diadem of Queen Shubad (detail), from the Royal Cemetery at Ur (*ca.* 2500 B.C.). Lapis lazuli beads mounted with tiny leaves, fruits, flowers, and figures of gold. (University Museum.)

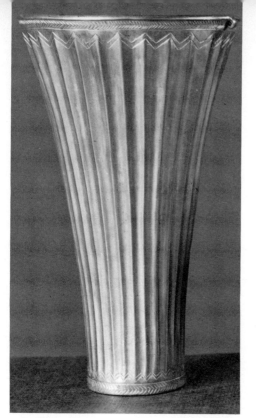

Fluted cup and spouted vessel of gold from the Royal Cemetery at Ur (*ca.* 2500 B.C.). (University Museum.)

Driver and chariot drawn by four asses (copper), found in the Shara Temple
at Tel Agrab (*ca.* 2700 B.C.). The chariot is lightly built. The driver stands
on two treads above the axle and grips a wooden centerpiece covered with
fleece with his legs. The span of four is guided by rings fixed in the upper
lips of the asses and by a whip, now lost. (O.I.P., LX, Plate 58, No. 310.)

Farmer's Almanac. Reverse of the tablet which gives instructions for a yearly cycle of agricultural activities. (University Museum.)

Bas-relief showing a herd of cows and various dairying activities from the temple at Al Ubaid (*ca.* 2500 B.C.). At the bottom, to the right of the central byre, a man is milking a cow; directly to the left of the byre a man is churning butter; while farther to the left three men are preparing and storing "samn," or clarified butter, which is still the main product of the pastoral population of Iraq. (Original in Iraq Museum; cast in University Museum.)

Various mythological scenes on cylinder seals. (*a*) The sun-god rising from the mountain. In the center Utu, the sun-god, rises from the mountain, with rays from his shoulders and a saw in his hand. To the right of Utu is Enki, the god of water and wisdom, who is accompanied by his two-faced minister, Isimud. To the left of Utu is a vegetation goddess, and next to her a hunter (*ca.* 2200 B.C.). (British Museum.) (*b*) The water-god in his sea house (Abzu) (*ca.* 2200 B.C.). On the extreme right is Enki, the water-god, enthroned in his sea house. To the left is Utu, the sun-god, with his rays and saw. The middle deity is unidentified. (British Museum.) (*c*) Divine journey (*ca.* 2200 B.C.). An unidentified deity holding a plow is traveling in a boat whose stern ends in a snake and whose prow ends in the body of a god propelling the boat. (Iraq Museum.)

Literary catalogue. Tablet and author's hand copy giving the titles of sixty-two literary works. (University Museum.)

The creation of man. Tablet, pieced together from three fragments, recounting the creation of man from the "clay that is over the abyss." (University Museum.)

Grammatical text from Nippur. This tablet originally contained sixteen columns, each subdivided into two. The left half contains a Sumerian grammatical unit, such as a substantive or verbal complex, while the right half gives its Semitic translation. (University Museum.)

Seated couple. A gypsum sculpture expressive of domestic affection and married contentment. (Joint Nippur Expedition of the Oriental Institute and the American Schools for Oriental Research.)

will indeed be unsurpassed. As she approaches the Abzu of Eridu, Enki—no doubt taken in by her charm—calls his messenger Isimud, whom he addressed as follows:

> Come, my messenger Isimud, give ear to my instructions,
> A word I shall say to you, take my word.
> The maid, all alone, has directed her step to the Abzu,
> Inanna, all alone, has directed her step to the Abzu,
> Have the maid enter the Abzu of Eridu,
> Give her to eat barley cake with butter,
> Pour for her cold water that freshens the heart,
> Give her to drink beer in the "face of the lion"
> At the holy table, the "table of heaven,"
> Speak to Inanna words of greeting.

Isimud did exactly as bidden by his master, and Inanna and Enki sit down to feast and banquet. After their hearts had become happy with drink, Enki exclaims:

> By the name of power, by the name of my power,
> To holy Inanna, my daughter, I shall present the divine
>   decrees.

He thereupon presents, several at a time, the more than one hundred divine decrees which, according to our author, control the culture pattern of civilization. Inanna is only too happy to accept the gifts offered her by the drunken Enki. She takes them and loads them on her "boat of heaven," and embarks for Erech with her precious cargo. But after the effects of the banquet have worn off, Enki notices that the *me*'s are gone from their usual place. He turns to Isimud, who informs him that he, Enki himself, presented them to his daughter, Inanna. Greatly upset, Enki regrets his munificence and decides to prevent at all costs the "boat of heaven" from reaching Erech. He therefore dispatches his messenger together with a group of sea monsters to follow Inanna and her boat to the first of the seven stopping stations that are situated between the Abzu of Eridu and Erech. Here the sea monsters are to seize the "boat of heaven" from Inanna; Inanna herself, however, must be permitted to continue her journey to Erech afoot.

Isimud does as bidden. He overtakes Inanna and the "boat of heaven" and informs her that Enki has changed his mind, and that while she is free to go on to Erech, he will have to take the boat and its precious cargo from her and bring it back to Erech. Whereupon Inanna berates Enki roundly for breaking his word and oath; she turns to her vizier, the god Ninshubur, for help, and the latter rescues her and the boat from Isimud and the sea monsters. Enki is persistent; again and again he sends Isimud accompanied by various sea monsters to seize the "boat of heaven." But on each occasion Ninshubur comes to the rescue of his mistress. Finally Inanna and her boat arrive safely at Erech, where, amidst jubilation and feasting on the part of the delighted inhabitants, she unloads the precious divine *me*'s one at a time.

In another Inanna myth a mortal plays an important role; its plot runs as follows: There once lived a gardener named Shukalletuda, whose diligent efforts at gardening had met with nothing but failure. Although he had carefully watered his furrows and garden patches, the plants had withered away; the raging winds smote his face with the "dust of the mountains"; all that he had carefully tended turned desolate. He thereupon lifted his eyes east and west to the starry heavens, studied the omens, observed and learned the divine decrees. As a result of this newly acquired wisdom, he planted the *sarbatu*-tree (as yet unidentified) in the garden, a tree whose broad shade lasts from sunrise to sunset. As a consequence of this ancient horticultural experiment, Shukalletuda's garden blossomed forth with all kinds of green.

One day, continues our myth, the goddess Inanna, after traversing heaven and earth, lay down to rest her tired body not far from Shukalletuda's garden. The latter, who had spied her from the edge of his garden, took advantage of Inanna's extreme weariness and had intercourse with her. When morning came and the sun rose, Inanna looked about her in consternation and determined to ferret out at all costs the mortal who had so shamefully abused her. She therefore sent three plagues against Sumer. First, she filled all the wells of the land with blood, so that all the palm groves and vineyards were saturated with blood. Second, she sent destructive winds and storms against the land. The nature of the third plague is uncertain since the relevant lines are too fragmentary. But in spite of all three plagues, she was unable to locate her defiler, for after each plague Shukalletuda went to his father's house and informed him of his danger. The father advised his son to direct his step to his brothers, the "black-headed people," that is, the people of Sumer, and to stay close to the urban centers. Shukalletuda followed this advice, and as a result, Inanna was unable to find him. After her third failure, Inanna realized bitterly that she was unable to avenge the outrage committed against her. She therefore decided to go to Eridu, to the house of Enki, the Sumerian god of wisdom, and ask his advice and help. Here, unfortunately, the tablet breaks off, and the end of the story remains unknown.

Except for references to mankind as a whole, mortals play little role in the Sumerian myths. In addition to the Inanna-Shukalletuda myth just recounted, there is only one other myth involving a mortal. This is the long-known Flood-story, so important for comparative Biblical studies. Unfortunately, only one tablet inscribed with this myth has been excavated to date, and only one-third of this tablet has been preserved. The beginning of the myth is broken away, and the first intelligible lines concern the creation of man, vegetation, and animals; the heavenly origin of kingship; the founding and naming of five antediluvian cities, which are presented to five tutelary deities. Next we learn that a number of deities are bitter and unhappy because of a divine decision to bring the flood and destroy mankind. Ziusudra, the Sumerian counterpart of the Biblical Noah, is then introduced in the story as a pious, god-fearing king who is constantly watching for divine dreams and revelations. He stations himself by a wall, where he hears the voice of a deity, probably Enki, informing him of the decision taken by the assembly of the gods to send a deluge and "destroy the seed of mankind."

The myth must have continued with detailed instructions to Ziusudra to build a giant boat and thus save himself from destruction. But all this is missing because of a rather large break in the tablet. When the text resumes, we find that the flood in all its violence has already come upon the earth where it rages for seven days and nights. At the end of that time, the sun-god, Utu, comes forth lighting and warming up the earth, and Ziusudra prostrates himself before him and offers him sacrifices of oxen and sheep. The last extant lines of the myth describe the deification of Ziusudra: after he had prostrated himself before An and Enlil, he was given "life like a god" and transported to Dilmun, the divine paradise-land, "the place where the sun rises."

Finally, there is a Sumerian myth which, although concerned with gods only, provides an interesting bit of anthropological information about the Semitic Bedu people known as Martu. The action of the story takes place in the city of Ninab, "the city of cities, the land of princeship" (a still unidentified locality in Mesopotamia). Its tutelary deity seems to have been Martu, god of the nomadic Semites who lived to the west and southwest of Sumer. The relative time when the events took place is described in cryptic, antithetical, and obscure phrases, thus:

> Ninab existed, Aktab existed not,
> The holy crown existed, the holy tiara existed not,
> The holy herbs existed, holy nitrum existed not. . . . .

The god Martu, the story begins, decides to marry. He asks his mother to find him a wife, but she advises him to go and find a wife for himself in accordance with his own desire. One day, the story continues, a great feast is prepared in Ninab, and to it comes Numushda, the tutelary deity of Kazallu, a city-state located to the northeast of Sumer, together with his wife and daughter. During this feast Martu performs some heroic deed which brings joy to the heart of Numushda. As a reward, the latter offers Martu silver and lapis lazuli. But Martu refuses; it is the hand of Numushda's daughter that he claims as a reward. Numushda gladly consents; so, too, does his daughter, although her girl friends try to dissuade her from marrying Martu since he is nothing but a barbaric, tent-dwelling Bedu who eats raw meat and "is not brought to burial when he dies."

CHAPTER FIVE

LITERATURE:

The Sumerian

Belles-Lettres

Archeology, and particularly the study of man's more ancient past as revealed in the excavations of long buried cities and villages, is by its very nature usually most articulate about his material culture; for archeological finds consist primarily of bricks and walls, tools and weapons, pots and vases, jewels and ornaments, statues and figurines, in short, all the varied products of man's arts and crafts. His social life, his economic and administrative organization, and particularly his world view as revealed in his religious beliefs, ethical ideals, and spiritual yearnings—all these usually have to be inferred and surmised from the artifacts, architecture, and burial customs and then only in the form of vague and loose generalizations.

The situation is quite different, however, in the case of Sumer, for here the excavators have unearthed tens of thousands of inscribed clay tablets—literally so—and these add what might be termed a dimension in depth to our understanding of its ancient culture. To be sure, more than 90 per cent of the inscribed material consists of economic and administrative documents, and these, significant as they are in many ways, reveal relatively little of the spiritual life of the ancient Mesopotamians. But a group of some five thousand tablets and fragments inscribed with a varied assortment of literary works have also been unearthed, and these enable us to penetrate to a certain extent into their very hearts and souls.

The Sumerian literary documents range in size from large

165

twelve-column tablets inscribed with hundreds of compactly written lines of text to tiny fragments containing no more than a few broken lines. The literary compositions inscribed on these tablets and fragments run into the hundreds and vary in length from hymns of less than fifty lines to myths of close to a thousand lines. As literary products, the Sumerian belles-lettres rank high among the aesthetic creations of civilized man. They compare not too unfavorably with the ancient Greek and Hebrew masterpieces and, like them, mirror the spiritual and intellectual life of an ancient culture which would otherwise have remained largely unknown. Their significance for a proper appraisal of the cultural and spiritual development of the entire ancient Near East can hardly be overestimated. The Akkadians, that is, the Assyrians and Babylonians, took these works over almost *in toto*. The Hittites, Hurrians, and Canaanites translated some of them into their own languages and no doubt imitated them widely. The form and content of the Hebrew literary works and, to a certain extent, even those of the ancient Greeks were profoundly influenced by them. As practically the oldest written literature of any significant amount ever uncovered—and there is little likelihood that any older literary documents will ever be uncovered outside of Sumer—it furnishes new, rich, and unexpected source material for all students of the history of civilization and particularly its more intellectual and spiritual aspects. It is not too much to predict that the recovery and restoration of this ancient and long forgotten literature will turn out to be a major contribution of our century to the humanities.

The full accomplishment of this task, however, is no simple matter; it will entail the devoted efforts of more than one cuneiform scholar over the coming years. For while most of the documents were excavated more than half a century ago, the piecing together and translation of the compositions inscribed on them made relatively little progress over the ensuing decades. In the first place, the great majority of the tablets came out of the ground broken and fragmentary, so that only a small part of their original content was preserved on each. Offsetting this disadvantage is the fact that the ancient scribes commonly prepared more than one copy of any given composition. The breaks and lacunae in one tablet or fragment may therefore frequently be restored from duplicating pieces that may themselves be in a fragmentary condition. To take full advantage of these duplications and the resulting restorations, however, it is essential to have available as much as possible of the source material in published form. This frequently entails copying by hand hundreds and hundreds of minutely inscribed tablets and fragments—a tedious and time-consuming task. No wonder that as late as 1935 only a relatively small portion of the Sumerian literary documents had been made available in spite of the devoted efforts of numerous cuneiformists: Hermann Hilprecht, Hugo Radau, Stephen Langdon, L. W. King, Heinrich Zimmern, Cyril Gadd, Henri de Genouillac, Arno Poebel, and Edward Chiera.

To help remedy this situation, at least to some extent, I have devoted much of the past twenty-five years to the study and copying of the unpublished Sumerian literary texts scattered throughout museums the world over. But with the passage of the years, it became ever more apparent that this was not a one-man task. Fortunately, in the past several years, a number of other scholars have shown no little zeal and zest to collaborate in the work: Edmund Gordon, whose work on the Sumerian proverbs and fables has opened up new vistas in the comparative study of world wisdom literature; Muazzez Çiğ and Hatice Kizilyay, the two curators of the tablet archives of the Museum of the Ancient Orient in Istanbul; Inez Bernhardt, assistant keeper of the Hilprecht Collection of the Friedrich-Schiller University in Jena; Eugen Bergmann of the Pontificio Instituto Biblico in Rome; and George Castellino, of the University of Rome. At the same time, J. A. van Dijk, a former student of De Liagre Böhl and Adam Falkenstein, has been copying and publishing Sumerian literary texts from the Iraq Museum in Baghdad and the Böhl collection in Leiden. And most important, several hundred Sumerian literary tablets excavated between 1923 and 1934 at Ur, which have been copied over the years by Cyril Gadd, are to be published in the near future. All in all, therefore, there is every reason to hope that the coming decade will witness the publication of a very considerable part of the Sumerian literary tablets and fragments that have been lying about for years in the museum cupboards.

But as experience has shown—and as more than one Sumerologist will testify—even given the complete text of a Sumerian literary work, its translation and interpretation present a difficult and at times heart-rending task. To be sure, the Sumerian grammatical problems are no longer as acute as in earlier days. The gratifying progress in this field is due largely to the past efforts of such eminent cuneiformists as Delitzsch, Thureau-Dangin, Zimmern, Landsberger, and particularly Poebel; it is Poebel's *Grundzüge der sumerischen Grammatik*, published about forty years ago, that has placed Sumerian grammar on a scientific basis. And even in the difficult and complicated area of Sumerian lexicology, the contributions of such scholars as Falkenstein, Jacobsen, and Landsberger—to name only the giants—show promise of surmounting some of the more frustrating obstacles. All in all, therefore, it is not unlikely that as a result of the cumulative and co-operative contributions of cuneiformists the world over, the coming decade will see relatively trustworthy translations of quite a number of the more significant literary compositions. Whatever may develop, we are at present in a position to take a new look at Sumerian literature as a whole, and this is what the following general survey aims to do.

Sumerian literature, as the term is used in this chapter, is restricted to myths and epic tales, hymns, lamentations and historiographic documents, essays long and short, precepts and proverbs; it will not include the votive inscriptions, some of which have no little literary value (see, for example, the Entemena historical inscriptions on pages 313–16), the Urukagina reform texts (see pages 317–23), and the political letters, some of which have a distinct literary flavor (see pages 331–35). The Sumerians probably first began to write down their literary works about 2500 B.C., although the earliest literary documents as yet recovered date from about 2400 B.C. Thus from approximately this century, we have a solid clay cylinder inscribed with twenty columns of text, consisting of a myth concerned primarily with the god Enlil and his sister, Ninhursag, and mentioning a number of other well-known Sumerian deities such as Inanna, Enki, and Ninurta. Its plot is still unintelligible, but the individual words, phrases, and motifs show a style and structure quite similar to that of the myths of a much later day, indicating that there was a continuous and consistent literary development over the centuries. This is corroborated by another fragmentary myth going back to the twenty-fourth century B.C. which concerns the son of Enlil, Ishkur, the storm-god, who had disappeared into the nether world. The distressed Enlil gathered the Anunnaki together to ask for help, and it was probably the fox who volunteered to bring back Ishkur from the nether world—a motif which is reminiscent to some extent of that found in the Paradise myth (see pages 147–48).

There is every reason to believe that the literary output of the Sumerians increased with the centuries, and no doubt they became quite prolific toward the end of the third millennium when the Sumerian school, the *edubba*, came to be an important center of education and learning. Sumerian literary activity continued unabated through the first half of the second millennium in spite of the fact that the Semitic Akkadian language was gradually replacing Sumerian as the spoken language of Sumer. In the *edubba*'s that functioned throughout the period of the Isin Dynasty and even later, the earlier literary works were studied, copied, and redacted with zest and zeal, with care and understanding; almost all the literary works that have come down to us are known only from copies and redactions prepared in what might be described as the post-Sumerian *edubba*'s. The presumably Akkadian-speaking teachers, poets, and writers who comprised the *edubba* personnel even created new Sumerian literary works, although, naturally enough, these followed closely the form and content, the style and pattern, of the earlier documents.

It has often been assumed that the Sumerian literary works were all religious in character and that they were composed and redacted by priests for use in the temple cult. With the possible exception of the hymns and lamentations, however, this view is hardly tenable. To begin with the most clear-cut cases, it is absurd to assume that the Sumerian proverbs and precepts or the essays dealing with the *edubba* were written either by priests or for priests or that they had any connection whatever with the temple cult. Nor is there any valid ground for assuming that the epic tales revolving about the heroes Enmerkar, Lugalbanda, and Gilgamesh were composed by priests and recited in the temple. Even in the case of the myths, there is no indication that they were recited at temple services and religious festivals, at least not during the Sumerian and early post-Sumerian periods. Only in the case of the hymns and lamentations does it seem reasonable to suppose that they were composed and redacted for use in the temple cult. But since—as we know from the recent excavations at Nippur—the tablets inscribed with the hymns and lamentations, like those inscribed with the other types of literary works, were found not in the temples but in the scribal quarter, they, too, must have been composed in the *edubba* by the members of its staff rather than by priests; in fact, priests are nowhere mentioned as part of the *edubba* personnel.

A key figure in the growth and development of Sumerian literature was the *nar,* or minstrel, who is mentioned sometimes side by side with the *dubsar,* or scribe, in the hymns, but his connection with the *edubba* is not clear. In any case, it is not improbable that some of the graduates of the *edubba* specialized in religious compositions and went into the service of the temple to teach its singers and musicians and to supervise and conduct the cult liturgies, while others, specializing in myths and epic tales, went into the service of the palace to train and instruct the court singers and entertainers. As yet, however, we have practically no information on these and similar details. Nor do we know anything about the audience or "reading public" for whom the Sumerian literary works were prepared. Only the *edubba* graduate could read and write, and it is hardly likely that even the "men of letters" made a practice of collecting private libraries for their own personal entertainment and instruction. In all probability, it was only the *edubba* that had a library, although the temple and the palace may also have possessed copies of those compositions that were relevant to their needs. It is hardly likely that Sumerian literary works stayed on the *edubba* "shelves" for teaching purposes only; in one way or another, they must have been used in public gatherings, whether these took place in the temple, the court, or the market place.

The large majority of the Sumerian literary works are written in poetic form. The use of meter and rhyme was entirely unknown, but practically all other poetic devices and techniques were utilized with no little skill, imagination, and effect: repetition and parallelism, metaphor and simile, chorus and refrain. Sumerian narrative poetry—the myths and epic tales, for example—

abounds in static epithets, lengthy repetitions, recurrent formulas, leisurely detailed descriptions, and long speeches. By and large, the Sumerian writers show little feeling for closely knit plot structure; their narratives tend to ramble rather disconnectedly and monotonously, with but little variation in emphasis and tone. Above all, the Sumerian poets seem to lack a sense of climax. The myths and epic tales show little intensification of emotion and suspense as the story progresses, and often the last episode is no more moving or stirring than the first. Nor is there any attempt at characterization and psychological delineation; the gods and heroes of the Sumerian narratives tend to be broad types rather than recognizable flesh-and-blood individuals.

The Sumerian myths at present recovered, wholly or in large part, are as follows: two in which the god Enlil plays the major role ("Enlil and Ninlil: The Birth of the Moon-God" and "The Creation of the Pickax"); four in which the god Enki is the protagonist ("Enki and the World Order: The Organization of the Earth and Its Cultural Processes," "Enki and Ninhursag: A Sumerian Paradise Myth," "Enki and Nimmah: The Creation of Man," and "Enki and Eridu"); one concerning the moon-god, Nanna-Sin ("The Journey of Nanna-Sin to Nippur"); two about Ninurta ("The Deeds and Exploits of Ninurta" and "The Return of Ninurta to Nippur"); five in which the goddess Inanna plays the major role ("Inanna and Enki: The Transfer of the Arts of Civilization from Eridu to Erech," "Inanna and the Subjugation of Mount Ebih," "Inanna and Shukalletuda: The Gardener's Mortal Sin," "Inanna's Descent to the Nether World," and "Inanna and Bilulu"); four in which the god Dumuzi plays the major role ("Dumuzi and Enkimdu: The Wooing of Inanna," "The Marriage of Dumuzi and Inanna," "The Death of Dumuzi," and "Dumuzi and the *Galla's*"); one myth concerned with the god of the Martu, the Semitic Bedu living west of Sumer ("The Marriage of Martu"); the Flood myth, in which the identity of the deity (or deities) who was the chief protagonist is still uncertain. (The plots of almost all of these myths have been sketched in chapter iv.)

An excellent illustration of the Sumerian mythological imagination is "Enki and the World Order," one of the longest and best preserved of the extant Sumerian narrative poems. Its text consists of approximately 466 lines, of which about 375 are preserved entirely or in large part; the most serious lacunae are at the very beginning and end and in the passage between lines 146 and 181. The available text, which is here presented in English for the first time, was pieced together from twelve tablets and fragments. The most important of these—the piece that proved basic for the restoration of the poem—is an eight-column tablet originally inscribed with the entire text of the myth. Unfortunately, this tablet had been found broken in two when unearthed in the old Nippur excavations, one half landing in the University Museum of the University of Pennsylvania in Philadelphia and the other in the Hilprecht Collection of the Friedrich-Schiller University in Jena. The text of the latter did not become available until quite recently, and the present restoration became possible as a result of a long-distance joining of the texts of the two long separated pieces.

The poet begins with a hymn of praise addressed to Enki; some of it is destroyed and unintelligible, but generally speaking, it seems to exalt Enki as the god who watches over the universe and is responsible for the fertility of field and farm, of flock and herd. A paean of self-glorification put into the mouth of Enki follows, which is concerned primarily with his relationship to the leading deities of the pantheon—An, Enlil, and Nintu—and to the lesser gods known collectively as the Anunnaki. Following a brief five-line passage which tells of the Anunnaki's homage to Enki, Enki, for a second time, utters a paean of self-glorification. He begins by exalting the power of his word and command in providing the earth with prosperity and abundance, continues with a description of the splendor of his shrine, the Abzu, and concludes with an account of his joyous journey over the marshland in his *magur*-boat, "the ibex of the Abzu," after which the lands of Magan, Dilmun, and Meluhha sent their heavily laden boats to Nippur with rich gifts for Enlil. At the conclusion of this passage, the Anunnaki once again pay homage to Enki, particularly as the god who "rides" and directs the *me*'s.

The poet now introduces a description of the various rites and rituals performed by some of the more important priests and spiritual leaders of Sumer in Enki's Abzu-shrine (unfortunately, the second half of the passage is almost entirely destroyed).

Following another fragmentary passage whose contents are altogether uncertain, we find Enki in his boat once again. With the sea creatures doing homage to him and abundance prevailing in the universe, Enki is ready to "decree the fates." Beginning, as might have been expected, with Sumer itself, he first exalts it as a chosen, hallowed land with "lofty" and "untouchable" *me*'s, where the gods have taken up their abode, then blesses its flocks and herds, its temples and shrines. From Sumer he proceeds to Ur, which he extols in lofty, metaphorical language and blesses with prosperity and pre-eminence. From Ur he goes to Meluhha and blesses it most generously with trees and reeds, oxen and birds, gold, tin, and bronze. He then proceeds to provide Dilmun with some of its needs. He is very unfavorably disposed toward Elam and Marhashi, two inimical lands, and proceeds to destroy them and carry off all their riches. To the nomadic Martu, on the other hand, he "presents cattle as a gift."

Enki now turns from the fates of the various lands which made up the Sumerian inhabited world and performs a whole series of acts vital to the earth's fertility and productiveness. Turning first to its physical features, he begins by filling the Tigris with fresh, sparkling, life-giving water—in the concrete metaphorical imagery of our poet, Enki is a rampant bull who mates with the river imagined as a wild cow. Then, to make sure that the Tigris and Euphrates function properly, he appoints the god Enbilulu, the "canal inspector," to take charge of them. Enki next "calls" the marshland and the canebrake, supplies them with fish and reeds, and appoints a deity "who loves fish"—the name is illegible—to take charge of them. He then turns to the sea, erects there his holy shrine, and places the goddess Nanshe, "the lady of Sirara," in charge. Finally, Enki "calls" the life-giving rain, makes it come down on earth, and entrusts it to the storm-god, Ishkur.

Enki now turns to the earth and its needs. He attends to the plow, yoke, and furrow, and appoints Enlil's farmer, Enkimdu, as their deity. He next "calls" the cultivated field, brings forth its varied grains and vegetables, and makes the grain-goddess, Ashnan, responsible for them. He looks to the pickax and brick mold, and puts the brick-god, Kulla, in charge of them. He lays foundations, aligns the bricks, builds "the house," and puts Mushdamma, "the great builder of Enlil," in charge.

Leaving farm, field, and house, Enki turns to the high plain, covers it with green vegetation, multiplies its cattle, and makes Sumugan, "the king of the mountains," responsible for them. He next erects stalls and sheepfolds, supplies them with the best fat and milk, and appoints the shepherd-god, Dumuzi, to take charge of them. Enki then fixes the "borders"—presumably of cities and states—sets up boundary stones, and places the sun-god, Utu, "in charge of the entire universe." Finally, Enki attends to "that which is woman's task," in particular the weaving of cloth, and puts Uttu, the goddess of clothing, in charge.

The myth now takes a rather unexpected turn, as the poet introduces the ambitious and aggressive Inanna, who feels that she has been slighted and left without any special powers and prerogatives. She complains bitterly that Enlil's sister, Aruru (alias Nintu), and her (Inanna's) sister-goddesses, Ninisinna, Ninmug, Nidaba, and Nanshe, have all received their respective powers and insignia, but that she, Inanna, has been singled out for neglectful and inconsiderate treatment. Enki seems to be put on the defensive by Inanna's complaint, and he tries to pacify her by pointing out that she actually does have quite a number of special insignia and prerogatives—"the crook, staff, and wand of shepherdship"; oracular responses in regard to war and battle; the weaving and fashioning of garments; the power to destroy the "indestructible" and to make the "imperishable" perish—as well as by giving her a special blessing. Following Enki's reply to Inanna, the poem probably closes with a four-line hymnal passage to Enki.

Here now is the translation of the extant text of the poem (omitting, however, the first fifty lines, which are fragmentary and obscure).

When father Enki comes out into the seeded Land, it brings forth fecund seed,
When Nudimmud comes out to my fecund ewe, it gives birth to the lamb,
When he comes out to my "seeded" cow, it gives birth to the fecund calf,
When he comes out to my fecund goat, it gives birth to the fecund kid,
When you have gone out to the field, to the cultivated field,
You pile up heaps and mounds on the high plain,
[You] . . . . the . . . of the parched (?) earth.

Enki, the king of the Abzu, overpowering (?) in his majesty, speaks up
with authority:
"My father, the king of the universe,
Brought me into existence in the universe,
My ancestor, the king of all the lands,
Gathered together all the *me*'s, placed the *me*'s in my hand.
From the Ekur, the house of Enlil,
I brought craftsmanship to my Abzu of Eridu.
I am the fecund seed, engendered by the great wild ox, I am the first
born son of An,
I am the 'great storm' who goes forth out of the 'great below,' I am
the lord of the Land,
I am the *gugal* of the chieftains, I am the father of all the lands,
I am the 'big brother' of the gods, I am he who brings full prosperity,
I am the record keeper of heaven and earth,
I am the ear and the mind (?) of all the lands,
I am he who directs justice with the king An on An's dais,
I am he who decrees the fates with Enlil in the 'mountain of wisdom,'
He placed in my hand the decreeing of the fates of the 'place where
the sun rises,'
I am he to whom Nintu pays due homage,
I am he who has been called a good name by Ninhursag,
I am the leader of the Anunnaki,
I am he who has been born as the first son of the holy An."

After the lord had uttered (?) (his) exaltedness,
After the great prince had himself pronounced (his) praise,
The Anunnaki came before him in prayer and supplication:
"Lord who directs craftsmanship,
Who makes decisions, the glorified; Enki, praise!"

For a second time, because of (his) great joy,
Enki, the king of the Abzu, in his majesty, speaks up with authority:
"I am the lord, I am one whose command is unquestioned, I am the
foremost in all things,
At my command the stalls have been built, the sheepfolds have been
enclosed,
When I approached heaven a rain of prosperity poured down from
heaven,
When I approached the earth, there was a high flood,
When I approached its green meadows,
The heaps and mounds were pi[led] up at my word.

I built my [house], a shrine, in a pure place, I called it with a good
   name,
I built my Abzu, a shrine, in a . . , I decreed a good fate for it.
My house—its shade stre[tches] over the 'snake'-marsh,
My house, its . . wears a beard among (?) the 'honey'-plants (?),
The ca[rps] wave the tail to him in (?) the sm[all *gizi*-reeds],
The sparrows chirp in their . . . . ,
The weapon-carrying . . . . ,
Came into my, Enki's,
The *abgal*'s,
. . [into my] . . .   . ,
The *enkum* (and) [*ninkum*] . . . ,
Sacred songs and spells filled my Abzu.
My *magur*-boat, the crown, the 'ibex of the Abzu'—
In its midst there is a great rejoicing.
The lofty marshland, my favorite spot,
Stretches out its arms to me, bends (?) its neck to me.
The *kara*'s drew (?) on (?) the oars in unison,
Sing sweet songs, cause the river to rejoice,
Nimgirsig, the *ensi* of my *ma*[*gur*-boat],
He[ld] the gold scepter [for me],
I, Enki, [. . .d] the boat 'ibex of the Abzu,'
I, the lord . . . . ,
I, Enki, ...
                    (Approximately five lines missing)
. . . . I would watch over its green cedars (?).
The l[ands] of Magan and Dilmun
Looked up at me, En[ki],
Moored (?) the Dilmun-boat to the ground (?),
Loaded the Magan-boat sky high;
The *magilum*-boat of Meluhha
Transports gold and silver,
Brings them to Nippur for Enlil, the [king] of all the lands."

To him who has no city, to him who has no horse,
The Martu—Enki pre[sen]ted cattle as a gift,

To the [great] prince who came forth in his [land],
The Anunnaki pay due homage:
"Lord who rides the great *me*'s, the pure *me*'s,
Who has charge of the universe, the widespread,
Who received the lofty 'sun-disk' in Eridu, the pure place, the mo[st
   prec]ious place,
Enki, lord of the universe, praise!"

For the great prince who comes forth in his land,
All the lords, all the chieftains,
The incantation priests of Eridu,
The "linen-wearers" of Sumer,
Perform the incantation rites of the Abzu,
To (?) father Enki in (?) the holy place . . . they direct (their) step,
In the sleeping chamber, the princely house, they . . . . ,
In the stations they call [his] name,
In (?) the lofty shrine, the Abzu [they] . . . . ,
            (About thirty-six lines destroyed in large part)
Nimgirsig, the *ensi* of the *magur*-boat,
He[ld] the holy scepter for the lord,
The *lahama*'s of the sea, the fifty, did ho[mage to him],
The *kara*'s . . d like a . . -bird of heaven.
For the king standing proudly, father Enki—in the Land—
The great prince who came forth in his Land,
Prosperity prevailed in the universe.

Enki decrees (the) fate:
"Sumer, 'great mountain,' 'country of the universe,'
Filled with enduring light, dispensing from sunrise to sunset the *me*'s
    to (?) the people,
Your *me*'s are lofty *me*'s, unreachable.
Your heart is profound, unfathomable.
The enduring . . , your place where gods give birth, is untouchable
    like heaven.
The born king, who dons the enduring diadem—
The born lord, who puts crown on head—
Your lord (is) an honored lord, he sits with the king An on An's dais,
Your king—the 'great mountain,' Father Enlil,
Has . . d him for you by (?) the . . . like a cedar—the father of all the
    lands.
The Anunnaki, the great gods,
Have taken up (their) dwelling place in your midst,
Eat (their) food in your tree-planted *giguna*.
House, Sumer, may your many stalls be built, may your cows mul-
    tiply,
May your many sheepfolds be erected, may your sheep be myriad,
May your *giguna* reach skyward,
May your enduring . . lift hand to heaven.
May the Anunnaki decree the fates in your midst."

He proceeded to the shrine Ur,
Enki, the king of the Abzu decrees (its) fate:
"City possessing all that is appropriate, water-washed, firm-standing ox,
Dais of abundance of the highland, knees open, green like a mountain,
Hashur-grove, wide of shade—he who is lordly because of his might (?)
Has directed your perfect *me*'s,
Enlil, the 'great mountain,' has pronounced your lofty name in the
     universe.
City whose fate has been decreed by Enlil,
Shrine Ur, may you rise heaven high."

He procee[ded] to the land Meluhha,
Enki, the king of the Abzu, [decrees] (its) fate:
"Black land, may your trees be large trees, [may they be 'highland']-
     trees,
[May] their thrones [fill] the royal palace,
May your reeds be large reeds, [may they be 'highland']-reeds,
May the heroes in the place of battle [wield their] weapons,
May your bulls be large bulls, [may they be] 'highland' bulls,
[May] their cry [be] the cry [of 'highland'] wild bulls,
May the great *me*'s of the gods be per[fected for you],
[May] all *dar*-birds of the highland [wear carneli]an beards,
[May] your bird be the *Haia*-bird,
[M]ay its calls fill the royal palace,
May your silver be gold,
May your copper be tin (and) bronze,
Land, may everything you have, [increase],
May your people [multiply],
May your . . go forth like a bull to his . . . ."

. . . the city of . .
He treated (?) like . . . . ,
He cleansed, purified the [land Di]lmun,
Placed Ninsikilla in charge of it,
He gave . . as . . , he eats its . . -fish,
He gave . . as a cultivated field (?), he eats [its da]tes.

. . . . Elam and Marhashi . . . .
Were (destined) to be devoured like . . -fish;
The king (presumably Enki) upon whom Enlil had bestowed might,
Destroyed their houses, destroyed their walls.
Their (precious) metal (and) lapis lazuli (and the contents of) their
     storehouses,
He brought to Nippur for Enlil—the king of all the lands.

To him who builds no city, builds no [house]—
The Martu—Enki presented cattle as a gift.

After he had cast his eye from that spot,
After father Enki had lifted it over the Euphrates,
He stood up proudly like a rampant bull,
He lifts the penis, ejaculates,
Filled the Tigris with sparkling water.
The wild cow mooing for its young in the pastures, the scorpion (-infested) stall,
[The Tigr]is surre[ndered] to him, as (to) a rampant bull.
He lifted the penis, brought the bridal gift,
Brought joy to the Tigris, like a big wild bull [rejoiced (?)] in its giving birth.
The water he brought is sparkling water, its "wine" tastes sweet,
The grain he brought, its checkered grain, the people eat it,
He fi[lled] the Ekur, the house of Enlil, with possessions,
With Enki, Enlil rejoices, Nippur [is delighted].

The lord don[ned] the diadem for lordship,
[Put on] the enduring tiara for kingship,
Trod the ground on his left side,
Prosperity came forth out of the earth for him.
After he had placed the scepter in his right hand,
In order to make the Tigris and Euphrates "eat together,"
He who utters the .. word in accordance with his .. ,
Who carries off like fat the "princely knee" from the palace,
The lord who decrees the fate, Enki the king of the Abzu,
Enbilulu, the inspector of canals,
[Enki] placed in charge of them.

He cal[led the marshland], placed in it carp (and) .. -fish,
He cal[led the canebrake], placed in it .. -reeds (and) green reeds,
                    (Two lines missing)
[He issued] a challen[ge . . . .].
Him who[se net] no fish escapes,
Whose trap no .. escapes,
Whose snare no bird escapes,
. . . . the son of . . . .
.. (a god) who loves fish,
Enki placed in charge of them.

The lord erected a shrine (?), a holy shrine—its heart is profound,
Erected a shrine (?) in the sea, a holy shrine—its heart is profound,
The shrine—its midst is a . . . , known to no one,
The [shrine]—its station is the . . *iku* constellation,
The lofty [shrine], above (?)—its station stands (?) by the "chariot"-
    constellation,
The . . . from the trembling . . . . its *melam's* . . ,
The Anunnaki came with [pray]er and supplication,
For Enki in the E-[engurra they set up] a lofty dais.
For the lord . . . . ,
The great prince . . , bor[n. . . .]
The *u*-bird . . . . ,
                    (Approximately three lines missing)
Her who is the great inundation of the deep,
Who . . s the *izi*-bird and the *lil*-fish, who . . . . ,
Who comes out from the *zipag*, who . . . . ,
The Lady of Sirar[a, Mother Nansh]e,
Of the sea, of its . . . . places,
Enki placed in charge.

He called the "two" rains, the water of the heaven,
Aligned them like floating clouds,
Drives (?) their (?) breath (of life) toward the horizon,
Turns (?) the hilly ground into fields.
Him who rides the great storm, who attacks with lightning (?),
Who closes the holy bolt in the "heart" of heaven,
The son of An, the *gugal* of the universe,
Ishkur . . , the son of An,
Enki placed in charge of them.

He directed the plow and the . . yoke,
The great prince Enki put the "horned oxen" in the . . . ,
Opened the holy furrows,
Made grow the grain in the cultivated field.
The lord who dons the diadem, the ornament of the high plain,
The robust, the farmer of Enlil,
Enkimdu, the man of the ditch and dike,
Enki placed in charge of them.

The lord called the cultivated field, put there the checkered grain,
Heaped up its . . grain, the checkered grain, the *innuba*-grain into
    piles,
Enki multiplied the heaps and mounds,
With Enlil he spread wide the abundance in the Land,

Her whose head and side are dappled, whose face is honey-covered,

The Lady, the procreatress, the vigor of the Land, the "life" of the black-heads,

Ashnan, the nourishing bread, the bread of all,

Enki placed in charge of them.

The great prince put the "net" upon the pickax, then directed the mold,

Fertilized the *agarin*, like good butter,

Him whose crushing pickax-tooth is a snake devouring the corpses,

. . . . ,

Whose . . mold directs . . . . ,

Kulla, the brick-maker (?) of the Land,

Enki placed in charge of them.

He built stalls, directed the purification rites,

Erected sheepfolds, put there the best fat and milk,

Brought joy to the dining halls of the gods,

In the vegetation-like plain he made prosperity prevail.

The trustworthy provider of Eanna, the "friend of An,"

The beloved son-in-law of the valiant Sin, the husband of holy Inanna,

The Lady, the queen of all the great *me*'s,

Who time and again commands the procreation of the . . . of Kullab,

Dumuzi, the divine *"ushumgal* of heaven," the "friend of An,"

Enki placed in [charge] of them.

He filled the Ekur, the house of Enlil, with possessions,

Enlil rejoiced with Enki, Nippur was joyous,

He fixed the borders, demarcated them with boundary stones,

Enki, for the Anunnaki,

Erected dwelling places in the cities,

Set up fields for them in the countryside,

The hero, the bull who comes forth out of the *hashur* (forest), who roars lion-(like),

The valiant Utu, the bull who stands secure, who proudly displays (his) power,

The father of the great city, the place where the sun rises, the gr[eat hera]ld of holy An,

The judge, the decision-maker of the gods,

Who wears a lapis lazuli beard, who comes forth from the holy heaven, the . . . . heaven,

Utu, the son born of [Ninga]l,

Enki placed in charge of the entire universe.

He wove the *mug*-cloth, directed the *temenos,*
Enki perfected greatly that which is woman's task,
For Enki, the people [. . d] the . . . -garment,
The tiara (?) of the palace, the jewel of the king,
Uttu, the trustworthy woman, the joyous (?),
Enki placed in charge of them.

Then all by her[self], having abandoned the royal scepter,
The woman, ... , the maid Inanna having abandoned the royal
  scepter
Inanna, to [her father] Enki,
Ente[rs] the house, (and) [humb]ly weeping, utters a plaint (?):
"The Anunnaki, the great gods—their fate
Enlil placed firmly in your [hand],
Me, the woman, [wh]y did you treat differently?
I, the holy Inanna,—where are [my prerogat]ives?
Aruru, [Enlil's sist]er,
Nintu, the queen [of the] moun[tain],
H[as taken for herself] her holy . . . . of lordship,
Has carried off for herself her . . . (and) leeks,
Has taken for herself her inlaid (?) *sila*-vessel of lapis lazuli,
Has carried off for herself her holy, pure *ala*-vessel,
She has become the midwife of the Land,
In her hand you have placed the born king, the born lord.
That sister of mine, the holy Ninisinna,
Has taken for herself the bright *unu*, has become the hierodule of An.
Has stationed herself near (?) An, utters the word which fills (?)
  heaven,
That sister of mine, the holy Ninmug,
Has taken for herself the gold chisel (and) the silver hammer (?),
Has become the met[alwor]ker (?) of the Land,
The [born] king, who dons the enduring diadem,
The born lord who puts crown on head, you have placed [in her
  hand].
That sister of mine, the holy Nidaba,
Has taken for herself the measuring rod,
Has fastened the lapis lazuli line (?) on her arm,
Proclaims all the great *me*'s,
Fixes the borders, marks off the boundaries—has become the scribe
  of the Land,
In her hands you have placed the food of the gods.
Nanshe, the lady, the lord—the holy . . . fell at her feet,

She has become the fishery inspector of the se[a] (?),
Fish, tasty, (and) . . . . ,
She presents to her [father] Enlil.
Me, the [woman], why did you treat differently?
I, holy Inanna, where are my prerogatives?"
(Approximately three lines missing)

. . . . his . . . . ,
"[E]nlil (?) . . . . ,
Has adorned (?) for you . . . . ,
You wear there the garment (?) 'might of the young lad,'
You have established the words spoken by the 'young lad,'
You have taken charge of the crook, staff, and wand of shepherdship,
Maid Inanna, what, what more shall we add to you?
Battles (and) onslaughts—of their oracles (?) you give (?) the answer,
In their midst, you who are not an *arabu*-bird, give (?) an unfavorable answer (?),
You twist the straight thread,
Maid Inanna, you straighten the twi[sted] thread,
You have fashioned garments, you wear garments,
You have woven *mug*-cloth, you have threaded the spindle,
In your . . . you have dyed (?) the many-colored . . thread.
Inanna, you have . . . . ,
Inanna, you have destroyed the indestructible, you have made perish the imperishable,
You have silenced (?) the . . with the 'timbrel (?) of lament,'
Maid Inanna, you have returned the *tigi*- and *adab*-hymns to their house.
You whose admirers do not grow weary to look at,
Maid Inanna, you who know not the distant wells, the fastening ropes (?);
Lo, the inundation has come, the Land is restored,
The inundation of Enlil has come, the Land is restored."
(Remaining nineteen lines destroyed)

To turn from myth to epic, there is little doubt that the Sumerians were the first to create and develop an epic literature consisting of heroic narrative tales in poetic form. Not unlike the ancient Greeks, Hindus, and Teutons, the Sumerians, early in their history, had passed through a heroic age, the spirit and temper of which are revealed in their epic lore. Impelled by the thirst for fame and name so characteristic of the ruling caste during a heroic age, the kings and princes had the bards and minstrels attached to the court improvise narrative poems or lays celebrating their adventures and achievements. These epic lays, with the primary object of providing entertainment at the frequent court banquets and feasts, were probably recited to the accompaniment of the harp or lyre.

None of the early heroic lays have come down to us in their original form, since they were composed when writing was either altogether unknown or, if known, of little concern to the illiterate minstrel. The written epics of the Greek, Indian, and Teutonic heroic ages date from much later days and consist of highly complex literary redactions in which only a selected number of the earlier lays are embedded and then only in a highly modified and expanded form. In Sumer, there is good reason to believe, some of the early heroic lays were first inscribed on clay five to six hundred years following the close of the heroic age after considerable transformation at the hands of priests and scribes.

The written epics of the three Indo-European heroic ages show a number of striking similarities in form and content. In the first place, all the poems are concerned primarily with individuals. It is the deeds and exploits of the individual hero that are the prime concern of the poet, not the fate or glory of the state or the community. While there is little doubt that some of the adventures celebrated in the poems have a historical basis, the poet does not hesitate to introduce unhistorical motifs and conventions, such as exaggerated notions of the hero's powers, ominous dreams, and the presence of divine beings. Stylistically, the epic poems abound in static epithets, lengthy repetitions, recurrent formulas, and descriptions that tend to be overleisurely and unusually detailed. Particularly noteworthy is the fact that all the epics devote considerable space to speeches. In all these respects, the pattern of Sumerian heroic poetry is similar to the pattern of Greek, Indian, and Teutonic epic material.

To be sure, there are a number of outstanding differences between the Sumerian epic material and that of the Greeks, Indians, and Teutons. For example, the Sumerian epic poems consist of individual, disconnected tales of varying length, each of which is restricted to a single episode. There is no attempt to articulate and integrate these episodes into a larger unit. There is relatively little characterization and psychological penetration in the Sumerian material. The heroes tend to be broad types, more or less undifferentiated, rather than highly personalized individuals. Moreover, the incidents and plot motifs are related in a rather static and conventionalized style; there is little of that plastic, expressive movement that characterizes such poems as Homer's *Iliad* and *Odyssey*. Mortal women play hardly any role in Sumerian epic literature, whereas they have a very prominent part in Indo-European epic literature. Finally, in the matter of technique, the Sumerian poet gets his rhythmic effects primarily from variations in the repetition patterns. He makes no use whatever of the meters or uniform line so characteristic of Indo-European epics. In spite of all these differences, it is hardly likely that a literary form so individual in style and technique as narrative poetry was created and developed independently and at different time intervals in Sumer, Greece, India, and Northern Europe. Since the narrative poetry of the Sumerians is by all odds the oldest of the four, it is not impossible that it was in Sumer that the epic genre first originated and that it spread from there to the lands around.

To date, we can identify nine Sumerian epic tales, varying in length from a little over one hundred to more than six hundred lines. Two of them revolve about the hero Enmerkar and may be entitled "Enmerkar and the Land of Aratta" and "Enmerkar and Ensukushsiranna" (see pages 269–73). Two center about the hero Lugalbanda, although Enmerkar plays a role in both; these may be entitled "Lugalbanda and Enmerkar" and "Lugalbanda and Mount Hurrum" (see pages 273–75). The remaining five revolve about the best known of Sumerian heroes, the hero without peer of the entire ancient Near East, Gilgamesh. Two of these, "Gilgamesh and the Bull of Heaven" and "The Death of Gilgamesh," are quite fragmentary. The remaining three are almost completely preserved. These are "Gilgamesh and Agga of Kish," which celebrates Gilgamesh as patriot and "defender of the realm"; "Gilgamesh and the Land of the Living," in which he plays the role of the adventurous dragon-killer, man's first St. George, as it were; and "Gilgamesh, Enkidu, and the Nether World," which depicts him as a surprisingly complicated individual: chivalrous, daring, tyrannical, loyal, plaintive, oracular, and inquisitive.

e poem "Gilgamesh and Agga" is the shortest of all Sumerian
ales; it consists of no more than one hundred fifteen lines.
ьrief as it is, however, it is of rather unusual interest. Its plot
deals with humans only; unlike all the other Sumerian epic tales,
it introduces no mythological motifs involving any of the Sumerian deities. The poem is historically significant; it sheds considerable new light on the early struggle of the Sumerian city-states.
Finally, it records the convening of man's first political assembly,
a "bicameral congress," which purportedly took place almost five
thousand years ago.

As is clear from the history of Sumer sketched in chapter ii,
Sumer, like Greece of a much later day, consisted of a number
of city-states vying for supremacy over the land as a whole. One
of the most important of these was Kish, a city which, according
to Sumerian legend, had received "kingship" from heaven immediately after the Flood. But in time, another city-state, Erech,
kept gaining in influence and power until it threatened Kish's
supremacy in Sumer. Agga, the last ruler of the Kish dynasty,
realized the danger and sent an ultimatum to Erech, where
Gilgamesh was "lord," to submit to Kish or suffer the consequences. Our poem begins with the arrival of Agga's envoys
bearing his ultimatum to Gilgamesh and the Erechites.

Gilgamesh is determined to fight rather than submit to Agga,
but first he has to get the approval of the citizens of Erech. He
therefore goes before "the convened assembly of the elders of
his city" with the urgent plea not to submit to Kish but to take
up arms and fight for victory. The "senators" are of a different
mind, however; they would rather yield to Kish and enjoy peace.
This decision is disappointing to Gilgamesh. He therefore comes
before the "convened assembly of the (younger) men of his city"
and repeats his plea. In a long statement ending with a eulogy
of Gilgamesh and encouraging words of victory, the assembly
of "men" declares for war and independence. Gilgamesh is now
well pleased, and in a speech to his faithful servant and constant
companion, Enkidu, shows himself highly confident of a victory
over Agga.

In a very short time, however—or as the poet puts it, "the days
were not five, the days were not ten"—Agga besieges Erech, and
in spite of their brave words, the Erechites are confounded. Gilga-

mesh then turns to the "heroes" of Erech and asks for a volunteer to go before Agga. One of them, Birhurturre by name, readily volunteers; he is confident that he can confound Agga's judgment.

But no sooner does Birhurturre pass through the city gates than he is seized, beaten, and brought before Agga. He begins to speak to Agga, but before he is finished, another hero, Zabardi-bunugga, ascends the wall. Upon seeing him, Agga asks Birhurturre if that is his king, Gilgamesh. When Birhurturre answers in the negative, Agga and his men are unimpressed and continue to besiege Erech and torture Birhurturre.

Now, however, Gilgamesh himself climbs the wall to meet Agga face to face, and the Erechites are terror-stricken. Upon learning from Birhurturre that this, at last, is his king, Agga, duly impressed, abandons the siege. Gilgamesh thereupon utters warm thanks to Agga for his generous attitude, and the poem closes with a paean of praise to Gilgamesh as the savior of Erech.

Here now is a tentative translation of the epic tale; much of it is still uncertain and obscure, but this is the best that can be done with it at the moment:

The envoys of Agga, the son of Enmebaraggesi
Proceeded from Kish to Gilgamesh in Erech,
The lord Gilgamesh before the elders of his city
Put the matter, seeks out their word:

"To complete the wells, to complete all the wells of the land,
To complete the wells, the small bowls of the land,
To dig the wells, to complete the fastening ropes—
Let us not submit to the house of Kish, let us smite it with weapons."

The convened assembly of the elders of his city
Answer Gilgamesh:
"To complete the wells, to complete all the wells of the land,
To complete the wells, the small bowls of the land,
To dig the wells, to complete the fastening ropes—
Let us submit to the house of Kish, let us not smite it with weapons."

Gilgamesh, the lord of Kullab,
Who performs heroic deeds for Inanna,
Took not the word of the elders of his city to heart.

A second time Gilgamesh, the lord of Kullab,
Before the "men" of his city, put the matter, seeks out their word:

"To complete the wells, to complete all the wells of the land,
 To complete the wells, the small bowls of the land,
 To dig the wells, to complete the fastening ropes,
 Do not submit to the house of Kish, let us smite it with weapons."

The convened assembly of the "men" of his city answer Gilgamesh:
"Of those who stand, those who sit,
 Of those who have been raised with the sons of kings,
 Of those who press the donkey's thigh,
 Who has their spirit!
 Do not submit to the house of Kish, let us smite it with weapons,
 Erech, the handiwork of the Gods,
 Eanna, the house ascending from heaven—
 It is the great gods who have fashioned its parts—
 Its great walls touching the clouds,
 Its lofty dwelling place established by An,
 You have cared for—you, king and hero.
 Conqueror, prince beloved of An,
 How should you fear his coming!
 That army is small, its rear totters,
 Its men hold not high their eyes."

Then, Gilgamesh, the lord of Kullab,
At the words of the "men" of his city his heart rejoiced, his spirit
    brightened,
He says to his servant Enkidu:
"Now, then, let the (peaceful) tool be put aside for the violence of
    battle,
 Let the battle weapons return to your side,
 Let them bring about fear and terror,
 He, when he comes—my great fear will fall upon him,
 His judgment will be confounded, his counsel will be dissipated."

The days were not five, the days were not ten,
Agga, the son of Enmebaraggesi besieged Erech,
Erech—its judgment was confounded.

Gilgamesh, the lord of Kullab,
Says to its heroes:
"My heroes with darkened faces,
 Who has heart, let him arise, I would have him go to Agga."

Birhurturre, the head man, to his king,
To his king, utters praise:

"I shall go to Agga,
His judgment will be confounded, his counsel will be dissipated."

Birhurturre went out through the city gate—
When Birhurturre had gone out through the city gate,
They seized him at the doors of the city gate,
Birhurturre—they crush his flesh,
Bring him before Agga,
Agga speaks to him.

He had not finished his words, when Zabardibunugga ascended the
  wall.
Agga saw him,
Says to Birhurturre:
"Slave, is that man your king?"

"That man is not my king,
Would that that man were my king,
That it were his strong forehead,
That it were his bison-like face,
That it were his lapis-like beard,
That it were his gracious fingers."

The multitude rose not, the multitude left not,
The multitude rolled not in the dust,
The foreigners, the lot of them, felt not overwhelmed,
The natives bit not the dust,
The prows of the longboats were not cut down,
Agga, the king of Kish, restrained not his troops,
They strike him, they beat him,
Birhurturre—they crush his flesh.

Following Zabardibunugga, Gilgamesh ascends the wall,
Terror fell upon the young and old of Kullab,
The doors of the city gate—they stationed themselves at their ap-
  proaches,
Enkidu went out through the city gate,
Gilgamesh peered over the wall,
Agga saw him:
"Slave, is that man your king?"
"That man is indeed my king."

No sooner had he said this,
The multitude rose, the multitude left,
The multitude rolled in the dust.

The foreigners, the lot of them, felt overwhelmed,
The natives bit the dust,
The prows of the longboats were cut down,
Agga, the king of Kish, restrained his troops.

Gilgamesh, the lord of Kullab,
Says to Agga:
"Agga, my lieutenant, Agga, my captain,
Agga, my army general,
Agga, you have filled with grain the fleeing bird,
Agga, you have given me breath, you have given me life,
Agga, you have brought the fugitive to your lap."

Erech, the handiwork of the god,
The great walls touching the sky,
The lofty dwelling established by An,
You have cared for, you, king and hero,
Conqueror, prince beloved of An,
Agga has set you free for the sake of Kish,
Before Utu, he has returned you the favor of former days,
Gilgamesh, lord of Kullab,
Your praise is good.

The motivating theme of the second of our Gilgamesh epic tales, "Gilgamesh and the Land of the Living," is man's anxiety about death and its sublimation in the notion of an immortal name. The plot of the tale is built around motifs and incidents pertinent to its predominantly poignant mood. Stylistically its somber tone is sustained and intensified by a skillful selection of the varied patterns of repetition and parallelism. Several of the crucial passages are still obscure. As of today, the story may be reconstructed as follows.

The lord Gilgamesh is burdened and oppressed with the thought of death. His heart is pained and his spirit heavy as he sees men die and perish in Erech, "dead bodies floating in the river's waters." Realizing bitterly that like all mortals, he, too, must die sooner or later, he is determined at least to raise up a name for himself before coming to his destined end. He therefore sets his heart on journeying to the far-distant "Land of the Living" to fell its famed cedars and bring them to Erech.

His mind made up, Gilgamesh informs Enkidu, his loyal servant, of his proposed undertaking. The latter advises him first to acquaint the sun-god, Utu, with his plan, for it is Utu who has charge of the "Land of the Living." Acting on this advice, Gilgamesh brings offerings to Utu and pleads for his support on the contemplated journey.

At first Utu is skeptical of Gilgamesh's qualifications, but Gilgamesh is insistent and repeats his plea in more persuasive language. Utu thereupon takes pity on him and promises to immobilize the seven weather demons who might otherwise have menaced Gilgamesh on his journey. Overjoyed, Gilgamesh gathers fifty volunteers from Erech—unattached men who have neither "house" nor "mother" and who are ready to follow him wherever he goes. After having weapons of bronze and wood prepared for himself and his companions, he and his followers set out from Erech to the "Land of the Living."

In the course of their journey they cross seven mountains, but it is not until they have crossed the seventh that Gilgamesh finds "the cedar of his heart." He fells it with his ax, and Enkidu cuts off its branches while his followers heap them up into a mound. But this act has aroused and disturbed Huwawa, the monster who guards the "Land of the Living," and he succeeds in having Gilgamesh fall into a heavy sleep or coma from which he is awakened only after considerable time and effort.

Thoroughly aroused by this unexpected delay, Gilgamesh swears by his mother, the goddess Ninsun, and by his father, the divine hero Lugalbanda, that he will not return to Erech until he has vanquished the monster Huwawa, be he man or god. Enkidu pleads with him to turn back, for he has seen this fearful monster and is certain that no one can withstand his attack. But Gilgamesh will have none of this caution. Convinced that if only they stand together no harm can befall them, he bids Enkidu put away fear and go forward with him.

The monster, however, is spying from his cedar house and makes frantic efforts to drive Gilgamesh off. But the latter refuses to be frightened, and seems to try to reassure Huwawa with the deceitful statement that he is bringing him gifts. In any case, we find Gilgamesh cutting down the seven trees which bar the approach to Huwawa's inner chamber, while his companions cut up their branches and arrange them in bundles at the foot of the mountain.

Gilgamesh has now come face to face with Huwawa. He slaps him gently on the cheek, throws a nose-ring over him, and fastens a rope about him. Whereupon Huwawa pleads tearfully with the sun-god, Utu, and humbles himself before Gilgamesh in an effort to obtain his freedom. Gilgamesh does indeed take pity on him, and in riddle-like phrases suggests to Enkidu that Huwawa be set free. But Enkidu advises against such generous actions as unwise and perilous. When the indignant Huwawa makes an insulting retort against Enkidu, the latter cuts off his neck.

The two heroes now bring Huwawa's severed head before Enlil, the king of the gods, eager, no doubt, for divine approbation and reward. But when Enlil sees Huwawa's severed head, he utters a curse which seems to doom them to eternal wandering over mountain and plain, scorched by the burning sun. Then perhaps as a protection against the mountains and forests and the wild beasts which prowl in them, Enlil presents Gilgamesh with what may perhaps be seven divine rays, known in Sumerian as *melam*'s. And on this rather obscure and ambivalent note, the poem comes to a close. A translation of the poem reads as follows:

The lord set his mind toward the "Land of the Living,"
The lord Gilgamesh set his mind toward the "Land of the Living,"
He says to his servant Enkidu:
"Enkidu, brick and stamp have not yet brought forth the fated end,
I would enter the 'land,' would set up my name,
In its places where names have been raised up, I would raise up my name,
In its places where names have not been raised up, I would raise up the names of the gods."

His servant Enkidu answers him:
"My master, if you would enter the 'land,' inform Utu,
Inform Utu, the valiant Utu,
The 'land,' it is Utu's charge,
The land of the felled cedar, it is the valiant Utu's charge,
Inform Utu."

Gilgamesh laid his hands on an all-white kid,
Pressed to his breast a speckled kid as an offering,
Placed in his hand the silver scepter of his command,
Says to heavenly Utu:
"Utu, I would enter the 'land,' be my ally,
I would enter the land of the felled cedar, be my ally."

Heavenly Utu says to him:
"True you are a princely warrior, but what are you to the 'land'?"

"Utu, a word I would speak to you, to my word your ear!
I would have it reach you, give ear to it!
In my city man dies, oppressed is the heart,
Man perishes, heavy is the heart,
I peered over the wall,
Saw the dead bodies floating in the river's waters,
As for me, I too will be served thus, verily it is so!
Man, the tallest, cannot reach to heaven,
Man, the widest, cannot cover the earth.
Brick and stamp have not yet brought forth the fated end,
I would enter the 'land,' would set up my name,
In its places where the names have been raised up, I would raise up
    my name,
In its places where the names have not been raised up, I would
    raise up the names of the gods.

Utu accepted his tears as an offering,
Like a man of mercy, he showed him mercy,
The seven weather heroes, the sons of one mother,
He brings into the caves of the mountains.

Who felled the cedar, was overjoyed,
The lord Gilgamesh was overjoyed,
Mobilized his city like one man,
Mustered (its men) like twin companions;
"Who has a house, to his house!
Who has a mother, to his mother!
Let single males who would do as I do stand at my side!"

Who had a house, to his house!
Who had a mother, to his mother!
Single males who would do as he did, fifty, stood at his side.

He directed his step to the house of the smiths,
Forged the sword, the crushing ax, his "might of heaven,"
He directed his step to the black forests of the plain,
Felled the willow, the apple, and the box tree,
The sons of his city who accompanied him took them in their hands,
The seven weather demons were brought into the caves of the moun-
    tains,

They cross the first mountain,
He found not the cedar of his heart,

After they had crossed the seventh mountain,
He found the cedar of his heart.

(Here a number of lines are destroyed, and it is not clear just
what happened. Perhaps Huwawa had become aware of the felling of the cedar, and had sent a strong sleep against Gilgamesh. In
any case, when the text becomes intelligible again, we find someone, probably Enkidu, trying to arouse Gilgamesh from his
slumber.)

He touches him, he rises not,
He speaks to him, he answers not,
"Who are asleep, who are asleep,
Gilgamesh, lord, son of Kullab,
How long will you sleep?
The land has become dark, it is full of shadows,
Dusk has brought forth its (dim) light,
Utu has gone with lifted head to his mother, Ningal,
O Gilgamesh, how long will you sleep!
Let not the sons of your city who have accompanied you
Stand waiting for you at the foot of the mountain,
Let not your mother who gave birth to you
Be driven off to the city's square.

He gave close heed,
Covered himself with his "word of heroism" like a garment,
Stretched about his breast the thirty-shekel garment he had carried
    in his hand,
Raised himself on the "great earth" like a bull,
Bit the dust, soiled his teeth:
"By the life of Ninsun, my mother who gave birth to me,
Of holy Lugalbanda, my father,
May I become as one who sits to be wondered at on the knee of
    Ninsun, my mother who gave birth to me."

A second time, moreover, he says to him:
"By the life of Ninsun, my mother who gave birth to me,
Of holy Lugalbanda, my father,
Until I will have vanquished that 'fellow,' whether he be a man,
Until I will have vanquished him, whether he be a god,
I shall not turn to the city my 'land'-turned step.

The faithful servant pleaded, clung to life,
Answers his master:

"My master, you who have not seen that 'fellow' are not terror-stricken,
I who have seen that 'fellow' am terror-stricken,
The warrior, his teeth are a dragon's teeth,
His face is a lion's face,
His roar is the onrushing flood water,
From his canebrake-devouring forehead, none escape.
My master, journey you to the land,
I will journey to the city,
Will tell your mother of your glory,
Let her squeal with laughter,
Then will tell her of your death,
Let her shed bitter tears."

"For me another will not die,
The loaded boat will not sink,
The three-ply cloth will not be cut,
On the wall no one will be overwhelmed,
House and hut, fire will not destroy,
Do you but help me, I will help you,
What can happen to us!
After it had sunk, after it had sunk,
After the Magan-boat had sunk,
After the boat 'Might of Magilum' had sunk,
All the living dwell in the 'boat of the living.'
Come, let us go forward, we will cast eyes upon him!
If when we go forward,
There be fear, there be fear, turn it back!
There be terror, there be terror, turn it back!"

"As your heart desires! Come, let us go forward!"

When they had not yet come within a distance of a quarter mile,
Huwawa stayed close to his cedar house,
Fastened his eye upon him, the eye of death,
Tossed his head against him, the guilt-covered head,
Cried out against him a terrifying cry.
Gilgamesh—his sinews, his feet trembled,
He was afraid,
He turned not back on the trodden path.

He (Huwawa) raised himself on his huge clawed feet,
Threw himself this way and that:
"Thick-maned, who wears the *uluhha*-garment,
Princely one, delight of the gods,

Irate bull, resolute in battle,
Who have made proud the mother who gave birth to you,
Who have made proud the nurse who suckled you, babe on lap,
Have no fear, put hand on ground."

Gilgamesh did not put hand on ground, said:
"By the life of Ninsun, my mother who gave birth to me,
Of holy Lugalbanda, my father,
You know well who lives in the 'land,'
For your little feet, I have made little shoes,
For your big feet, I have made big shoes."

He (Gilgamesh) himself uprooted the first,
The sons of his city who accompanied him,
Cut down the branches, bundle them up,
Lay them at the foot of the mountain,
After he himself had finished off the seventh, he approached his
    chamber,
Pressed him to his wall like the "wine-quay" snake,
Slapped his cheek as if he were pressing a kiss on him,
Tied a nose-ring on him, like a caught ox,
Fastened a rope about his arms like a caught warrior.

Huwawa—his teeth shook,
He clasped the lord Gilgamesh by the hand:
"I would say a word to Utu."
"Utu, I know not the mother who gave birth to me,
Know not the father who had reared me,
The 'land' gave birth to me, you have reared me."

He adjured Gilgamesh by Heaven, Earth, and Nether World,
Took him by the hand, groveled before him.

Then the princely Gilgamesh—his heart took pity on him,
He says to Enkidu, his servant:
"Enkidu, let the caught bird go to its home,
Let the caught warrior return to his mother's bosom."

Enkidu answers Gilgamesh:
"The tallest who has no judgment,
Fate will devour—Fate who knows no distinctions.
If the caught bird go to its home,
The caught warrior return to his mother's bosom,
You will not return to the city of your mother who gave birth to you."

Huwawa says to Enkidu:
"Hired man, hungry, thirsty, and obsequious,
Why did you speak ill of me to him!"

When he had thus spoken,
Enkidu, in his anger, cut off his neck,
Threw it into an arm-sack,
They brought it before Enlil,
Opened the arm-sack, drew out his (severed) head,
Placed it before Enlil.

Enlil looked at the head of Huwawa,
Was angered by the words of Gilgamesh:
"Why did you act thus!
Because you have laid hands on him,
Have destroyed his name,
May your faces be scorched,
May the food you eat be eaten by fire,
May the water you drink be drunk by fire."

(Then follows the presentation of the seven *melam*'s by Enlil to Gilgamesh and an obscure three-line passage which ends the poem.)

In the third of our epic tales, "Gilgamesh, Enkidu, and the Nether World," the hero is depicted in turn as a chivalrous knight, an oppressive bully, a despairing whiner, a counseling sage, a loyal master, and a saddened mortal anxious to learn about life in the nether world. His servant Enkidu plays the role of a faithful and courageous friend who, however, fails to heed his master's admonition at a crucial moment and loses his life as a consequence. And in the background stands Inanna, the Sumerian Aphrodite, with her irresistible tears and her ill-fated, death-tainted gifts.

The poem begins with a prologue consisting of two brief passages which have nothing to do with Gilgamesh and the plot of the story. The first passage concerns divine acts of creation, including the separation of heaven and earth, and is thus of major significance in Sumerian cosmogony and cosmology. The second part of the prologue depicts the struggle between Enki, the Sumerian Poseidon, and the nether world embodied in a monstrous dragon. It seems to have taken place not long after the separation of heaven and earth, after the goddess Ereshkigal had been abducted into the nether world by force—all of which calls to mind the Greek myth of the rape of Persephone. As to the outcome of this battle, we are left in the dark by the poet, who was anxious to get on with his Gilgamesh story, which, as far as it can be understood at present, runs as follows:

Once upon a time, a *huluppu*-tree (perhaps a willow), planted on the bank of the Euphrates and nurtured by its waters, was uprooted by the South Wind and carried away on the waters of the Euphrates. There it was seen by the goddess Inanna, who was roving about in the vicinity terrified—for some unexplained reason—by the "word" of An and Enlil, the two leading deities of the Sumerian pantheon. Inanna took the tree in her hand and brought it to her city Erech, where she planted it in her fruitful garden. There she tended it carefully in the hope that when the tree had grown big she could make of its wood a throne and a couch for herself.

Years passed. The tree matured and grew big, but its trunk stood bare without branch or leaf. For at its base, the snake who knows no charm had built its nest; in its crown, the fierce *Imdugud*-bird had placed its young; and in its middle, the vampire Lilith had built her house. And so Inanna, the lighthearted and ever joyful, shed bitter tears.

As dawn broke, and her brother, the sun-god, Utu, came forth from his "princely field," Inanna tearfully told him all that had befallen her *huluppu*-tree. But Utu would do nothing to help her.

Inanna then repeated her plaint to her "brother" Gilgamesh, and he decided to stand by her. He donned his armor weighing fifty minas, took in his hand the "ax of the road," and slew the snake who knows no charm at the base of the tree. Seeing this, the *Imdugud* fled with its young to the distant mountains, and Lilith tore down her house in the middle of the tree and fled to her desolate haunts. Gilgamesh and the men of Erech who accompanied him then cut down the tree and gave it to Inanna for her throne and couch.

What did Inanna do? From the base of the tree she fashioned a *pukku* (probably a drum); and from its crown, she fashioned a *mikku* (probably a drumstick); and then she presented both of them to Gilgamesh. But Gilgamesh used them to oppress the citizens of Erech, particularly, it seems, by summoning the young men to war and thus making widows of their wives. In any case, "because of the cries of the young maidens," to use the words of our poet, the *pukku* and the *mikku* fell into the "great dwelling," that is, the nether world. Gilgamesh did his best to retrieve them but was unsuccessful. And so he sat down at the *ganzir*, described as the "eye" of the nether world, and bemoaned his loss.

Now when Enkidu, Gilgamesh's servant, saw his master's distress, he bravely volunteered to descend to the nether world to bring up the *pukku* and the *mikku*. Whereupon Gilgamesh warned him of the nether world taboos that he must guard against "lest the cry of the nether world" hold him fast, particularly the cry for the mother of the healing god, Ninazu, who was lying asleep, altogether nude and uncovered, in the nether world. But Enkidu failed to heed the admonition of his master and so was held fast by the nether world and was unable to reascend to the earth.

Gilgamesh, distraught because of this new misfortune, proceeded at once to Nippur, the home of Enlil, the king of the gods. Tearfully he told him what had befallen Enkidu. But Enlil was unmoved and refused to help him.

Gilgamesh then proceeded to Eridu, the home of Enki, the god of wisdom, and repeated his plaint. Enki decided to help Gilgamesh, at least as far as was possible under the circumstances. At his order, the sun-god, Utu, opened a vent in the nether world through which Enkidu's ghost—for that was all that was now left of Enkidu—ascended to the earth. Master and servant—or rather the servant's ghost—embraced, and Gilgamesh proceeded to question Enkidu about what he had seen in the lower regions. And with this depressing colloquy, the poem which began with the happy days of creation comes to a far from happy end. Here now is the text of the poem as far as it is available to date:

In days of yore, in the distant days of yore,
In nights of yore, in the far-off nights of yore,
In days of yore, in the distant days of yore,

After in days of yore all things needful had been brought into being,
After in days of yore all things needful had been ordered,
After bread had been tasted in the shrines of the Land,

After bread had been baked in the ovens of the Land,
After heaven had been moved away from earth,
After earth had been separated from heaven,
After the name of man had been fixed,
After An had carried off heaven,
After Enlil had carried off earth,
After Ereshkigal had been carried off into the nether world as its
    prize—

After he had set sail, after he had set sail,
After the father had set sail for the nether world,
Against the king, the small were hurled,
Against Enki, the large were hurled,
Its small stones of the hand,
Its large stones of the dancing reeds,
The keel of Enki's boat,
Overwhelm in battle like an attacking storm,
Against the king, the water at the head of the boat,
Devours like a wolf,
Against Enki, the water at the rear of the boat,
Strikes down like a lion.

Once upon a time, a tree, a *huluppu,* a tree—
It had been planted on the bank of the Euphrates,
It was watered by the Euphrates—
The violence of the South Wind plucked up its roots,
Tore away its crown,
The Euphrates carried it off on its waters.

The woman, roving about in fear at the word of An,
Roving about in fear at the word of Enlil,
Took the tree in her hand, brought it to Erech:
"I shall bring it to pure Inanna's fruitful garden."

The woman tended the tree with her hand, placed it by her foot,
Inanna tended the tree with her hand, placed it by her foot,
"When will it be a fruitful throne for me to sit on," she said,
"When will it be a fruitful bed for me to lie on," she said.

The tree grew big, its trunk bore no foliage,
In its roots the snake who knows no charm set up its nest,
In its crown the *Imdugud*-bird placed its young,
In its midst the maid Lilith built her house—
The always laughing, always rejoicing maid,
The maid Inanna—how she weeps!

As light broke, as the horizon brightened,
As Utu came forth from the "princely field,"
His sister, the holy Inanna,
Says to her brother Utu:
"My brother, after in days of yore the fates had been decreed,
After abundance had sated the land,
After An had carried off heaven,
After Enlil had carried off earth,
After Ereshkigal had been carried off into the nether world as its
    prize—
After he had set sail, after he had set sail,
After the father had set sail for the nether world . . .

(Inanna now repeats the entire passage, ending with the following lines:)

The always laughing, always rejoicing maid,
I, the maid Inanna, how I weep!"

Her brother, the hero, the valiant Utu,
Stood not by her in this matter.

As light broke, as the horizon brightened,
As Utu came forth from the "princely field,"
His sister, the holy Inanna,
Speaks to the hero Gilgamesh:
"My brother, after in days of yore the fates had been decreed,
After abundance had sated the land,
After An had carried off heaven,
After Enlil had carried off earth,
After Ereshkigal had been carried off into the nether world as its
    prize—
After he had set sail, after he had set sail,
After the father had set sail for the nether world . . .

(Inanna again repeats the entire passage, ending with the following lines:)

The always laughing, always rejoicing maid,
I, the maid Inanna, how I weep."

Her brother, the hero Gilgamesh,
Stood by her in this matter,
He donned armor weighing fifty minas about his waist—
Fifty minas were handled by him like thirty shekels—

His "ax of the road"—
Seven talents and seven minas—he took in his hand,
At its roots he struck down the snake who knows no charm,
In its crown the *Imdugud*-bird took its young, climbed to the mountains,
In its midst the maid Lilith tore down her house, fled to the wastes.
The tree—he plucked at its roots, tore at its crown,
The sons of the city who accompanied him cut off its branches,
He gives it to holy Inanna for her throne,
Gives it to her for her bed,
She fashions its roots into a *pukku* for him,
Fashions its crown into a *mikku* for him.

The summoning *pukku*—in street and lane he made the *pukku* resound,
The loud drumming—in street and lane he made the drumming resound,
The young men of the city, summoned by the *pukku*—
Bitterness and woe—he is the affliction of their widows,
"O my mate, O my spouse," they lament,
Who had a mother—she brings bread to her son,
Who had a sister—she brings water to her brother.

After the evening star had disappeared,
And he had marked the places where his *pukku* had been,
He carried the *pukku* before him, brought it to his house,
At dawn in the places he had marked—bitterness and woe!
Captives! Dead! Widows!

Because of the cry of the young maidens,
His *pukku* and *mikku* fell into the "great dwelling,"
He put in his hand, could not reach them,
Put in his foot, could not reach them,
He sat down at the great gate *ganzir*, the "eye" of the nether world,
Gilgamesh wept, his face turns pale:
"O my *pukku*, my *mikku*,
My *pukku* with zest irresistible, with rhythm irrepressible—
If only my *pukku* had once been in the carpenter's house,
If only it had been with the carpenter's wife, like the mother who gave birth to me,
If only it had been with the carpenter's child, like my little sister—
My *pukku*, who will bring it up from the nether world!
My *mikku*, who will bring it up from the nether world!"

Enkidu, his servant, says to him:
"My master, why do you weep!
Why is your heart grievously sick!
I will bring up your *pukku* from the nether world,
I will bring up your *mikku* from the 'eye' of the nether world!"

Gilgamesh says to Enkidu:
"If now you will descend to the nether world,
A word I speak to you, take my word,
Instruction I offer you, take my instruction:

"Wear not clean clothes,
Lest the beadles come against you like an enemy.
Anoint not yourself with the beaker's sweet oil,
Lest at its smell they crowd about you.
Throw not the throw-stick in the nether world,
Lest those struck by the throw-stick surround you.
Carry not a staff in your hand,
Lest the shades flutter all about you.
Tie not sandals on your feet,
Raise not a cry in the nether world,
Kiss not the wife you love,
Strike not the wife you hate,
Kiss not the child you love,
Strike not the child you hate,
Lest the cry of the nether world hold you fast—
The cry for her who is sleeping, who is sleeping,
For the mother of Ninazu, who is sleeping,
Whose holy body no garment covers,
Whose holy breast no cloth drapes."

Enkidu descended to the nether world,
Heeded not the words of his master—
He wore his clean clothes,
The beadles came against him like an enemy.
He anointed himself with the beaker's sweet oil,
At its smell they crowded about him.
He threw the throw-stick in the nether world,
Those struck by the throw-stick surrounded him.
He carried a staff in his hand,
The shades fluttered all about him.
He put sandals on his feet,
Raised a cry in the nether world,

Kissed the wife he loved,
Struck the wife he hated,
Kissed the child he loved,
Struck the child he hated,
The cry of the nether world held him fast—
The cry for her who is sleeping, who is sleeping,
For the mother of Ninazu, who is sleeping,
Whose holy body no garment covers,
Whose holy breast no cloth drapes.

Enkidu was not able to ascend from the nether world—
Not fate holds him fast,
Not sickness holds him fast,
The nether world holds him fast.
Not demon Nergal, the unsparing, holds him fast,
The nether world holds him fast.
In battle, the "place of manliness" he fell not,
The nether world holds him fast.

Then went Gilgamesh to Nippur,
Stepped up all alone to Enlil in Nippur, wept:
"Father Enlil, my *pukku* fell into the nether world,
My *mikku* fell into *Ganzir*,
I sent Enkidu to bring them up,
The nether world holds him fast.
Not fate holds him fast,
Not sickness holds him fast,
The nether world holds him fast.
Not demon Nergal, the unsparing, holds him fast,
The nether world holds him fast.
In battle, the 'place of manliness,' he fell not,
The nether world holds him fast."

Father Enlil stood not by him in this matter,
He went to Eridu,
Stepped up all alone to Enki in Eridu, wept:
"Father Enki, my *pukku* fell into the nether world,
My *mikku* fell into *ganzir*,
I sent Enkidu to bring them up,
The nether world holds him fast.
Not fate holds him fast,
Not sickness holds him fast,
The nether world holds him fast.
Not demon Nergal, the unsparing, holds him fast,

The nether world holds him fast.
In battle, the 'place of manliness,' he fell not,
The nether world holds him fast."

Father Enki stood by him in this matter,
Says to the hero, the valiant Utu,
The son born of Ningal:
"Open now the vent of the nether world,
Raise Enkidu's ghost out of the nether world."

He opened the vent of the nether world,
Raised Enkidu's ghost out of the nether world.
They embrace, they kiss,
They sigh, they hold counsel:
"Tell me, what saw you in the nether world?"
"I will tell you, my friend, I will tell you."

The poem ends with a rather poorly preserved question-answer colloquy between the two friends concerned with the treatment of the dead in the nether world.

Hymnography—to turn from epic to hymn—was a carefully cultivated, highly sophisticated art in Sumer. Scores of hymns, varying in length from less than fifty to well-nigh four hundred lines, have come down to us, and there is every reason to believe that this is only a fraction of the hymns composed in Sumer throughout the centuries. To judge from their contents, the extant Sumerian hymns may be divided into four major categories: (1) hymns extolling the gods; (2) hymns extolling kings; (3) hymnal prayers in which paeans of praise to the gods are interspersed with blessings and prayers for kings; and (4) hymns glorifying Sumerian temples.

The divine hymns are in the form of either an address by the poet to the deity or a glorification of the deity and his achievements in the third person. Among the longer and more important are the following: (1) a hymn to Enlil noteworthy for its poetic summary of civilization's debt to his beneficence; (2) a hymn to the god Ninurta addressed to him not only under that name but under the names Pagibilsag and Ningirsu as well; (3) a hymn to the goddess Inanna by Enheduanna, long known as the daughter of Sargon the Great; (4) a hymn to Inanna as the Venus star, noteworthy for its description of the *hieros-gamos* ceremony celebrating the union of the goddess and the king Iddin-Dagan of

Isin on New Year's Day; (5) a hymn to Inanna as the goddess of
war and wrath; (6) a hymn to Utu as the god of justice who
regulates and supervises the world order; (7) a hymn to the
goddess Nanshe as the guardian of man's ethics and morals; (8) a
hymn to Hendursag, Nanshe's especially selected vizier in charge
of judging man's deeds and misdeeds; (9) a hymn to the goddess
Ninisinna as the "great physician of the black-heads," the patron-
deity of the art of medicine and healing; (10) a hymn to Ninkasi
as the goddess of intoxicating drink; (11) a hymn to Nidaba as
the goddess of writing, accounting, and wisdom; and (12) a hymn
to the goddess Nungal, the daughter of Ereshkigal, as judge and
protector of the "black-heads."

Of the hymns exalting kings, the most important group belongs
to Shulgi, the second ruler of the Third Dynasty of Ur; five of
them are now restorable wholly or in large part. Two hymns sing
the praises of Shulgi's father, Ur-Nammu. There are quite a number of hymns celebrating the rulers of the Isin dynasty that followed the Third Dynasty rulers, particularly Iddin-Dagan,
Ishme-Dagan, and Lipit-Ishtar. Most of the royal hymns are ex-
travagantly self-laudatory; the kings themselves are purported to
have uttered grandiloquent, inflated, and vain-sounding paeans
of self-glorification without hesitation and inhibition. This unusual
and, from our point of view, rather unworthy kingly behavior is
not without psychological significance; it fits in with the drive for
prestige and superiority characteristic of Sumerian behavior in
general (see chapter vii).

A high favorite with the Sumerian hymnographers was the type
of composition in which paeans to the gods were interlarded with
blessings and prayers for the kings. Except, rather unexpectedly,
for the mother-goddess, Ninhursag, practically all the major deities are represented in this hymnal category: An, Enlil, Enki,
Nanna, Utu, Ninurta, Nergal, Inanna, Bau, and Ninisinna. As for
the kings blessed and prayed for, all the rulers of the Third
Dynasty of Ur as well as the earlier rulers of the First Dynasty of
Isin are represented. One of these hymns is addressed to the goddess Bau as the friend and supporter of Eannatum of Lagash,
which indicates rather conclusively that this hymnal type was
already current in Sumer in pre-Sargonic days.

Finally, the temple hymns are represented by a song of praise to the Ekur, Enlil's temple in Nippur; by a hymn to the temple of the goddess Ninhursag at Kesh; and best of all, by a composition of over four hundred lines containing brief hymns to all the more important temples of Sumer and Akkad. One of the most noteworthy of all extant temple hymns is that inscribed on the long known Gudea cylinders, which consists of close to fourteen hundred lines of text and celebrates the rebuilding of the Eninnu temple in Lagash.

Turning to the formal aspects of Sumerian hymnography, it is worth noting that hymn-writing had become so sophisticated a literary art in Sumer that it was subdivided into various categories by the ancient poets themselves, and many of the extant hymns are ascribed to their appropriate categories by a special subscription at the end of the composition. The common Sumerian word for hymns is *sir*, which may or may not have anything to do with the Hebrew *shir*. Some of the categories of *sir* are *sir-hamun*, perhaps "harmony hymns"; *sir-namnar*, "musical hymns"; *sir-namgala*, "hymns of *gala*-ship"; *sir-namursagga*, "hymns of heroship"; and *sir-namsipad-inanna-ka*, "hymns of shepherdship of (the goddess) Inanna," the shepherd in this case being, no doubt, the god Dumuzi. Hymnal categories that seem to be named from the musical instruments accompanying them are *tigi*, probably a hymn accompanied by lyre; *irshemma*, perhaps a hymn accompanied by drum; and *adab*, a hymn accompanied by some still unidentified stringed instrument. The *tigi* and *adab* hymns are broken up by the ancient poets into sections bearing the notations *sagarra* and *sagidda*, which seem to mean literally "the set strings (?)" and "the long strings," respectively—further proof that these hymns were accompanied by musical instruments. The *adab* hymns also include special sections bearing the notations *barsud* and *shabatuku*, the meaning of which is still unknown; they usually end with a three-line prayer for the king, designated as *urunbim*, a rubric of uncertain meaning. Both the *adab* and the *tigi* categories also make use of an antiphon consisting of from one to four lines, something like a choral refrain, bearing the still obscure notation which may tentatively be read *izkig*. Finally, there are a number of hymns that are divided into stanzas with the notation *kirugu*, "genuflexion" (?), which is often followed by the refrain-like passage designated as *izkig*.

The Sumerian lamentations are primarily of two kinds: those bewailing the destruction of Sumerian cities and city-states and those lamenting the death of the god Dumuzi or one of his counterparts. Of the former kind, two of the best preserved concern the destruction of Ur. A third concerns the destruction of Nippur; it begins as a lament but ends on a note of joy with the restoration of the city by Ishme-Dagan of Isin. As for the Dumuzi laments, they range in size from long compositions of over two hundred lines to brief laments of less than fifty lines. Quite a few of these Dumuzi texts have been published to date. But there is still no trustworthy translation available for many of them, especially those written in a phonetic rather than in the historical orthography, which makes even word-division uncertain, let alone meaning and interpretation.

Related to the lamentation is the elegy or funeral song. This Sumerian literary genre was entirely unknown until 1957 when, in the course of a visit to the Soviet Union, I came across a tablet in the Pushkin Museum inscribed with two such elegies. A detailed edition of the text was prepared with the co-operation of the Pushkin Museum and appeared in 1960. The sketch of the content of the two poems and the translation presented here are based on this study.

The tablet, which was no doubt inscribed in the ancient city of Nippur about 1700 B.C.—it may, of course, have first been composed considerably earlier—was divided by the ancient scribe into four columns. It contains two compositions of unequal size separated by a ruled line. The first and longer of the two consists of 112 lines of text, whereas the second has only 66 lines. Following the text of the two compositions, and separated from it by a double line, is a three-line colophon giving the title of each of the compositions as well as the number of lines which they contain individually and together. Both of the compositions consist in large part of funeral dirges uttered by a single individual named Ludingirra. In the first, Ludingirra laments the death of his father, Nanna, who, if I have understood the relevant passage correctly, had died from wounds received in some kind of physical struggle. In the second dirge, the same Ludingirra bewails the death of his good and beloved wife, Nawirtum, who seems to have died a natural death.

In both compositions, the dirges are preceded by prologues which serve to set the scene. The prologue to the first dirge consists of 20 lines and is therefore relatively brief compared with the rest of the composition. The prologue to the second dirge, however, consists of 47 lines and is therefore about two-and-a-half times as long as the remainder of the poem. Stylistically, both compositions make use of highly poetic diction characterized by various types of repetition, parallelism, choral refrains, similes, and metaphors. The deeds and virtues of the deceased, as well as the grief and suffering of those left behind, are sung in inflated and grandiloquent phrases; but this is an understandable feature of funeral songs and orations the world over and at all times.

The prologue to the first composition begins with a rather prosaic two-line statement which seems to relate that a son who had gone away to a distant land was called back to Nippur where his father lay mortally sick. Six lines follow, each of which describes the father with some highly flattering phrases and ends with the refrain "(he) had become ill." These lines are followed by a passage depicting the intensity of the father's illness and suffering and his eventual death. News of the catastrophe reaches the son "on a distant journey"; whereupon, we may assume, he returns to Nippur and, overcome with grief, he writes the lament which follows.

The dirge itself begins by depicting the desperate grief of the deceased's wife, who was presumably Ludingirra's mother, of an unnamed *lukur*-priestess of the god Ninurta, of an unnamed *en*-priestess of the god Nusku, and of the deceased's sons and their brides. Following what seems to be a brief prayer for Nanna's welfare, the dirge continues with a description of the mourning for the deceased by his daughters, by the elders and the matrons of Nippur, and by his slaves. At this point, rather surprisingly, what seems to be a one-line prayer involving the eldest son of the deceased is interposed. Following this prayer comes a passage containing a number of curses against Nanna's murderer and the latter's offspring. The dirge concludes with a series of prayers: for the welfare of the deceased in the nether world, for his favorable treatment at the hands of his personal god and the god of his city, and for the well-being of his wife, children, and kin.

In the second elegy it is the prologue to the dirge that, as men-

tioned earlier, takes up the greater part of the poem. It begins
with the announcement of Nawirtum's death in a series of par-
allel-phrased similes and metaphors and continues with a description of the ensuing grief on the part of the inhabitants of Nippur.
Following two very obscure passages—the first of which seems to
describe the interruption of important religious rites in Nippur
as a result of Nawirtum's death—Nawirtum's husband, Ludingirra,
comes on the scene to utter his mournful lament. The dirge itself
may be divided into two parts: a bitter lament for Ludingirra's
bereavement, consisting of a succession of parallel clauses, each
followed by an identical refrain; and a series of prayers for the
deceased and for her husband, children, and household.

As for the importance and significance of the two elegies, it
needs no saying that they have considerable intrinsic merit as
literary efforts; they attempt to convey in imaginative poetic form
the deep human passions and emotions generated by the tragic
loss, through inevitable death, of the closest and dearest of kin.
From the point of view of the history of literature, they are our
first precious examples of the elegiac genre—they precede by
many centuries the Davidic dirges for Saul and Jonathan and
the Homeric laments for Hector which close the *Iliad* on so sad
a note—and should therefore prove to be invaluable for purposes
of comparative study. The first of the two poems is also of some
importance for our understanding of Sumerian cosmology; for
from it we learn that the Sumerian sages—or at least some of them
—held the beliefs that the sun, after setting, continued its journey
through the nether world at night and that the moon-god, Nanna,
spent his "day of sleep," that is, the last day of each month, in the
nether world. Most important of all, the two poems, and particularly the first, shed considerable new light on the Sumerian ideas
about life in the nether world. Thus, for example, we now learn
for the first time of the "judgment of the dead" and that, as might
have been expected, it was the sun-god, Utu—the judge par excellence of mankind—who made the decisions; we also learn that
the moon-god, Nanna, in some way "decreed the fate" of the dead
on the day he visited the nether world.

As for the authorship of the two elegies and the motivation for
their composition, there is little doubt that the writer of the poems
was one of the *ummia*'s who worked and taught in the Sumerian

edubba and that the compositions themselves were used as texts to be studied and copied by the students of the *edubba*. In fact, one of the lines of the first elegy has now been found inscribed on a small practice-tablet excavated at Nippur in the handwriting of both teacher and pupil. On the surface, the author writes as if he himself were merely composing the prologues to the two poems, while the dirges themselves are presumably being given as the *ipsissima verba* of Ludingirra. Moreover, at least in the first elegy, the author states that Ludingirra had written down his lament, which might lead to the presupposition that the author had, in fact, a copy of Ludingirra's dirges before him. But all this seems rather unlikely, especially in view of the uniformity of style that characterizes the prologues and the dirges. All in all, one is left with the impression that the two elegies are purely imaginative creative efforts on the part of a poet moved by the aesthetic urge to compose an eloquent and moving funeral chant, just as he might have been inspired, for example, to compose a mythological or epic poem.

Here now is a literal translation of the two elegies, with all the question marks and breaks, awkward as these are; parts of the text are unfortunately quite difficult and obscure:

First Elegy

[A father] sent to a far-off place for his son,
The son who had gone to the distant place did not [neglect] the instructions "of those days."
The city-dwelling father had become ill,
The precious brilliant, found (only) in remote mountains, had become ill,
Who was fair (and) attractive (?) of speech, who . . . . , had become ill,
Who had an attractive (?) figure as well as (?) an (attractive) head, had become ill,
Who was wise of plan, highly qualified for the assembly, had become ill,
Who was a man of truth, god-fearing, had become ill,
Had become ill—and had not eaten—was languishing away (?),
With mouth (?) shut tight (?) he tasted no food, lay famished,
Like a tablet (?), like a kid (?), he . . . . ,
The hero, the leader (?), [moves (?)] not a foot (?),

From (?) his sick ... he was consumed with wail[ing (?)] for (?) his
  children (?),
Heart anguished, [shaken (?)] with wailing,
The scholar died in Nippur (of wounds received) in an attack (?).

This matter reached his son on a distant journey,
Like a son who had not been separated (?) from his father,
He returned (?) not the garment (?) which had been sent (?) to him,
The son shed tears, threw himself to the dust, utters for him a "hymn
  of song,"
Ludingirra out of his burning (?) heart writes a lament:
"O father, who has died in an attack (?),
O Nanna, who through the evil planned against him, has been carried
  off to the nether world,
Your wife—lo, formerly (?) she was his wife, (but) now she is a
  widow—
Wheels (?) about you like a whirlwind, ... for joy ... ,
Like a ... she acts for you, (yes) you—gone is her reason,
She has set up [a cry (of pain)] as if she were about to give birth,
Turns the ... , [moans (?)] like a cow,
... has issued a cry (of pain), sheds tears,
Has covered up its (?) ... , and (?) has taken (?) what is just (?),
... in darkness (?) ... ,
Who gathers (?) ... ,
Touches you, the (?) heart ... is (?) heavy (?).

"Who (?) ... rises (?) ... at dawn (?),
From among the ... who dwell in ... , the *lukur*-priestess of Ni-
  nurta (?) from the ... has thrown herself [to the dust (?)],
Like a mourning (?) god (?), she ... ,
Her shouts (?) (of anguish) ... evil,
In (?) the midst (?) of the cloister (?) she (?) ... , ... ,
Has made (?) the wide(spread) [pe]ople (?) ... grain, water (?).

"The confusion (?) of (?) battles (?) the *en*-priestess of
  Nusku (?) ... ,
... tears apart (?) for you (?), for you her (?) ... , ... ,
... ,
... from your lap ... ,
... ,
... .

"Your sons [who (?)] were treated (?) like king's sons,
Whatever they (?) eat ... ,
Whatever they (?) drin[k] ... ,

Honey (and) ghee they (?) . . . ,
The table they (?) load (?) with (?) oil (for) you,
The tears which they shed for him are piteous (?) tears,
Their mourning (?) for him is (that) of loving (and) pure-hearted
   (ones),
Like shriveled grain they . . .
The birdlings return (?) . . . , raise (?) . . . ,
The brides of (?) your sons, who have said: 'Where, (oh) where is he
   now?'—
Over them has fallen (?) your . . . ,
In their . . . has been silenced (?) for you—
On the laps of the (members of the) house(hold)(?) . . . for you,
Your . . . sweet sounds . . . sleep . . . ,
Like . . . . has been . . . ,
The . . . lament for you (?) . . . does not (?) cease.

"O my father, [may] your heart [be at rest],
O Nanna, [may] your spirit [be pleased],
The *en*'s (and) *ensi*'s . . . ,
[May (?)] those who have escaped the hand of death . . . —
The hand of death has been . . . in (?) their (?) . . . . , [no] one . . . ,
Death is the favor (?) of the gods, the place where the fate is
   decreed . . . —
May your offspring . . . your knee (?).
Your daughters have . . . . for you in their (?) . . . ,
The elders of your city [have set up (?)] mourning (?) [for you],
The matrons of your city have . . . . for you,
The slave [by (?)] the millstone . . . has [shed (?)] tears for you,
The house(hold) where (?) he (?) is placed (?) . . . ,
He has . . . silver (?), he has acquired (?) grain, he has [multiplied
   (?)] with possessions.

"May the eldest son [establish (?)] for you your . . . firm foundations.
"The man who killed you, [who (?)] like one who . . . the heart . . . ,
Who assaulted (?) you, (yes) you, with cruel strength—
True (?) vengeance belongs to the king (?), the shepherd, your (per-
   sonal) god,
True (?) counsel belongs to Utu—
That man, [ma]y he be a man accursed, death [shall be his lot],
His bones [let no] one [bury (?)],
His offspring, ... , [may] their name [be eradicated (?)],
May their possessions like flying (?) . . . sparrows (?) . . . .

"May the . . . . of the Land (?) . . .

Bring (?) your favorable . . . words, may they make you content,

O Nanna, may your spirit (?) be pleased, may your heart be at rest,

Utu, the great lord (?) of Hades,

After turning the dark places to light, will judge your case (favorably),

May Nanna decree your fate (favorably) on the "day of sleep,"

[May] Nergal, the Enlil of the nether world, ... before (?) it (?),

May the bread-eating heroes (?) utter your name, . . . food,

[May] the . . . of the nether world . . . pity . . . ,

May (?) the . . . -drinkers [satisfy (?)] your thirst with fresh water,

[May (?)] . . . . ,

In strength [may (?)] Gilgamesh . . . your (?) heart (?),

[May] Nedu and Etana [be] your allies,

The gods of the nether world will [utter (?)] prayers for you,

May your (personal) god say 'Enough!' May he [decree (?)] (favorably) your fate,

May the god of your city . . . for you a . . . heart,

May he [annul] for you (your) promises (?) (and) debts,

May he [erase] the guilt of the house(hold) [from] the accounts (?),

[May he bring to nought] the evil planned against you . . . ,

May those you leave behind be happy, [may] . . . ,

May the . . . take (?) . . . ,

May the (good) spirits (and) genii [protect (?)] your . . . ,

May the children you begot be written (?) down (?) for leader-sh[ip(?)],

May (all) your daughters marry,

May your wife stay well, may your kin multiply,

May prosperity (and)well-being (?) envelop (them) day in, day out,

In your . . . may beer, wine, (and all) good things never cease,

May the invocation (?) of your (?) house(hold) be forever the invocation (?) of your (personal) (?) god!"

Second Elegy

An evil day [came (?)] upon the matron in (?) her (?) . . . ,

Upon the fair lady, the well-favored matron, the evil eye [came (?)],

Upon the birdling overstepping (?) its nest the net has [fallen] (?),

The fecund mother, the mother of (many) children is [held (?) fast (?)] by the snare (?),

The fawn-colored cow, the fertile (?) wild cow, [lies (?) crushed (?)] like a *gakkul*-vessel,

Nawirtum, the fertile (?) wild cow [lies (?) crushed (?)] like a
  gakkul-vessel,
She who did not (ever) say "I am sick!" was not cared for,
Who did not (ever) . . . did not . . . the place divine (?),
Like their (?) resting place, their (?) hurled . . . was not . . .

Nippur is cloud-bedecked (?), in the city . . . ,
Over the multitudes has fallen a cry (?) of woe (?) . . . ,
. . . . ,
. . . . ,
Pity for her whose life has come to an end overcomes (?) them,
At her being (?) laid (?) like a golden statue they (?) are
  anguished (?)—
He who looks upon her, (how) will he not mourn (?)?
The weeping women . . . . ,
The best (?) songs of the bards (?) of sweet words
Are turned everywhere into laments (and) moans (?).

Because (?) . . . had been returned (?), [they (?) utter (?)] it (?)
  as a song for her,
Because (?) from her small . . .
The . . . -stone . . . . ,
Because (?) in the lap of her husband (her) days were not prolonged,
  (and so) weeping ceased not,
Because (?) from his . . . Ninurta returned (?) not the joyful shout,
Because (?) his beloved *en*-priestess entered not the *gipar*,
The donkey mare which had been chosen (?) as (?) a wife (?) is not
  accepted (?) as a sacrifice (?).

Because (?) . . . was brought to an end (?) at his side,
He (?) rises (?) in (?) greatness (and (?)) favor, utters a lament
  for her,
To her (?) mother who had given birth to her (?), he . . . , he . . . .
  for her,
Their (?) shares (?), their (?), he makes for her into (?) a . . . . ,
Their souls (?) have come forth before (?) her, their evil (?) bodies
  (?) (are (?)) rent (?) apart (?),
Their (?) . . , workers (?), (and (?)) kin are . . . . , their (?) . . .
  [are (?)] . . . .

Because (?) . . . from the knee (?) . . . . ,
They did [n]ot (?) stand . . . ,
(All) their nursemaids were . . . . ,
. . . . ,

Like men enraged, stones . . . . sick (?),
From her (?) city the light from above . . . did not increase (?).

Then [her] belo[ved] husband all alone . . . . ,
In his city, in Nippur, the city (?) . . . . ,
Ludingirra, her [belo]ved husband, all al[one] . . . . ,
In his city, in Nippur, the city (?) . . . . ,
Approached her with (?) suffering (?) heart (?) [in (?)] . . . , the
    great dwelling place,
They (?) took (?) his (?) hand, their (?) hearts were overwhelmed (?),
His . . . was cut off (?) from nourishment, his breath was stifled (?),
[Moans (?)] like a cow he uttered, he who had no . . . . -garments (?),
Their (?) . . . . he wears, he weeps before her:

"O where now is . . . ! I would cry out to you,
Where now are (the goddess) Meme (and) the genii, the
    alluring (?)! I would cry out to you,
Where now is the [comely (?)] mouth (?), the attractive (?) mouth
    (?), the gracious mouth (?)! I would cry out to you,
Where now is my attractive (?) weapon (?), the gloriously (?) fash-
    ioned (?) quiver! I would cry out to you,
Where now is that which brightens the face (?), my princely counsel!
    I would cry out to you,
Where now is my . . . . , my precious brilliant! I would cry out to you,
Where now are my sweet songs which rejoice the heart! I would cry
    out to you,
Where now is my attractive (?) weapon (?), the golden quiver which
    brightens the spirit! I would cry out to you,
Where now are my dancing, 'hand-lifting,' (and) frolicking (?)! I
    would cry out to you.

"May your way (of life) not perish (from memory), may your name
    be pronounced (in days to come),
May the guilt of your house(hold) be erased, may your debts be
    annulled,
May your husband stay well, may he make good as (both) man of
    valor (and) elder (?),
May the fate of your children be propitious, may well-being be in store
    for them,
May your house(hold) move to the fore, may its future be ample,
May Utu bring forth for you light from the nether world—he who . . . ,
May Ninkurra . . . by (?) you, may she raise you high,
Because the bitter storm has been turned (?) against you, may the
    horizon turn (?) it back (?),

The demon who has brought his hand against you—may a cruel curse
be uttered (?) against him,
Because the kindly matron lies like an ox in her splendor (?)—[bit]ter
is the lament for you!"

Historiography, as had already been noted earlier in this book,
was hardly a favorite literary form among the Sumerian men of
letters, and the compositions about to be listed can be designated
as "historiographic" only by generously stretching the accepted
meaning of the word. The longest and best preserved of the
Sumerian "historiographic" compositions is "The Curse of Agade:
The Ekur Avenged," which attempts to explain the catastrophic
destruction of the city by the barbaric Gutian hordes (see pages
62–66). Another well-preserved historiographic document revolves
about the defeat of these same Gutians by Sumer's "savior,"
Utuhegal. A third and rather brief, but historically quite significant, document concerns primarily the successive restorations of
the Tummal, Ninlil's shrine in the city of Nippur (see pages 46–
49). There are also tablets and fragments which indicate that a
series of legendary tales had existed clustering about Sargon the
Great and his deeds, particularly those relating to his contemporaries Ur-Zababa and Lugalzaggesi; but as yet not enough of this
material has been recovered to provide us with a clear picture of
its contents. Finally there is the composition concerned with Ur-
Nammu's life in the nether world, which may have been his-
toriographically motivated (see pages 130–31).

The last group of Sumerian literary documents to be considered in this chapter is the "wisdom" compositions, consisting of
disputations, essays long and short, and collections of precepts
and proverbs. The disputation, a high favorite among the Sumerian men of letters, is the prototype and predecessor of the literary
genre known as "tenson," which was popular in Europe in late
antiquity and in the Middle Ages. Its major component is a debate, a battle of words, between two opposing protagonists usually
personifying a pair of contrasting animals, plants, minerals, occupations, seasons, or even man-made tools and implements. The
argument, which goes back and forth several times between the
two rivals, consists primarily of "talking up" in most flattering
terms one's own value and importance and of "talking down"
those of the opponent. All of this is written in poetic form, how-

ever, since the Sumerian men of letters were the direct heirs of
the illiterate minstrels of much earlier days, and poetry came to
them more naturally than prose. The disputation composition was
often rounded out formally with an appropriate mythological introduction which told of the creation of the protagonists and
with a fitting ending in which the dispute was settled in favor of
one or the other of the rivals by divine decision.

As of today, seven such disputations are known: (1) "The
Dispute between Summer and Winter," (2) "The Dispute between Cattle and Grain," (3) "The Dispute between the Bird
and the Fish," (4) "The Dispute between the Tree and the Reed,"
(5) "The Dispute between Silver and Mighty Copper," (6) "The
Dispute between the Pickax and the Plough," and (7) "The Dispute between the Millstone and the *gulgul*-stone." Except for the
last named, these compositions range in size from close to two
hundred to just over three hundred lines. The two largest and
best preserved are "The Dispute between Summer and Winter"
and "The Dispute between Cattle and Grain"; the following
sketch of their contents will illustrate the style and structure, the
tone and flavor of the genre as a whole.

"The Dispute between Summer and Winter" begins with a
mythological introduction which informs us that Enlil, the leading
deity of the Sumerian pantheon, has set his mind to bring forth
all sorts of trees and grain and to establish abundance and prosperity in the land. For this purpose, two semidivine beings, the
brothers Emesh, "Summer," and Enten, "Winter," are created,
and Enlil assigns to each his specific duties, which they executed
thus:

> Enten made the ewe give birth to the lamb, the goat to give birth to
>   the kid,
> Cow and calf to multiply, fat and milk to increase,
> In the plain he made rejoice the heart of the wild goat, sheep, and
>   donkey,
> The birds of heaven—in the wide earth he made them set up their
>   nests,
> The fish of the sea—in the canebrake he made them lay their eggs,
> In the palm grove and vineyard he made honey and wine abound,
> The trees, wherever planted, he caused to bear fruit,
> The gardens he decked out in green, made their plants luxuriant,

Made grain increase in the furrows,
Like Ashnan (the grain-goddess), the kindly maid, he made it come
forth sturdily.
Emesh brought into being the trees and fields, made wide the stalls
and the sheepfolds,
In the farms he multiplied produce, bedecked the earth . . . . ,
Caused the abundant harvest to be brought into the houses, the
granaries to be heaped high,
Cities and habitation to be founded, houses to be built in the land,
Temples to rise mountain high.

Their mission accomplished, the two brothers decide to come
to Nippur to the "house of life" and bring thank-offerings to their
father Enlil. Emesh brings sundry wild and domestic animals,
birds, and plants as his gift, while Enten chooses precious metals
and stones, trees and fish as his offering. But at the door of the
"house of life," the jealous Enten starts a quarrel with his brother.
The arguments go back and forth between them, and finally
Emesh challenges Enten's claim to the position of "farmer of the
gods." And so they betake themselves to Enlil's great temple, the
Ekur, and each states his case. Thus Enten complains to Enlil:

Father Enlil, you have given me charge of the canals,
I brought the water of abundance,
Farm I made touch farm, heaped high the granaries,
I made grain increase in the furrows,
Like Ashnan, the kindly maid, I made it come forth sturdily,
Now Emesh, the . . . . , who has no understanding for fields,
Has jostled by . . . arm and . . . shoulder,
At the king's palace. . . . .

Emesh's version of the quarrel, which begins with several flattering phrases cunningly directed to win Enlil's favor, is brief but
as yet unintelligible. Then

Enlil answers Emesh and Enten,
"The life-producing waters of all the lands—Enten is in charge of them.
Farmer of the gods—he produces everything,
Emesh, my son, how do you compare yourself with your brother
Enten!"
The exalted word of Enlil, with meaning profound,
Whose verdict is unalterable, who dares transgress it!
Emesh bent the knee before Enten, offered him a prayer,

Into his house he brought nectar, wine, and beer,
They sate themselves with heart-cheering nectar, wine, and beer,
Emesh presents Enten with gold, silver, and lapis lazuli,
In brotherhood and companionship they pour joyous libations. . . . .

In the dispute between Emesh and Enten,
Enten, the faithful farmer of the gods, having proved himself the
    victor over Emesh,
. . . Father Enlil, praise!

In "The Dispute between Cattle and Grain," the two protagonists are the cattle-goddess, Lahar, and her sister, the grain-goddess, Ashnan. These two, according to our myth, were created in
the creation chamber of the gods in order that the Anunnaki, the
children of the heaven-god, An, might have food to eat and clothes
to wear. But the Anunnaki were unable to make effective use of
cattle and grain until man was created. All this is told in an introductory passage which reads:

After on the mountain of heaven and earth,
An (the heaven-god) had caused the Anunnaki (his followers) to be
    born,
Because the name Ashnan had not been born, had not been fashioned,
Because Uttu (the goddess of clothing) had not been fashioned,
Because to Uttu no *temenos* had been set up,
There was no ewe, no lamb was dropped,
There was no goat, no kid was dropped,
The ewe did not give birth to its two lambs,
The goat did not give birth to its three kids,
Because the name of Ashnan, the wise, and Lahar,
The Anunnaki, the great gods, did not know,
The *shesh*-grain of thirty days did not exist,
The *shesh*-grain of forty days did not exist,
The small grains, the grain of the mountain, the grain of the pure
    living creatures did not exist.

Because Uttu had not been born, because the crown (of vegetation)
    had not been raised,
Because the lord . . . had not been born,
Because Sumugan, the god of the plain, had not come forth,
Like mankind when first created,
They (the Anunnaki) knew not the eating of bread,
Knew not the dressing of garments,

Ate plants with their mouths like sheep,
Drank water from the ditch.

In those days, in the creation chamber of the gods,
In their house Duku, Lahar and Ashnan were fashioned;
The produce of Lahar and Ashnan,
The Anunnaki of the Duku eat but remain unsated;
In their pure sheepfolds *shum*-milk, the good,
The Anunnaki of the Duku drink but remain unsated;
For the sake of their pure sheepfolds, the good,
Man was given breath.

The passage following the introduction describes the descent of
Lahar and Ashnan from heaven to earth and the cultural benefits
which they bestow on mankind:

In those days Enki says to Enlil:
"Father Enlil, Lahar and Ashnan,
They who have been created in the Duku,
Let us cause them to descend from the Duku."

At the pure word of Enki and Enlil,
Lahar and Ashnan descend from the Duku,
For Lahar they (Enlil and Enki) set up the sheepfold,
Plants and herbs in abundance they present to her.

For Ashnan they establish a house,
Plough and yoke they present to her.
Lahar standing in her sheepfold,
A shepherdess increasing the bounty of the sheepfold is she;
Ashnan standing among the crops,
A maid kindly and bountiful is she.

Abundance which comes from heaven,
Lahar and Ashnan caused to appear (on earth),
In the assembly they brought abundance,
In the land they brought the breath of life,
The *me*'s of the god they direct,
The contents of the warehouses they multiply,
The storehouses they fill full.

In the house of the poor, hugging the dust,
Entering they bring abundance;
The pair of them, wherever they stand,
Bring heavy increase into the house;

The place where they stand they sate, the place where they sit they
   supply,
They made good the heart of An and Enlil.

But then Lahar and Ashnan drank much wine, and so they began to quarrel in the farms and fields. In the arguments which
ensued, each deity extolled her own achievements and belittled
those of the other. Finally, Enlil and Enki intervened and declared Ashnan the victor.

There are four compositions of the disputation type which in
one way or another concern the Sumerian school and its personnel
and graduates. Two of these, "The Disputation between Enkimansi and Girnishag" and "The Colloquy between an *ugula* and
a Scribe," are treated in detail in the chapter on education (chapter vi). To these can now be added "The Disputation between
Enkita and Enkihegal" and "The Disputation between Two School
Graduates."

The "Disputation between Enkita and Enkihegal," which consists of about two hundred and fifty lines, begins with the rather
surprising statement, "Fellows, today we don't work," and continues with a series of about twenty paragraphs, most of which
are from four to five lines in length, replete with insults and taunts
hurled by the two protagonists against each other. Here, for example, we find one saying to the other caustically:

Where is he, where is he (this fellow), who compares his pedigree
to my pedigree! Neither on the female side nor on the male side
can he compare his pedigree to my pedigree. Neither on the master's
side nor on the slave's side is your pedigree like mine.

To which the other retorts:

Wait now, don't brag so, you have no future.

which only adds fuel to the fire:

What do you mean I have no future! My future is every bit as good
as your future. Both from the point of view of wealth, as well as of
pedigree, my future is as good as your future.

Or take this acrimonious paragraph in which the one taunts the
other as a most unmusical fellow:

You have a harp, but know no music,
You who are the "water boy" of (your) colleagues,

(Your) throat (?) can't sound a note,
You stutter (your) Sumerian, can't make a straight speech,
Can't sing a hymn, can't open (your) mouth,
And you are an accomplished fellow!

Finally, after one of the antagonists had cast aspersions on the members of the family of his opponent, they decided to go to their "city" and have their colleagues decide between them. But, if I understand correctly the rather obscure and ambiguous text at this point, they were advised to go to the *ugula,* "the supervisor(?)," in the *edubba,* and he, the *ugula,* decided that both were at fault and scolded them for wasting their time in quarrels and disputes.

"The Disputation between the Two School Graduates" is a composition of about one hundred and forty lines which begins with a highly boastful address by one of the protagonists introduced by the sentence "Old grad, come, let us debate." The rival responds accordingly, and the insults fly back and forth to the very end of the composition, which closes with a vituperative blast by one of the antagonists consisting of twenty-eight lines full of vitriolic abuse.

Finally, there is a disputation between two unnamed ladies (it is written not in the main Sumerian dialect but in the Emesal, the dialect ordinarily reserved in the Sumerian literary texts for the female of the species) which is every bit as vituperative and venomous as that between the rival schoolmen. The composition consists of over two hundred lines divided into some twenty-five paragraphs which are filled with derisive taunts and scurrilous, sarcastic sneers.

Unlike the disputation-type of composition, the essay seems to have found little favor among the Sumerian men of letters; at present, at least, we have but few compositions that could be classified as essays. There are the Job-like poetic document concerned with human suffering and submission (see pages 126–29); two essays, partly in dialogue form, concerned with life in the *edubba* and the value of education (both treated in detail in chapter vi); and a rather brief essay inscribed on a tablet in the Hilprecht Collection at Jena, which appears to describe an evil and hated man by the name of Tani, who practiced violence, hated righteousness and truth, was arbitrary in the assembly, and in fact acted abominably all around. There are also, perhaps, a number of very brief or miniature essays on various subjects, but at the moment little can be said of the true nature of their content.

There are three Sumerian collections of precepts and instructions: "The Farmers' Almanac" (see pages 340–42), "The Instructions of Shuruppak to His Son Ziusudra," which consists of practical admonitions for wise and effective behavior, and a third, which seems to consist of moral and ethical admonitions, although it is only fragmentarily preserved. The second of these, "The Instructions of Shuruppak to His Son Ziusudra," is rather interesting because of its stylistic device of ascribing whole wisdom collections to presumably very wise rulers of the distant past, a characteristic feature of the Biblical Book of Proverbs. For although these precepts were probably compiled sometime around 2000 B.C., they were attributed to King Shuruppak, who was the father of Ziusudra, the Sumerian Noah, evidently a suitable candidate for the position of sage par excellence. The Biblical flavor of this composition is evident even in its initial lines, which read in part:

> Shuruppak gave instructions to his son,
> Shuruppak, the son of Ubartutu,
> Gave instructions to his son Ziusudra:

> "My son, I would instruct you, take my instruction,
> Ziusudra, I would utter a word to you, give heed to it;
> Do not neglect my instruction,
> Do not transgress the word I uttered,
> The father's instruction, the precious, carry out diligently."

And so we come to the last type of composition in the wisdom genre, the proverb. The total extant Sumerian proverb material consists roughly of about seven hundred tablets and fragments, the great majority of which were unidentified until 1953. A fair proportion of the tablets had originally contained whole collections of proverbs or extensive excerpts from such collections. The rest were school practice tablets containing either very short excerpts of the collections or, often enough, only a single proverb. Edmund Gordon, my former student and assistant, has now studied carefully the entire extant proverb material; he concludes that the ancient Sumerian scribes had produced at least fifteen to twenty different standard proverb compilations, of which about ten to twelve can now be reconstructed in large part. These contain more than a thousand proverbs between them. In about half of the collections, the proverbs were arranged in groups according to the initial signs. In the others, the proverbs were not arranged in groupings based on key words, and although proverbs with similar subject matter occasionally appear side by side, the criterion for the order of arrangement is not apparent. Be that as it may, the Sumerian proverbs reveal a keen if not always flattering evaluation of the human scene and the drives and motives, the hopes and longings, and the paradoxes and contradictions which pervade it. Here now are a selected few of the more intelligible proverbs as translated in large part by Edmund Gordon:

1 Let what's mine stay unused; but let me use what is yours—this will (hardly) endear a man to his friends' household.

2 You don't tell me what you have found;
you only tell what you have lost.

3 Possessions are sparrows in flight which can find no place to alight.

4 Don't pick it now; later it will bear fruit.

5 He who eats much can't sleep.

6 It's not the heart which leads to enmity;
it's the tongue which leads to enmity.

7 Tell a lie; then if you tell the truth it will be deemed a lie.

8 Into an open mouth, a fly enters.

9 The traveler from distant places is a perennial liar.

10 Build like a lord—live like a slave;
build like a slave—live like a lord.

11 Hand to hand—a man's house is built;
stomach to stomach—a man's house is destroyed.

12 Poorly fed—grandly living!

13 When walking, come now, keep your feet on the ground.

14 Friendship lasts a day;
kinship lasts forever.

15 Who has much silver may be happy;
who has much grain may be glad;
but he who has nothing can sleep.

16   A sweet word is everybody's friend.

17   A loving heart builds the home;
     a hating heart destroys the home.

18   The desert canteen is a man's life;
     the shoe is a man's eye;
     the wife is a man's future;
     the son is a man's refuge;
     the daughter is a man's salvation;
     the daughter-in-law is a man's devil.

19   Marry a wife according to your choice;
     have a child as your heart desires.

20   A "delinquent," his mother should never have given birth to him,
     his god should never have fashioned him.

21   A scribe who knows not Sumerian, what kind of scribe is he?

22   A scribe whose hand moves as fast as the mouth, that's a scribe for
     you.

23   A singer whose voice is not sweet is a poor singer indeed.

24   In a city without (watch)dogs, the fox is the overseer.

25   The fox trod upon the hoof of the wild ox, saying, "Didn't it hurt?"

26   A cat—for its thoughts!
     A mongoose—for its deeds!

In conclusion, we must say just a word about the ancient Sumerian literary catalogues which developed no doubt out of the
need of handling, storing, and recording the thousands of tablets
of varied shapes and sizes that were inscribed with hundreds of
literary compositions. As of today, seven catalogues dating from
the second millennium B.C. have been unearthed and are now
located as follows: one in the Iraq Museum in Baghdad; one in
the Louvre; one in the University Museum of the University of
Pennsylvania; one in the Berlin Museum; two in the Hilprecht
Collection in the Friedrich-Schiller University in Jena; and one
temporarily in the British Museum. All in all, these seven catalogues list the titles of over two hundred Sumerian compositions,
or "books," the title usually consisting of the first part of the first
line. Two of the catalogues restrict their listings to hymns. The
remaining five are not so limited, but contain the titles of various
types of compositions. The principles which guided their writers

are by no means clear; a priori one might have expected the nature of the contents of the compositions to have been the determining criterion, but this is only rarely the case. One of the catalogues, that at the Iraq Museum, specifically states that it is a list of tablets assembled in certain containers, and this may be true of several of the other catalogues.

Only recently, an eighth literary catalogue of a rather different kind from the other seven has been identified by the editors of the Assyrian Dictionary of the Oriental Institute of the University of Chicago, who also translated a few lines from it. This text is of particular importance, since, to judge from the script, it dates from as early as the Third Dynasty of Ur, a period from which almost no literary documents have been recovered to date. Unfortunately, the text, just because it has no later parallels, is very difficult to interpret, and the following translation, which owes a great deal to my former assistant Miguel Civil, is to be taken as a pioneer and preliminary effort:

From the initial tablet (of the composition entitled) "Enki Has Ascended to the Dining Hall" to (the tablet beginning with the words) "Heaven's zenith" (are the following four tablets beginning with the words):

Who knows the eclipses, the mother of him who knows the incantations,
At the nodding canebrake,
The . . . gods of battle,
The inimical, fighting twins;

(All these tablets are inscribed with) consecutive sections of (the composition entitled) "Enki Has Ascended to the Dining Hall" (and are found) inside one "well."

From the initial tablet (of the composition entitled) "The God Lilia" to (the tablet beginning with the words) "The . . . of the journey are seven" (are the following three tablets beginning with the words):

In the seven . . . I made enter,
Let the young man have (his) arms fastened,
The . . . of the great . . . ;

(All these tablets are inscribed with) consecutive sections of (the composition entitled) "The God Lilia" (and are found) inside one "well."

(As for the composition entitled) "The Feet of the Man of Trust-worthy Words Who . . . ," (the tablets inscribed with) its consecutive sections have not been found.

(The tablets inscribed with) the consecutive sections of (the composition entitled) "Who Goes Forth against the Inimical City."

It is not impossible that this particular catalogue was prepared to list the tablets recovered from wells, where they may have been hidden for one reason or another; the statement near the end that one of the compositions has not been found, if the rendering is correct, seems to corroborate this surmise. As for the last two lines, these seem to be left hanging in mid-air, and there is no way of knowing what the ancient scribes meant by this notation.

CHAPTER SIX

EDUCATION:

The Sumerian

School

From the point of view of the history of civilization, Sumer's supreme achievements were the development of the cuneiform system of writing and the formal system of education which was its
direct outgrowth. It is no exaggeration to say that had it not been
for the inventiveness and perseverance of the anonymous, practically oriented Sumerian pundits and teachers who lived in the
early third millennium B.C., it is hardly likely that the intellectual
and scientific achievements of modern days would have been possible; it was from Sumer that writing and learning spread the
world over. To be sure, the inventors of the earliest Sumerian
signs, the pictographs, could hardly have anticipated the system
of schooling as it developed in later days. But even among the
oldest known written documents—those found in Erech—consisting of more than a thousand small pictographic clay tablets inscribed primarily with bits of economic and administrative mem-
oranda, there are several which contain word lists intended for
study and practice; that is, as early as 3000 B.C., some scribes were
already thinking in terms of teaching and learning. Progress was
slow in the centuries that followed; but by the middle of the
third millennium B.C., there must have been a number of schools
throughout Sumer where writing was taught formally. In ancient
Shuruppak, the home city of the Sumerian Noah, quite a number
of school "textbooks" dating from about 2500 B.C. were excavated
some fifty years ago, consisting of lists of gods, animals, artifacts,
and a varied assortment of words and phrases.

However, it was in the course of the last half of the third millennium that the Sumerian school system matured and flourished. From this period tens of thousands of clay tablets have already been excavated, and there is little doubt that hundreds of thousands more lie buried in the ground awaiting the future excavator. The vast majority are administrative in character and cover every phase of Sumerian economic life. From these we learn that the number of scribes who practiced their craft throughout those years ran into the thousands; there were junior scribes and "high" scribes, royal and temple scribes, scribes who were highly specialized for particular categories of administrative activities, and scribes who became leading officials in state and government. There is every reason to assume, therefore, that numerous scribal schools of considerable size and importance flourished throughout the land.

But none of these early tablets deals directly with the Sumerian school system, its organization and method of operation. For this type of information, we must go to the first half of the second millennium B.C. From this later period excavators have discovered hundreds of practice-tablets filled with all sorts of exercises prepared by the pupils themselves as part of their daily schoolwork; their script ranges from the sorry scratches of the "first-grader" to the elegantly made signs of the far-advanced student about to become a "graduate." By way of inference, these ancient copybooks tell us not a little about the method of teaching current in the Sumerian school and about the nature of the curriculum. Better yet, the ancient professors and teachers themselves liked to write about school life, and several of their essays on this subject have been recovered at least in part. From all these sources we get a picture of the Sumerian school, its aims and goals, its students and faculty, its curriculum and teaching techniques, which is quite unique for so early a period in the history of man.

The Sumerian school was known as *edubba*, "tablet house." Its original goal was what we would term "professional," that is, it was first established for the purpose of training the scribes necessary to satisfy the economic and administrative needs of the land, primarily, of course, those of the temple and palace. This continued to be the major aim of the Sumerian school throughout its existence. However, in the course of its growth and development, and particularly as a result of the ever widening curriculum, it came to be the center of culture and learning in Sumer. Within its walls flourished the scholar-scientist, the man who studied whatever theological, botanical, zoölogical, geographical, mathematical, grammatical, and linguistic knowledge was current in his day and who in some cases added to this knowledge.

Moreover, rather unlike present-day institutions of learning, the Sumerian school was also the center of what might be termed creative writing. It was here that the literary creations of the past were studied and copied; it was here, too, that new ones were composed. While it is true, therefore, that the large majority of graduates from the Sumerian schools became scribes in the service of the temple and palace and among the rich and powerful of the land, there were some who devoted their lives to teaching and learning. Like the university professor of today, many of these ancient scholars depended for their livelihood on their teaching salaries and devoted themselves to research and writing in their spare time. The Sumerian school, which probably began as a temple appendage, became in time a secular institution; the teachers were paid, as far as we can see, out of the tuition fees collected from the students. The curriculum, too, was largely secular in character.

Education was, of course, neither universal nor compulsory. The greater part of the students came from the more wealthy families; the poor could hardly afford the cost and the time which a prolonged education demanded. Until recently this was assumed a priori to be the case. But about a decade ago, a Luxembourg cuneiformist by the name of Nikolaus Schneider ingeniously proved it from contemporary sources. In the thousands of published economic and administrative documents from about 2000 B.C., some five hundred individuals list themselves as scribes, and for further identification many of them add the names of their fathers and their occupations. Schneider compiled a list of these data and found that the fathers of the scribes, that is, of the school graduates, were governors, "city fathers," ambassadors, temple administrators, military officers, sea captains, high tax officials, priests of various sorts, managers, supervisors, foremen, scribes, archivists, and accountants—in short, all the wealthier citizens of an urban community. Only one single woman is listed as a scribe in these documents, and the likelihood is, therefore, that the student body of the Sumerian school consisted of males only.

The head of the Sumerian school was the *ummia,* "expert," "professor," who was also called "school-father," while the pupil was called "school-son" and the alumnus "the school-son of days past." The assistant professor was known as "big brother," and some of his duties were to write the new tablets for the pupils to copy, examine the students' copies, and hear them recite their studies from memory. Other members of the faculty were, for example, "the man in charge of drawing" and "the man in charge of Sumerian." There were also monitors in charge of attendance and special proctors responsible for discipline. We know nothing of the relative rank of the school personnel, except, of course, that the headmaster was the "school-father."

If we now turn to the curriculum of the Sumerian school, we have at our disposal a wealth of data from the schools themselves, which is indeed unique in the history of early man. For in this case there is no need to depend on the statements made by the ancients or on inference from scattered bits of information; we have the actual written products of the schoolboys themselves, from the beginner's first attempts to the copies of the advanced student, which were so well prepared that they were hardly to be distinguished from those of the professor. It is from these school products that we realize that the Sumerian school's curriculum consisted of two primary groups; the first may be described as semiscientific and scholarly and the second as literary and creative.

In considering the first, or semiscientific, group of subjects, it is important to stress that it did not stem from what we may call the scientific urge, the search for truth for truth's sake; rather, it grew and developed out of the main school aim, which was to teach the scribe how to write the Sumerian language. For in order to satisfy this pedagogical need, the Sumerian scribal teachers devised a system of instruction which consisted primarily of linguistic classification; that is, they classified the Sumerian language into groups of related words and phrases and had the students memorize and copy them until they could reproduce them with ease. In the course of the third millennium B.C., these textbooks became ever more complete and gradually grew to be more or less stereotyped and standard for all the schools of Sumer. Among them we find long lists of names of trees and reeds, of all sorts of animals (including insects and birds), of countries, cities, and villages, and of all sorts of stones and minerals. All in all, these compilations show a considerable acquaintance with what might be termed botanical, zoölogical, geographical, and mineralogical lore, a fact that is only now beginning to be realized by historians of science.

Our schoolmen also prepared all sorts of mathematical tables and many detailed mathematical problems together with their solutions. And in the field of linguistics, we find the study of Sumerian grammar well represented; a number of the school tablets are inscribed with long lists of substantive complexes and verbal forms which indicate a highly sophisticated grammatical approach. Moreover, as a result of the gradual conquest of the Sumerians by the Semitic Akkadians in the last quarter of the third millennium B.C., our ancient professors prepared what are by all odds the oldest dictionaries known to man. For the Semitic conquerors not only borrowed the Sumerian script; they also treasured highly the Sumerian literary works and studied and imitated them long after Sumerian had become extinct as a spoken language—hence, the pedagogical need for dictionaries in which the Sumerian words and phrases were translated into the Akkadian language. (See Fig. 5.)

As for the literary and creative aspects of the Sumerian curriculum, they consisted primarily of studying, copying, and imitating the large and diversified group of literary compositions that must have originated and developed primarily in the latter half of the third millennium B.C. The number of these ancient works ran into the hundreds; they were almost all poetic in form and ranged in length from close to a thousand to less than fifty lines. As recovered to date, they are seen to consist in the main of the following genres: myths and epic tales in the form of narrative poems celebrating the deeds and exploits of the Sumerian gods and heroes; hymns to gods and kings; lamentations, that is, poems bewailing the not infrequent destruction of the Sumerian cities; wisdom compositions, including proverbs, fables, and essays. Of the approximately five thousand literary tablets and fragments recovered from the ruins of Sumer, not a few are in the immature hand of the ancient pupils themselves.

Little is known as yet of the teaching methods and techniques practiced in the Sumerian school. In the morning, upon his arrival in school, the pupil studied the tablet that he had prepared the day before. After this, the "big brother," that is, the assistant

Sumerian	Sign	Akkadian Translation	Meaning
i l - a r		ti-il-pa-nu	throwing stick
t a - a l		ru-up-šum	width
n a - g á		e-si-tum	mortar
g a - a z		pa-ḫa-su-um	to break into pieces
"		da-a-ku-um	to kill
n i n - d a		mi-i-rum	bull
"		pa-ar-si-ik-tum	a measure
"		it-tu-ú-um	funnel of a seed-plow

Fig. 5.—*Extract from a Sumero-Akkadian Vocabulary*

professor, prepared a new tablet, which the student then proceeded to copy and study. Both the "big brother" and "school-father" would examine his copies to see if they were correct. Memorizing, no doubt, played a very large role in the student's work. Then, too, the teacher and the assistants must have supplemented the bare lists, tables, and literary texts that the student was copying and studying with considerable oral and explanatory material. But these "lectures," which would no doubt prove invaluable for our understanding of Sumerian scientific, religious, and literary thought, were in all probability never written down and hence are lost to us forever.

While the Sumerian school was in no way "tainted" by what we could call progressive education, the curriculum was pedagogically oriented at least to some extent. Thus the neophyte began his studies with quite elementary syllabic exercises such as tu-ta-ti, nu-na-ni, bu-ba-bi, zu-za-zi, etc. This was followed by the study and practice of a sign list of some nine hundred entries which gave single signs along with their pronunciation. Then came lists containing hundreds of words that had come to be written, for one reason or another, not by one sign but by a group of two or more signs. These were followed by collections containing literally thousands of words and phrases arranged according to meaning. Thus in the field of the "natural sciences," there were lists of the parts of the animal and human body, of wild and domestic animals, of birds and fishes, of trees and plants, of stones and stars. The lists of artifacts included wooden objects—more than fifteen hundred items ranging from pieces of raw wood to boats and chariots; objects made of reed, skin, leather, and metal; assorted types of pottery, garments, foods, and beverages. A special group of these lists dealt with place names—lands, cities, and hamlets as well as rivers, canals, and fields. A collection of the most common expressions used in administrative and legal documents was also included as well as a list of some eight hundred words denoting professions, kinship relations, deformities of the human body, etc.

It was only when the student had become well acquainted with the writing of the complex Sumerian vocabulary that he began to copy and memorize short sentences, proverbs, and fables, and also collections of "model" contracts, this last being essential for the redaction of legal documents, which played a large role in the economic life of Sumer. Along with this linguistic training, the student was also given instruction in mathematics, which took the form of studying and copying metrological tables, with the equivalence of measures of capacity, length, and weight, as well as multiplication and reciprocal tables for computation purposes. Later, the student was put to solving practical problems dealing with wages, canal-digging, and construction work.

In the matter of discipline—and as will be seen below, disci-

pline seems to have been a major problem in the Sumerian school
—there was no sparing of the rod. While the teachers no doubt
encouraged their students to do good work by means of praise
and commendation, they depended primarily on the cane for cor-
recting the student's faults and inadequacies. The student did not
have an easy time of it. He attended school daily from sunrise to
sunset; he must have had some vacation throughout the year, but
we have no information on the point. He devoted many years to
his school studies; he stayed in school from his early youth to the
day when he became a young man. It would be most interesting
to know if—and when and to what extent—the students were expected to specialize in one study or another. But on this point, as
indeed on many other matters concerned with school activities,
our sources fail us.

In conclusion, we may say just a word about the school building. In the course of several Mesopotamian excavations, buildings
have been uncovered which for one reason or another were identified as possible schoolhouses; one in Nippur, another in Sippar,
and a third in Ur. But except for the fact that a large number of
tablets were found in the rooms, there seems little to distinguish
them from ordinary house rooms, and the identification may be
mistaken. However, some fifteen years ago, the French who excavated ancient Mari far to the west of Nippur uncovered two
rooms which definitely seem to show physical features that might
be characteristic of a schoolroom; in particular, they contain several rows of benches made of baked brick, capable of seating
one, two, and four people.

There may be a reference to the shape and form of the school
building in an enigmatic riddle that an ancient Sumerian professor contrived, which reads as follows:

> (What is it:)
> A house which like heaven has a plow,
> Which like a copper kettle is cloth-covered,
> Which like a goose stands on a base,
> He whose eyes are not open enters it,
> He whose eyes are (wide) open comes out of it?
>
> Its solution is: It's the school.

While the first part of this riddle, which is found on a still unpublished tablet excavated at Ur and copied by Cyril J. Gadd of

the British Museum, is altogether obscure, the last two lines sum up succinctly the purpose of the school; to turn the ignorant and illiterate into a man of wisdom and learning.

As already noted, we have at our disposal quite a number of essays relating to education which the ancient schoolmen themselves prepared for the edification of their students, and these give a graphic and vivid picture of various aspects of school life, including the interrelationships between faculty, students, parents, and graduates. Following are four of the better preserved essays, which, to judge from the contents, may be entitled (1) "Schooldays," (2) "School Rowdies (The Disputation between Enkimansi and Girnishag)," (3) "A Scribe and His Perverse Son," and (4) "Colloquy between an *ugula* and a Scribe."

The essay "Schooldays," which deals with the day-to-day activities of the schoolboy as recounted by an "old grad" with some of the nostalgic details that the modern alumnus recounts at his class reunion, is one of the most human documents excavated in the ancient Near East. Originally composed by an anonymous schoolteacher who lived about 2000 B.C., its simple, straightforward words reveal how little human nature has really changed throughout the millenniums. We find our ancient schoolboy, not unlike his modern counterpart, terribly afraid of coming late to school "lest his teacher cane him." When he awakes he hurries his mother to prepare his lunch. In school he misbehaves and is caned more than once by the teacher and his assistants; we are quite sure of the rendering "caning" since the Sumerian sign consists of "stick" and "flesh." As for the teacher, his pay seems to have been as meager then as it is now; at least, he is only too happy to make a "little extra" from the parents to eke out his earnings.

The composition, which was no doubt the creation of one of the *ummia*'s in the *edubba,* begins with a direct question to an old alumnus which reads: "Old Grad, where did you go (when you were young)?" The latter answers: "I went to school." The professor-author then asks: "What did you do in school?" This is the cue for the old grad to reminisce about his school activities thus:

I recited my tablet, ate my lunch, prepared my (new) tablet, wrote it, finished it; then my model tablets were brought to me; and in the afternoon my exercise tablets were brought to me. When school was dismissed, I went home, entered the house, and found my father sitting there. I explained (?) my exercise-tablets to my father, (?) recited my tablet to him, and he was delighted, (so much so) that I attended him (with joy).

The author now has the schoolboy turn to the house servants (it was evidently quite a well-to-do home) with these words:

I am thirsty, give me water to drink; I am hungry, give me bread to eat; wash my feet, set up (my) bed, I want to go to sleep. Wake me early in the morning, I must not be late lest my teacher cane me.

Presumably all this was done, for we next find our schoolboy saying:

When I arose early in the morning, I faced my mother and said to her: "Give me my lunch, I want to go to school!" My mother gave me two rolls, and I set out; my mother gave me two rolls, and I went to school. In school the fellow in charge of punctuality said: "Why are you late?" Afraid and with pounding heart, I entered before my teacher and made a respectful curtsy.

But curtsy or not, it was a bad day for our ancient pupil—at least as the old grad remembered it rather nostalgically—he had to take canings from various members of the school staff. Or, in the words which the author puts in the mouth of the alumnus:

My headmaster read my tablet, said:
"There is something missing," caned me.
        (There follow two unintelligible lines)
The fellow in charge of neatness (?) said:
"You loitered in the street and did not straighten up (?) your
    clothes (?)," caned me.
        (There follow five unintelligible lines)
The fellow in charge of silence said:
"Why did you talk without permission," caned me.
The fellow in charge of the assembly (?) said:
"Why did you 'stand at ease (?)' without permission," caned me.
The fellow in charge of good behavior said:
"Why did you rise without permission," caned me.
The fellow in charge of the gate said:
"Why did you go out from (the gate) without permission," caned me.
The fellow in charge of the whip said:
"Why did you take . . without permission," caned me.
The fellow in charge of Sumerian said:

"Why didn't you speak Sumerian," caned me.

My teacher (*ummia*) said:

"Your hand is unsatisfactory," caned me.

(And so) I (began to) hate the scribal art, (began to) neglect the scribal art.

My teacher took no delight in me; (even) [stopped teaching (?)] me his skill in the scribal art; in no way prepared me in the matters (essential) to the art (of being) a "young scribe," (or) the art (of being) a "big brother."

In despair, according to our old grad, he turned to his father, saying:

Give him a bit extra salary, (and) let him become more kindly (?); let him be free (for a time) from arithmetic; (when) he counts up all the school affairs of the students, let him count me (too among them; that is, perhaps, let him not neglect me any longer).

From here on, the author himself takes over, describing the events as if he had been there and had witnessed them, thus:

To that which the schoolboy said, his father gave heed. The teacher was brought from school, and after entering in the house, he was seated on the "big chair." The schoolboy attended and served him, and whatever he learned of the scribal art, he unfolded to his father. Then did the father in the joy of his heart say joyfully to the headmaster of the school: "My little fellow has opened (wide) his hand, (and) you made wisdom enter there; you showed him all the fine points of the scribal art; you made him see the solutions of the mathematical and arithmetical (problems), you (taught him how) to make deep (?) the cuneiform script (?).

The author now has the father turn to his household servants, saying:

Pour for him *irda*-oil, bring it to the table for him. Make fragrant oil flow like water on his stomach (and) back; I want to dress him in a garment, give him some extra salary, put a ring on his hand.

The servants do as they are bidden, and then the teacher speaks to the schoolboy:

Young fellow, (because) you hated not my words, neglected them not, (may you) complete the scribal art from beginning to end. Because you gave me everything without stint, paid me a salary larger than my efforts (deserve), (and) have honored me, may Nidaba, the queen of guardian angels, be your guardian angel; may your pointed stylus write well for you; may your exercises contain no faults. Of your brothers, may you be their leader; of your friends may you be their chief; may you rank the highest among the school graduates, satisfy (?) all who walk (?) to and from in (?) the palaces. Little fellow, you "know" (your) father, I am second to him; that homage be paid to you, that you be blessed—may the god of your father bring this about with firm hand; he will bring prayer and supplication to Nidaba, your queen, as if it were a matter for your god. Thus, when you put a kindly hand on the . . . of the teacher, (and) on the forehead of the "big brother," then (?) your young comrades will show you favor. You have carried out well the school's activities, you are a man of learning. You have exalted Nidaba, the queen of learning; O Nidaba, praise!

From the preceding essay it is not easy to decide whether the faculty of the Sumerian school consisted largely of sadists or whether its student body consisted of rowdies and roughnecks. That the latter may have been true at least in part seems to be corroborated by the second of our essays, "The Disputation between Enkimansi and Girnishag." According to this document, the ancient pedagogues seem to have had their hands full trying to control pupils who took pleasure in pushing, shouting, quarreling, and cursing.

This one hundred and sixty line Sumerian essay has only recently been pieced together from seven tablets and fragments by Cyril J. Gadd, professor emeritus of the School of Oriental and African Studies of the University of London, and the author of this book. Two of these were excavated at Ur by Sir Leonard Woolley about twenty-five years ago; they were published in part by Professor Gadd in 1956, under the title "Teachers and Students in the Oldest Schools," as an inaugural lecture at the School of Oriental and African Studies. But these two tablets contained only the beginning and end of the essay. A fuller text is now available as a result of the identification of five pieces excavated at Nippur, one of which, a large eight-column tablet containing a whole collection of Sumerian essays, proved to be of particular importance for the restoration of the text of our essay. Excavated some sixty years ago, it is now in the Hilprecht Collection of the Friedrich-Schiller University of Jena in East Germany, and its contents were only recently made available. It must be stressed, however, that in spite of the more complete text now available, much of the meaning of the essay and not a few of its implications are still quite uncertain, since many of the passages are only partially preserved. The sketch here presented must therefore be taken as preliminary and tentative, and future discoveries may modify the interpretation considerably.

One rather unexpected and not uninteresting bit of comparative cultural information provided by our essay concerns the literal meaning and derogatory implications of the word "sophomore," which is first known to have been used as an English word in Cambridge in 1688. There is reason to believe that this word, "sophomore," is the English form of a Greek compound word "sophos-moros," which means literally "clever-fool." Now, as Professor Gadd was first to point out, our Sumerian essay contains the exact equivalent of the Greek "sophos-moros." In the course of the bitter and abusive arguments between the two school rivals which constitute the main part of the essay, one of them taunts the other with being a *"galam-huru,"* a Sumerian compound word meaning literally "clever-fool," that is, "sophomore." The composition consists primarily of a bitter verbal contest between two schoolmates named Enkimansi and Girnishag, both of whom are far advanced in their studies; in fact, Girnishag may have reached the height of being "big brother," that is, an assistant instructor in the school. In the course of the disputation each talks up his own virtues and talents in glowing terms and talks down his opponent with withering sneers and vituperative insults. Thus near the very beginning of the document, one of these worthies addresses the other as follows:

You dolt, numskull, school pest, you illiterate, you Sumerian ignoramus, your hand is terrible; it cannot even hold the stylus properly; it is unfit for writing and cannot take dictation. (And yet you say) you are a scribe like me.

To this the other worthy answers:

What do you mean I am not a scribe like you? When you write a document it makes no sense. When you write a letter it is illegible (?). You go to divide up an estate, but are unable to divide up the estate. For when you go to survey the field, you can't hold the measuring line. You can't hold a nail in your hand; you have no sense. You

don't know how to arbitrate between the contesting parties; you aggra-
vate the struggle between the brothers. You are one of the most in-
competent of tablet writers. What are you fit for, can any one say (?)?

To which his rival retorts:

Why, I am competent all around. When I go to divide an estate,
I divide the estate. When I go to survey the field, I know how to hold
the measuring line. I know how to arbitrate between the contesting
parties. I know how to pacify the struggle between the brothers and
soothe their feelings. But you are the laziest (?) of scribes, the most
careless (?) of men. When you do multiplication, it is full of mistakes
(?) . . . In (computing) areas you confuse (?) length with width.
Squares, triangles, circles (?), and sectors—you treat them all without
understanding as if . . . You chatterbox, scoundrel, sneerer, and bully,
you (dare say) that you are the "heart" of the student body!

Taking this sentence as a cue, his opponent begins with the query:
"What do you mean I am not the 'heart' of the student body?" He
then continues with a description of his talents as a keeper of
accounts and ends with these lines:

Me, I was raised on Sumerian, I am the son of a scribe. But you are
a bungler, a windbag. When you try to shape a tablet, you can't even
smooth (?) the clay (?). When you try to write a line, your hand can't
manage (?) the tablet . . . You "sophomore," cover your ears! cover
your ears! (Yet) you (claim to know) Sumerian like me!

At this point a long passage follows which is so poorly preserved that it is difficult to follow even the shift of speakers. Finally, someone (probably the *ugula*, that is, a monitor of some
sort) became so incensed at one student—Enkimansi—that he was
ready to lock him up and put him in chains, to judge from the
following passage toward the very end of the composition, which
in the following tentative translation reads:

Why do you behave like this! Why do you push, curse, and hurl
insults at each other! Why do you raise a commotion in the school! . . . .
(There follow four unintelligible lines.) The commotion has reached him!
Why were you insolent (?), inattentive (?), (why do you) curse, and hurl
insults against him who is your "big brother" and has taught you the
scribal art to your own advantage (?)! Even the *ummia* who knows everything shook his head violently (?) (saying): "Do to him what you please."
If I (really) did to you what I pleased—to a fellow who behaved like
you (and) was inattentive (?) to his "big brother"—I would (first)
beat you with a mace—what's a wooden board (when it comes to beat-

ing!)—(and) having put copper chains on your feet, would lock you up in the house (and) for two months would not let you out of the school (building).

Following four unintelligible lines, the composition closes with the words: "In the dispute between Girnishag and Enkimansi the *ummia* gave the verdict."

As can be surmised from the two preceding essays, the Sumerian school was rather formidable and uninviting; the curriculum was "stiff," the teaching methods drab, the discipline harsh. No wonder, then, that at least some of the pupils played truant when possible and became "problem children" to their teacher and parents. Which brings us to the third of our school essays, "A Scribe and His Perverse Son," a text pieced together from more than a score of tablets and fragments. This essay is noteworthy as one of the first documents in the history of man in which the word "humanity" (Sumerian, *namlulu*) is used not only to designate mankind but in the sense of conduct and behavior befitting human beings.

The composition, which is about one hundred eighty lines in length, begins with an introduction consisting of a more or less friendly dialogue between father and son in which the latter is admonished to go to school, work diligently, and report back without loitering in the streets. To make sure the lad has paid close attention, the father has him repeat his words verbatim.

From this point on, the essay is a monologue on the part of the father. It starts with a series of practical instructions to help make a man of his son: not to gad about in the streets and boulevards; to be humble before his monitor; to go to school and learn from the experience of man's early past. There follows a bitter rebuke to the wayward son, who, his father claims, has made him sick unto death with his perennial fears and inhuman behavior. He, the father, is deeply disappointed at the son's ingratitude; he never made him work behind plow or ox, nor did he ever ask him to bring firewood or to support him as other fathers make their sons do. And yet his son has turned out to be less of a man than the others.

Like many a disappointed parent of today, the father seems to be especially hurt that his son refuses to follow his professional footsteps and become a scribe. He admonishes him to emulate his companions, brothers, and friends and to follow his own profession, the scribal art, in spite of the fact that it is the most difficult of all professions that the god of arts and crafts thought up and brought into being. It is most useful, the father argues, for the poetic transmission of man's experiences. But in any case, he continues, it is decreed by Enlil, the king of all the gods, that a son should follow his father's profession.

After a final upbraiding for the son's pursuit of materialistic success rather than humanistic endeavor, the text becomes rather obscure; it seems to consist of brief, pithy sayings intended, perhaps, to guide the son in true wisdom. In any case, the essay closes on a happy note, with the father blessing his son and praying that he find favor in the eyes of his personal god, the moon-god, Nanna, and his wife, the goddess Ningal.

Here now is a quite literal, if tentative, translation of the more intelligible portions of the essay, omitting only here and there an obscure phrase or a broken line. The father begins by asking his son:

"Where did you go?"

"I did not go anywhere."

"If you did not go anywhere, why do you idle about? Go to school, stand before your 'school-father' (professor), recite your assignment, open your schoolbag, write your tablet, let your 'big brother' write your new tablet for you. After you have finished your assignment and reported to your monitor, come to me, and do not wander about in the street. Come now, do you know what I said?"

"I know, I'll tell it to you."

"Come, now, repeat it to me."

"I'll repeat it to you."

"Tell it to me."

"I'll tell it to you."

"Come on, tell it to me."

"You told me to go to school, recite my assignment, open my schoolbag, write my tablet, while my 'big brother' is to write my new tablet. After finishing my assignment, I am to proceed to my work and to come to you after I have reported to my monitor. That's what you told me."

"Come now, be a man. Don't stand about in the public square or wander about the boulevard. When walking in the street, don't look all around. Be humble and show fear before your monitor. When you show terror, the monitor will like you.

(About fifteen lines destroyed)

"You who wander about in the public square, would you achieve success? Then seek out the first generations. Go to school, it will be of benefit to you. My son, seek out the first generations, inquire of them.

"Perverse one over whom I stand watch—I would not be a man did I not stand watch over my son—I spoke to my kin, compared its men, but found none like you among them.

"What I am about to relate to you turns the fool into a wise man, holds the snake as if by charms, and will not let you accept false phrases.

"Because my heart had been sated with weariness of you, I kept away from you and heeded not your fears and grumblings—no, I heeded not your fears and grumblings. Because of your clamorings, yes, because of your clamorings, I was angry with you—yes, I was angry with you. Because you do not look to your humanity, my heart was carried off as if by an evil wind. Your grumblings have put an end to me, you have brought me to the point of death.

"I, never in all my life, did I make you carry reeds to the canebrake. The reed rushes which the young and the little carry, you, never in your life did you carry them. I never said to you 'Follow my caravans.' I never sent you to work, to plow my field. I never sent you to work, to dig up my field. I never sent you to work as a laborer. 'Go, work and support me,' I never in my life said to you.

"Others like you support their parents by working. If you spoke to your kin and appreciated them, you would emulate them. They provide 10 *gur* of barley each—even the young ones provided their fathers with 10 *gur* each. They multiplied barley for their father, maintained him in barley, oil, and wool. But you, you're a man when it comes to perverseness, but compared to them you're not a man at all. You certainly don't labor like them—they are the sons of fathers who make their sons labor, but me—I didn't make you work like them.

"I, night and day am I tortured because of you. Night and day you waste in pleasures. You have accumulated much wealth, have expanded far and wide, have become fat, big, broad, powerful, and puffed. But your kin waits expectantly for your misfortune and will rejoice at it because you looked not to your humanity."

(Here follows an obscure passage of forty-one lines which seems to consist of proverbs and old saws; the essay then concludes with the father's poetic blessing:)

From him who quarrels with you may Nanna, your god, save you,
From him who attacks you may Nanna, your god, save you,
May you find favor before your god,

May your humanity exalt you, neck and breast,
May you be the head of your city's sages,
May your city utter your name in favored places,
May your god call you by a good name,
May you find favor before your god Nanna,
May you be regarded with favor by the goddess Ningal.

If in spite of the heavy and far from exciting curriculum, the harsh punishments by his teachers, and the bitter rivalry of his more aggressive fellow classmates the ambitious and persevering student succeeded in graduating from school, there were several job possibilities open to him; he could, for example, enter the services of the palace or temple, or he could become the managing scribe and accountant of one of the larger estates which dotted the land. In the fourth of the school essays, "Colloquy between an *ugula* and a Scribe," we find the *edubba* graduate, now a full-fledged scribe on one such estate, having an argument with the *ugula* (probably its superintendent), who himself was an alumnus of the *edubba.* The composition, which consists of seventy-eight lines reconstructed from a dozen tablets and fragments, begins with an address by the *ugula* which reads:

Old Grad, come here to me (and) let me tell you what my *ummia* (the professor in charge of the *edubba*) told me.

I, too, like you was (once) a little fellow and had a "big brother."

The *ummia* would assign me work (that was even too much) for a (grown) man.

(But) I darted about like a darting reed, became absorbed in the work, neglected not my *ummia*'s words, did not act according to my own self(ish spirit), (and as a result) the "big brother" was pleased with my accomplishment.

He rejoiced because I humbled myself before him and spoke (?) in my favor (?).

Whatever he sketched for me I made, I put everything in its place—(even) a fool could easily (?) follow (?) his instructions.

He guided my hand on the clay, showed me how to behave properly, "opened" my mouth with words, uttered good counsel, focused (?) (my) eyes on the rules which guide the man of achievement: diligence is the very essence (literally "lot") of achievement, time-wasting is taboo, the fellow who gads about (and) wastes time at his assignment has failed his assignment.

He (the "big brother") vaunted not his knowledge, his words are restrained—had he vaunted his knowledge, eyes would "pop."

Attend him (therefore) before the sun rises (and) before the night cools; do not turn back the pleasure of being by the side of the "big brother"; having come close to the "big foreheads" your words will become honored.

He (the "big brother"(?)) did not turn back a second time the fastened eyes . . . , he bound about your neck a garland (?) of man's courtesy and respect (?).

The heart of the afflicted (?) having been soothed, he is freed of guilt.

The man (who brings) milk (?) sacrifices (?), made adequate (?) his gift; the man of wealth has pressed his knee-bent kid to his breast —so (?) must you be courteous to man, supervisor, and owner, must make their heart content.

So much for the *ugula's* rather diffuse and long-winded speech. Following an introductory line which reads; "The learned scribe humbly answers his *ugula*," the text continues with what seems to be a far from humble response:

You recounted to me . . like a . . , (but) now I will let you have the answer to it; as for your ox-like bellow, you will not turn me into an ignoramus with its lack of understanding—I will answer it fully (?) (literally, perhaps, "sixty times").

Like a puppy (your) eyes are wide apart (?) (even if) you act (like) a human being.

Why do you lay down rules for me as if I am an idler?

Anyone who heard you would drop (?) his hands in despair (?).

Let me explain to you carefully (literally, "let me put into your hand") the art of being a scribe since (?) you have mentioned it.

You have put me in charge over your house (and) never have I let you find me idling about.

I held the slave girls, slaves, and (the rest of) your household to their task; saw to it that they enjoyed their bread, clothing, and fat (and) that they work properly (literally, "as is their way").

You did not (have to) follow your slave in the house of your master; I did the unpleasant (?) task (?) (and) followed him like a sheep.

I have said daily the protecting (?) prayers which you have ordered; your sheep (and) your oxen are pleasing (and) bring joy to your god; on the day when your god's boat is moored they (the priests (?)) lay hands on you (in blessing). You assigned me the breast (that is, perhaps, the high, unirrigated part) of the field (and) I made the men work there—a challenging task which permits no sleep either by night or in the heat of day.

(Yet) all the . . . . (and (?)) the sons of the farmers nod (?) approval (?).

I applied the kindly hand in your field (and) folks spoke well of me; I made the ox bring in whatever filled (?) your path (?), made him carry (?) his load for you.

From my youth you raised me, watched over my behavior, treated me kindly like goodly silver, (and) did not . . . . I (therefore) kept away (?) from you that which "walks not in greatness," like something which is taboo for you; I kept away from you the "small winds (?)" (and) did not let them exist for you.

Raise now your head high, you who were formerly a little fellow, you can (now) turn your hand against (?) (any) man, (so) act (?) as is befitting.

Here probably ends the scribe's answer, although there is no introductory line to indicate a change of speaker. The rather unexpectedly amiable response of the *ugula*, which concludes the composition, reads as follows:

You who paid homage (?) to me, who blessed (?) me, who brought instruction into my body like edible milk (and) fat—because (?) you stood not about in idleness I have obtained the earth's favors, have not suffered its misfortunes. The *ummia*, the "word-knowers" nod (?) approval (?), tell (?) all about you in their houses (?), wherever they are (?). Your name is uttered (only) for good, your commands are well received (?). The ox-drivers (?) [halt (?)] their strife at your sweet songs; at your sweet songs the contenders (?) will drop (?) [(their) contention (?)]. The *ummia* pays you (?) homage with joyful heart (saying): "You who (as a) little fellow sat at my words, pleased my heart—Nidaba (the patron goddess of the *edubba*) has given in your hand the honor of (being an) *ummia;* you are the consecrated of Nidaba, may you rise heaven high. May you be blessed with joyous heart, [suffer] no heartache; may you [excel (?)] in whatever is in the *edubba*, the house of learning; [may] the loftiness of Nidaba [bring (?) you un]rivaled (?) rejoicing. At your kindly wisdom strife [will halt (?)]; the little fellows will drop (?) [their contention (?) in] . . . . . The craftsmen will utter [your name for good]; the . . . . will recount [your] . . . In the song-echoing (?) street, the street where . . . , you have brought the unrivaled *me;* you have mastered (?) the direction of harmonious (?) conduct."

There follows the typical closing phrase: "O Nidaba, praise!" To all of which the modern professor and teacher might well respond with a wistful and envious "Amen!"

CHAPTER SEVEN

CHARACTER:

Drives, Motives, and Values

By and large, studies devoted to Sumerian culture and civilization approach their subject from the descriptive point of view only. Usually, they proceed to break up Sumerian culture into its various aspects; social, political, economic, administrative, legal, religious, technological, artistic, and literary. Each of these subdivisions is then described with as much detail as the available data permit and the particular purpose of the study calls for. Rarely is Sumerian culture approached from the psychological point of view, that is, from a consideration of the character and personality of the people who created it. To help fill this gap, I have devoted a series of studies in the past several years to the psychological aspects of Sumerian civilization, especially as revealed in their literary documents. In a paper entitled "Rivalry and Superiority: Two Dominant Features of the Sumerian Culture Pattern,"[1] I tried to isolate and describe one of the major motivating forces of Sumerian behavior, the drive for superiority and pre-eminence with its great stress on competition and success. In an article entitled "Love, Hate and Fear: Psychological Aspects of Sumerian Culture,"[2] I sketched the role of love, hate, and fear as motivating emotional drives in Sumerian conduct. In this chapter, I shall try to summarize the results of these two studies. It cannot be stressed strongly enough that the conclu-

[1] *Selected Papers of the Fifth International Congress of Anthropological and Ethnological Sciences* (1960), pp. 287–91.

[2] *Eretz-Israel,* V (1958), 66–74.

sions here presented are preliminary and tentative in character; even the literary documents whose texts are complete cannot be fully understood, let alone those—and they are in the majority—which still have numerous gaps and breaks. Nevertheless, it can be safely said that at least some of the results sketched in this chapter are reasonably trustworthy and will stand the test of time.

Let us start with the three emotional drives which motivate not a few of man's values: love, hate, and fear. The Sumerian word for "love" is a compound verb which seems to mean literally "to measure the earth," "to mete out a place"; just how this developed into the meaning "love" is uncertain.

As is true of all mankind, love among the Sumerians was an emotion which varied in character and intensity. There was the passionate, sensuous love between the sexes, which usually culminated in marriage; the love between husband and wife, between parents and children, between the various members of the family; the love between friends and intimates; and the love between gods, kings, and people. We may begin our sketch of love in Sumer with the natural, passionate love between "man and maid."

It is well known that marriage in ancient Sumer, and indeed in the ancient Near East in general, was usually a practical arrangement in which the carefully weighed shekel counted more than love's hot desire. Nevertheless, there is considerable evidence that there was no little wooing and cooing before marriage; much of it was no doubt surreptitious and all the sweeter for it. A very illuminating example is furnished by a poem inscribed on a tablet in the Hilprecht Collection of the Friedrich-Schiller University of Jena, which might well be entitled "Love Finds a Way" or "Fooling Mother." The two main characters in the poem are Inanna, "Queen of Heaven," the Sumerian Venus, and Dumuzi, her sweetheart and husband-to-be. The poem, which is designated by the ancient scribe himself as a *tigi*, that is, probably a song recited to the accompaniment of the lyre, is divided into two stanzas. The first begins with a soliloquy by Inanna in which she relates that one day while she was innocently singing and dancing about in heaven, Dumuzi met her, took her hand, and embraced her; she then begged him to let go of her, since she did not know how she could keep this clandestine love from her mother Ningal, wife of the moon-god, Sin. Whereupon Dumuzi suggests that she deceive her mother by telling her that she whiled away the hours with a girl friend in the public square. And with this as a ready excuse, they make love by the moonlight. Here now are the poet's own words:

Last night as I the queen was shining bright,
Last night as I the queen of heaven was shining bright,
As I was shining bright, was dancing about,
As I was singing away while the bright light overcame (?) the night,

He met me, he met me,
The lord Kuli-Anna (Dumuzi) met me,
The lord put his hand into my hand,
Ushumgal-Anna (Dumuzi) embraced me.

There then follows a rather engaging, tender, and amorous tête-à-tête between the two lovers, with Inanna pleading:

Come (?) now (?) set me free, I must go home,
Kuli-Enlil, (Dumuzi) set me free, I must go home,
What can I say to deceive my mother!
What can I say to deceive my mother, Ningal!

But this does not stop Dumuzi, who has a ready answer:

I will tell you, I will tell you,
Inanna, most deceitful of women, I will tell you,
(Say) "My girl friend, she took me with her to the public square,
There a player (?) entertained (?) us with dancing,
His chant, the sweet, he sang for us,
In sweet rejoicing he whiled away the time for us";
Thus deceitfully stand up to your mother,
While we by the moonlight take our fill of love,
I will prepare (?) for you a bed pure, sweet, and noble,
The sweet day will bring you joyful fulfilment."

The second stanza consists of an exulting monologue by Inanna —and no wonder—since it seems that after their night of pleasure, Dumuzi had agreed to marry her. The first part of the stanza is destroyed; when the text picks up again, Inanna is making a joyful announcement that Dumuzi is about to speak to her mother, presumably to ask for her hand in marriage. The poem concludes, naturally enough, with Inanna's ecstatic eulogy of her husband-to-be and the future victim of her dire wrath.

I (Inanna) have come to my mother's gate,
Walking in joy,
I have come to Ningal's gate,
Walking in joy,
To my mother he (Dumuzi) will say the word,
Will sprinkle cypress oil on the floor,
To my mother Ningal he will say the word,
Will sprinkle cypress oil on the floor,
He whose dwelling is fragrant,
Whose word brings joy.

My lord of pure and seemly limbs,
Ama-Ushumgal-Anna, the son-in-law of Sin,
My lord, sweet is your increase,
Tasty your plants and herbs in the plain,
Ama-Ushumgal-Anna, sweet is your increase,
Tasty your plants and herbs in the plain.

Although according to this poem, Inanna and Dumuzi keep their love a secret and are even prepared to deceive Inanna's mother, there is another version of the affair in which Dumuzi woos his bride in the open and with her mother's full approbation. According to this myth, Dumuzi, the shepherd, comes to Inanna's house and asks for admittance. At her mother's advice, she bathes and anoints herself, puts on her queenly robes, adorns herself with precious stones, and opens the door for Dumuzi. They embrace in joy and probably cohabit.

In still another version of the Dumuzi-Inanna courtship and marriage, the permission of Inanna's father, the moon-god, Sin, seems to be an essential condition. According to this poem, which consists of two stanzas, Inanna, after bedecking the various parts of her body with jewels of precious metals and stones, is met by Dumuzi in the *gipar* of the Eanna temple in Erech. She is eager to bed with him at once, but evidently finds it advisable to get her father's consent; in any case, we find her sending a messenger to her father with the request that Dumuzi be allowed to dally with her.

While according to the three versions summarized above, Inanna's love for Dumuzi seems every bit as warm and passionate as that of Dumuzi for her—even more so in some respects—we get quite a different picture from another Sumerian poem which belongs to the disputation genre of literary works. According to this myth, which is in the form of a playlet, Inanna actually loves the farmer Enkimdu and not the shepherd Dumuzi. In spite of the persuasive efforts of her brother, the sun-god Utu, Inanna first turns Dumuzi down "flat" and only changes her mind after a rather angry and aggressive speech by Dumuzi in which he emphasizes the superiority of his possessions over those of Enkimdu. In fact, Dumuzi is so upset by Inanna's preference that he tries to pick a fight with his rival, Enkimdu, and it is only after the latter appeases him with friendly words and promises that the two rivals become reconciled.

Nor were Dumuzi and Inanna the only deities whose marriage was preceded by a passionate love affair. Enlil, the leading deity of the Sumerian pantheon, Nippur's "young man," fell in love at first sight with Ninlil, Nippur's "young maid," when he saw her on the bank of Nippur's stream, Nunbirdu, after she had bathed in its "pure waters." When she turned down his ardent advances, he had his messenger Nusku bring up a boat, where he raped her and impregnated her with the seed of the moon-god, Nanna. For this violent act he was punished by the fifty great gods with banishment to the nether world, but the faithful Ninlil followed him and had there three more children by him. At some time the couple must have gotten married, for Ninlil is known throughout the Sumerian literary documents as Enlil's worthy and respectable wife.

The Bedu-god Martu, on the other hand, had no need to rape the lady of his choice, Adnigkishar, daughter of Numushda, the tutelary deity of the city Kazallu. When at a divine banquet in the city of Aktab Martu expressed his wish for her to become his wife, she joyfully agreed in spite of a friend who tried hard to dissuade her because Martu was known as

A tent-dweller [buffeted (?)] by wind and rain, [he knows (?) not (?)] prayers,
With the weapon he [makes (?)] the mountain his habitation,
Contentious to excess, he turns (?) against the lands, knows not to bend the knee,
Eats uncooked meat,
Has no house in his lifetime,
Is not brought to burial when he dies.

Finally the important role which love and sex played before marriage, at least in some cases, may be inferred from the love songs purported to be sung by priestesses selected as brides for the king on the occasion of the *hieros-gamos* celebrated on New Year's Day. Two such songs have come down to us, and these ring out with passionate love and sexual ecstasy. Here, for example, is one of these poems addressed to the king Shu-Sin by his beloved "bride":

Bridegroom, dear to my heart,
Goodly is your beauty, honeysweet,
Lion, dear to my heart,
Goodly is your beauty, honeysweet.

You have captivated me, let me stand tremblingly before you,
Bridegroom, I would be taken by you to the bedchamber,
You have captivated me, let me stand tremblingly before you,
Lion, I would be taken by you to the bedchamber.

Bridegroom, let me caress you,
My precious caress is more savory than honey,
In the bedchamber, honey-filled,
Let me enjoy your goodly beauty,
Lion, let me caress you,
My precious caress is more savory than honey.

Bridegroom, you have taken your pleasure of me,
Tell my mother, she will give you delicacies,
My father, he will give you gifts.

Your spirit, I know where to cheer your spirit,
Bridegroom, sleep in our house until dawn,
Your heart, I know where to gladden your heart,
Lion, sleep in our house until dawn.

You, because you love me,
Give me pray of your caresses,
My lord god, my lord protector,
My Shu-Sin, who gladdens Enlil's heart,
Give me pray of your caresses.

Your place goodly as honey, pray lay (your) hand on it,
Bring (your) hand over like a *gishban*-garment,
Cup (your) hand over it like a *gishban-sikin*-garment.

Thus there is reason to believe that not all marriages in Sumer were for practical advantages and that at least in some instances they were motivated by love and desire. It is not surprising therefore to find a Sumerian proverb reading:

> Marry a wife according to your choice;
> have a child as your heart desires!

To be sure, marriage was no light burden for the Sumerian, as is evident from the proverb:

> Who has not supported a wife or child,
> has not borne a leash.

Moreover, the Sumerian husband frequently found himself neglected, or as one of them puts it:

> My wife is at the outdoor shrine,
> my mother is down by the river,
> and here am I starving of hunger.

Indeed, the Sumerian male at least at times regretted his marriage, as can be seen from the saying:

> For his pleasure—marriage;
> on his thinking it over—divorce.

Whether there was love or not before marriage, once married, the couple settled down to humdrum, day-by-day existence in which love receded more and more to the background. Even so, it is not altogether unknown, and such phrases as "beloved husband" and "beloved wife" are not infrequent in the Sumerian documents. Thus, for example, in the poem "Gilgamesh, Enkidu, and the Nether World," we find Gilgamesh advising his loyal servant Enkidu, who is about to descend to the nether world to bring up Gilgamesh's *pukku* and *mikku*:

> Kiss not your beloved wife,
> Strike not your hated wife,
> Kiss not your beloved son,
> Strike not your hated son.

Or when the king Ur-Nammu, having died and gone to the nether world, finds no peace and sets up a long and bitter lament in part because of his wife whom he can no longer press to his bosom and his child whom he can no longer fondle on his knee. The king is frequently designated as the "beloved husband" of Inanna. On the votive inscriptions, the husband not infrequently includes his wife and children, that is, he dedicates the object to the deity not only for his own life but also for that of his wife and children.

This brings us to the family, the basic unit of Sumerian society. That the members of the family were knit closely together by love, respect, and familial obligations is clear from the proverb:

The desert canteen is a man's life; the shoe is a man's eye; the wife is man's future; the son is a man's refuge; the daughter is a man's salvation; the daughter-in-law is a man's devil.

And from a lamentation passage such as:

The storm which knows not the mother, the storm which knows not the father,
The storm which knows not the wife, the storm which knows not the child,
The storm which knows not the sister, the storm which knows not the brother,
The storm which knows not the male friend, the storm which knows not the female friend.

And from this passage which describes the lamentable conditions which were to prevail in the city of Ur in accordance with a decision reached by the angry gods:

The mother will not care for her son,
The father will not cry out, O my wife,
The concubine will not rejoice in the lap,
The children will not be fondled on their knees.

Similarly, when the Sumerian "Job," afflicted with dire suffering and pain, beseeches his own personal god, his "guardian angel," the father who begot him, as it were, he calls on his family to stand by him with tears and lament:

Lo, let not my mother who bore me cease my lament before you,
Let not my sister utter the happy song and chant,
Let her utter tearfully my misfortunes before you,
Let my wife voice mournfully my suffering,
Let the expert singer bemoan my bitter fate.

Revealing, too, in this respect, is the more or less stereotyped description of the *galla's*, the underworld's inhuman, loveless, and cruel demons, as beings who

Take away the wife from the man's lap,
Take away the child from the nursemaid's breast;

or, more extensively, who

Sate not with pleasure the wife's lap,
Kiss not the well-fed children,
Take away the man's son from his knee,
Carry off the daughter-in-law from the house of the father-in-law.

Turning from the family as a whole to the parent-child relationship, it is clear from the passages just quoted that it was normal for Sumerian parents to love and care for their children and for children to love and heed their parents. In the *edubba* essays dealing with the Sumerian schools and schoolmen, the relationship between father and son, in particular, is revealed as close, intimate, and full of understanding. In the Sumerian myths, admonition and advice by parents for the good and well-being of their children are common and stereotyped. The goddess Ninmah, the mother of the storm-god, Ninurta, was filled with compassion for her son, who had performed dangerous and heroic deeds in his struggle with the monsters of the Kur, to such an extent that she was unable to rest and sleep until she had traveled to the Kur, in spite of the "fear and terror of the battle" raging all about. Even animals are thought of as loving their children dearly. The love between cow and calf is proverbial throughout the literature. The love of a bitch for its pup is admirably expressed in this succinct proverb:

This is what the . . . (?) bitch says, "Whether I make them fawn (colored) or whether I make them brindled, I love my young ones!"

Even the monstrous *Imdugud*-bird and his wife raise a bitter cry when they approach their nest and find their young missing.

Normally, too, there must have been a close and warm relationship between brother and sister as well as between parents and children. The brother, especially, seems to have taken the place of the father in some respects. Inanna, for example, turns to her brother, Utu, for help when her sacred tree in Erech is invaded by the snake, the *Imdugud*-bird, and the vicious Lilith. When the time comes for Inanna to choose a husband, it is her brother, Utu, who tries to guide her choice and to persuade her, for her own good, to marry the shepherd Dumuzi rather than the farmer Enkimdu. When the gardener Shukalletuda tries to escape Inanna's wrath, he takes his father's advice and "stay(s) close to his brothers' cities"; and while the word "brothers" here refers to the "black-headed" people as a whole, the fact is that it was because they were looked upon as "brothers" that Shukalletuda felt safe and secure. Enmerkar, when besieged by the Martu in his city Erech, sends Lugalbanda to his "sister" Inanna in Aratta for help. When Dumuzi is seized by the demons, he pleads with Utu to transform him into a gazelle that he may "betake his soul" to his sister, the goddess Geshtinanna, who loves him dearly and tenderly. When Enki falls sick and the mollified Ninhursag proceeds to heal him, she asks repeatedly and tenderly: "My brother, what hurts you?"

To judge from the proverb, "Friendship lasts a day; kinship endures forever," love between friends was not as strong and lasting as that between blood relations. Nevertheless, friendship and loyalty were highly prized in Sumer. The friendship between Gilgamesh and Enkidu was legendary and proverbial throughout the ancient Near East. Lugalbanda's friends were deeply concerned about his contemplated journey to Aratta, which involved the crossing of high mountains and the dreaded river of Kur. When in the course of the march of the Erechites on Aratta, Lugalbanda became deathly ill on Mount Hurum, his grieving friends abandoned him only after they had tried in every way to revive him and believed all hope gone—even so, they promised themselves to pick up his body and return it to Erech on their way back. The Sumerian Job's anguish and bitterness is due not a little to the fact that he finds himself betrayed by his friends and companions.

As for love divine, the love of god for man, it is to be borne in mind that, theoretically at least, the Sumerian theologians taught that man was created by the gods solely to serve and tend them and presumably, therefore, that the god-man relationship corresponded to that of master-slave. But religious attitudes and practices rarely accord with theory and theology, and the love of god for man on the pattern of love between parents and children as well as between husband and wife is a not infrequent phenomenon in the Sumerian documents. To start with, there was the doctrine of the personal god—the "my god" of the worshipper, whom he thought of as his father or mother. It was the love of Inanna for Erech and its people that prompted her to go to Eridu and carry off the *me*'s, the "divine laws," in the "boat of heaven," dangerous though this was. In the lamentation literature, the gods again and again manifest their love and affection. Ningal, the wife of the moon-god, for example, is depicted by the authors of "The Lamentation over the Destruction of Ur" as begging, pleading, and weeping before An and Enlil not to destroy her city and its people. According to a second Ur lamentation, it is Nanna himself who pleads with Enlil to spare his city and its people. When the flood had been decreed, Nintu weeps and Inanna sets up a lament for the people. Even Enlil, aloof and awe-inspiring, is conceived as a beneficent, fatherly deity.

On occasion, individual mortals were treated with love, affection, and compassion by the gods. Both An and Enlil cherished the Flood-hero, Ziusudra, presented him with eternal life, and took him up to dwell among the gods in the "place where the sun rises." When Enmerkar was besieged in Erech by Martu, he sent Lugalbanda with a plea for help to his "sister" Inanna in Aratta, which said in part:

> If she (Inanna) loves the city (Erech) but hates me,
> Why should she link the city with me?
> If (on the other hand) she hates the city but loves me,
> Why should she link me with the city?

Lugalbanda, sick to death, abandoned and forsaken on Mount Hurum, raised his eyes to heaven and wept before the gods Utu, Inanna, and Sin, and in each case—even in the case of Inanna— the poet says that he wept before the deity "like his father who begot him." When Gilgamesh brought an offering to Utu and pleaded for his support as he was about to march off to the "Land of the Living," the poet writes:

> Utu accepted his tears as an offering,
> Like a "man of mercy" he showed him mercy.

According to another poem, Gilgamesh is "the prince beloved of An." Gudea, the man "whom Ningirsu loves," pleads with the goddess Gatumdug:

> I have no mother, you are my mother,
> I have no father, you are my father.

King Shulgi is the beloved of Ninlil. His son, Shu-Sin, is "the Beloved of Enlil, whom Enlil has chosen as the beloved of his heart." Finally, the kings of Sumer are known as the "beloved husbands" of Inanna throughout the Sumerian documents from the time of Enmerkar down to post-Sumerian days, since they seem to have been mystically identified with Dumuzi, an early deified king of the city of Erech, who according to the Sumerian mythographers had actually married Inanna and, at least according to one version, had been handed over by her to the demons, who carried him off to the nether world.

Patriotism, love of country, and particularly love of the home city, was a strongly moving force in Sumerian thought and action. Love of the city-state naturally came first in time and was never altogether superseded by love of Sumer as a whole. The inhabitants of a city were known as its "sons" and were considered a closely related, integrated unit. Normally, they took pride in their city, god, and ruler and were ever ready to take up arms in their behalf. The struggle between the city-states, which in a sense proved to be Sumer's undoing, was bitter and persistent; and they stubbornly refused to give up their independence. At what time Sumer began to think of itself as a political entity consisting of a land divided into numerous city-states is uncertain; it must have occurred some centuries before 2500 B.C. As the royal hymns show, it was the king's sacred, patriotic duty to defend the land from the enemies and bring security and well-being to "the Land," as Sumer was often designated. At least from the time of the Third Dynasty of Ur, the Sumerians, "the sons of Sumer," are known as "the black-heads" and "brothers." The love of the people for their city and state makes itself manifest particularly in the bitter, heartbreaking lamentations in which the Sumerian poets bewail the destruction of both city and state.

Where there is love there is hate, and Sumer was no exception in this respect. Gilgamesh contrasts the beloved wife and the hated wife, the beloved son and the hated son, in the following four lines, which were cited above:

> Kiss not your beloved wife,
> Kiss not your beloved son.
> Strike not your hated wife,
> Strike not your hated son.

Enmerkar contrasts love and hate with telling effect in his plea to Inanna quoted above (page 259). The god Hendursag is a king who "loves justice" but "hates violence." Indeed, if I am not mistaken, hatred played a rather dominant role in Sumerian behavior. As will be shown later, the Sumerian political, economic, and educational institutions were deeply colored by aggressive competition, by a drive for prestige and pre-eminence, which must have inspired a high degree of hatred, scorn, and contempt.

The gods, too, not infrequently displayed hatred and wrath. Enlil, himself, "with frowning forehead," puts "the people of Kish to death" and crushes "the houses of Erech into dust." Then, because his Ekur in Nippur has been pillaged and defiled, Enlil, "the raging flood which had no rival," brings about the well-nigh total destruction of all Sumer by bringing down the barbarous Gutians from their mountains. All four leading deities, An, Enlil, Enki, and Nintu, are implacable in their decision to destroy Ur and Sumer in the reign of Ibbi-Sin. Ninhursag angrily pronounces a curse of death upon Enki, who had eaten the eight plants which she had brought into being. Ninurta angrily curses the stones who had acted inimically toward him in his struggle with the Asag demon. Ereshkigal, the queen of the nether world, "bit her thigh, was filled with wrath" when her chief gatekeeper, Neti, announces the arrival of her sister, Inanna, at the "palace of the nether world."

But the great hater in Sumerian mythology, as might have been anticipated, is also the great lover: the cruel, ambitious, aggressive, but evidently not unattractive, Inanna. When "Dumuzi put on a noble robe" and "sat high on his seat" instead of groveling before his wife, Inanna, who had just ascended from the nether world, she became enraged and turned him over to the seven nether world demons who had accompanied her. As the poet puts it:

> She fastened the eye upon him, the eye of death,
> Spoke the word against him, the word of wrath,
> Uttered the cry against him, the cry of guilt.

When the gardener Shukalletuda took advantage of weary Inanna and raped her, she was so enraged that she sent three destructive plagues against Sumer in a vain effort to locate her abuser. When Gilgamesh rejected Inanna's love proposals, she sent down the vicious "bull of heaven" to ravage Gilgamesh's city of Erech. Even in the hymnal literature, she is depicted at times as a goddess of bitter wrath and dire destruction.

Fear, like hatred, tended to color deeply and darkly the Sumerian way of life. From birth to death the Sumerian had cause at times to fear his parent, his teachers, his friends and fellow citizens, his superiors and rulers, the foreign enemy, the violence of nature, wild animals, vicious monsters and demons, sickness, death, and oblivion. No wonder, then, that the most significant feature of man's golden age, according to Sumerian thinkers, was freedom from fear, or as the poet puts it:

> Once upon a time, there was no snake, there was no scorpion,
> There was no hyena, there was no lion,
> There was no wild dog, no wolf,
> There was no fear, no terror,
> Man had no rival.

Let us turn now from the emotional drives and motivations to the values which pervaded Sumerian life and begin with what is basic and fundamental in all cultures, life itself and the importance attached to it. Love of life pervades Sumerian civilization in all its forms and aspects: social, political, economic, and religious. On the numerous votive objects which the Sumerians dedicated to one god or another, they state frankly and expressly that they do so for the prolongation of their own life or for the life of those close to them. The royal hymnal prayers are replete with special prayers for the long life of the king. The vain and pathetic quest for eternal life is a favorite theme of the Mesopotamian epic. While all peoples and cultures cherish life and value it dearly, the Sumerians clung to it with particular tenacity because of their theological conviction that after death the emasculated spirit descended to the dark and dreary nether world, where life was at best but a dismal, wretched reflection of life on earth. There was no heart-lifting, soul-soothing hope of a life in paradise, although paradoxically enough, there are indications that the good and deserving did have a happier fate than the wicked and evil.

Closely allied to the love of life was the value put on material prosperity and well-being. The Sumerians prized highly wealth and possessions, rich harvests, well-stocked granaries, folds and stalls filled with cattle large and small, successful hunting on the plain and good fishing in the sea. The kings constantly boast in their hymns of bringing prosperity and well-being to the land and its people. The disputation texts, such as those involving Emesh and Enten, and Lahar and Ashnan, are replete with passages exalting the products of farming and cattle-raising. In the lamentations, the poets constantly and in no uncertain terms bemoan the loss of material possessions. To take only one example, here is a revealing passage from a lamentation over the destruction of Ur:

My possessions like heavy locusts on the move have been carried off,
O my possessions, I will say,
My possessions, who comes from the lands below, to the lands below
  has carried off,
O my possessions I will say,
My possessions, who comes from the lands above, to the lands above
  has carried off,
O my possessions, I will say,
My precious metal, stone, and lapis lazuli have been scattered about,
O my possessions, I will say.

The Sumerian proverbs contain many a jibe at the weakness, ineffectualness, and wretchedness of the poor; for example:

When a poor man dies do not try to revive him.

When he had bread he had no salt, when he had salt he had no bread,
When he had meat he had no condiment, when he had the condiment
  he had no meat.

Wealth is hard to come by, but poverty is always with us.

The poor have no power.

How lowly is the poor man; the edge of the oven is his mill.
His ripped garment stays unmended; what he has lost remains unsought for.

There seems to be no trace of such consoling promises to the Sumerian poor as "inheritance of the earth" in some coming millennium or "pie in the sky," to use an American phrase. We may therefore conclude that the pursuit of wealth, no doubt, played an important role in Sumerian life.

Finally, on the level of ethics and morals, the documents reveal that the Sumerians cherished and valued goodness and truth, law and order, justice and freedom, wisdom and learning, courage and loyalty—in short, all of man's most desirable virtues and qualities. Even mercy and compassion were treasured and practiced, at least in the breach, to judge from the numerous references to the special protective treatment accorded to widows, orphans, and refugees as well as to the poor and oppressed. The step-by-step evolution of these ethical values is as difficult to trace for the ancient Sumerian culture as it is for our own. At least in part, they must have grown out of the extension of the love motive from the individual and his immediate family to the community at large and even to humanity as a whole. For the Sumerians, the "black-heads," as they came to be known, realized quite clearly that they were only part of a larger humanity which inhabited the four *ubda*'s, that is, the four regions into which they divided the world as a whole. In fact, as recently pointed out by the young scholar, J. J. A. Van Dijk, the Sumerian word for "mankind," *namlulu*, came to designate in Sumerian not only humans in the collective sense but, like the English word "humanity," all conduct and behavior characteristic of humanity and worthy of it. (For the Sumerian ideas of the world about them, see pages 269–89.) Thus, for example, in the *edubba* essay cited above, "A Scribe and His Perverse Son," the father upbraids his son not only for shocking ingratitude and for failing to follow in his footsteps and become a scribe, but for actions not worthy of his humanity.

But in spite of their lofty ideals and sublime ethics, the chances are that the Sumerians could never have come as far or achieved as much either materially or spiritually, had it not been for one very special psychological drive which motivated much of their behavior and deeply colored their way of life—the ambitious, competitive, aggressive, and seemingly far from ethical drive for pre-eminence and prestige, for victory and success. I first came upon the idea that the will to superiority, the driving ambition for victory over a rival, was a pervading source of motivation in Sumerian behavior in the course of piecing together and translating the Sumerian poems and essays which the ancient scribes themselves categorized as "contests" or "disputations." Quite a number of these uninhibited and quarrelsome literary debates have come down to us, and their very popularity indicates that they reflect a behavioral pattern well known to the Sumerians and approved by them. To cite just a few typical examples of the style used in these contest dialogues, here is first one of the more intelligible portions of a speech addressed by Copper to Silver in the "Copper-Silver" debate:

Silver, only in the palace do you find a station, that's the place to which you are assigned. If there were no palace, you would have no station; gone would be your dwelling place . . . . . (Four lines unintelligible.) . . . . In the (ordinary) home, you are buried away in its darkest spots, its graves, its "places of escape" (from this world). When irrigation time comes, you don't supply man with the stubble-loosening copper mattock; that's why nobody pays any attention to you! When planting time comes, you don't supply man with the plough-fashioning copper adz; that's why nobody pays any attention to you! When winter comes, you don't supply man with the firewood-cutting copper ax; that's why nobody pays any attention to you! When the harvest time comes, you don't supply man with the grain-cutting copper sickle; that's why nobody pays any attention to you! . . . . (Four lines unintelligible.) Silver, if there were no palace, you would have neither station nor dwelling place; only the grave, the "place of escape," would be your station. Silver, if it were not for these places, you would have no place to be assigned to! . . . . (One and a half lines unintelligible.) . . . . Like a god you don't put your hand to any (useful) work. How dare you then to assail (?) me like a wolf (?)? Get into your dark shrines (?); lie down in your graves!

Thus ends Copper's speech. The author then continues:

The taunts which mighty Copper had hurled against him made him (Silver) feel wretched; the taunts filled with shame (?) and bitterness made him smart (?) and wince (?) like water from a salty well. . . . . (One line unintelligible.) . . . . Then did Silver give the retort to mighty Copper: . . . . (There follows Silver's bitter address to Copper, much of which is unintelligible at the moment.)

Or, to take a passage from the "Dispute between Summer and Winter":

Then did Summer give the retort to Winter, who had hurled taunts against him: "Winter, don't brag about your extraordinary strength! I know your lair (?). Let me tell where you "hole up" in the city; you cannot find enough cover (?). You are a sickly (?) fellow and weak-kneed! The fireplace (?), the very edge of the fire, the oven, that's your mountain (?)! Your shepherds and herdsmen with (their) heavy (flocks of) ewes and lambs, the weak-kneed fellows, run before you like sheep from fireplace (?) to oven and from oven to fireplace (?). During the height of the storm you sentence them to constant coughing (?). Because of you, the city people set up a constant chattering of teeth. During the water-drenched (?) days, no one walks the streets. The slave rejoices with the fireplace (?) and spends his days inside the house. The slave girl does not go out into the downpour, and spends her time with clothes. During the winter, the fields are not worked, their furrows are not attended to . . . . (Three lines unintelligible.) . . . Don't you boast of your extraordinary strength; let me keep you straight on the rules and regulations (which govern you)!"

Finally, there is a sample of a bragging speech by the shepherd-god, Dumuzi, whose plea for marriage has just been rejected by the goddess Inanna in favor of the farmer-god, Enkimdu.

The competitive drive for superiority and pre-eminence played a large role in Sumerian formal education, which entailed many years of school attendance and study. Together with the whip and the cane, it was consciously utilized by both parents and teachers to make the student exert himself to the utmost to master the complicated but far from exciting curriculum in order to become a successful scribe and a learned scholar. Thus in the "Schooldays" essay discussed in chapter vi, we find the teacher encouraging the ambitious student with the following persuasive words: "Of your brothers may you be their leader, of your friends may you be their chief; may you rank the highest among the school graduates." Or, to take the essay "The Disputation of Enkimansi and Girnishag," the rival students' speeches bristle with such insulting and vituperative name-calling as "dolt," "numskull," "pest," "illiterate," "bungler," "windbag," etc. Moreover, this particular essay ends in a sentence which prompts a rather startling, but not unilluminating, conjecture concerning another important facet of Sumerian culture, the emphasis on law and legality, the penchant for compiling law codes and writing legal documents, which has long been recognized to have been a predominant feature of Sumerian economic and social life. This sentence reads: "In the dispute between Enkimansi and Girnishag, the teacher gives the verdict." The Sumerian word used here for "verdict" is the same term used for verdicts at court trials, and one cannot hold back the thought that the extraordinary importance which the Sumerians attached to law and legal controls is due, at least in part, to the contentious and aggressive behavioral pattern which characterized their culture.

Turning to the political scene, we now have at least two epic tales celebrating the victory of the head of the Sumerian city-state of Erech over a presumptuous rival who ruled the city-state of Aratta, which was situated not in Sumer but perhaps somewhere in the neighborhood of the Caspian Sea. To judge from the contents of these two poems, it was the driving ambition of each of these rulers to break down the morale of his rival by a kind of "war of nerves" and thus to make submissive vassals of him and his subjects. The tales are replete with taunts and threats carried back and forth by messengers and heralds as well as with challenges and contests. It is finally Enmerkar, the lord of Erech, who emerges as victor and to whom, according to one of the poems, his defeated rival, the lord of Aratta, offers abject submission in these rather revealing words:

You are the beloved of Inanna, you alone are exalted,
Inanna has truly chosen you for her holy lap;
From the lower (lands) to the upper (lands) you are their lord,
I am second to you,
From the (moment of) conception, I was not your equal, you are the
"big brother,"
I cannot compare with you ever!

Quite revealing, too, for the Sumerian drive for victory, prestige, and glory on the political front are the numerous self-laudatory royal hymns in which the Sumerian king recites his own virtues and achievements unblushingly and uninhibitedly in rather hyperbolic and extravagant language.

It is thus fairly obvious that the drive for superiority and prestige deeply colored the Sumerian outlook on life and played an important role in their education, politics, and economics. This suggests the tentative hypothesis that not unlike the strong emphasis on competition and success in modern American culture, the aggressive penchant for controversy and the ambitious drive for pre-eminence provided no little of the psychological motivation which sparked and sustained the material and cultural advances for which the Sumerians are not unjustly noted: irrigation expansion, technological invention, monumental building, the development of a system of writing and education. Sad to say, the passion for competition and superiority carried within it the seed of self-destruction and helped to trigger the bloody and disastrous wars between the city-states and to impede the unification of the country as a whole, thus exposing Sumer to the external attacks which finally overwhelmed it. All of which provides us with but another historic example of the poignant irony inherent in man and his fate.

CHAPTER EIGHT

THE LEGACY

OF SUMER

On the assumption that civilization is of some value for man, the long-dead Sumerians might well point with "fingerless" pride to the numerous innovations, inventions, and institutions which they helped to originate. To be sure, it might be said that these would have come to be in any case, Sumerians or no Sumerians. But this hardly seems to the point—the Sumerians were there first, and it seems not unfair to give credit where credit is due. Be that as it may, in this chapter I shall attempt to sketch rather briefly and hesitatingly some of their more palpable and significant contributions to the culture of man. However, before turning to the legacy of Sumer to later generations, let us take a look at the give-and-take between the Sumerians and their neighbors near and far in the days when they were alive and making history instead of being made into history. And let us start with Aratta, a far-off city-state probably situated in northwestern Iran near the Caspian Sea, which owes its fame and name not to its own achievements, though these seem to have been quite a few, but to the bards and poets of Sumer who, for some as yet undiscovered reason, sang of its metals and stones, its craftsmen and artisans, its boldly challenging *en*, its boastfully confident *mashmash*, and its beloved goddess, who seems to be none other than Inanna of Sumer.

In 1952 I published a Sumerian poem entitled "Enmerkar and the Lord of Aratta: A Sumerian Epic Tale of Iraq and Iran"; it consists of over six hundred fairly well-preserved lines of text pieced together from twenty tablets and fragments now located in the Istanbul Museum of the Ancient Orient and in the University Museum of the University of Pennsylvania at Philadelphia.

The two main protagonists of this epic tale are Enmerkar, a priestly lord—or *en*, to use the Sumerian word—of Erech, an ancient Sumerian city which the Germans have been excavating on and off for the past thirty years, and an unnamed *en* of Aratta, an important but still unidentified city-state in ancient Iran. Briefly sketched, the content of this Sumerian epic tale runs as follows.

Once upon a time, Enmerkar, son of the sun-god, Utu, having determined to make a vassal state of Aratta, implores his sister, Inanna, the powerful Sumerian goddess of love and war, to see to it that the people of Aratta bring gold, silver, lapis lazuli, and precious stones and build for him various shrines and temples, particularly the Abzu, the sea temple of Enki, in Eridu.

Inanna, heeding Enmerkar's plea, advises him to seek out a suitable herald to cross the imposing mountains of Anshan and assures him that the people of Aratta will submit to him and carry out the building operations he desires. Enmerkar selects his herald and sends him to the *en* of Aratta with a message containing a threat to destroy and make desolate his city unless he and his people bring down silver and gold and build and decorate Enki's temple. To further impress him, Enmerkar instructs his herald to repeat to him the "spell of Enki," which relates how the god Enki had put an end to man's "golden age" under Enlil's universal sway over the earth and its inhabitants.

The herald, after traversing seven mountains, arrives at Aratta, duly repeats his master's words to its *en*, and asks for his answer. The latter, however, refuses to yield to Enmerkar, claiming that he is Inanna's protégé and that she had brought him to Aratta as its ruler. Thereupon, the herald informs him that Enmerkar had brought Inanna to Erech and had made her queen of its temple, Eanna, and that the goddess had promised Enmerkar that Aratta would submit to him.

The *en* of Aratta is stunned by this news. He composes an answer for the herald to take back to his king in which he admonishes Enmerkar for resorting to arms and says that he prefers a "contest," that is, a fight between two selected champions. He goes on to say that, since Inanna has become his enemy, he is ready to submit to Enmerkar only if he will send him large quantities of grain. The herald returns to Erech posthaste and delivers the message to Enmerkar in the courtyard of the assembly hall.

Before making his next move, Enmerkar performs several acts apparently ritualistic in character. First, he takes counsel with Nidaba, the Sumerian goddess of wisdom. Then he has his beasts of burden loaded with grain. They are led to Aratta by the herald, who is to deliver to its lord a message eulogizing Enmerkar's scepter and commanding the lord to bring Enmerkar carnelian and lapis lazuli. On arrival, the herald piles up the grain in the courtyard and delivers his message. The people, delighted with the grain, are ready to present Enmerkar with the desired carnelian (nothing seems to be said of the lapis lazuli) and to have the "elders" build his "pure house" for him. But the hysterical *en* of Aratta, after eulogizing his own scepter, refuses and insists, in words identical with those of Enmerkar, that the latter bring *him* carnelian and lapis lazuli.

On the herald's return to Erech, Enmerkar seemingly consults the omens, in particular one involving a *sushima*-reed, which he brings forth from "light to shade" and from "shade to light," until he finally cuts it down "after five years, after ten years had passed." He sends the herald forth once again to Aratta, this time merely placing the scepter in his hand without any accompanying message. The sight of the scepter seems to arouse terror in the *en* of Aratta. He turns to his *shatam* and, after speaking bitterly of the plight of his city as a result of Inanna's displeasure, seems ready to yield to Enmerkar. Nevertheless, he once again issues a challenge to Enmerkar. This time he demands that Enmerkar select, as his representative, one of his "fighting men" to engage in single combat with one of his own "fighting men." Thus "the stronger will become known." The challenge, in riddle-like terms, asks that the selected retainer be neither black nor white, neither brown, yellow, nor dappled—which seems to make little sense when speaking of a man.

On the herald's arrival at Erech with this new challenge, Enmerkar bids him return to Aratta with a three-part message: (1) He (Enmerkar) accepts the *en* of Aratta's challenge and is prepared to send one of his own retainers to fight his representative to a decision. (2) He demands that the *en* of Aratta heap up gold, silver, and precious stones for the goddess Inanna in Erech. (3) He once again threatens Aratta with total destruction unless its *en* and its people bring "stones of the mountain" to build and decorate the Eridu shrine for him.

In the first part of the message, Enmerkar's words appear to clear up the lord of Aratta's riddle-like terms about the color of the retainer to be selected. Enmerkar substitutes the word "garment" for "fighting man." Presumably, the colors were meant to refer to garments worn by the combatants rather than to their bodies.

A remarkable passage follows which, if correctly interpreted, informs us that Enmerkar was, in the opinion of the poet, the first to write on clay tablets and that he did so because his herald seemed "heavy of mouth" and unable to repeat the message, perhaps because of its length. The herald delivers the inscribed tablet to the *en* of Aratta and awaits his answer. But help now seems to come to the *en* from an unexpected source. The Sumerian god of rain and storm, Ishkur, brings to Aratta wild wheat and beans and heaps them up before the *en*. At the sight of the wheat the *en* takes courage. His confidence regained, he informs Enmerkar's herald that Inanna had by no means abandoned Aratta or her house and bed there.

From here on, the text becomes fragmentary and the context difficult to follow, except for the statement that the people of Aratta did bring gold, silver, and lapis lazuli to Erech and heaped them up in the courtyard of Eanna for Inanna.

In another Sumerian epic poem, which consists of close to three hundred lines and which has been only partially published to date, we again find Enmerkar, the *en* of Erech, in a bitter contest with an *en* of Aratta, but with one in this case who bears the good Sumerian name Ensukushsiranna. Its plot, very briefly put, is as follows.

In the days when a certain Ennamibaragga-Utu was king of an empire presumably including Sumer and parts of ancient Iran, Ensukushsiranna, the *en* of Aratta, issued a challenge to Enmerkar, the *en* of Erech, demanding that the latter recognize him as his overlord and that the goddess Inanna be brought to Aratta. Enmerkar is contemptuous of the challenge and in a long address, in which he depicts himself as the favorite of the gods, declares that Inanna will remain in Erech and demands that Ensukushsiranna become his vassal. Ensukushsiranna gathers the members of his council and asks them for advice. They counsel him to submit to Enmerkar, but this he indignantly refuses to do. Whereupon the *mashmash*-priest of Aratta comes to his aid and boasts that he will subdue Erech—and indeed, all the lands "above and below, from the sea to the cedar mountain"—by his magical power. Ensukushsiranna is delighted and gives him five minas of gold and five minas of silver as well as the necessary supplies. The *mashmash* arrives in Erech in due course but is outwitted by the goddess Nidaba's two shepherds and a wise old crone by the name of Sagburru, who finally kills him and throws his dead body into the Euphrates. When Ensukushsiranna hears of what has befallen his *mashmash*, he hurriedly sends a messenger to Enmerkar and capitulates completely, admitting abjectly that Enmerkar is his superior.

Another Sumerian epic tale whose contents are revealing of the extraordinarily close political, religious, and cultural contacts between Erech and Aratta is one which may be entitled "Lugalbanda and Enmerkar." It consists of approximately four hundred lines, and the relevant details of its plot are as follows.

Lugalbanda, one of the heroes of Erech belonging to Enmerkar's military entourage, has just returned to Erech from a perilous journey, only to find his lord and liege in great distress. For many years past, the Semitic Martu have been ravaging both Sumer and Uri (roughly the later Akkad). Now they are laying siege to Erech itself, and Enmerkar finds that he must get a call for help through to his sister (none other than the goddess Inanna of Aratta). But he can find no one to undertake the dangerous journey to Aratta to deliver the message. Whereupon Lugalbanda steps up to his king and bravely volunteers for the task. Upon Enmerkar's insistence on secrecy, he swears that he will make the journey alone unaccompanied by his followers. After receiving from Enmerkar the exact words of his message to Inanna, Lugalbanda hastens to his friends and followers and informs them of his imminent journey. They try to dissuade him, but with no success. He takes up his weapons, crosses the seven mountains that reach from one end of Anshan to the other—or, as the poet puts it, "from the 'shoulder' of Anshan to the 'head' of Anshan"—and finally arrives with joyful step at his destination.

In Aratta, Lugalbanda is given a warm welcome by Inanna. She asks what has brought him all alone from Erech to Aratta, and he repeats verbatim Enmerkar's message and call for help.

Inanna's answer is obscure; it seems to involve a river and the river's unusual fish which Enmerkar is to catch; also involved are certain water vessels which he is to fashion. Enmerkar does as directed, and the poem closes with a paean of praise to Aratta, which seems to have supplied Enmerkar with metal- and stone-workers.

The contents of the three Sumerian epic tales sketched above are of unusual significance for the light they shed on the otherwise practically unknown ancient Iranian city-state of Aratta; they provide us with a number of revealing details regarding Aratta's political organization, economy, and religion, all of which are quite new and unexpected. Thus we find, according to our Sumerian poet, that the political head of Aratta, just as in the Sumerian city-state of Erech, was a military and religious leader known as the *en* and that he bore a Sumerian name. We also find that there were other high political officials in Aratta with such Sumerian titles as *ensi, sukkal, shatam, ragaba,* and *ugula;* and that Aratta, like the Sumerian city-state, had an advisory assembly, whose opinion, however, could be ignored by the city's ruler if he felt disposed to do so.

In regard to religion, we learn that the Sumerian pantheon was worshipped in Aratta. Its tutelary deity was the Sumerian goddess Inanna who, to judge from the first of our epic poems, "Enmerkar and the Lord of Aratta," was only later made the "Queen of Eanna" in Erech by Enmerkar. Another favorite deity of Aratta was Dumuzi—long known as a deified ruler of Erech—the shepherd who, according to the Sumerian mythographers, became Inanna's beloved and death-doomed husband. The god Enki, on the other hand, whose special protégé Enmerkar seems to have been, was rather inimically disposed toward Aratta and its *en.*

Aratta's economic wealth, to judge from our poems, consisted primarily of gold, silver, and all kinds of stone; it was noted, moreover, for its skilled metal- and stone-workers, its masons and sculptors. It was for this reason, no doubt, that the rulers of Erech, a region destitute of stones and metals, were eager to add Aratta to their domain. On the other hand, Aratta was not rich in grain, which Erech had in surplus—hence, perhaps, the readiness on the part of her people to yield to Erech in spite of the wishes of their ruler.

Let us now turn to the geographic indications in our poems and try to figure out the probable location of Aratta on the map. First of all, we are reasonably certain that Aratta was located in Iran, since our poems depict it as separated from Erech, in southern Mesopotamia, by the entire land of Anshan, from its "shoulder" to its "head," and Anshan, most scholars agree, is situated in southwestern Iran. A problem arises, however, in trying to locate Aratta in relation to Anshan. Is it to be sought north of Anshan in the direction of Lake Urmia and the Caspian Sea, or to the east in the direction of Baluchistan and India, or to the south in the direction of Laristan and the Persian Gulf? Once again, it is a Sumerian epic tale which may give us the answer. This poem, which may be entitled "Lugalbanda and Mount Hurum," remained largely unintelligible until 1955, when a large six-column tablet from the Hilprecht Collection of the Friedrich-Schiller University in Jena became available; it tells the following story.

Enmerkar, the lord of Erech, has decided to journey to Aratta in order to make it a vassal state. Accompanied by a vast host of Erechites under the command of seven unnamed heroes and Lugalbanda, who, to quote the words of the poem, "was their eighth," he arrives at Mount Hurum. Then and there Lugalbanda falls ill. His brothers and friends do all they can to revive him, but to no avail. Taking him for dead, they decide that they will leave his corpse on Mount Hurum, proceed on their journey to Aratta, and on their return from the campaign, pick up his body and carry it back to Erech. But Lugalbanda is not dead. Abandoned and forsaken, he prays to the gods of the sun, moon, and the Venus star, and they restore his health. He wanders all over the highland steppe, and there we must leave him for the present, since our available texts break off at this point.

It is clear from this poem that Mount Hurum was situated somewhere between Erech and Aratta, and since it is not unreasonable to assume that Mount Hurum was the original home of the Hurrian people from the neighborhood of Lake Van, we may conclude that Aratta lay in the vicinity of Lake Urmia or perhaps even farther east. In fact, Enmerkar's campaign to Aratta might be compared to some extent with that of Sargon II more than two thousand years later (714 B.C.) to the land of the Mannai, the account of which, interestingly enough, mentions the crossing of a river called Aratta, a name reminiscent, perhaps, of the city Aratta.

From mountain-perched Aratta near the Caspian Sea, let us turn to two lands which often go together in the inscriptions, Magan and Meluhha; their location is still in doubt, although they may turn out to be Egypt and Ethiopia. In fact, most cuneiformists agree that by the first millennium B.C. Magan and Meluhha did correspond roughly to Egypt and Ethiopia. It is for the earlier periods—for the days of Sargon the Great, Gudea, and the Third Dynasty of Ur, for example—that this identification has been generally thought to be most unlikely, since it would involve the seemingly incredible assumption that the peoples of those early days had seagoing ships that could reach the east coast of Africa. This has led to the hypothesis that over the millenniums there was a shift in toponymy, that is, that in the third and second millenniums B.C. the names Magan and Meluhha corresponded to the lands bordering the east and southeast Arabian coasts but that for one reason or another these names were later transferred to Egypt and Ethiopia.

Now methodologically speaking, the verification of a hypothesis involving a name shift in the cuneiform documents for countries of such recognized importance as those referred to by the names Magan and Meluhha should be based on evidence that is reasonably assured and decisive. But as of today, there does not seem to me to be that kind of evidence; there is still a strong possibility, as will become evident from what follows, that there was no toponymic shift and that Magan and Meluhha correspond more or less to Egypt and Ethiopia in the third millennium B.C. as well as in the first millennium.

Magan and Meluhha are mentioned in both Sumerian and Akkadian texts from at least the time of Sargon the Great down to the middle of the first millennium B.C. Sargon the Great, in his own inscriptions, writes that the boats of Magan, Meluhha, and Dilmun rode at anchor in his capital, Agade. His grandson, Naram-Sin, captured Manium, the king of Magan, brought back booty from Magan, and had stones quarried there; a number of alabaster vases dedicated by Naram-Sin and inscribed with the words "booty of Magan" have been excavated. Gudea writes that he obtained diorite for his statues from Magan and wood for the building of his temple Eninnu from both Magan and Meluhha. Ur-Nammu, in the prologue to his law code, speaks of returning the Magan-boat of Nanna on the boundary—an enigmatic statement, but one which seems to point to the importance attached to trade relations between Magan and Sumer. Economic documents from the time of the Third Dynasty of Ur mention such imports from Magan and Meluhha as copper, ivory, carnelian, and onions. In the post-Sumerian periods, we find Meluhha mentioned several times as a place of "black men," which leads naturally to an identification of Meluhha with Ethiopia.

There are also a number of references to Magan and Meluhha in the Sumerian literary texts, published and unpublished, which are highly significant of the close relationship between Magan, Meluhha, and Sumer and which point to the identification of Magan and Meluhha with Egypt and Ethiopia.[1] The references are as follows:

1. A three-line passage in the poem "Gilgamesh and the Land of the Living" which reads:

> After it had sunk, after it had sunk,
> After the Magan-boat had sunk,
> After the boat "The Might of Magilum" had sunk.

These lines are part of a hortatory address by Gilgamesh to Enkidu, who, terrified by the thought of encountering Huwawa, the guardian monster of the "land of the cut cedar," is reluctant to accompany his master on his dangerous journey. The implications of the passage are quite uncertain, but it proves that the theme of the Magan-boat and its sinking was current lore among the Sumerians. Moreover, there is some possibility that the third line, which mentions a boat called "The Might of Magilum," actually refers to Meluhha.

2. A line toward the very end of the myth "Enki and Ninhursag" reads: "Let Nintulla be the lord of Magan." These words are uttered by the god Enki, who is decreeing the fates of eight deities born by the goddess Ninhursag to heal his eight bodily organs

[1] The Sumerian texts as well as detailed references will be found in my "Magan and Meluhha according to the Sumerian Literary Texts," prepared for the Huitième Rencontre Assyriologique.

which had become sick and ailing as a consequence of his eating eight forbidden plants. The name Nintulla has all the earmarks of a Sumerian complex and has the meaning "the lord of *tul*," in which the syllable *tul* represents a word unknown at present. We learn from this line, therefore, that a god of Magan bore a Sumerian name and that the Sumerian poets and men of letters found no difficulty in originating and propagating the idea that their own god Enki had appointed him as the god of Magan. This speaks for a rather close and intimate relationship between the lands and peoples of Sumer and Magan.

3. An eight-line passage from "The Curse of Agade" reads as follows:

The Martu of the highland, who know not grain,
Bring him (Naram-Sin) unblemished oxen, unblemished kids;
The Meluhhaites, the men of the black land,
Bring to him all kinds of exotic wares;
The Elamites and Subarians carry the loads for him like load-carrying
    donkeys;
All the *ensi's* and the *sanga's*,
The comptrollers of the Guedinna,
Lead (their) gifts straight (to Agade) monthly and at new years.

Here, then, we find the Meluhhaites listed as bringing tribute to Naram-Sin in his capital, Agade, alongside the Martu, Elamites, and Subarians. To be sure, it is rather surprising that Magan is not mentioned here, since according to the long-known contemporary votive inscriptions, Naram-Sin conquered Magan and brought back booty from it; in fact, it would seem not unlikely on general grounds that—to paraphrase a well-known American election dictum—"as went Magan, so went Meluhha." Be that as it may, what is of no little importance in "The Curse of Agade" passage is the fact that the Meluhhaites are designated as "the men of the black land," a phrase which closely parallels the expression "the black Meluhhaites" found in the first millennium inscriptions mentioned above. For this similarity tends to indicate that the land known by the name of Meluhha to the authors of that poem, who probably lived some time about 2000 B.C., was identical with that known as Meluhha to the first-millennium scribes, and that there had been no toponymic shift over the years.

4. A two-line passage in a Ninurta hymn published as text No. 61 in my *Sumerian Literary Texts from Nippur*, reads: "Carnelian and lapis lazuli you brought (?) from the land Meluhha." This statement is part of a passage extolling the god Ninurta as the "bringer" of metals, stones, and minerals from the countries in which they are found. Carnelian is indeed well known as a product characteristic of Meluhha, but it is rather surprising to find Meluhha noteworthy also for lapis lazuli.

5. A still unpublished variant of a passage from the myth "Enki and Ninhursag," consisting largely of a blessing uttered no doubt by Enki to Dilmun, reads as follows:

May the land Tukrish transport to you gold [from] Harali, lapis lazuli, (and) .. ;

May the land Meluhha [bring(?)] to you tempting, precious carnelian, *messhagan*-wood, fine "sea"(?)-wood, (and) large boats;

May the land Marhashi [bring (?)] to you "precious" stone (and) crystal,

May the land Magan [bring (?)] to you mighty copper, the strength of .. , diorite, *u*-stone, and *shuman*-stone;

May the "Sea-land (?)" bring (?) to you ebony (?), the ornament ... of the king,

May the land Zalamgar transport to you wool, (?), good ore (?), (and) .. ;

May the land Elam transport to you wool (?) .. , (and) heavy (?) tribute;

May Ur, the dais of kingship, the city .... , [bring (?)] to you grain, sesame oil, noble garments, fine garments, (and) large boats;

May the wide sea bring (?) you its abundance;

The city—its dwellings are good dwellings,

Dilmun—its dwellings are good dwellings;

Its barley is very small barley,

Its dates are very large dates,

Its harvests bring three ... ,

Its trees ..... .

Here, then, Meluhha is depicted as a land noted for carnelian and two types of wood, while Magan is depicted as noted for copper and three types of stone. Since several of these products are known from the economic documents as characteristic of Magan and Meluhha, it would seem not unreasonable to assume that the Sumerian men of letters had a moderately good idea of the economic importance of the two countries and probably of their location as well. Moreover, while this passage tells us relatively little about Magan and Meluhha, it is invaluable for the picture it draws of Dilmun and may even prove significant for the location of that country.

6. A passage from the myth "Enki and the World Order" reads:

The lands Magan and Dilmun
Looked up at me, Enki,
Moored (?) the Dilmun-boat to the ground (?),
Loaded the Magan-boat sky high;
The Magilum-boat of Meluhha,
Transports silver and gold,
Brings them to Nippur for Enlil, the king of all the lands.

Although the meaning of several of the words and phrases is uncertain, the sense of the passage as a whole is quite clear: the people of Magan and Meluhha are depicted as bringing their products by boat—note that the Magilum-boat is here clearly identified with Meluhha—to Enlil's temple in Nippur, that is, of course, to Sumer. It is hardly likely that this description of third millennium B.C. "international relations" was nothing more than an invention on the part of our poets; it must have been common knowledge that these three countries supplied Sumer with many of its economic necessities either through forced tribute or commercial exchange or both.

7. A second relevant passage from the same myth, consisting of sixteen lines, contains Enki's blessing of Meluhha. While some of the words and phrases of this passage are still obscure, it is obvious that the poet knew Meluhha (designated here, too, as "the black land") as a prosperous and populous country rich in trees, reeds, bulls, *dar*-birds—note that the *dar*-birds of Meluhha are also known from the economic documents, which provides additional proof that the poet did not invent his description of the country—*haia*-birds, and sundry metals.

All of this evidence hardly solves with finality the problem of Meluhha's location and identification. But no matter where situated, the fact that the Sumerian poets and men of letters were so favorably disposed toward it would tend to indicate that there was a rather close and intimate relationship between Meluhha and Sumer, far closer and far more intimate than has hitherto been generally thought.

The land Dilmun, to which we now turn, seems to have been even more intimately related to Sumer than Magan and Meluhha. Dilmun is identified by most scholars with the island of Bahrein in the Persian Gulf; a large and highly competent Danish archeological expedition has been excavating there for the past ten years largely because of its faith in this identification. As the following analysis of the relevant literary material will show, however, there is considerable room for skepticism on this point. In fact, there is even some possibility that Dilmun may turn out to include the region in Pakistan and India where a remarkable urban, literate culture flourished toward the end of the third millennium B.C., the so-called Harappan, or Indus Valley, culture.[2]

A fairly obvious clue to the general direction in which Dilmun is to be sought is found in the last extant lines of the Sumerian deluge myth, according to which Ziusudra, the Sumerian Flood-hero, is given eternal life and transplanted by the great gods An and Enlil to Dilmun, which is described as "the place where the sun rises." Now the epithet "the place where the sun rises" hardly fits the island of Bahrein, which hugs the Arabian coast and is almost directly south of Sumer; it is much more likely to refer to the region of the Indus River, or perhaps to Baluchistan.

In the Lugalannemundu inscription (see pages 50–52), eight lands over which Lugalannemundu claims control are named several times in the same order, thus: "The Cedar Land," Elam, Marhashi, Gutium, Subir, Martu, Sutium, and Eanna. On the not unreasonable assumption that this list is geographically oriented, "The Cedar Land" referred to would not be identical with the Lebanon to the west but with a land to the east of Elam. This is borne out by the fact that the sun-god, Utu, is described in the Sumerian literature as the god who "rises from the land of aromatics and cedar." It is not unlikely that this land, which is certainly to be sought in the east, is the same as the "Cedar Land" of the Lugalannemundu inscription. Moreover, since the "Cedar Land" is the place from which the sun rises, it would not be surprising to find that the "Cedar Land" and Dilmun, "the place where the

[2] For a discussion of this culture, see Sir Mortimer Wheeler's *Early India and Pakistan* (1959).

sun rises," are roughly identical. And, indeed, the cedar is mentioned as a tree native to Dilmun in a cryptic and still enigmatic passage in a Dumuzi lament which reads:

> My shoulder is the cedar, my breast is the cypress,
> My . . . . is the consecrated cedar,
> The cedar, the consecrated of Hashur,
> The shade of Dilmun.

If the identification of the "Cedar Land," the place where the sun rises, with Dilmun should turn out to be correct, then the land to which Gilgamesh and Enkidu make their dangerous and adventurous journey in the epic tale "Gilgamesh and the Land of the Living" might also turn out to be Dilmun, although it is never explicitly so called in the poem. For this land, too, is characterized as a land of cedars, and the deity in charge of it is none other than the sun-god, Utu. Moreover, its epithet "the Land of the Living" may point to its identification with Dilmun; for Dilmun, according to the poem "Enki and Ninhursag: A Sumerian Paradise Myth," is described as a land where

> The sick-eyed says not "I am sick-eyed,"
> The sick-headed says not "I am sick-headed,"
> Its (Dilmun's) old woman says not "I am an old woman,"
> Its old man says not "I am an old man."

lines which seem to say indirectly and obliquely that Dilmun is a land of deathlessness and immortality. This would explain, of course, why Ziusudra had been transplanted to Dilmun once the gods had granted him immortality. In fact, it may yet turn out that Gilgamesh traveled to "the Land of the Living" in quest of immortality, in spite of the fact that the initial passages in the poem "Gilgamesh and the Land of the Living" point to the drive for name and fame as the impelling motivation.

But no matter where Dilmun is located, it is clear from what has already been said that it was looked upon by the Sumerians as a blessed paradise land, intimately related to Sumer especially on the religious and spiritual level. According to the myth "Enki and Ninhursag," it appears to have been Enki's home ground, as it were, where he begot quite a number of deities. The great goddess Ninhursag, too, seems to have been quite at home in Dilmun; indeed, it seems to have been the place where all the gods meet.

Its tutelary deity was a goddess bearing the good Sumerian name, Ninsikil, "the pure lady," and her husband, whom Enki begot, was Enshag, "the fair lord." From the variant passage from Ur in the "Enki and Ninhursag" poem quoted above (see pages 147–49), we get the impression that Dilmun was one of the richest and most powerful countries in the ancient world.

Now Dilmun is not just a literary fiction, a never-never land created by the fertile imagination of the Sumerian bards and poets. It has a long history, to judge from the votive and economic documents, beginning with Ur-Nanshe, who records that "the ships of Dilmun brought him wood as a tribute from foreign lands." The boats of Dilmun anchored at the Agade docks alongside those of Magan and Meluhha in the time of Sargon the Great. According to the economic documents from the time of the Third Dynasty of Ur and the Isin-Larsa period which followed, the imports from Dilmun consisted of gold, copper and copper utensils, lapis lazuli, tables inlaid with ivory, "fisheyes" (perhaps pearls), ivory and ivory objects (combs, breastplates, and boxes as well as human- and animal-shaped figurines and end pieces for furniture), beads of semiprecious stones, dates, and onions. "Dilmun onions," in fact, are mentioned in the economic texts dating from as early as the twenty-fourth century B.C. Long after the Sumerians had ceased to exist, throughout the second and first millenniums B.C., we find Dilmun mentioned in the Akkadian documents. There are Dilmun messengers and caravans. The Assyrian king Tukulti-Ninurta uses in his titles the expression "king of Dilmun and Meluhha," reminiscent, in a way, of the Biblical "from India to Ethiopia" used of King Ahasuerus in the Book of Esther. There is a king of Dilmun by the name of Uperi, who paid tribute to Sargon II of Assyria. There is another king by the name of Hundaru, in whose days booty taken from Dilmun consisted of bronze, objects made of copper and bronze, sticks of precious wood, and large quantities of kohl, used as eye paint. In the days of Sennacherib, a crew of soldiers is sent from Dilmun to Babylon to help raze that city, and they bring with them bronze spades and spikes which are described as a characteristic product of Dilmun. Just how to interpret the Sumerian literary evidence which treats Dilmun as a Sumerian Elysium in the light of the "down to earth" Dilmun of the economic and historical documents must remain more or less a mystery until intelligible written documents are found in Dilmun itself, whether it turns out to be the island of Bahrein or the region of Southern Iran and the Indus Valley.

As is evident from what has been said above about Aratta, Magan and Meluhha, and Dilmun, Sumerian influence, particularly at the religious and spiritual level, reached out for thousands of miles and in all directions. It is obvious, too, that over the centuries the Sumerians had accumulated no little information concerning foreign lands and alien peoples. Sumerian merchants roving far and wide by land and sea brought back with them reports of the strange places they visited and of the folk that inhabited them. So, too, no doubt, did the soldiers returning from successful military expeditions. Within the Sumerian cities themselves, there were considerable numbers of foreigners: soldiers captured in battle and brought back as slaves as well as freemen who had come to settle in the city for one reason or another. All in all, therefore, the Sumerian courtiers, administrators, priests, and teachers had considerable knowledge of foreign countries: their geographic location and physical features, their economic resources and political organization, their religious beliefs and practices, their social customs and moral tenets. In fact, not only did the Sumerians *know* a good deal about foreign countries and peoples; they also *judged* them, that is, they assessed their conduct and character and evaluated their way of life in accordance with their own Sumerian standards and values.

To judge from the available evidence, both archeological and literary, the world known to the Sumerians extended no farther than India on the east; Anatolia, the Caucasus region, and the more westerly parts of central Asia on the north; the Mediterranean Sea on the west, although perhaps Cyprus and even Crete might be included; and Egypt and Ethiopia on the south. There is at present no evidence known to me that the Sumerians had any contact with, or knowledge of, peoples living in northern Asia, China, or anywhere on the European continent. The Sumerians themselves divided the world into four *ubda*'s, that is, four regions or districts, which seem to correspond roughly to the four points of the compass. The oldest known grouping of this type is in the golden-age passage of the poem "Enmerkar and the Lord of Aratta," the relevant portion of which reads as follows:

> Once upon a time, the lands Shubur and Hamazi,
> Many (?)-tongued Sumer, the great land of princeship's
>   divine laws,
> Uri, the land having all that is appropriate,
> The land Martu, resting in security,
> The whole universe, the people in unison,
> To Enlil in one tongue give praise.

If this passage is correctly translated, it seems to indicate that the Sumerians thought that their own land Sumer formed the earth's southern boundary; that the district Uri, usually equated with Akkad, though it may at that time have been thought to include a much larger territory, formed the earth's northern boundary; that the eastern district was comprised of Shubur and Hamazi; and that the western region was designated by the name of the land Martu, a word which actually came to mean "west" in the Sumerian language. In the Akkadian omen literature of a later date, which may of course go back to an earlier Sumerian counterpart, the four districts are usually given as Akkad (in place of Sumer) in the south; Elam or Gutium in the east; Shubur in the north (instead of the east as it seems to be in the golden-age passage); and Martu again in the west. Unfortunately, neither the Sumerian nor the Akkadian writers go into detail. Nowhere did they indicate what they thought was the actual extent of these four regions, which seem to leave out of account such countries as India, Egypt, and Ethiopia, for example, countries which were certainly known to both the Sumerians and Akkadians. In any case, according to the Sumerian thinkers, the boundaries of these districts and of the lands in them were marked off by the gods at the time of the creation of the universe, and at least by about 2400 B.C., the credo was accepted throughout Sumer that the air-god, Enlil, was the king of the entire inhabited earth, "the king of all the lands," and not merely of Sumer alone.

Inhabiting the four corners of the earth were the *nam-lulu;* this is a Sumerian compound word probably consisting of *lu,* "man," reduplicated and the particle *nam,* used to form abstract nouns—it therefore corresponds in formation to the English "mankind." The Sumerian people—the "black-heads" as they called themselves from at least 2000 B.C. on—were only a part of this larger mankind but, needless to say, a very important part. In fact, they were so

important a part that at least in one case the "black-heads" seem
to be identified with humanity as a whole. Thus there is a passage
in the first part of the long-known Sumerian Flood myth which
reads:

> After An, Enki, and Ninhursag
> Had fashioned the black-headed people,
> Vegetation luxuriated from the earth,
> Animals, four-legged (creatures) of the plain were
>   brought artfully into existence.

Here, then, "black-heads" seem to be juxtaposed with plants and
animals, as if the word referred to mankind as a whole. Again, according to the same Flood-myth, when the gods had decided to
send down "kingship" on earth, they founded all of the first five
royal cities in Sumer. And when the Flood came "to destroy the
seed of *mankind*," it was the Sumerian king Ziusudra of Shuruppak who was saved by the gods as "the preserver of the name of
vegetation and the seed of *mankind*."

There is little doubt that the Sumerians considered themselves
a kind of "chosen people," "the salt of the earth," as it were. In the
myth "Enki and the World Order," which treats of the god Enki's
creating and organizing the natural and cultural entities and
processes essential to civilized society, we find him blessing Sumer in winged words which reveal that the Sumerians thought of
themselves as a rather special and hallowed community more intimately related to the gods than mankind in general—a community noteworthy not only for its material wealth and possessions,
not only for its powerful kings, but also for its honored spiritual
leaders, the *en*'s—a community which all the fate-decreeing
heaven-gods, the Anunnaki, had selected as their abode.

Naturally enough by no means all foreign lands and peoples
were looked upon with such favor as Meluhha, Dilmun, and
Aratta. Bitterness, scorn, and hatred, however, were heaped primarily on the enemies at whose hands they suffered. The Gutians,
for example, who in the days of the Dynasty of Akkad brought
death and destruction to Sumer and its people, were described
bitterly as "a people which brooks no control," "a stinging viper
of the mountains," "an enemy of the gods." The Elamites and Subarians are termed "men of destruction" in the Sumerian lamen-

tations. Moreover, in the case of the Elamites, we find an attempt at succinct characterization of their personality in two sayings (from a Sumerian proverb collection) which Edmund Gordon is preparing for publication. The first reads literally: "The Elamite —one house for him to live in is not good," that is, presumably, the Elamite was not satisfied with one house. If this interpretation is correct, it is clear that rightly or wrongly the Sumerians looked upon the Elamites as unusually greedy and ambitious. The second proverb reads literally: "The Elamite is sick: his teeth are chattering." If the meaning is that the Elamite could not help wincing from pain, then it is clear that the Sumerians thought the Elamites to be "cry-babies" and unmanly.

In the case of two other peoples, the Hurrians and the Martu, it is not improbable that we have a contemptuous capsule-like characterization wrapped in one word. The Hurrians, as is well known, lived originally on Mount Hurum, the region about Lake Van. Now a word *hurum* is found in Sumerian literature with the meaning "boor," "fool." In fact, in the *edubba* essay "The Disputation between Enkimansi and Girnishag," the word *hurum* is combined with the word *galam,* which means "clever," to describe one of the students as a "clever-fool," or sophomore. Now if the word *hurum,* "fool," is identical with the word *hurum* in the phrase *kur-hurum,* the "land Hurum," this one word would say a whole pageful about what the Sumerians thought of the Hurrians.

Similarly, in the case of the people known as Martus, it is the etymology of the Sumerian word *arad,* "slave," which may prove revealing. For it has been suggested, and in my opinion not without reason, that the word *arad* derives from the word (*m*)*art*(*u*); if this is true, it would indicate that the Sumerians characterized the Martu as of a slavish, servile disposition.

In the case of the Martu, too, there is a Sumerian proverb of cultural significance; it reads literally: "Wheat is prepared with (?) *gu-nunuz*-grain as a confection; the Martu eat it but know not what it contains." This proverb fits in well with an epithet of Martu well known from the literary documents which reads: "Martu who knows not grain."

The Martu, as is well known, were Semites. But if the Sumerians spoke critically of them, it was only with regard to their culture, not their ethnic origin. This leads us to the problem of the

relationship between Semites—particularly those Semites which
came to be known as Akkadians—and the Sumerians. Until recently the history of early Mesopotamia was viewed as a bitter,
deadly struggle between the two racial groups. Some years ago,
however, Thorkild Jacobsen collected some fairly convincing evidence which led him to the conclusion that Semites and Sumerians lived "peacefully side by side in Mesopotamia." This, however, can only be partially true. For when, for example, the Semite
Sargon the Great dedicated his statues and steles in the most
Sumerian of Sumerian temples, the Ekur of Nippur, he (and also
his successors Rimush and Manishtushu) had them inscribed in
both Sumerian and Akkadian and primarily in the latter, which
indicates, of course, that Sargon and his successors were quite
conscious of their Semitic origin and background. Similarly, in
order to keep the conquered Sumerian cities under their control,
Sargon and his successors appointed their Akkadian kin to the
higher administrative posts and garrisoned them with all-Akka-
dian troops, to such an extent, in fact, that economic documents
written in the Akkadian language began to appear all over Sumer
—all of which would hardly endear them to the Sumerians. Thus,
it seems not unlikely that there was considerable friction and
hard feeling between the Sumerians and the Semitic-speaking
and kin-conscious Akkadians who, during the period of the Sargonic dynasty, were striving to become the lords and masters of
Sumer—a rather intolerable situation which may explain in part
the desecration and destruction of the Ekur at Nippur by Naram-
Sin, as described with such bitterness and chagrin by the author
of "The Curse of Agade."

In any case, it was a Semitic people—the Amorites—who put an
end to the Sumerians as a political, ethnic, and linguistic entity.
To be sure, the conquered conquered the conquerors, and the
Amorites, commonly known as Babylonians because their capital
was the city of Babylon, took over Sumerian culture and civilization lock, stock, and barrel. Except for the language, the Babylonian educational system, religion, mythology, and literature are
almost identical with the Sumerian, excluding, of course, the expected changes and variations due to political developments and
the passing of time. And since these Babylonians, in turn, exercised no little influence on their less cultured neighbors, particu-

larly the Assyrians, Hittites, Hurrians, and Canaanites, they, as much as the Sumerians themselves, helped to plant the Sumerian cultural seed everywhere in the ancient Near East. And this brings us to the legacy of Sumer down through the ages, including our own, although in our age this heritage is no longer an active and creative source of cultural growth but a rather melancholy if not altogether uninspiring theme for antiquarian history.

The tracking-down of Sumer's legacy may well begin with the socio-political institution commonly known as the city-state, which, in Sumer, developed out of the village and town in the second half of the fourth millennium B.C. and was a flourishing institution throughout the third millennium. The city—with its free citizens and assembly, its nobles and priests, its clients and slaves, its ruling god and his vicar and representative on earth, the king, its farmers, craftsmen, and merchants, its temples, walls, and gates —is found all over the ancient world from the Indus to the western Mediterranean. Some of its specific features may vary from place to place, but by and large it bears a strong resemblance to its early Sumerian prototype, and its seems not unreasonable to conclude that not a few of its elements and counterparts go back to Sumerian roots. It may well be, of course, that the city would have come into being in the ancient world whether Sumer had existed or not. But this is not at all certain; in Egypt, for instance, the city-state never took root, and the same might have happened in other parts of the ancient world.

One of the most characteristic features of the Sumerian city-state throughout the greater part of the third millennium B.C. was written law, beginning with the writing of legal documents such as sales and deeds and culminating in the promulgation of specially prepared law codes. Written legal documents and law codes are found in later periods all over the ancient Near East, and there is little doubt that although these may differ in details they all go back to Sumerian prototypes; even Greece and Rome would probably never have had their written laws had it not been for the Sumerian penchant for keeping a record of their legal transactions.

In the matter of scientific achievement, it is probably in the field of mathematics that the Sumerians made their major contribution to future generations by devising the sexagesimal system of place notation, which may have been the forerunner of the Hindu-Arabic decimal system now in use. Traces of the Sumerian sexagesimal system exist even today in the measurement of the circle and angle by degrees and in some of the weights and measures that were current until relatively recent times.

In the field of technology, the potter's wheel, the wheeled vehicle, and the sailboat are all probably Sumerian inventions. And while metallurgy is certainly not of Sumerian origin, the products of the Sumerian metalworkers were dispersed all over the ancient Near East, and some even reached as far as Hungary and Central Europe.

Architecture was the major art of Sumer from earliest times, in particular the construction of temples with their stone foundations and platforms, niched cellas, painted walls and altars, mosaic-covered columns, and impressive façades; it would not seem unlikely that at least some of these architectural techniques were diffused over the ancient world. Sumerian architects also made use of the dome, vault, and arch, and it is not improbable that the arch first came to Greece and Rome from contact with Babylonia, which had inherited it from Sumer. Near Eastern sculpture, too, particularly the practice of fashioning statues of gods and men, may go back to Sumerian origins, since it was the Sumerian theologians who first conceived of the idea that the statue represented the ruler, or even some other high official, standing before his god in unceasing prayer, as it were, for his life. The Sumerian cylinder seal "rolled" its way all over the ancient world from India to Cyprus and Crete, and there is many a church in Europe today whose capitals are ornamented with conventionalized motifs going back to scenes first imagined and engraved by the Sumerian artist and craftman.

The achievements of the Sumerians in the areas of religion, education, and literature left a deep impress not only on their neighbors in space and time but on the culture of modern man as well, especially through their influence, indirect though it was, on the ancient Hebrews and the Bible. The extent of the Hebrew debt to Sumer becomes more apparent from day to day as a result of the gradual piecing together and translation of the Sumerian literary works; for as can now be seen, they have quite a number of features in common with the books of the Bible. This chapter will close, therefore, with a sketch of the Biblical parallels found in Sumerian literature by isolating and analyzing the various beliefs, tenets, themes, motifs, and values which seem to be common to the ancient Hebrews and the much more ancient Sumerians.

The form and content of the Sumerian literary works have been discussed and analyzed in great detail in chapter vi of this book, and no further elaboration is needed at this point. It goes without saying that a written literature so varied, comprehensive, and time-honored as the Sumerian left a deep impress on the literary products of the entire Near East. Particularly was this so since at one time or another practically all the peoples of western Asia—Akkadians, Assyrians, Babylonians, Hittites, Hurrians, Canaanites, and Elamites (to name only those for which positive and direct evidence is available at the moment)—had found it to their interest to borrow the cuneiform script in order to inscribe their own records and writings. The adoption and adaptation of this syllabic and logographic system of writing, which had been developed by the Sumerians to write their own agglutinative and largely monosyllabic tongue, demanded a thorough training in the Sumerian language and literature. To this end, no doubt, learned teachers and scribes were imported from Sumer to the schools of the neighboring lands, while the native scribes traveled to Sumer for special instruction in its more famous academies. The result was a wide dissemination of Sumerian culture and literature. The ideas and ideals of the Sumerians—their cosmology, theology, ethics, and system of education—permeated to a greater or lesser extent the thoughts and writings of all the peoples of the ancient Near East. So, too, did the Sumerian literary forms and themes— their plots, motifs, stylistic devices, and aesthetic techniques. And the Hebrews of Palestine, the land where the books of the Bible were composed, redacted, and edited, were no exception.

To be sure, even the earliest parts of the Bible, it is generally agreed, were not written down in their present form much earlier than 1000 B.C., whereas most of the Sumerian literary documents were composed about 2000 B.C. or not long afterward. There is, therefore, no question of any contemporary borrowing from the Sumerian literary sources. Sumerian influence penetrated the Bible through the Canaanite, Hurrian, Hittite, and Akkadian literatures—particularly through the latter, since, as is well known, the

Akkadian language was used all over Palestine and its environs in
the second millennium B.C. as the common language of practically
the entire literary world. Akkadian literary works must therefore
have been well known to Palestinian men of letters, including the
Hebrews, and not a few of these Akkadian literary works can be
traced back to Sumerian prototypes, remodeled and transformed
over the centuries.

However, there is another possible source of Sumerian influence on the Bible which is far more direct and immediate than
that just described. In fact, it may well go back to Father Abraham himself. Most scholars agree that while the Abraham saga as
told in the Bible contains much that is legendary and fanciful, it
does have an important kernel of truth, including Abraham's birth
in Ur of the Chaldees, perhaps about 1700 B.C., and his early life
there with his family. Now Ur was one of the most important
cities of ancient Sumer; in fact, it was the capital of Sumer at
three different periods in its history. It had an impressive *edubba*;
and in the joint British-American excavations conducted there
between the years 1922 and 1934, quite a number of Sumerian
literary documents have been found. Abraham and his forefathers
may well have had some acquaintance with Sumerian literary
products that had been copied or created in their home town
academy. And it is by no means impossible that he and the members of his family brought some of this Sumerian lore and learning
with them to Palestine, where they gradually became part of the
traditions and sources utilized by the Hebrew men of letters in
composing and redacting the books of the Bible.

Be that as it may, here are a number of Biblical parallels from
Sumerian literature which unquestionably point to traces of Sumerian influence:

1   *Creation of the Universe*   The Sumerians, like the ancient
Hebrews, thought that a primeval sea had existed prior to creation. The universe, according to the Sumerians, consisted of a
united heaven and earth engendered in some way in this primeval
sea, and it was the air-god, Enlil—perhaps not unlike the *ruach-
elohim* of Genesis—who separated heaven from earth.

2   *Creation of Man*   Man, according to both the Hebrews and
the Sumerians, was conceived as having been fashioned of clay

and imbued with the "breath of life." The purpose for which he was created was to serve the gods—or Jahweh alone, in the case of the Hebrews—with prayer, supplication, and sacrifices.

3 *Creation Techniques* Creation, according to both Biblical and Sumerian writers, was accomplished primarily in two ways: by divine command and by actual "making" or "fashioning." In either case, the actual creation was preceded by divine planning, though this need not have been explicitly stated.

4 *Paradise* No Sumerian parallels to the story of the Garden of Eden and the Fall of Man have yet been found. There are, however, several paradise motifs that are significant for comparative purposes, including one that may help to clarify the rib episode in Genesis 2:21–23. Moreover, there is some reason to believe that the very idea of a divine paradise, a garden of the gods, is of Sumerian origin (see pages 147–49).

5 *The Flood* As has long been recognized, the Biblical and Sumerian versions of the Flood story show numerous obvious and close parallels. Noteworthy, too, is the fact that according to at least one Mesopotamian tradition there were ten antediluvian rulers, each with a life span of extraordinary length, which is reminiscent of some of the Biblical antediluvian patriarchs.

6 *The Cain-Abel Motif* The rivalry motif depicted in the undoubtedly much abbreviated Cain-Abel episode of the Bible was a high favorite with the Sumerian writers and poets (see pages 217–23 for fuller details).

7 *The Tower of Babel and the Dispersion of Mankind* The story of the building of the Tower of Babel originated, no doubt, in an effort to explain the existence of the Mesopotamian ziggurats. To the Hebrews, these towering structures, which could often be seen in a state of ruin and decay, became symbols of man's feeling of insecurity and the not unrelated lust for power which brings upon him humiliation and suffering. It is most unlikely, therefore, that a parallel to this story will be found among the Sumerians, to whom the ziggurat represented a bond between heaven and earth, between god and man. On the other hand, the idea that there was a time when all peoples of the earth "had one language and the same words" and that this happy state was

brought to an end by an irate deity may have a parallel in a golden-age passage which is part of the Sumerian epic tale "Enmerkar and the Lord of Aratta" (see pages 262 and 285).

8 *The Earth and Its Organization* The Sumerian myth "Enki and the World Order: The Organization of the Earth and Its Cultural Processes" (see pages 174–83) provides a detailed account of the activities of Enki, the Sumerian god of wisdom, in organizing the earth and in establishing what might be termed law and order on it; this poem has its Biblical echoes in, for example, Deuteronomy 32:7–14 (note especially verse 8) and Psalm 107.

9 *Personal God* To judge from the covenant between God and Abraham—note, too, the reference to a "god of Nahor" in Genesis 31:53—the ancient Hebrews were familiar with the idea of a personal god. The belief in the existence of a personal god was evolved by the Sumerians at least as early as the middle of the third millennium B.C. According to Sumerian teachers and sages, every adult male and family head had his "personal god," or a kind of good angel whom he looked upon as his divine father. This personal god was in all probability adopted by the Sumerian paterfamilias as the result of an oracle or a dream or a vision involving a mutual understanding or agreement not unlike the covenant between the Hebrew patriarchs and Jahweh.

To be sure, there could have been nothing mutually exclusive about the covenant between the Sumerian and his tutelary deity, and in this respect, therefore, it differed very significantly from that between Abraham and his god. All that the Sumerian expected of his personal god was that he speak in his behalf and intercede for him in the assembly of the gods whenever the occasion demanded and thus insure for him a long life and good health. In return, he glorified his god with special prayers, supplications, and sacrifices, although at the same time he continued to worship the other deities of the Sumerian pantheon. Nevertheless, as the Sumerian literary document "Man and His God" indicates, there existed a close, intimate, trusting and even tender relationship between the Sumerian and his personal god, one which bears no little resemblance to that between Jahweh and the Hebrew patriarchs and, in later days, between Jahweh and the Hebrew people as a whole.

10 *Law*   That the Biblical laws and the long-known Hammurabi law code show numerous similarities in content, terminology, and even arrangement is recognized by practically all students of the Bible. But the Hammurabi code itself, as has been shown in recent years, is an Akkadian compilation of laws based largely on Sumerian prototypes (see pages 79–88). In fact, there is good reason to infer that the extraordinary growth and development of legal concepts, practices, precedents, and compilations in the ancient Near East goes back largely to the Sumerians and their rather one-sided emphasis on rivalry and superiority (see pages 266–67).

11 *Ethics and Morals*   The ethical concepts and moral ideals developed by the Sumerians (see pages 123–25) were essentially identical with those of the Hebrews, although they lacked their almost palpable ethical sensitivity and moral fervor, especially as these qualities are exemplified in the Biblical prophetic literature. Psychologically, the Sumerian was more distant and aloof than the Hebrew—more emotionally restrained, more formal and methodical. He tended to eye his fellow men with some suspicion, misgiving, and even apprehension, which inhibited to no small extent the human warmth, sympathy, and affection so vital to spiritual growth and well-being. And in spite of his high ethical attainments, the Sumerian never reached the lofty conviction that a "pure heart" and "clean hands" were more worthy in the eyes of his god than lengthy prayers, profuse sacrifices, and elaborate ritual.

12 *Divine Retribution and National Catastrophe*   Jahweh's wrath and the humiliation and destruction of the people that incurs it constitute an often repeated theme in the Biblical books. Usually the national catastrophe comes about through a violent attack by some neighboring people, especially selected as Jahweh's scourge and whip. To this theme the historiographic document "The Curse of Agade" offers a rather interesting parallel: Enlil, the leading deity of the Sumerian pantheon, having been deeply angered by the blasphemous act of a ruler of Agade, lifted his eyes to the mountains and brought down the barbarous and cruel Gutians, who proceeded to destroy not only Agade but almost all of Sumer as well.

13　*The Plague Motif*　The Sumerian myth "Inanna and Shukalletuda: The Gardener's Mortal Sin" (see pages 162–63) contains a plague motif which parallels to some extent the Biblical plague motif in the Exodus story: in both cases, a deity angered by the misdeeds and obduracy of an individual sends a series of plagues against an entire land and its people.

14　*Suffering and Submission: The "Job" Motif*　Quite recently, a Sumerian poetic essay which is of rather unusual significance for Biblical comparative studies has become available. Its central theme, human suffering and submission, is identical with that treated so sensitively and poignantly in the Biblical Book of Job. Even the introductory plot is the same: A man—unnamed in the Sumerian poem—who had been wealthy, wise, righteous, and blessed with friends and kin is overwhelmed one day, for no apparent reason, by sickness, suffering, poverty, betrayal, and hatred. Admittedly, however, the Sumerian essay, which consists of less than one hundred and fifty lines, compares in no way with the Biblical book in breadth, depth, and beauty; it is much closer in mood, temper, and content to the more tearful and plaintive psalms of the Book of Psalms.

15　*Death and the Nether World*　The Biblical Sheol, and, for that matter, the Hades of the Greeks, has its counterpart in the Sumerian Kur. Like the Hebrew Sheol, the Kur was the dark, dread abode of the dead. It was a land of no return, from which only exceptionally the shade of a once prominent figure might be called up for questioning. In the Sumerian literary documents, there are several other interesting parallels with Hebrew ideas relating to the nether world: its depiction as the pitiful home of former kings and princes; the raising of the shades of the dead from it; and the imprisonment in it of the god Dumuzi, the Biblical Tammuz, for whom the women of Jerusalem were lamenting as late as the days of the prophet Ezekiel.

So much for some of the more obvious and significant Biblical parallels from Sumerian literature. Needless to say, this list only scratches the surface. Thus, while revising the translation of the Farmers' Almanac for this book, I was struck by two Biblical parallels of an ethical character which the earlier translation had missed: the touching exhortation to the farmer to show compassion to the "gleaners" during the harvesting and to the oxen during the threshing. In the coming years, as more and more of the Sumerian literary documents become available, the number of Sumerian parallels will grow and multiply—particularly for such books as Psalms, Proverbs, Lamentations, and Song of Songs. These considerations bring us to a question which may already have occurred to the reader: If the Sumerians were a people of such outstanding literary and cultural importance for the ancient Near Eastern world as a whole that they even left their indelible impress on the literary works of the Hebrew men of letters, why is it that there seems to be little trace of them in the Bible? In Genesis, chapters 10 and 11, for example, we find lists of quite a number of eponyms, lands, and cities. But except for the rather obscure word "Shinar," which scholars usually identify with Sumer, but which actually stands for the Sumerian equivalent of the compound word "Sumer-Akkad," there seems to be no mention of the Sumerians in the entire Bible, a fact which is hardly reconcilable with their purported pre-eminence and influence.

Interestingly enough, a solution to this rather puzzling enigma was suggested over a quarter of a century ago by my teacher and colleague, Arno Poebel, in the form of a brief comment in an article published in the *American Journal of Semitic Languages* (LVIII [1941], 20–26). Poebel's suggestion has found no responsive echo among Orientalists, and it seems to have been relegated to scholarly oblivion. It is my conviction, however, that it will stand the test of time and in due course be recognized as a significant contribution to Hebrew-Sumerian interconnections.

Before evaluating Poebel's explanation, however, the reader will have to bear in mind a rather curious, but well-founded and generally accepted, Sumerian phonetic law which is essential to an intelligent approach to the problems involved. This law, the formulation of which marked a milestone in the study of the Sumerian language, may be stated as follows: Sumerian *final* consonants were *amissible* and were not pronounced in speech unless followed by a grammatical particle beginning with, or consisting of, a vowel. Thus, for example, the Sumerian word for field, *ashag,* was pronounced *asha* (without the final *g*). But when this same word appeared in the Sumerian complex *ashag-a,* "in the field," in which the *-a* is a grammatical element equated with the English "in," it was pronounced *ashag*, not *asha*. Similarly, the Sumerian word for "god," *dingir*, was actually pronounced *dingi*, with the final *r* silent. But in the complex, *dingir-e*, "by god," in which the *-e* stands for the English "by," the word was pronounced *dingir*, not *dingi*.

Now to return to our problem and the quest for the word "Sumer," or rather "Shumer," to use the form found in the cuneiform documents. Poebel was struck by the word's resemblance to the name "Shem," Noah's eldest son, and the distant ancestor of such eponyms as Ashur, Elam, Aram, and above all, Eber, the eponym of the Hebrews.

The equation of "Shem" and "Shumer," however, presented two difficulties: the interchange of the vowels *e* and *u* and the omission of the final *er*. Now the first of these presents no difficulty at all; the cuneiform *u* often becomes *e* in Hebrew—a particularly pertinent example is the Akkadian *shumu*, "name," and the Hebrew *shem*. As for the second difficulty—the omission of the final *er* of "Shumer" in its Hebrew counterpart "Shem"—this can now be explained by applying the Sumerian law of amissibility of final consonants. For the word "Shumer" was pronounced *Shumi* or, even more probably, *Shum* (the final *i* is a very short, *shewa*-like vowel), and the Hebrews thus took it over from Sumerian as "Shem."

Nor is Shem the only example of a Hebrew name borrowed from a Sumerian word without its final consonant. The name of the city where Abraham was born is written as Ur in the Bible. But the Sumerian name, as has long been known, is not *Ur* but *Urim*; "in Ur," for example, is *urim-a*, not *ur-a*. In this case, too, therefore, the Biblical authors had borrowed the name as actually pronounced in Sumerian when not followed by a grammatical element beginning with a vowel.

If Poebel's hypothesis turns out to be correct, and Shem is identical with Shumer-Sumer, we must assume that the Hebrew authors of the Bible, or at least some of them, considered the Sumerians to have been the original ancestors of the Hebrew people. Linguistically speaking, they could not have been more mistaken: Sumerian is an agglutinative tongue unrelated to the inflected Semitic family of languages of which Hebrew forms a part. But there may very well have been considerable Sumerian blood in Abraham's forefathers, who lived for generations in Ur or some other Sumerian cities. As for Sumerian culture and civilization, there is no reason to doubt that these proto-Hebrews had absorbed and assimilated much of the Sumerian way of life. In brief, Sumerian-Hebrew contacts may well have been more intimate than hitherto suspected, and the law which went forth from Zion (Isaiah 2:2) may have had not a few of its roots in the soil of Sumer.

APPENDIXES

Appendixes A and B were prepared to give the reader an idea of the Sumerian writing and language.

Appendix C includes translations of thirty-five votive inscriptions based largely on an unpublished manuscript of Arno Poebel, prepared in connection with the GRUNDZUEGE DER SUMERISCHEN GRAMMATIK. Appendixes F (1) and G (1–3) are also based on this manuscript. For references to the original text of the votive inscriptions, see especially Thureau Dangin's DIE SUMERISCHEN UND AKKADISCHEN KÖNIGSIN-SCHRIFTEN; George Barton's ROYAL INSCRIPTIONS OF SUMER AND AKKAD; and Edmond Sollberger's valuable compendium CORPUS DES INSCRIP-TIONS "ROYALES" PRÉSARGONIQUES DE LAGASH.

Appendix D includes sample date-formulas from various sources.

Appendix E is a revised rendering of the Sumerian King List based on Thorkild Jacobsen's KING LIST, F. R. Kraus's "Zur Liste der aelteren Koenige von Babylonien," and the author's copies of the relevant fragments published in UNIVERSITY MUSEUM BULLETIN (see Section II of the Bibliography).

Sections 2–4 of Appendix F are based on a preliminary study of the relevant tablet material by the author.

Appendix G (see above under Appendix C).

Appendix H is based on Francis R. Steele's THE CODE OF LIPIT-ISHTAR.

Appendix I is a translation of the Farmer's Almanac, prepared in collaboration with Thorkild Jacobsen, Benno Landsberger, and Michel Civil.

A. THE ORIGIN AND DEVELOPMENT OF THE CUNEIFORM SYSTEM OF WRITING

The cuneiform system of writing was probably originated by the Sumerians. The oldest inscriptions unearthed to date—more than one thousand tablets and fragments from about 3000 B.C.—are in all likelihood written in the Sumerian language. Whether or not it was the Sumerians who invented the script, it was certainly they who, in the third millennium B.C., fashioned it into an effective writing tool. Its practical value was gradually recognized by the surrounding peoples, who borrowed it from the Sumerians and adapted it to their own languages. By the second millennium B.C., it was current throughout the Near East.

The cuneiform script began as pictographic writing. Each sign was a picture of one or more concrete objects and represented a word whose meaning was identical with, or closely related to, the object pictured. The defects of a system of this type are twofold: the complicated forms of the signs and the great number of signs required render it too unwieldy for practical use. The Sumerian scribes overcame the first difficulty by gradually simplifying and conventionalizing the forms of the signs until their pictographic originals were no longer apparent. As for the second difficulty, they reduced the number of signs and kept them within limits by resorting to various helpful devices. The most significant device was substituting phonetic for ideographic values. Figure 6 was prepared to illustrate this development.

NO. 1 is a picture of a star. It represents primarily the Sumerian word *an,* "heaven." The same sign is used to represent the word *dingir,* "god."

NO. 2 represents the word *ki,* "earth." It is obviously intended to be a picture of the earth, although the interpretation of the sign is still uncertain.

NO. 3 is probably a stylized picture of the upper part of a man's body. It represents the word *lu,* "man."

NO. 4 is a picture of the pudendum. It represents the word *sal,* "pudendum." The same sign is used to represent the word *munus,* "woman."

NO. 5 is a picture of a mountain. It represents the word *kur,* whose primary meaning is "mountain."

NO. 6 illustrates the ingenious device developed early by the inventors of the Sumerian system of writing whereby they could represent pictorially words for which the ordinary pictographic representation entailed a certain amount of difficulty. The sign for the word *geme,* "slave girl," is actually a combination of two signs—that for *munus,* "woman," and that for *kur,* "mountain" (signs 4 and 5 in our table). Literally, therefore, this compound sign expresses the idea "mountain-woman." But since the Sumerians obtained their slave girls largely from the mountainous regions about them, this compound sign adequately represented the Sumerian word for "slave girl," *geme.*

NO. 7 is a picture of a head. It represents the Sumerian word *sag,* "head."

NO. 8 is also a picture of a head. The vertical strokes indicate the particular part of the head which is intended—that is, the mouth. The sign therefore represents the Sumerian word *ka,* "mouth." The same sign represents the word *dug,* "to speak."

NO. 9 is probably a picture of a bowl used primarily as a food container. It represents the word *ninda,* "food."

NO. 10 is a compound sign consisting of the signs for mouth and food (Nos. 8 and 9 in our table). It represents the word *ku,* "to eat."

NO. 11 is a picture of a water stream. It represents the word *a,* "water." This sign furnishes us with an excellent illustration of the process by which the Sumerian script gradually lost its unwieldy pictographic character and became a phonetic system of writing. Although the Sumerian word *a,* represented by sign No. 11, was used primarily for "water," it also had the meaning "in." The word "in" is a word denoting relationship and stands for a concept which is difficult to express pictographically. The originators of the Sumerian script had the ingenious idea that, instead of trying to invent a complicated picture-sign to represent the word "in," they could use the sign for *a,* "water," since the words sounded exactly alike. The early Sumerian scribes came to realize that a sign belonging to a given word could be used for another word with an altogether unrelated meaning if the *sounds* of the two words were identical. With the gradual spreading of this practice, the Sumerian script lost its pictographic character and tended more and more to become a purely phonetic script.

NO. 12 is a combination of the signs for "mouth" and "water" (Nos. 8 and 11). It represents the word *nag,* "to drink."

NO. 13 is a picture of the lower part of the leg and foot in a walking position. It represents the word *du,* "to go," and also the word *gub,* "to stand."

NO. 14 is a picture of a bird. It represents the word *mushen,* "bird."

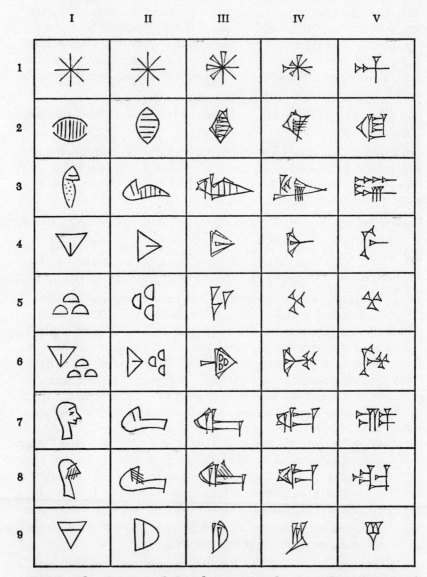

Fig. 6.—*The Origin and Development of the Cuneiform System of Writing. A table showing the forms of eighteen representative signs from about 3000 B.C. to about 600 B.C.*

Fig. 6.—*Continued*

NO. 15 is a picture of a fish. It represents the word *ha*, "fish." This sign furnishes another example of the phonetic development of the Sumerian script. The Sumerian word *ha* means not only "fish" but also "may"—that is, the Sumerians had two words which were identical in pronunciation but quite unrelated in meaning. And so, early in the development of the script, the Sumerian scribes began to use the sign for *ha*, "fish," to represent also the phonetically identical *ha*, "may."

NO. 16 is a picture of the head and horns of an ox. It represents the word *gud*, "ox."

NO. 17 is a picture of the head of a cow. It represents the word *ab*, "cow."

NO. 18 is the picture of an ear of barley. It represents the word *she*, "barley."

The signs in the first column are from the earliest known period in the development of Sumerian writing. Not long after the invention of the pictographic script, the Sumerian scribes found it convenient to turn the tablet in such a way that the pictographs lay on their backs. As the writing developed, this practice became standard, and the signs were regularly turned 90 degrees. The second column in the table gives the pictographic signs in this turned position. The next column represents the "archaic" script current around 2500 B.C. Column IV represents the forms of the signs of about 1800 B.C. in which most of the literary documents were written. The more simplified forms depicted in the last column were the signs used by the royal scribes of Assyria in the first millennium B.C.

B. THE SUMERIAN LANGUAGE

Sumerian is an agglutinative tongue, not an inflected one like Indo-European or Semitic. Its roots, by and large, are invariable. Its basic grammatical unit is the word complex rather than the individual word. Its grammatical particles tend to retain their independent structure rather than become inextricably attached to the word roots. In structure, therefore, Sumerian resembles no little such agglutinative languages as Turkish, Hungarian, and some of the Caucasian languages. In vocabulary, grammar, and syntax, however, Sumerian still stands alone and seems to be unrelated to any other language, living or dead.

Sumerian has six vowels: three open vowels, *a*, *e*, *o*, and three corresponding close vowels, *ā*, *ê*, *u*. The vowels were not sharply articulated and were frequently modified in accordance with a law of vowel harmony. This was especially true of vowels in grammatical particles, which were short and unaccented. At the end of a word, or between two consonants, they were often elided.

Sumerian has fifteen consonants: *b, p, t, d, g* (hard), *k, z, s, sh, ch* (as in the Scottish "loch"), *r, l, m, n,* and *g* (like the ng in "lung"). The consonants were amissible; they were not pronounced at the end of a word unless followed by a grammatical particle beginning with a vowel.

Sumerian roots are monosyllabic in large part, although there are a considerable number of polysyllabic words. Reduplication of roots is used to indicate plurality of objects or actions. Substantives frequently consist of compound words: *lu-gal,* "king" ("big man"); *dubsar,* "scribe" ("tablet-writer"); *di-ku,* "judge" ("judgment-determiner"). Abstracts are formed with the help of *nam* (English "-ship"): *lu-gal,* "king"; *nam-lu-gal,* "kingship." The substantives have no grammatical gender. Instead, they are divided into two categories, animate and inanimate. Animals belong to the inanimate category, grammatically speaking.

The Sumerian sentence consists of (1) a series of substantive complexes related to the predicate either as subject, indirect object, dimensional object, or direct object; (2) the grammatical particles expressing these relationships; (3) the predicate consisting of the verbal root preceded by a thematic particle and a series of infixes recapitulating the relationship between the root and the substantive complexes. The substantive complex may consist of a noun alone or of a noun and all its modifiers, such as adjectives, genitives, relative clauses, and possessive pronouns. The relationship particles always come at the end of the entire substantive complex and are therefore known as postpositions.

Sumerian is rather poor in adjectives and often uses genitival expressions instead. Copulas and conjunctions are rarely used;* the relevant words, complexes, and clauses are usually arranged asyndetically. There is no relative pronoun in Sumerian; a nominalizing particle is used at the end of the clauses instead. Relative clauses, moreover, are used to a limited extent only; their place is often taken by a passive participle which is identical with the infinitive in form.

In addition to the main Sumerian dialect, which was probably known as *Emegir,* "the princely tongue," there were several others which were less important. One of these, the *Emesal,* was used primarily in speeches made by female deities, women, or eunuchs.

* "And" should therefore regularly be in parentheses, but the translations throughout the book have not been consistent in this respect.

C. VOTIVE INSCRIPTIONS

1   AANNEPADA OF UR (tablet)

Aannepada, the king of Ur, the son of Mesannepada, the king of Ur, built a house for Ninhursag.

2   LUGALKIGINNEDUDU OF ERECH AND UR (vase)

When Enlil, the king of all the lands, directed a firm call to Lugal-kiginnedudu and gave him the *en*-ship together with the kingship—the *en*-ship he exercised in Erech, and the kingship in Ur. Then Lugal-kiginnedudu, for his life, with great joy, dedicated (this vase) to Enlil, his beloved king.

3   LUGALKIGINNEDUDU (pieced together from three large blocks of un-hewn red granite and white marble)

Lugalkiginnedudu dedicated (this block) to Enlil.

4   ENSHAKUSHANNA (text pieced together from two vases)

Enshakushanna, the *en* of Sumer, the king of the Land, when the gods had bidden him, made war on Kish and took prisoner Enbi-Ishtar, the king of Kish. (Thereupon) the people of Akshak and the people of Kish [begged him] that he should not lay waste the cities as well [but he should take] their possessions (instead) . . . . . He returned their cities to them (as they requested), (but) he dedicated in Nippur their statues (that is, of Akshak and Kish), their precious metal, precious stone, and their wooden possessions to Enlil, the king of the lands.

5   ENSHAKUSHANNA (vase)

Enshakushanna dedicated to Enlil the possessions of Kish, against which he had made war.

6   UR-NANSHE OF LAGASH (door socket)

Ur-Nanshe, the king of Lagash, the son of Gunidu, the son of Gurmu, built the house of Ningirsu; built the house of Nanshe; built the house of Gatumdug; built the harem; built the house of Ninmar. The ships of Dilmun brought him wood as a tribute from foreign lands. He built the Ibgal; built the Kinir; built the scepter (?)-house.

7   UR-NANSHE OF LAGASH (tablet)

Ur-Nanshe, the king of Lagash, the son of Gunidu, the son of Gurmu, built the house of Nanshe; fashioned (the statue of) Nanshe, queen and *en;* built the temple enclosure of Girsu; fashioned (the statue of) Shulshagga; built the Ibgal; fashioned (the statue of) Lugalur. . . . . ; fashioned (the statue of) Lugaluru; built the Kinir; fashioned (the statue of) Ninab. . . . ; fashioned (the statue of) Ningidri; built the house of Gatumdug; fashioned (the statue of) Gatumdug; built the Bagara; built the harem; built the Abzu of the canals; built the Tirash.

8 UR-NANSHE OF LAGASH (door socket)

When Ur-Nanshe, the king of Lagash, the son of Gunidu, built Girsu, the dwelling place, for Ningirsu, he dedicated (this door socket to him). He (also) built the house of Nanshe; built the Ibgal; built the Bagara; built the harem; built the house of Gatumdug; built the Tirash.

9 EANNATUM OF LAGASH (brick)

Eannatum, the *ensi* of Lagash, who was granted might by Enlil, who constantly is nourished by Ninhursag with (her) milk, whose name Ningirsu had pronounced, who was chosen by Nanshe in (her) heart, the son of Akurgal, the *ensi* of Lagash, conquered the land Elam; conquered Urua; conquered Umma; conquered Ur. At that time he built a well made of baked bricks for Ningirsu in his wide temple courtyard. His (Eannatum's) god is Shulutula. Then did Ningirsu love Eannatum.

(Here the text ends; but this is probably an extract from a longer inscription which tells what Ningirsu did for Eannatum because of his love for him.)

10 EANNATUM OF LAGASH (boulder)

FOR NINGIRSU—Eannatum, the *ensi* of Lagash, whose name Enlil had pronounced, to whom Ningirsu had given strength, whom Nanshe had chosen in (her) heart, whom Ninhursag had constantly nourished with (her) milk, whom Inanna had called by a good name, to whom Enki had given understanding, the beloved of Dumuzi-Abzu, the trusted one of Hendursag, the beloved friend of Lugaluru, the son of Akurgal, the *ensi* of Lagash—his (Eannatum's) grandfather was Ur-Nanshe, the *ensi* of Lagash—restored Girsu for Ningirsu; built for him the wall of the "holy city"; (and) built Nina for Nanshe.

Eannatum conquered Elam, the lofty mountain, (and) heaped up their (that is, the Elamites') burial mounds. He conquered the *ensi* of Urua, who had planted the standard of the city (Urua) at their head (that is, at the head of the people of Urua), (and) heaped up their burial mounds. He conquered Umma (and) heaped up their twenty burial mounds; returned Guedinna, his beloved field, to Ningirsu. He conquered Erech; conquered Ur; conquered Kiutu; laid waste to Uruaz (and) killed its *ensi*; laid waste to Mishime; destroyed Adua.

With Eannatum, whose name Ningirsu had pronounced, the foreign lands fought. In the year that the king of Akshak rose up (to do battle), Eannatum, whose name Ningirsu had pronounced, smote Zuzu, the king of Akshak, from the Antasurra of Ningirsu up to Akshak and destroyed him. At that time, he (Eannatum) dug a new canal for

Ningirsu (and) named it Lummagimdug after his Tidnu name, Lumma —Eannatum was his Sumerian name.

To Eannatum, the *ensi* of Lagash, whom Ningirsu had conceived of (in his mind), Inanna, because she loved him, gave the kingship of Kish in addition to the *ensi*-ship of Lagash.

With Eannatum, (the people of) Elam fought; he (Eannatum) drove (the people of) Elam back to their land. Kish fought with him; he drove the king of Akshak back to his land.

Eannatum, the *ensi* of Lagash, who makes the foreign lands submit to Ningirsu, smote Elam, Shubur, (and) Urua from the Asuhur (canal). He smote Kish, Akshak, and Mari from the Antasurra of Ningirsu.

He reinforced (the walls of the canal) Lummagimdug for Ningirsu and presented it to him as a gift. (Then) Eannatum, to whom Ningirsu had given strength, built the reservoir of (the canal) Lummagimdug containing (?) 3,600 *gur* of 2 *ul* (probably about 57,600 gallons).

Eannatum, whom Ningirsu had conceived of (in his mind), (and) whose (personal) god is Shulutula, built for him (Ningirsu) the palace, Tirash.

11   EANNATUM OF LAGASH (excerpts from the inscription on the Stele of the Vultures)

a) Divine favors bestowed on Eannatum

In [Eannatum] .... Inanna rejoiced; Inanna grasped (his) arm (and) called him by the name Eanna-Inanna-Ibgalkakatum (that is, He-who-is-worthy-of-the-Eanna-of-the-Inanna-of-the-Ibgal). (Thereupon) she sat him on the right knee of Ninhursag, (and) Ninhursag [reached out] her right breast to him.

In Eannatum, the seed implanted in the womb by Ningirsu, Ningirsu rejoiced. Ningirsu measured off (for him) (one extra) span, measured off (for him) cubits up to 5 cubits, (thus making) 5 cubits and 1 span. Ningirsu in great joy .... .

b) The oath of the covenant

Eannatum laid the *shushgal*-net of Enlil upon the Ummaite, (and) he (the Ummaite) swore to him (Eannatum). (And this is) what the Ummaite swore to Eannatum: "By the life of Enlil, the king of heaven and earth! The fields of Ningirsu I will eat (only) up to one *karu*, (and only) up to the old dike will I claim (as my right); but never unto wide eternity will I violate the boundaries of Ningirsu, nor will I infringe upon their (the boundaries') dikes (and) canals; nor will I rip out their steles. (However) if I violate (the boundaries), then may the *shushgal*-net of Enlil, by which I have sworn, be hurled down on Umma from heaven."

Eannatum, moreover, acted very knowingly. Two doves on whose eyes he had put spices (and) on whose heads he had strewn cedar (?) he caused to be eaten for Enlil at Nippur (with the plea): "As long as days exist (and) as long as words are spoken, if the Ummaite, no matter at whose command or at whose request, breaks (his) word to my king Enlil, the king of heaven and earth, (then), on the day that he violates that word, may the *shushgal*-net of Enlil, by which he (the Ummaite) swore, be hurled down on Umma from heaven."

Eannatum (thereupon) laid the *shushgal*-net of Ninhursag upon the Ummaite, (and) he (the Ummaite) swore to him (Eannatum). (And this is) what the Ummaite swore to Eannatum: "By the life of Ninhursag! The fields of Ningirsu I will eat (only) up to one *karu*, (and only) up to the old dike will I claim (as my right): but never unto wide eternity will I violate the boundaries of Ningirsu, nor will I infringe upon their (the boundaries') dikes (and) canals, nor will I rip out their steles. (However) if I violate (the boundaries), then may the *shushgal*-net of Ninhursag be hurled down on Umma from heaven."

Eannatum, moreover, acted very knowingly. Two doves on whose eyes he had put spices (and) on whose heads he had strewn cedar (?) he caused to be eaten for Ninhursag at Kesh (with the plea): "As long as days exist (and) as long as words are spoken, if the Ummaite, no matter at whose command or at whose request, breaks (his) word to my mother Ninhursag, (then), on the day he violates that word, may the *shushgal*-net of Ninhursag, by which he (the Ummaite) swore, be hurled down on Umma from heaven.

Eannatum (thereupon) laid the *shushgal*-net of Enki, the king of the Abzu upon the Ummaite, (and) he (the Ummaite) swore to him (Eannatum). (And this is) what the Ummaite swore to Eannatum: "By the life of Enki, the king of the Abzu! The fields of Ningirsu I will eat (only) up to one *karu*, (and only) up to the old dike will I claim (as my right); but never unto wide eternity will I violate the boundaries of Ningirsu, nor will I infringe upon their (the boundaries') dikes (and) canals; nor will I rip out their steles. (However) if I violate (the boundaries) may the *shushgal*-net of Enki, the king of the Abzu, by which I have sworn, be hurled down on Umma from heaven."

Eannatum, moreover, acted very knowingly. He set free . . . in the . . . . of Ningirsu, (and) the *suhur*-fish of the Abzu he bit to pieces (with the plea): "As long as days exist (and) as long as words are spoken, if the Ummaite, no matter at whose command or at whose request, breaks (his) word to my king Enki, (then), on the day that he violates that word, may the *shushgal*-net of Enki, the king of the Abzu, by which he swore, be hurled down from heaven on Umma."

Eannatum (thereupon) laid the *shushgal*-net of Sin, the spirited young bull of Enlil, upon the Ummaite, (and) he (the Ummaite) swore to him (Eannatum). (And this is) what the Ummaite swore to Eannatum: "By the life of Sin, the spirited young bull of Enlil! The fields of Ningirsu I will eat (only) up to one *karu*, (and only) up to the old dike will claim (as my right); but never unto wide eternity will I violate the boundaries of Ningirsu, nor will I infringe on their (the boundaries') dikes (and) canals, nor will I rip out their steles. (However) if I violate (the boundaries), may the *shushgal*-net of Sin, the spirited young bull of Enlil, by which I have sworn, be hurled down from heaven on Umma."

Eannatum, moreover, acted very knowingly. (Of) four doves on whose eyes he had put spices (and) on whose heads he had strewn cedar (?), two [he caused to be eaten] at Ur [for Nanna (?), two he caused to be eaten at Gaesh (?) for S]in (with the plea): "As long as days exist and as long as words are spoken, if the Ummaite, no matter at whose command or at whose request, breaks (his) word to my king Sin, the spirited young bull of Enlil, (then), on the day that he violates that word, may the *shushgal*-net of Sin, the spirited young bull of Enlil, by which he swore, be hurled down from heaven on Umma."

Eannatum (thereupon) laid the *shushgal*-net of Utu, the king of . . . , upon the Ummaite, (and) he (the Ummaite) swore to him (Eannatum). (And this is) what the Ummaite swore to Eannatum: "By the life of Utu, the king of . . . ! The fields of Ningirsu I will eat (only) up to one *karu*, (and only) up to the old dike will I claim (as my right); but never unto wide eternity will I violate the boundaries of Ningirsu, nor will I infringe upon their (the boundaries') dikes (and) canals, nor will I rip out their steles. (However) if I violate (the boundaries), then may the *shushgal*-net of Utu, the king of . . . , by which I swore, be hurled down from heaven on Umma."

Eannatum, moreover, acted very knowingly. Two doves on whose eyes he had put spices (and) on whose heads he had strewn cedar (?) he caused to be eaten for Utu, the king of . . . , (in) Larsa at the . . . Ebabbar (with the plea): "As long as days exist and as long as words are spoken if the Ummaite, no matter at whose command or at whose request, breaks (his) word to my king Utu, (then), on the day that he violates that word, may the *shushgal*-net of Utu, the king of . . . , by which he swore, he hurled down on Umma from heaven."

Eannatum (thereupon) [placed (?)] the serpent of Ninki [before (?)] the Ummaite, (and) he (the Ummaite) utters the name of (that is, "swears by") Ninki. (And this is) what the Ummaite swore to Eannatum: "By the life of Ninki! The fields of Ningirsu I will eat (only) up to one *karu*, (and only) up to the old dike will I claim (as my right); but never unto wide eternity will I violate the boundaries of Ningirsu, nor will I infringe upon their (the boundaries') dikes (and) canals, nor will I rip out their steles. (However) if I violate them (the boundaries), (then) may Ninki, whose name I have uttered, cause the serpent (rising up) out of the earth to sink its fangs into the foot of Umma; (the moment) that Umma crosses that dike, may Ninki snatch away his foot from the earth.

Eannatum, moreover, acted very knowingly. . . .* (with the plea): "As long as days exist and as long as words are spoken, if the Ummaite, no matter at whose command or at whose request, breaks (his) word to my mother Ninki; (then), on the day that he violates that word, may Ninki, by whom he has sworn, cause the serpent (rising up) out of the earth to sink its fangs into the foot of Umma; (the moment) that Umma crosses over that dike, may Ninki snatch away his foot from the earth."

c) The name of the stele

The name of the stele is Ningirsu, Lord-of-the-Fruitful-Crown, Life-of-the-Canal-Ugedinna—this is not the name of a man; rather, it is its (the stele's) name; the name (that is,) of the stele of the Guedinna, the beloved field of Ningirsu, which Eannatum returned to Ningirsu.

d) Inscription above the shoulder of Eannatum

Eannatum, Ningirsu's prostrator of the enemy lands.

12 ENANNATUM I OF LAGASH (diorite mortar)

FOR NINGIRSU, ENLIL'S FOREMOST WARRIOR—Enannatum, the *ensi* of Lagash, Ningirsu's prostrator of the enemy lands, the son of Akurgal, the *ensi* of Lagash, had a mortar made for the crushing of onions (and) dedicated it for (the prolongation of) his life to Ningirsu in the Eninnu.

13 ENANNATUM I OF LAGASH (stone mace head)

Barakisumun (?), the servant of Enannatum, the *ensi* of Lagash, the *sukkal*, dedicated it (this mace head) to Ningirsu of the Eninnu for the life of his king Enannatum.

14 ENTEMENA OF LAGASH (cones)

Enlil, the king of all the lands, the father of all the gods, marked off the boundary for Ningirsu (and) Shara by his steadfast word, (and) Mesilim, the king of Kish, measured it off in accordance with the word of Sataran (and) erected a stele there. (But) Ush, the *ensi* of Umma, violated (both) the decree (of the gods) (and) the word

---

* In this break we expect a description of some ritual act by Eannatum, corresponding, for example, to the sending of doves in some of the parallel preceding passages.

(given by man to man), ripped out its (the boundary's) stele, and entered the plain of Lagash.

(Then) did Ningirsu, Enlil's foremost warrior, do battle with (the men of) Umma in accordance with his (Enlil's) straightforward word; by the word of Enlil he hurled the great net upon them (and) heaped up their skeleton (?) piles in the plain in their (various) places. (As a result) Eannatum, the *ensi* of Lagash, the uncle of Entemena, the *ensi* of Lagash, marked off the boundary with Enakalle, the *ensi* of Umma; made its (the boundary's) ditch reach from the Idnun (canal) to the Guedinna; inscribed (several) steles along that ditch; restored Mesilim's stele to its (former) place; (but) did not enter the plain of Umma. He (then) built there the Imdubba of Ningirsu, the Nam-nunda-kigarra, (as well as) the shrine of Enlil, the shrine of Nin-hursag, the shrine of Ningirsu, (and) the shrine of Utu.

(Moreover, following the boundary settlement,) the Ummaites could eat the barley of (the goddess) Nanshe (and) the barley of Ningirsu to the amount of one *karu* (for each Ummaite and only) for interest; (also) he (Eannatum) levied a tax on them (and thus) brought in for himself (as revenue) 144,000 "large" *karu*.

Because this barley remained unpaid—(besides) Ur-Lumma, the *ensi* of Umma, deprived of water the boundary ditch of Ningirsu (and) the boundary ditch of Nanshe; ripped out its (the boundary ditch's) steles (and) put them to fire; destroyed the dedicated (?) shrines of the gods which had been built in the Namnunda-kigarra; obtained (the help of) the foreign lands; and (finally) crossed the boundary ditch of Ningirsu—Enannatum fought with him in the Gana-ugigga, (where) the fields and farms of Ningirsu (are), (and) Entemena, Enannatum's beloved son, defeated him. Ur-Lumma (then) fled, (while) he (Entemena) slew (the Ummaite forces) up into Umma (itself); (moreover) his (Ur-Lumma's) elite force (consisting of) sixty soldiers he wiped out (?) on the bank of the Lummagirnunta canal. (As for) its (Umma's fighting) men, he (Entemena) left their bodies in the plain (for the birds and beasts to devour) (and then) heaped up their skeleton (?) piles in five (separate) places.

At that time (however) Il, the temple-head of Zabalam, ravaged (?) (the land) from Girsu to Umma. Il took to himself the *ensi*-ship of Umma; deprived of water the boundary ditch of Ningirsu, the bound-ary ditch of Nanshe, the Imdubba of Ningirsu, that tract (of arable land) of the Girsu tracts which lies toward the Tigris, (and) the Nam-nunda-kigarra of Ninhursag; (and) paid (no more than) 3,600 *karu* of the barley (due) Lagash. (And) when Entemena, the *ensi* of Lagash, repeatedly sent (his) men to Il because of that (boundary) ditch, Il, the *ensi* of Umma, the plunderer of fields and farms, the speaker of evil, said: "The boundary ditch of Ningirsu, (and) the boundary ditch of Nanshe are mine"; (indeed) he (even) said: "I shall exercise control from the Antasurra to the Dimgal-Abzu temple." (However) Enlil (and) Ninhursag did not grant this to him.

Entemena, the *ensi* of Lagash, whose name Ningirsu had pronounced, made this (boundary) ditch from the Tigris to the Idnun in accordance with the straightforward word of Enlil, in accordance with the straightforward word of Ningirsu, (and) with the straightforward word of Nanshe, (and) restored it for his beloved king Ningirsu and for his beloved queen Nanshe (after) he had constructed of bricks the foundation of the Namnunda-kigarra. May Shulutula, the god of Entemena, the *ensi* of Lagash, whom Enlil gave the scepter, whom Enki gave understanding, whom Nanshe chose in (her) heart, the great *ensi* of Ningirsu, the man who had received the words of the gods, stand forever (literally, "unto distant days") before Ningirsu and Nanshe (and plead) for the life of Entemena.

The Ummaite who (at any future time) will cross the boundary ditch of Ningirsu (and) the boundary ditch of Nanshe in order to take to himself fields and farms by force—whether he be (really) an Ummaite or a foreigner—may Enlil destroy him; may Ningirsu, after hurling his great net on him, bring down on him his lofty hand (and) his lofty foot; may the people of his city, having risen in rebellion, strike him down in the midst of his city.

15 ENTEMENA OF LAGASH (brick)

For Ningirsu, Enlil's foremost warrior, Entemena, the *ensi* of Lagash, whom Nanshe had chosen in (her) heart, the great *ensi* of Ningirsu, made the Emah of the boundary which was set up by Enlil for Ningirsu; for Ningirsu, his king who loved him, Entemena made it (the Emah) reach from the Idnun to the Mubikur (?); (and) the steles of the fields (and) farms of the boundaries of Ningirsu he erected for him (there). The god of Entemena, who built the Emah of Ningirsu, is Shulutula.

16 ENTEMENA OF LAGASH (door socket)

For Ningirsu, the foremost warrior of Enlil, Entemena built the chariot house. The god of Entemena, who built the chariot house, is Shulutula.

17 ENTEMENA OF LAGASH (brick)

May Shulutula, god of Entemena, the *ensi* of Lagash, whom Nanshe had chosen in (her) heart, the great *ensi* of Ningirsu, the son of Enannatum, the *ensi* of Lagash, the man who built the Eshgi of Ningirsu, stand forever (literally, "unto distant days") before Ningirsu—Ningirsu, the foremost warrior of Enlil—in the Eninnu (and plead) for his (Entemena's) life.

18   ENTEMENA OF LAGASH (clay nail)

For Nanshe of the E-engurra, Entemena, the *ensi* of Lagash, whom Nanshe had chosen in (her) heart, the great *ensi* of Ningirsu, the son of Enannatum, the *ensi* of Lagash, built the E-engurra (the "house of the deep"), the date "orchard," (and) decorated it for her with gold and silver. He brought it (the clay nail) into (the E-engurra) (and) deposited it (there) for her (Nanshe).

19   ENTEMENA OF LAGASH (stone)

FOR NINGIRSU, THE FOREMOST WARRIOR OF ENLIL—Entemena, the *ensi* of Lagash, the son of Enannatum, the *ensi* of Lagash, built the palace of the Antasurra for Ningirsu (and) decorated it with gold and silver. He built for him the . . -garden (and) laid out wells of burnt bricks in it. At that time, his servant Dudu, the *sanga* of Ningirsu, built the *dasila*-wall of the Guedinna (and) called it E-igi-il-edinna (the "eye-lifting-house-of-the-plain"). He built the walls of the quays for the ferryboats of Girsu, (and) called it Enzishagal ("The-lord-who-gives-the-breath-of-life"). May his god Shulutula prostrate himself (in prayer) before Ningirsu in the Eninnu for his (Entemena's) life.

20   ENTEMENA OF LAGASH (silver vase)

FOR NINGIRSU, THE FOREMOST WARRIOR OF ENLIL—Entemena, the *ensi* of Lagash, whom Nanshe had chosen in (her) heart, the great *ensi* of Ningirsu, the son of Enannatum, the *ensi* of Lagash, made for Ningirsu, the king who loved him, a vase of pure silver (and) stone (?) out of which Ningirsu drinks, (and) brought it to Ningirsu of the Eninnu for his life.

At that time Dudu was the *sanga* of Ningirsu.

21   DUDU (small square block of stone)

For Ningirsu of the Eninnu, Dudu, the *sanga* of Ningirsu, brought it (this stone) from Urua (and) made it into (his) mace top.

Dudu, the head *sanga* of Ningirsu. (Inscription near carving of man.)

22   ENANNATUM II OF LAGASH (door socket)

FOR NINGIRSU, THE FOREMOST WARRIOR OF ENLIL—Enannatum, the *ensi* of Lagash, whom Nanshe had chosen in (her) heart, the great *ensi* of Ningirsu, the son of Entemena, the *ensi* of Lagash, restored for Ningirsu his brewery. The god of Enannatum, the man who restored the brewery of Ningirsu, is Shulutula.

23 URUKAGINA OF LAGASH (olive-shaped clay label)

The name of (this clay label) is—Ningirsu spoke (favorably) with Bau in the temple of Erech about the welfare of Urukagina.

24 URUKAGINA OF LAGASH (cones)

For Ningirsu, the foremost warrior of Enlil, Urukagina, the king of Lagash, built the palace Tirash; built the Antasurra for him; built the house of Bau for her (Bau); built the Bursag, his *sadug*-house for him (Ningirsu); built the sheep-shearing shed in the "Holy City" for her (Bau); dug for Nanshe the Idninadu ("the-canal-going-to-Nina"), her beloved canal, (and) made its reservoir like unto the mid-ocean for her; built the wall of Girsu for him (Ningirsu).

Formerly, from days of yore, from (the day) the seed (of man) came forth, the man in charge of the boatmen seized the boats. The head shepherd seized the donkeys. The head shepherd seized the sheep. The man in charge of the fisheries seized the fisheries. The barley rations of the *guda*-priests were measured out (to their disadvantage) in the Ashte (presumably the storehouse of the *ensi*). The shepherds of the wool-bearing sheep had to pay silver (to the *ensi*) for (the shearing of) the white sheep. The man in charge of field surveyors, the head *gala*, the *agrig*, the man in charge of brewing, (and) all of the *ugula*'s had to pay silver for the shearing of the *gaba*-lambs. The oxen of the gods plowed the onion patches of the *ensi*, (and) the onion (and) cucumber fields of the *ensi* were located in the god's best fields. The *birra*-donkeys (and) the prize oxen of the *sanga*'s were bundled off (presumably as taxes for the *ensi*). The attendants of the *ensi* divided the barley of the *sanga*'s (to the disadvantage of the *sanga*'s). The wearing apparel (here follows a list of fifteen objects, principally garments, most of which are unidentifiable) of the *sanga*'s were carried off as a tax (to the palace of the *ensi*). The *sanga* (in charge) of the food (supplies) felled the trees in the garden of the indigent mother and bundled off the fruit.

He who brought the dead man to the cemetery (for burial)—his beer (that is, the beer he received in return) was 7 pitchers (and) his (loaves of) bread were 420. The . . (an unidentifiable official) received 2 *ul hazi*-barley, 1 garment, 1 head-support, (and) 1 bed. The *ludimma* received 1 (*ul*) barley.

He who brought a citizen to rest among the reeds of Enki—his beer was 7 pitchers (and) his (loaves of) bread were 420. The . . (an unidentifiable official) received 2 *ul* of barley, 1 bed, (and) 1 chair. The *ludimma* received 1 (*ul*) of barley.

The artisans had to beg for their bread (literally, "took bread of supplication"). The apprentices had to take the food leavings (?) of the great gate.

The houses of the *ensi* (and) the fields of the *ensi*, the houses of the (palace) harem (and the fields of the (palace) harem, the houses of the (palace) nursery (and) the fields of the (palace) nursery crowded each other side by side. From the borders of Ningirsu to the sea, there was the tax collector.

If the king's retainer dug a well in the highest part of his field, he seized a blind man (to draw water and presumably did not provide him with adequate food and drink). He (the king's retainer) seized a blind man for the *mushdu*-water which is in the field (presumably to drain it off if necessary and did not provide him with adequate food and drink).

These were the (social) practices of former days.

(But) when Ningirsu, the foremost warrior of Enlil, gave the kingship of Lagash to Urukagina, (and) his (Ningirsu's) hand had grasped him out of the multitude (literally, "36,000 men"); then he (Ningirsu) enjoined upon (literally, "set up for") him the (divine) decrees of former days.

He (Urukagina) held close to the word which his king (Ningirsu) spoke to him. He banned (literally, "threw off") the man in charge of the boatmen from (seizing) the boats. He banned the head shepherds from (seizing) the donkeys and sheep. He banned the man in charge of the fisheries from (seizing) the fisheries. He banned the man in charge of the storehouse from (measuring out) the barley ration of the *guda*-priests. He banned the bailiff from (receiving) the silver (paid for the shearing) of the white sheep and of the *gaba*-lambs. He banned the bailiffs from the tax of (that is, levied on) the *sanga*'s which (used to be) carried off (to the palace).

He made Ningirsu king of the houses of the *ensi* (and) of the fields of the *ensi*. He made Bau queen of the houses of the (palace) harem (and) of the fields of the (palace) harem. He made Shulshaggana king of the houses of the (palace) nursery (and) of the fields of the (palace) nursery. From the borders of Ningirsu to the sea, there was no tax collector.

He who brought the dead to the cemetery (for burial)—his beer was (only) 3 pitchers (and) his (loaves of) bread were (only) 80. The . . (an unidentifiable official) received (only) 1 bed (and) 1 head-support. The *ludimma* received (only) 3 *ban* (½ of an *ul*) of barley. He who brought a citizen (to rest) among the reeds of Enki—his beer was (only) 4 pitchers and his (loaves of) bread were (only) 240. The . . (an unidentifiable official) received (only) 1 *ul* of barley. The *ludimma* received (only) 3 *ban* of barley. The *nindingir* received 1 woman's headband and 1 *sila* of butter.

(At this point the text records a reform which seems to be an innovation rather than a rectification of an earlier abuse: various amounts and kinds of bread and beer were to be given as a permanent ration to such peoples as the *gala*-priest of Girsu and the *gala*-priest of Lagash as well as to the other *gala*-priests, the craftsmen's guilds, unidentifiable officials from the city of Nina, certain blind laborers, and other workers. Following this, the text continues with the reforms of former abuses:)

He did away with (the necessity of) the apprentices (to take) the food leavings (?) of the gate. He did away with (the necessity of) the artisans to beg for their bread. The *sanga* (in charge) of the food (supplies) did not (dare) enter the garden of the indigent mother (for the purpose of felling the trees and carrying off the fruit).

He (Urukagina) (also) promulgated (these two ordinances): (1) When a good donkey is born to a king's retainer, (and) his supervisor says to him, "I want to buy it from you," and when he (the supervisor) is about to buy it from him, he (the king's retainer) says to him (the supervisor), "Pay me as much as I think fair" (literally, "Weigh out for me the silver pleasing to my heart"), then when he refuses to sell it (literally, "does not let it be bought from him"), the supervisor must not coerce him to do so (literally, "he must not strike him" in order to compel his assent to it). (2) When the house of a king's retainer was next to the house of a "big man" (and) that "big man" says to him, "I want to buy it from you," and if when he (the "big man") is about to buy it from him, he (the king's retainer) says, "Pay me as much as I think fair" or "Pay me in barley equivalent to my house," then when he refuses to sell it, that "big man" must not coerce him to do so.

He (Urukagina) amnestied the "citizens" (literally, "the sons") of Lagash who (were imprisoned because of) the debts (which they) had incurred, (or because of) the amounts (of grain claimed by the palace as its) due, (or because of) the barley (claimed by the palace for its) stores, (or because of) theft (or) murder, and set them free.

(Finally) Urukagina made a covenant with Ningirsu that a man of power must not commit an (injustice) against an orphan or widow.

During this year he (Urukagina) dug for Ningirsu the little canal belonging (?) to Girsu (literally, perhaps, "which Girsu has"); gave it its former name (or perhaps conversely, set aside its former name), calling it "Ningirsu-who-is-powerful-out-of-Nippur." He joined it to the Ninadu canal, (saying) "May the pure canal, whose 'heart' is bright, bring clear water to Nanshe."

25   URUKAGINA OF LAGASH (cone)

(This inscription begins with a list of the building activities performed by Urukagina in Lagash for its numerous deities. Following the list, it continues with reforms of the numerous abuses current in Sumer before his days:)

In those days, when Ningirsu, the foremost warrior of Enlil, gave the kingship of Girsu to Urukagina, (and) his (Ningirsu's) hand had grasped him out of the multitude (literally, "36,000 men"), then he (Urukagina) [freed] the Lagashites (from the following abuses):

The man in charge of the boatman used to seize the boats. The head shepherds used to seize the donkeys and sheep. The man in charge of the fisheries used to seize the fisheries. The barley rations of the *guda*-priests used to be measured out (to their disadvantage) in Ashte. The shepherds of the wool-bearing sheep used to pay silver for the (shearing of) the white sheep. (All) such (officials) as the man in charge of the field surveyors, the head *gala*, the man in charge of brewing, the *agrig*, (and) the *ugula's* used to pay silver for (the shearing of) the *gaba*-lambs.

(Following a small lacuna, the inscription continues as follows:)

The *sanga* (in charge) of the food (supplies) did not (dare) enter the garden of the indigent mother, did not fell the trees there, (and) did not bundle off the fruit.

He who brought the dead to the cemetery (for burial)—his beer was (only) 3 pitchers (and) his (loaves of) bread were (only) 80. The .. (an unidentifiable official) received (only) 1 bed (and) 1 head-support. The *ludimma* received (only 1) *ban* of barley. He who brought a citizen (to rest) among the reeds of Enki—his beer was (only) 4 pitchers and his (loaves of) bread were (only) 240. The .. (an unidentifiable official) received (only) 1 *ul* of barley. The *ludimma* received (only) 3 *ban* of barley.

Of the houses of the *ensi*, of the fields of the *ensi*, (and) of the possessions of the *ensi*—Ningirsu was (now) the king. Of the houses of the (palace) harem, of the fields of the (palace) harem, (and) of the possessions of the (palace) harem—Bau was (now) the queen. Of the houses of the (palace) nursery, of the fields of the (palace) nursery, (and) of the possessions of the (palace) nursery—Shulshaggana was (now) the king.

(Here follows the innovation described in the preceding document. Following this, the text continues with the reform of former abuses:)

He did away with (the necessity of) the apprentices (to take) the food leavings (?) of the gate. He did away with (the necessity of) the artisans to beg for their bread.

The "citizens" (literally, "sons") of Lagash who (were imprisoned because of) the debts (which they) had incurred, (or because of) the amounts (of grain claimed by the palace as its) due, (or because of) the barley (claimed by the palace for its) stores, (or because of) theft (or) murder—Urukagina, who had received the kingship of Girsu, set free.

26 URUKAGINA OF LAGASH (oval plaque)

(Following a large lacuna, the text begins with a description of an abuse whose meaning is rather obscure. It reads as follows:)

If sheep were bought, the (influential) man used to carry off the best of these sheep for himself.

(The text then continues:) The barley rations of the *guda*-priests were measured out (to their disadvantage) in the Ashte. (In fact) their barley-ration storehouses were built in the Ashte, (and) were . . .

If the *agrig's*, the *ugula's*, (and) *gala's*, the plowmen, (and) the men in charge of brewing brought wool-bearing sheep to the palace (and) had them shorn there, (and) if the sheep were white, they had to pay 5 shekels of silver for the wool of the sheep (literally, "their wool") which had been brought to the palace.

The oxen of the gods plowed the onion patches of the *ensi*, (and) the onion and cucumber fields of the *ensi* were located in the god's best fields.

(Large lacuna)

If a king's retainer seized a blind man for the *mushdu*-water which is in the field, he would give him to eat (nothing but) the food leavings (?); nor would he give him drinking water; nor would he give the donkey (used by the blind man) drinking water.

If the son of a poor man laid out a fish pond, the (influential) man would take away its fish, (and) that man went unpunished.

If a man divorced (his) wife, the *ensi* took 5 shekels of silver and the *sukkalmah* took 1 shekel of silver. If a perfumer (?) made a "head"-oil preparation (?), the *ensi* took 5 shekels of silver, the *sukkalmah* took 1 shekel of silver, (and) the *abgal* took 1 shekel of silver.

(There follows the description of an abuse which is obscure because the text is fragmentary. Then following a large lacuna, the text continues with the reforms which can be restored in part as follows:)

If a man divorced (his) wife, neither the *ensi*, nor the *sukkalmah* received any silver (in payment). If a perfumer (?) made a "head"-oil preparation (?), neither the *ensi* nor the *sukkalmah* nor the *abgal* received any silver (in payment).

If the son of a poor man laid out a fish pond, the (influential) man did not (dare) take away its fish.

The thief was stoned with stones (upon which was inscribed his evil) intent. Missing possessions (where found or recovered from a thief) were hung up in the great gate (where they could be claimed by the rightful owner).

If a woman said to a man ". . . ." (unfortunately, the text is unintelligible at this crucial point), her teeth were crushed with burnt bricks, (and) these burnt bricks (upon which her guilt was inscribed) were hung up in the great gate (for all to see). The women of former days used to take two husbands, (but) the women of today (if they attempted this) were stoned with stones (upon which was inscribed their evil) intent.

(Following a reform relating to various kinds of seers and diviners which is fragmentary and unintelligible, there is a large lacuna. The text resumes in the midst of the recapitulation of the struggle between Umma and Lagash as recounted in the Entemena cone (pages 311–15) and concludes with a résumé of Urukagina's (?) building activities.)

27   URUKAGINA OF LAGASH (tablet)

The Ummaite has set fire to the Ekisurra. He has set fire to the Antasurra, carried off its precious metal (and) lapis lazuli. He has laid hands on the palace Tirash. He has laid hands on the Abzubanda. He has laid hands on the shrine (or perhaps, "dais") of Enlil (and) the shrine (or perhaps, "dais") of Utu. He has laid hands on the Ahush, carried off its precious metal (and) lapis lazuli. He has laid hands on the Ebabbar, carried off its precious metal (and) lapis lazuli. He has laid hands on the *giguna* of (the goddess) Ninmah of the holy grove, carried off its precious metal (and) lapis lazuli. He has laid hands on the Bagara, carried off its precious metal (and) lapis lazuli. He has set fire to the Dukuru, carried off its precious metal (and) lapis lazuli. He has laid hands on the Abzu of the canals. He has set fire to the house of Gatumdug, carried off its precious metal (and) lapis lazuli, destroyed its statues. He has set fire to the Ibgal-Eanna of Inanna, carried off its precious metal (and) lapis lazuli, destroyed its statues. He has laid hands on the Shapada, carried off its precious metal (and) lapis lazuli. In the Henda he has overturned the . . . He has laid hands on Kiab (and) the house of Nindar, carried off its precious metal (and) lapis lazuli. He has set fire to Kinunir (and) the house of Dumuzi-Abzu, carried off its precious metal (and) lapis lazuli. He has set fire to the house of Lugaluru, carried off its precious metals (and) lapis lazuli. He has laid hands on the E-engurra of Nanshe, carried off its precious metal (and) lapis lazuli. He has laid hands on .. (and) the house of Amageshtin—from (the statue) of (the goddess) Amageshtin he carried off her precious metal (and) lapis lazuli, threw it (the statue) into its well (that is, the well of the house of Amageshtin). He has ruined the barley of the field of Ningirsu, as much as had been plowed.

Because the Ummaite destroyed the bricks of Lagash, he committed a sin against Ningirsu; he (Ningirsu) will cut off the hands which had been lifted (?) against him. It is not the sin of Urukagina, the king of Girsu. May Nidaba, the (personal) goddess of Lugalzaggesi, the *ensi* of Umma, make him (Lugalzaggesi) bear all (these) sins.

28 LUGALZAGGESI (vase)

Enlil, the king of all the lands—to Lugalzaggesi, the king of Erech, the king of the Land (that is, Sumer), the *ishib* of An, the *lumah* of Nidaba, the son of Uu, the *ensi* of Umma (and) the *lumah* of Nidaba, *upon* whom An, the king of all the lands, looked with steadfast eye, the great *ensi* of Enlil, to whom Enki gave understanding, whose name Utu had pronounced, the great *sukkal* of Sin, the *shakannak* of Utu, the sustenance of Inanna, son born of Nidaba, who is constantly nourished by Ninhursag with (her) milk, the "man" of (the god) Messanga-Unugga, the foster child of (the goddess) Ninabuhadu, the queen of Erech, the lofty *agrig* of the gods.

When Enlil, the king of all the lands, had given the kingship of the Land to Lugalzaggesi, had directed to him the eyes (of all the people) of the Land from east to west (literally, "from the rising of the sun to the setting of the sun"), had prostrated (all the people) for him— then (all the people) from the lower sea, along the Tigris (and) Euphrates to the upper sea directed their feet toward him; from east to west, Enlil gave him no rival; (the people of) all the lands lie (peacefully) in the meadow under his rule (literally, "under him"); the Land rejoiced under his rule; all the chieftains of Sumer (and) the *ensi*'s of all the foreign lands bowed down before him in Erech in accordance with the *me* of princeship.

In those days, Erech spent its days in good cheer. Ur, like a bull, raised its head to heaven. Larsa, the beloved city of Utu, uttered cries of joy. Umma, the beloved city of Shara, "raised a lofty arm." Zabalam made the walls re-echo (with cries of joy) like the mother sheep whose lamb has been returned (to her). Der "raised neck to heaven."

Lugalzaggesi, the king of Erech, the king of the Land, dedicated, for his life, various vases to Enlil, his beloved king; in these he brought large food offerings to Enlil, his king, in Nippur, (and) out of these he poured libations of sweet water—with (this) inscription, "May Enlil, the king of the lands, plead for me before An, his beloved father; may he add 'life to my life'; under my rule (literally, "under me") may the lands lie peacefully in the meadows; may all mankind thrive like plants and herbs; may the sheepfolds of An increase; may (the people of) the Land look upon a 'fair earth'; the good fortune which (the gods) have decreed for me, may they never alter; (and) unto eternity may I be the foremost (?) shepherd."

29 SARGON (tablet)

Sargon, the king of Akkad, the *mashkim* of Inanna, the king of Kish, the *guda*-priest of An, the king of the Land, the great *ensi* of Enlil, laid waste the city Erech, destroyed its wall; fought with the men of Erech, conquered them; fought with Lugalzaggesi, the king of Erech, took him prisoner (and) brought him in a neck-stock to the gate of Enlil.

Sargon, the king of Akkad, fought with the men of Ur, conquered them, laid waste their city, (and) destroyed its walls; laid waste E-Ninmar, destroyed its walls, laid waste its territory from Lagash to the sea, washed his weapons in the sea; fought with the men of Umma, conquered them, laid waste their city, (and) destroyed its walls.

To Sargon, the king of the Land, Enlil gave no rival; (indeed) Enlil gave him the entire territory from the sea above to the sea below. Akkadians (literally, "sons of Akkad") held the *ensi*-ships (everywhere) from the lower sea and above; the men of Mari (and) the men of Elam served Sargon, the king of the Land (as their master).

Sargon, the king of the Land, restored Kish (and) gave that city to them (the men of Kish) as a dwelling place.

Whoever destroys this inscription—may Utu tear out his foundation (from under him); may he bereave him of his seed.

THE INSCRIPTION OF ITS (THE STATUE'S) PEDESTAL

30 SARGON (tablet)

Sargon, the king of Kish, triumphed in thirty-four battles (over the cities) up to the edge of the sea (and) destroyed their walls. He made the ships from Meluhha, the ships from Magan, (and) the ships from Dilmun tie up alongside the quay of Agade.

Sargon, the king, prostrated himself before Dagan (and) made supplication to him; (and) he (Dagan) gave him the upper land, (namely) Mari, Yarmuti, (and) Ibla, up to the Cedar Forest (and) up to the Silver Mountain.

Sargon, the king, to whom Enlil permitted no rival—5,400 warriors ate bread daily before him.

Whoever destroys this inscription—may An destroy his name; may Enlil exterminate his seed; may Inanna . . . . .

31 RIMUSH (tablet)

[From days of yore] no one had made a statue of lead, (but) Rimush, the king of Kish, had a statue of himself made of lead. It stood before Enlil; (and) it recited (?) his (Rimush's) virtues in the *idu* of the gods.

Whoever destroys this inscription—may Enlil (and) Utu tear out his foundations (from under him); may they bereave him of his seed.

THE INSCRIPTION OF . . . .

32 NAMMAHNI OF UMMA (clay nail)

In those days when Yarlagan was king of Gutium, Nammahni, the *ensi* of Umma, built for (the goddess) Ninurra, the mother of Umma, her old house and restored it.

33 UTUHEGAL (tablet)

ENLIL—Enlil, the king of all the lands, commissioned Utuhegal, the mighty man, the king of Erech, the king of the four quarters (of the world), the king whose command no one can gainsay, to destroy the name of Gutium, the snake (and) the scorpion of the mountain, who lifted his arm against the gods, who carried off the kingship of Sumer to the (foreign) land, who filled Sumer with enmity, who tore away the wife from him who had a wife, who tore away the child from him who had a child, (and) set up enmity (and) rebellion in the Land.

(Whereupon) he (Utuhegal) went to Inanna, his queen, (and) made supplication to her: "My queen, lioness in battle, who attacks all the (foreign) lands! Enlil commissioned me to bring back the kingship of Sumer. Be you my ally (in this)! Tirigan, the king of Gutium, apportioned (?) the . . of . . . . . (Although) no one marched forth against him, he seized the Tigris and the seacoast. In Sumer he closed off fields below, closed off roads above. He made the weeds grow tall on the highways of the Land."

Utuhegal, the king who was granted might by Enlil, whom Inanna had chosen in (her) heart, the mighty man, marched forth to battle from Erech against him (Tirigan). In the house of (the god) Ishkur, he made an offering (?) (and) spoke to his city: "Enlil has given me Gutium; Inanna, my queen, as my ally, has given my destiny into the charge of Dumuzi, the *ama-ushumgal* of heaven, has given me Gilgamesh, the son of (the goddess) Ninsun, as a *mashkim*."

The citizens of Erech (and) the citizens of Kullab (a district of Erech) were filled with joy. Like one man, (the people of) his city followed him, (and) he directed the troops chosen (?) (from among them).

After departing from the house of Ishkur, he made an offering (?) on the fourth day in the *nagsu* of (the river) Iturungal; on the fifth day he made an offering (?) at the shrine of the goddess Ilitabba. He took prisoner Ur-Ninazu (and) Nabi-Enlil, the *shakannak*'s of Tirigan, whom he had sent to Sumer as ambassadors (and) placed "stocks" of wood upon their hands.

After he (Utuhegal) departed from the shrine of Ilitabba, on the sixth day he made an offering (?) in Muru; he went before Ishkur (and) made supplication to him: "Ishkur, Enlil has given me weapons. Be you my ally (in this)!"

In that very night, ... ; he went to Utu (and) made supplication to him: "Utu, Enlil has given me Gutium. Be you my ally (in this)!"

At (?) that place, Gutium gathered (?) its (?) forces (?) (and) sent forth the troops against him. Utuhegal, the mighty man, conquered them (and) took their *shakannak*'s prisoner.

Then Tirigan, the king of Gutium, fled all by himself back (toward Gutium). In Dubrum, where he had taken refuge, he was treated kindly (?). (But) since the men of Dubrum knew that Utuhegal was the king to whom Enlil had granted might, they did not set Tirigan free. The envoy of Utuhegal took Tirigan (and) his family prisoner in Dubrum, placed "stocks" of wood upon his hands, (and) blindfolded (?) him. He (Tirigan) was (then) brought before Utuhegal, threw himself at his feet, (and) he (Utuhegal) set his foot upon his neck. He (then) prostrated (?) and . . . . Gutium, the scorpion (and) the snake of the mountain, removed (?) the . . . . from (?) its territory, (and thus) returned the kingship to Sumer.

34　UR-BAU OF LAGASH (statue)

For Ningirsu, the mighty warrior of Enlil, Ur-Bau, the *ensi* of Lagash, son born of Ninagal, whom Nanshe has chosen in her heart, who was granted might by Ningirsu, whom Bau has called by a good name, to whom Enki has given understanding, whom Inanna has conceived of (in her mind), the beloved servant of Lugaluru, the beloved of Dumuzi-Abzu—

I, Ur-Bau, dug for Ningirsu, my king, the . . ground to . . ells deep; its (that is, the excavated earth's) mound, I crushed (?) like stone, fired (?) it like metal, spread (?) it out (literally, "turned it into 'wide earth'") like *ninda*, returned that (excavated) earth into its midst (that is, into the area which had been dug), (and) heaped up the earth foundation. On this (foundation) I built a platform 10 ells high, (and) on the platform I built for him (Ningirsu) the Eninnu-Nigibarbar 12 ells (high).

For Ninhursag, the mother of the gods, I built her Girsu-house. For Bau, the gracious lady, the daughter of An, I built her Urukuga-house. For Inanna, the holy, princely queen, I built her Uru-house.

For Enki, the king of Eridu, I built his Girsu-house. For Nindara, the king (and) *en*, I built his house. For Ninagal, his goddess, I built her house. For Ninmar, the gracious lady, the foremost daughter of Nanshe, I built the Eshgutur, the house she chose in her heart. For Ensignun, the donkeyherd of Ningirsu, I built his "prize-donkey" house. For Geshtinanna, the all-powerful (?) (literally, perhaps, "greater than all"), I built her Girsu-house. For Dumuzi-Abzu, the lord of Kinunir, I built his Girsu-house.

35 SINGASHID OF ERECH (clay nail)

For Lugalbanda, his god, (and) for Ninsun, his mother, Singashid, the king of Erech, the king of Amnanum, the sustenance of Eanna, at the time that he built the Eanna, (also) built the Ekikal, their dwelling house, in which their hearts rejoiced.

During his reign—his years were years of great prosperity—3 *gur* of barley, 12 *mina*'s of wool, 10 *mina*'s of copper, (and) $\frac{1}{10}$ of a *gur* of oil, each sold for 1 shekel of silver in accordance with the (extraordinarily low) market price (current) in his land.

D. SAMPLE DATE-FORMULAS

"Year (in which) Sargon destroyed Adab (?)"	Sargon, number of year unknown
"Year (in which) Naram-Sin destroyed Sabum"	Naram-Sin, number of year unknown
"Year (in which) Pirig-midashu, daughter of the king, was elevated to the sovereignty of Marhashi"	Shulgi, year 17
"Year (in which) the citizens of Ur were organized as spearmen"	Shulgi, year 19
"Year (in which) Ganhar was destroyed"	Shulgi, year 25
"Year (in which) Simurum was destroyed"	Shulgi, year 26
"Year (in which) Simurum was destroyed a second time"	Shulgi, year 27
"Year (in which) Simurum and Lulubum were destroyed a ninth time"	Shulgi, year 45
"Year (in which) Kimash, Humurtu, and the surrounding country were destroyed in one day"	Shulgi, year 47
"Year (in which) Shu-Sin, the king of Ur, built the western wall (called) 'Muriq-Tidnim'"	Shu-Sin, year 4
"Year (in which) Ibbi-Sin, the king of Ur, struck down like a storm Susa, Adamdun, and the land of Awan, subdued them in one day, and took their *en*'s captive"	Ibbi-Sin, year 17

E. SUMERIAN KING LIST

After kingship had descended from heaven, Eridu became (the seat) of kingship. In Eridu Alulim reigned 28,800 years as king; Alalgar reigned 36,000 years—two kings reigned 64,800 years. Eridu was abandoned, (and) its kingship was carried off to Badtibira.

In Badtibira, Enmenluanna reigned 43,200 years; Enmengalanna reigned 28,800 years; Dumuzi, the shepherd, reigned 36,000 years—three kings reigned 108,000 years. Badtibira was abandoned, (and) its kingship was carried off to Larak.

In Larak, Ensipazianna reigned 28,800 years—one king reigned 28,800 years. Larak was abandoned, (and) its kingship was carried off to Sippar.

In Sippar, Enmeduranna reigned 21,000 years as king—one king reigned 21,000 years. Sippar was abandoned, (and) its kingship was carried off to Shuruppak.

In Shuruppak, Ubartutu reigned 18,600 years as king—one king reigned 18,600 years.

(Total) five cities, eight kings reigned 241,200 years.

The Flood then swept over (the land). After the Flood had swept over (the land) and kingship had descended from heaven (a second time), Kish became (the seat) of kingship. In Kish, Gaur reigned 1,200 years as king; Gulla-Nidaba-annapad reigned 960 years; Palakinatim reigned 900 years; Nangishlishma reigned . . . . years; Bahina reigned . . . . years; Buanum reigned 840 years; Kalibum reigned 960 years; Galumum reigned 840 years; Zukakip reigned 900 years; Atab reigned 600 years; Mashda, the son of Atab, reigned 840 years; Arurim, the son of Mashda, reigned 720 years; Etana, the shepherd, he who ascended to heaven, who made firm all the lands, reigned 1,560 years as king; Balih, the son of Etana, reigned 400 years; Enmenunna reigned 660 years; Melam-Kish, the son of Enmenunna, reigned 900 years; Barsalnunna, the son of Enmenunna, reigned 1,200 years; Meszamug, the son of Barsalnunna, reigned 140 years; Tizkar, the son of Meszamug, reigned 305 years; Ilku reigned 900 years; Iltasadum reigned 1,200 years; Enmebaraggesi, he who smote the weapons of the land Elam, reigned 900 years as king; Agga, the son of Enmebaraggesi reigned 625 years. (Total) twenty-three kings reigned 24,510 years, 3 months, 3½ days. Kish was defeated (in battle), (and) its kingship was carried off to Eanna.

In Eanna, Meskiaggasher, the son of (the sun-god) Utu reigned (both) as *en* (and) king 324 years—Meskiaggasher entered the sea (and) ascended the mountains; Enmerkar, the son of Meskiaggasher, the king of Erech who had built Erech, reigned 420 years as king; Lugalbanda, the shepherd, reigned 1,200 years; Dumuzi, the fisherman, whose city was Kua, reigned 100 years; Gilgamesh, whose father was a nomad(?), reigned 126 years; Urnungal, the son of Gilgamesh, reigned 30 years; Udulkalamma, the son of Urnungal reigned 15 years; Labasher reigned 9 years; Ennundaranna reigned 8 years; Meshede reigned 36 years; Melamanna reigned 6 years; Lugalkidul reigned 36 years. (Total) twelve kings reigned 2,310 years. Erech was defeated (in battle), (and) its kingship was carried off to Ur.

In Ur, Mesannepadda reigned 80 years as king; Meskiagnunna, the son of Mesannepadda reigned 36 years as king; Elulu reigned 25 years; Balulu reigned 36 years. (Total) four kings reigned 177 years. Ur was defeated (in battle), (and) its kingship was carried off to Awan.

(In Awan, there were three kings who reigned 356 years, but their names are destroyed in large part; the text then continues:) Awan was defeated (in battle), (and) its kingship was carried off to Kish.

In Kish . . . . reigned (more than) 201 years as king; Dadasig reigned . . . . years; Mamagal reigned 420 years; Kalbum, the son of Mamagal, reigned 132 years; Tuge reigned 360 years; Mennumna reigned 180 years; Lugalmu reigned 420 years; Ibbi-Ea reigned 290 (?) years. (Total) eight kings reigned 3,195 years. Kish was defeated (in battle), (and) its kingship was carried off to Hamazi.

In Hamazi, Hadanish reigned 360 years. (Total) one king reigned 360 years. Hamazi was defeated, (and) its kingship was carried off to Erech.

In Erech . . . . reigned 60 years as king; Lugalure reigned 120 years; Argandea reigned 7 years. (Total) three kings reigned 187 years. Erech was defeated, (and) its kingship was carried off to Ur.

In Ur (the names of the rulers of the Second Dynasty of Ur, who were four in number and probably reigned 116 years, are destroyed). Ur was defeated, (and) its kingship was carried off to Adab.

In Adab, Lugalannemundu reigned 90 years as king. (Total) one king reigned 90 years. Adab was defeated, (and) its kingship was carried off to Mari.

In Mari, Ilshu reigned 30 years as king; . . , the son of Ilshu reigned 17 years; . . reigned 30 years; . . reigned 20 years; . . reigned 30 years; . . reigned 9 years. (Total) six kings reigned 136 years. Mari was defeated, (and) its kingship was carried off to Kish.

In Kish, Ku-Bau, the innkeeper, she who made firm the foundations of Kish, reigned 100 years as "king." (Total) one king reigned 100 years. Kish was defeated, (and) its kingship was carried off to Akshak.

In Akshak, Unzi reigned 30 years as king; Undalulu reigned 12 years; Urur (perhaps to be read, Zuzu) reigned 6 years; Puzur-Nirah reigned 20 years; Ishu-Il reigned 24 years; Shu-Sin, the son of Ishu-Il, reigned 7 years. (Total) six kings reigned 99 years. Akshak was defeated (and) its kingship was carried off to Kish.

In Kish, Puzur-Sin, son of Ku-Bau, reigned 25 years as king; Ur-Zababa, the son of Puzur-Sin, reigned 400 years. Simudarra reigned 30 years; Usiwatar, the son of Simudarra, reigned 7 years; Ishtar-muti reigned 11 years; Ishme-Shamash reigned 11 years; Nannia, the stone-worker, reigned 7 years. (Total) seven kings reigned 491 years. Kish was defeated, (and) its kingship was carried off to Erech.

In Erech, Lugalzaggesi reigned 25 years as king. (Total) one king reigned 25 years. Erech was defeated, (and) its kingship was carried off to Agade.

In Agade, Sargon, whose father (?) was a gardener, the cupbearer of Ur-Zababa, the king of Agade who built Agade, reigned 56 years as king; Rimush, the son of Sargon, reigned 9 years; Manishtushu, the older brother of Rimush, son of Sargon, ruled 15 years; Naram-Sin, the son of Manishtushu, reigned 56 years; Sharkalisharri, the son of Naram-Sin, reigned 25 years. Who was king? Who was not king? (that is, a period of anarchy). Igigi, the king; Nanum, the king; Imi, the king; Elulu, the king—the four of them were kings (but) reigned (only) 3 years. Dudu reigned 21 years; Shudurul, the son of Dudu, reigned 15 years. (Total) eleven kings reigned 197 years. Agade was defeated, (and) its kingship was carried off to Erech.

In Erech, Urnigin reigned 7 years as king; Urgigir, the son of Urni-gin, reigned 6 years; Kudda reigned 6 years; Puzur-ili reigned 5 years; Ur-Utu reigned 6 years. (Total) five kings reigned 30 years. Erech was smitten with weapons, (and) its kingship was carried off to the Gutium hordes.

In the Gutium hordes, (first reigned) a nameless king; (then) Imta reigned 3 years as king; Inkishush reigned 6 years; Sarlagab reigned 6 years; Shulme reigned 6 years; Elulumesh reigned 6 years; Inim-bakesh reigned 5 years; Igeshaush reigned 6 years; Iarlagab reigned 15 years; Ibate reigned 3 years; . . . reigned 3 years; Kurum reigned 1 year; . . . reigned 3 years; . . . reigned 2 years; Irarum reigned 2 years; Ibranum reigned 1 year; Hablum reigned 2 years; Puzur-Sin, the son of Hablum, reigned 7 years; Iarlaganda reigned 7 years; . . . reigned 7 years; . . . reigned 40 days. (Total) twenty-one kings reigned 91 years, 40 days. The Gutium hordes were defeated, (and) their kingship was carried off to Erech.

In Erech, Utuhegal reigned 7 years, 6 months, 15 days as king.

(Total) one king reigned 7 years, 6 months, 15 days. Erech was smitten with weapons, (and) its kingship carried off to Ur.

In Ur, Ur-Nammu reigned 18 years as king; Shulgi, the son of Ur-Nammu, reigned 48 years; Amar-Sin, the son of Shulgi, reigned 9 years; Shu-Sin, the son of Amar-Sin (an error for "the son of Shulgi"), reigned 9 years; Ibbi-Sin, the son of Shu-Sin, reigned 24 years. (Total) five kings reigned 108 years. Ur was defeated, (and) its kingship was carried off to Isin.

In Isin, Ishbi-Erra reigned 33 years as king; Shuilishu, the son of Ishbi-Erra, reigned 10 years; Idin-Dagan, the son of Shuilishu, reigned 21 years; Ishme-Dagan, the son of Idin-Dagan, reigned 20 years; Lipit-Ishtar, the son of Ishme-Dagan, reigned 11 years; Ur-Ninurta reigned 28 years; Bur-Sin, the son of Ur-Ninurta, reigned 21 years; Lipit-Enlil, the son of Bur-Sin, reigned 5 years; Erraimitti reigned 8 years; Enlil-bani reigned 24 years; Zambia reigned 3 years; Iterpisha reigned 4 years; Urdukuga reigned 4 years; Sinmagir reigned 11 years. (Total) fourteen kings reigned 203 years.

F. LETTERS

1   LETTER FROM LUENNA TO ENETARZI

To Enetarzi, the *sanga* of Ningirsu, say: This is what Luenna, the *sanga* of (the goddess) Ninmar, says—

Luenna, the *sanga*, fought with 600 Elamites who were carrying off booty (literally, "removable goods") from Lagash to Elam. He defeated the Elamites and (took) 540 Elamites (prisoner). Ur-Bau, the man in charge of the *shubur* (?)-slaves, (and) Niglunutum, the *ugula* of the smiths, were among them, (and) they are in the Eninmar. He [Luenna (?) recovered (?) from them] 5 vessels (?) of pure silver, 20 . . . . , 5 royal garments, (and) 15 hides of food sheep (that is, sheep raised to be eaten rather than sheared for wool).

As long as . . the *ensi* of Lagash lives (and) as long as Enannatum-sipad-zi, the *agrig*, lives, their . . . . shall be brought to Ninmar.

2   LETTER FROM ARADMU TO SHULGI

To my king speak; thus says your servant Aradmu:

You have commissioned me to keep in good condition the expedition roads to the land of Subir, to stabilize the borders of your country, to make known the ways of country, to counsel the wise of the assembly against (?) the "foul (?) seed (?)," (and) to make all obedient—that the word of the day might be brought into their mouths. When I came to the gate of the palace, no one asked for the "peace" of my king. Those who were sitting did not rise (and) did not prostrate themselves. When I approached (I found that) he had . . . "the house of the expedition" which had been ornamented with "combs," gold and silver "lance heads," carnelian, (and) covering (?) lapis lazuli . . . ; he "glorified" constantly silver and gold; he seated himself on a throne placed loftily on a dais; he put his foot on a golden footstool (and) did not move his foot from it. The bailiffs in charge (?) of his slaves (?)—each in charge of 5,000 (men)—stood at his right (and) left. He [had himself served with (?)] . . . as a meal (and) obtained. . . . Then I was brought into . . . [As I entered] a golden chair with a foot-rest was brought to me, (and) I was told to sit down. In accordance with the order of my king I said, "I will remain standing, I will not sit down." I was brought 1 fatted ox, 6 fatted sheep, (and) . . . ; when the . . . (and) the bailiffs of my king overturned my table, I was afraid (and) terrified. The fifth day of the month Ezen-Ninazu has past, (and) I sent to you a . . . man. (Now) the first day of the month Ubiku has past. My king, you have commissioned me, (but) in half a month (?) . . . has approached. My king Shulgi, may you know (this).

3   LETTER FROM SHULGI TO ARADMU

To Aradmu speak; thus says your king Shulgi:

The man, whom you sent, is no help to you; he does not take hold of the instructions from your hand. As for me I urge (?) you just as if you were in my place to stabilize the country, to direct the people, to make them obedient, (and) to take (firm) hold of the cities of the country. Of their "big men" make known their word. Let my terror cover all the foreign lands. Let my mighty power, "the power of hero-ship," fall upon the foreign lands. Let my South Wind cover the land. Cause to flee all supervisors of the plain (and) all watchers (?) of the fields. As long as that "foul (?) seed (?)" does not . . . their (?) wise man of the assembly. Bring him out before you (?), let him enter before you. If the wise man of the assembly—like me—had not remained silent (?), he (the "foul (?) seed (?)") would not have seated himself on a throne placed loftily on a dais; he would not have put his foot on a golden footstool; he would not have terrified the *ensi* together with the *ensi*-ship, the royal supervisor with royal supervisor, and would not make them serve (him); he would smite (and) hurt no one; the man upon whom he looks (with favor) would not wax strong. Is this how you make firm the land! If you love me do not join up with him. You are puffed up; you know not (my) bailiffs; keep in mind their (the bailiffs') humanity and my heroship. If you are my father and mother, you should speak before your fathers . . . Make them (the people of Subir) obedient; make firm the foundation of the land. It is urgent.

4 LETTER FROM ISHBI-ERRA TO IBBI-SIN

To Ibbi-Sin my king speak; thus says your servant Ishbi-Erra:

You have charged me with an expedition to Isin and Kazallu to buy grain. The grain has reached the price (of) 1 *gur* for each (shekel), . . . (and to date) 20 talents of silver have been spent for buying grain. But now having heard the report that the hostile Martu have entered your country, I brought into Isin the 72,000 *gur* of grain—all of it. Now the Martu—all of them—have entered the midst of the land (Sumer) (and) have seized the great fortresses one after the other. Because of the Martu, I am not able to transport (?) that grain; they are too strong for me, (and) I am immobilized. Let my king have 600 boats (with the capacity of) 120 *gur* each caulked; let him (?) . . . a boat (of?) 72 . . . ; let him (?) . . . 50 . . (and) 1 door (and) . . . boat; and let him (collect?) all (these) boats. (Then) let them be brought down to the narrow (?) . . . by (way of) the river, "the river of the mountain," and the dug canals; and I will . . . before him. Put me in charge of the places where the boats are to be moored, (and) . . . all the grain will be stored (?) in good condition. If you shall lack grain, I will bring you the grain. My king, the Elamites have been weakened in battle; their grain . . . has come to an end. Do not weaken. Do not agree to become their slave, and do not walk behind them. I have (enough) grain for 15 years (to satisfy) the hunger of your palace and its cities. My king, put me in charge of watching over Isin (and) Nippur.

5 LETTER FROM PUZUR-NUMUSHDA TO IBBI-SIN

To Ibbi-Sin my king speak; thus says your servant Puzur-Numushda:

The messenger of Ishbi-Erra . . has put his eyes on me (saying): "My king Ishbi-Erra sent the (following) message:

'My king Enlil (by) his command gave me the shepherdship of the land, (and) Enlil commanded me to bring before the goddess Nini-sinna the cities, the gods, and the camps of the banks of the Tigris and Euphrates, of the banks of the Nunme canal and the banks of the Me-Enlil canal, from the land Hamazi until the sea of Magan; to set up Isin as the *ganun*-ship of Enlil; to make it have a (great) name; to make . . ; and to make its (Sumer's) cities inhabited. Why now do you resist me? I swear by the name of Dagan, my god, I have nothing but peaceful intentions for Kazallu. (As for) the cities (and) the land which Enlil has commanded me (to take charge of), in the midst of Isin I will build their . . . ; I will make them celebrate their feasts; (and) I will set up in their *gipar* my statue, my emblem, my high priest, (and) my high priestess. Before Enlil in the Ekur (and) before Nanna (in) the Ekishnugal, the sons of . . . will utter their prayers. And why did you . . . your trusted one from his land? I will build Isin's wall, (and) I will call (its) name Idilpashunu.' "

It was just as he said; he built Isin's wall (and) called (its) name Idilpashunu. He seized Nippur, put watches over it, and pronounced (?) all the commands (?)—he seized Nippur. He took Zinnum, the *ensi* of Subir, as a prisoner; plundered Hamazi; (and) returned Narahi, the *ensi* of Eshnuna, Shu-Enlil, the *ensi* of Kish, (and) Puzur-Tutu, the *ensi* of Badzi-Abba, (each) to his place. Ishbi-Erra stood at the head of his troops, seized the banks of the Tigris, the Euphrates, the Nunme and the Me-Enlil canals; and Idil-Malgi entered . . . (When) Girbubu, the *ensi* of Girkal, resisted, he (Ishbi-Erra) cut . . . (and) seized him. His terror lies heavy on me; he has put his eyes on me. Let my king know that I have no ally, no one to walk at my side; and (that) since his . . . overtook me, I walk alone.

6   LETTER FROM IBBI-SIN TO PUZUR-NUMUSHDA

To Puzur-Numushda, the governor of Kazallu, speak; thus says your king Ibbi-Sin:

Since I have selected for you . . . troops (and) have put them at your disposal as the governor of Kazallu, are not, as in my case, your troops your renown? Why did you send me thus: "Ishbi-Erra has his eyes on me, and (only) after he has left me will I come." How is it that you did not know when Ishbi-Erra will return to (his) land? Why did not you together with Girbubu, the governor of Girkal, march forth the troops which had been placed in your hand before him? How is it that you delay to turn back the . . . ? . . . Enlil has sent evil upon Sumer. Its enemy descending from the land . . . he has raised unto the shepherdship of the land. Now did Enlil give the kingship to a worthless man, to Ishbi-Erra, who is not of Sumerian seed. Lo, in the assembly of the gods, Sumer has been prostrated. Father Enlil, whose commands are . . . , verily commanded thus: "As long as evildoers exist in Ur, Ishbi-Erra, the man of Mari, will tear down its foundations, will measure out Sumer." And (so) when you were appointed governor of the several cities, they went over to Ishbi-Erra in accordance with Enlil's word. (Even) after you, like a . . . . , hand over the city to the enemy and have become a faithful servant, Ishbi-Erra does not know (you). Now bring you (help) hither in order to restore the good word and to put an end to the false; let them perform . . . among its people. Do not turn away; do not go against me. His hand will not reach over the city; the man of Mari will not exercise lordship in accordance with (his) inimical plan. (For) now Enlil has stirred up the Martu from out of their land; they will strike down the Elamites and capture Ishbi-Erra. With the restoration of the land to its (former) place, (its) might will become known throughout all the lands. It is urgent, do not . . .

G. *DITILLA'S* (court decisions)

1.

Sheshkalla, the son of Ur-Lamma, declared: "I am not the slave of Ur-Sahar-Bau." (But the fact was that) Ur-Lamma, Sheshkalla's father, was given as a slave by Alla, the scribe, into the house of Ur-Sahar-Bau, the son of Namu, (in exchange for) a pension (?) of barley and wool. Moreover, Ludugga and Dudima swore that Ur-Lamma engendered Sheshkalla, the slave, in the house of Ur-Sahar-Bau. (Therefore) the slave was confirmed (as belonging to) the heirs of Ur-Sahar-Bau.

Tiemahta—the *mashkim*
Lu-Shara—the judge
(Date-formula follows.)

2.

Akalla, the son of Luninshubur, (and) Urshuanna were witnesses (to the fact that) Kaku, the son of Ninshubur, had bought the 12 large date-palm saplings from Lunanna, the father of Urabu, for 3 shekels of silver (as) its full price. Urabu (however) repudiated the witnesses. (Whereupon) Kaku took an oath (that he had actually bought the saplings from the father of Urabu, Lunanna). (Therefore) the garden was confirmed (as belonging to) Kaku.

Tiemahta—the *mashkim*
Lu-Shara (and) Ur-Sataran—the judges
(Date-formula follows.)

3.

Innashagga, the wife of Dudu, the son of Titi, bought a . . . house of 2⅔ *sar* with her own money. As long as Dudu lived, Ur-Eninnu, the son of Dudu, had possession of his house. Since Innashagga had bought the house, he (Ur-Eninnu) had the tablet (recording) the purchase of the house made over to him by Innashagga. Innashagga took the oath that she bought the house with her own money (and) not with the property of Dudu.

Dudu had given Ninana, the son of Niza, the goldsmith, (as a slave) to Innashagga, his wife. After the death of Dudu, the heirs of Dudu, through Arad-Nanna, the *ensi* (and) *sukkalmah,* claimed title (to the slave) from her. Urgula, the son of the *sanga* of Ninshubur, Nammah, the *guzala* of Gizi, (and) Alul, the singer, testified that Dudu had given the slave to Innashagga; (and) the heirs of Dudu confirmed this testimony. Since (their statements) were confirmed by the statements of the heirs, the witnesses were not compelled to take the oath.

(Therefore) Ninana, the son of Niza, (and) the house were then confirmed (as belonging to) Innashagga, the wife of Dudu.

Geme-Tirash, Magina, (and) Sag-Bautuku, the daughters of Ninana, the son of Niza, were given their freedom by Innashagga, the wife of Dudu, before the judges. The heirs of Dudu swore by the name of the king that they would not change their mother's word.

Urbagara, the son of Ur- . . . —the *mashkim*

Lu-Shara, Ludingirra, (and) Ur-Sataran—their judges

(that is, of the lawsuits here recorded)

(Date-formula follows.)

H. LIPIT-ISHTAR LAW CODE

PROLOGUE

When the great An, the father of the gods, (and) Enlil, the king of all the lands, the lord who determines ordinances, had . . to Nini-sinna, the daughter of An, the . . . for her . . . (and) the rejoicing . . . for her bright forehead; when they had given her the kingship of Sumer (and) Akkad (and) a favorable reign in her (city) Isin, the . . . established by An; when An (and) Enlil had called Lipit-Ishtar— Lipit-Ishtar, the wise shepherd, whose name had been pronounced by Nunamnir—to the princeship of the land in order to establish justice in the land, to banish complaints, to turn back enmity (and) rebellion by the force of arms, (and) to bring well-being to the Sumerians and Akkadians, then I, Lipit-Ishtar, the humble shepherd of Nippur, the stalwart farmer of Ur, who abandons not Eridu, the suitable lord of Erech, king of Isin, king of Sumer and Akkad, who am fit for the heart of Inanna, established justice in Sumer and Akkad in accordance with the word of Enlil. Verily, in those days I procured . . . the freedom of the sons and daughters of Nippur, the sons and daughters of Ur, the sons and daughters of Isin, the sons and daughters of Sumer and Akkad upon whom . . . slaveship . . . had been imposed. Verily, in accordance with . . . , I made the father support his children, (and) I made the children support their father; I made the father stand by his children, (and) I made the children stand by their father; in the father's house (and) in the brother's house, I . . . . Verily, I, Lipit-Ishtar, the son of Enlil, brought seventy into the father's house (and) the brother's house; into the bachelor's house, I brought . . . for ten months . . . . the wife of a man, . . . the child of a man . . . . .

THE LAWS

1 . . . which had been set up . . . . .

2 . . . the property of the father's house from its . . . . .

3 . . . the son of the state official, the son of the palace official, the son of the supervisor . . . . .

4 . . . a boat . . . a boat he shall . . . . .

5 If a man hired a boat (and) set it on a . . . journey for him . . . . .

6 . . . the gift . . . he shall . . . . .

7 If he gave his orchard to a gardener to raise . . . (and) the gardener . . . to the owner of the garden . . . . .

8 If a man gave bare ground to (another) man to set out an orchard (and the latter) did not complete setting out that bare ground as an orchard, he shall give to the man who set out the orchard the bare ground which he neglected, as part of his share.

9 If a man entered the orchard of (another) man (and) was seized there for stealing, he shall pay 10 shekels of silver.

10 If a man cut down a tree in the garden of (another) man, he shall pay ½ mina of silver.

11 If adjacent to the house of a man the bare ground of (another) man has been neglected and the owner of the house has said to the owner of the bare ground, "Because your ground has been neglected someone may break into my house; strengthen your house," (and) this agreement has been confirmed by him, the owner of the bare ground shall restore to the owner of the house any of his property that is lost.

12 If a slave girl or slave of a man has fled into the heart of the city (and) it has been confirmed that he (or she) dwelt in the house of (another) man for one month, he shall give slave for slave.

13 If he has no slave, he shall pay 15 shekels of silver.

14 If a man's slave has compensated his slaveship to his master (and) it is confirmed (that he has compensated) his master twofold, that slave shall be freed.

15 If a *miqtum* is a grant of the king, he shall not be taken away.

16 If a *miqtum* went to a man of his own free will, that man shall not hold him; he (the *miqtum*) may go where he desires.

17 If a man without authorization bound (another) man to a matter to which he (the latter) had no knowledge, that man is not affirmed; he (the first man) shall bear the penalty in regard to the matter to which he has bound him.

18 If the master of an estate or the mistress of an estate has defaulted on the tax of the estate (and) a stranger has borne it, for three years he (the owner) may not be evicted. (Afterward) the man who bore the tax of the estate shall possess that estate, and the (former) owner of the estate shall not raise any claim.

19 If the master of an estate . . . . .

20 If a man from the heir(s) seized . . . . .

21 [If] . . . . the house of the father . . . he married, the gift of the house of her father which was presented to her as her heir he shall take.

22 If the father (is) living, his daughter whether she be a *nindingir*, a *lukur*, or a hierodule shall dwell in the house like an heir.

23 If the daughter in the house of (her) living father . . . . .

24 If the second wife whom he had married bore him children, the dowry which she brought from her father's house belongs to her children; (but) the children of (his) first wife and the children of (his) second wife shall divide equally the property of their father.

25 If a man married a wife (and) she bore him children (and) those children are living, and a slave also bore children for her master (but) the father granted freedom to the slave and her children, the children of the slave shall not divide the estate with the children of their (former) master.

26 If his first wife dies (and) after her (death) he takes his slave as a wife, the children of his first wife are his heirs; the children which the slave bore for her master shall be like . . . , his house they shall . . . . .

27 If a man's wife has not borne him children (but) a harlot (from) the public square has borne him children, he shall provide grain, oil, and clothing for that harlot; the children which the harlot has borne him shall be his heirs, and as long as his wife lives the harlot shall not live in the house with his wife.

28 If a man turned his face away from his first wife . . . (but) she has not gone out of the house, his wife whom he married as his favorite is a second wife; he shall continue to support his first wife.

29 If a (prospective) son-in-law has entered the house of his father-in-law (and if) he made his betrothal (but) afterward they made him go out (of the house) and gave his wife to his companion,

they shall present to him the betrothal gifts which he brought (and) that wife may not marry his companion.

30 If a young man married a harlot (from) the public square (and) the judges have ordered him not to visit her, (but) afterward he divorced his wife, money . . . . .

31 [If] . . . . he has given him, after their father's death the heirs shall divide the estate of their father, (but) the inheritance of the estate they shall not divide; they shall not "cook their father's word in water."

32 If the father while living has set aside a betrothal gift for his eldest son (and) in the presence of the father who was still alive he (the son) married a wife, after the father's (death) the heir . . . . .

33 If it has been confirmed that the . . . had not divided the estate, he shall pay 10 shekels of silver.

34 If a man rented an ox (and) injured the flesh at the nose-ring, he shall pay one-third of (its) price.

35 If a man rented an ox (and) damaged its eye, he shall pay one-half of (its) price.

36 If a man rented an ox (and) broke its horn, he shall pay one-fourth of (its) price.

37 If a man rented an ox (and) damaged its tail, he shall pay one-fourth of (its) price.

38 [If] . . . . he shall pay.

EPILOGUE

Verily, in accordance with the true word of Utu, I caused Sumer and Akkad to hold to true justice. Verily, in accordance with the pronouncement of Enlil, I, Lipit-Ishtar, the son of Enlil, abolished enmity and rebellion; made weeping, lamentations, outcries . . . taboo; caused righteousness and truth to exist; brought well-being to the Sumerians and the Akkadians . . . .

Verily, when I had established the wealth of Sumer and Akkad, I erected this stele. May he who will not commit any evil deed with regard to it, who will not damage my handiwork, who will not erase its inscription, who will not write his own name upon it—be presented with life and breath of long days; may he rise high in the Ekur; may Enlil's bright forehead look down upon him. (On the other hand) he who will commit some evil deed with regard to it, who will damage my handiwork, who will enter the storeroom (and) change its pedestal, who will erase its inscription, who will write his own name upon it, (or) who, because of this curse, will substitute someone else for himself—that man, whether he be a . . . , whether he be a . . . , may he take away from him . . (and) bring to him . . . in his . . . his . . . whoever; may Ashnan and Sumugan, the lords of abundance, take away from him . . . his . . . may he abolish . . . . May Utu, the judge of heaven and earth . . . take away . . . his . . . its foundation . . . as . . . may he be counted; let not the foundation of his land be firm; its king, whoever he may be, may Ninurta, the mighty hero, the son of Enlil . . .   .

I. FARMERS' ALMANAC

In days of yore a farmer instructed his son (as follows):

When you are about to take hold of your field (for cultivation), keep a sharp eye on the opening of the dikes, ditches, and mounds (so that) when you flood the field the water will not rise too high in it. When you have emptied it of water, watch the field's water-soaked ground that it stay virile ground for you. Let shod oxen (that is, oxen whose hooves are protected in one way or another) trample it for you; (and) after having its weeds ripped out (by them) (and) the field made level ground, dress it evenly with narrow axes weighing (no more than) two-thirds of a pound each. (Following which) let the pickax wielder eradicate the ox hooves for you (and) smooth them out; have all crevices worked over with a drag, and have him go with the pickax all around the four edges of the field (lines 1–12).

While the field is drying, let your obedient (household) prepare your tools for you, make fast the yoke bar, hang up your new whips on nails, and let the hanging handles of your old whips be mended by the artisans. Let the bronze . . . . your tools "heed your arm"; let the leather "headbinder," goad, "mouth-opener," (and) whip uphold you (in matters requiring discipline and control); let your *bandu*-basket crackle; (all this) will make a mighty income for you (lines 13–21).

When your field has been supplied with what is needed, keep a sharp eye on your work. After adding an extra ox to the plow-ox—when one is harnessed to another ox, their plow is larger than (an ordinary) plow—make them . . . . one *bur;* they will make for you a . . . . like a storm, so that three *gur* barley will be planted in that one *bur.* Sustenance is in a plow! (Thus) having had the field worked with the *bardil*-plow—(yes) the *bardil*-plow—(and then) having had it worked over with the *shukin*-plow, repeat (the process). (After) having had it (the field) harrowed (and) raked three times and pulverized fine with a hammer, let the handle of your whip uphold you; brook no idleness. Stand over them (the field laborers) during their work, (and) brook no interruptions. Do not [distract] your field workers. Since they must carry on by day (and by) heaven's stars for ten (days), their strength should be spent on the field, (and) they are not to dance attendance on you (lines 22–40).

When you are about to plow your field, let your plow break up the stubble for you. Leave your "mouth-cover" of the plow . . . . , (and) leave your . . . . on a narrow nail. Let your moldboards spread to the side, set up your furrows—in one *garush* set up eight furrows. Furrows which have been deeply dug—their barley will grow long (lines 41–47).

When you are about to plow your field, keep your eye on the man who puts in the barley seed. Let him drop the grain uniformly two fingers deep (and) use up one shekel of barley for each *garush*. If the barley seed does not sink in properly, change your share, the "tongue of the plow." If the . . . . , (then) plow diagonal furrows where you have plowed straight furrows, (and) plow straight furrows where your have plowed diagonal furrows. Let your straight furrows make your borders into *tulu*-borders; let the *lu*-furrows make straight your borders; (and) plow *ab*-furrows where . . . . . (Then) let all its clods be removed; all its high spots be made into furrows; (and) all its depressions be made into low furrows—(all this) will be good for the sprout (lines 48–63).

After the sprout has broken through (the surface of) the ground, say a prayer to the goddess Ninkilim, (and) shoo away the flying birds. When the barley has filled the narrow bottom of the furrow, water the top seed. When the barley stands up high as (the straw of) a mat in the middle of a boat, water it (a second time). Water (a third time) its royal barley. If the watered barley has turned red, what you say is: "It is sick with the *samana*-disease." But if it has succeeded in producing kernel-rich barley, water it (a fourth time), (and) it will yield you an extra measure of barley in every ten (lines 64–72). When you are about to harvest your field, do not let the barley bend over on itself (but) harvest it at the moment of its (full) strength. A reaper, a man who bundles the mown barley, and a man who [sets up the sheaves] before him—these three (as a team) shall do the harvesting for you. The gleaners must do no damage; they must not tear apart the sheaves. During your daily harvesting, as in "days of need," make the earth supply the sustenance of the young and the gleaners according to their number (that is, presumably, he must leave the fallen kernels on the ground for needy children and gleaners to pick), (and) let them sleep (in your field) as (in) the (open) marshland. (If you do so) your god will show everlasting favor. After you have obtained . . . . , do not . . . . , (but) roast (some of) the mown barley (so that) the "prayer of the mown barley" will be said for you daily (lines 73–86).

When you are about to winnow the barley, let those who weigh your barley [prepare] for you (bins of) thirty *gur*. Have your threshing floor made level (and) the *gur* (-bins) put in order (ready for) the road. When your tools have been [readied] for you (and) your wagons put in order for you, have your wagons climb the (barley) mounds—your "mound-threshing" (is to take) five days. When you are about to "open the mound," bake *arra*-bread. When you "open" the barley, have the teeth of your threshing sledges fastened with leather and let bitumen cover the . . . . . When you are about to hitch the oxen (to the threshing sledge), let your men who "open" the barley stand by with (their—that is, the oxen's) food (lines 87–99).

When you have heaped up the barley, say the "prayer of the (still) uncleaned barley." When you winnow the barley, pay attention to the men who lift the barley from the ground—two "barley-lifters" should lift it for you. On the day the barley is to be cleaned, have it laid on sticks, (and) say a prayer evening and night. (Then) have the barley "unloosed" (from the chaff) like (with) an overpowering wind, (and) the "unloosed" barley will be stored for you (lines 100–108).

(These are) the instructions of Ninurta, the son of Enlil. O Ninurta, trustworthy farmer of Enlil, your praise is good (lines 109–11)!

SELECTED
BIBLIOGRAPHY

GENERAL

Braidwood, Robert J. *The Near East and the Foundations of Civiliza-tion.* Eugene, Ore., 1952.

Chiera, Edward. *They Wrote on Clay.* 2d ed. Chicago: University of Chicago Press, 1955.

Childe, Vere Gordon. *New Light on the Most Ancient Near East.* 4th ed. New York: Frederick Praeger, 1953.

Gadd, Cyril J. *"The Cities of Babylonia,"* in *The Cambridge Ancient History* (rev. ed.; Cambridge: University Press, 1962), I, chap. xiii, 1–60.

Jacobsen, Thorkild. *"Mesopotamia,"* in *The Intellectual Adventure of the Ancient Man.* By H. Frankfort *et al.* Chicago: University of Chicago Press, 1946.

Kramer, Samuel N. *From the Tablets of Sumer.* Indian Hills, Colo.: The Falcon's Wing Press, 1956. (Reprinted in 1959 as *History Begins at Sumer.* New York: Doubleday & Co., Inc.)

Pallis, S. A. *The Antiquity of Iraq.* Copenhagen: Einar Monksgaard, 1956. A rather capricious but not unuseful book which contains a comprehensive bibliography of the more important Sumerological publications up to 1954.

Pritchard, James B. (ed.). *Ancient Near Eastern Texts.* 2d ed. Princeton, N.J.: Princeton University Press, 1955.

Rowton, M. B. *"Chronology: Ancient Western Asia,"* in *The Cambridge*

Ancient History (rev. ed.; Cambridge: University Press, 1962), I, chap. vi, 23–69.

Saggs, H. W. F. *The Greatness That Was Babylon*. New York: Hawthorn Books, 1962.

I ARCHEOLOGY AND DECIPHERMENT

Fossey, Charles. *Manuel d'Assyriologie*. Vol. I. Paris: Leroux, 1904.

Parrot, André. *Archéologie mésopotamienne*. Vols. I (1946) and II (1953). Paris: Albin Michel.

——. *Tello. Vingt campagnes de fouilles (1877–1933)*. Paris: Albin Michel, 1948.

II HISTORY

Edzard, Dietz Otto. *Die "Zweite Zwischenzeit" Babyloniens*. Wiesbaden: Otto Harrossowitz, 1957.

——. "Enmebaragesi von Kis," in *Zeitschrift für Assyriologie*, LIII (1959), 9–26.

Jacobsen, Thorkild. *The Sumerian King List*. Chicago: University of Chicago Press, 1939.

——. "Early Political Development in Mesopotamia," in *Zeitschrift für Assyriologie*, LII (1957), 91–140.

Kramer, Samuel N. "A 'Fulbright' in Turkey," *University Museum Bulletin*, XVII/2 (1952).

Kraus, F. R. "Zur Liste der aelteren Koenige von Babylonien," in *Zeitschrift für Assyriologie*, L (1952), 29–60.

——. "Nippur und Isin nach altbabylonischen Rechtsurkunden," in *Journal for Cuneiform Studies*, III (1951).

Lambert, Maurice. "La période présargonique. Essai d'une histoire sumérienne," in *Sumer*, VIII (1952), 57–77, 198–216.

Landsberger, Benno. "Die Anfaenge der Zivilisation in Mesopotamien," in *Journal of the Faculty of Languages, History, and Geography of the University of Ankara*, II (1944), 431–37.

Sollberger, Edmond. "Sur la chronologie des rois d'Ur," in *Archiv für Orientforschung*, XVII (1955), 10–48.

Speiser, E. A. *Mesopotamian Origins*. Philadelphia: University of Pennsylvania Press, 1930.

Woolley, C. Leonard. *Excavations at Ur*. London: Ernest Benn, Ltd., 1954.

——. *The Sumerians*. Oxford: Clarendon Press, 1929.

III SOCIETY

Diakonoff, N. M. *Sumer: Society and State in Ancient Mesopotamia.* Moscow: Academy of Sciences, U.S.S.R., 1959. In Russian with English résumé.

Falkenstein, Adam. *Die neusumerische Gerichtsurkunden.* Vols. I–III. Munich: Verlag der Bayerischen Akademie der Wissenschaften, 1956–57.

———. "La cité-temple sumérienne," in *Journal of World History,* I (1954), 784–814.

Forbes, R. J. *Metallurgy in Antiquity.* Leiden: Brill, 1950.

———. *Studies in Ancient Technology.* 6 vols. Leiden: Brill, 1955–58.

Frankfort, Henri. *The Art and Architecture in the Ancient Orien.* Baltimore: Penguin Books, Inc., 1955.

Hallo, William W. Early Mesopotamian Royal Titles. New Haven: American Oriental Society, 1957.

Lenzen, H. *Die Sumerer.* Berlin: Gebr. Mann, 1948.

Lloyd, Seton. *The Art of the Ancient Near East.* New York: Frederick Praeger, 1961.

Neugebauer, O. *The Exact Sciences in Antiquity.* 2d ed. Providence, R.I.: Brown University Press, 1957.

Neugebauer, O., and Sachs, A. *Mathematical Cuneiform Texts.* New Haven, Conn.: American Oriental Society and the American Schools for Oriental Research, 1945.

Oppenheim, A. L., and Hartman, Louis F. *On Beer and Brewing Techniques in Ancient Mesopotamia.* (Supplement No. 10 to the *Journal of the American Oriental Society,* December, 1950.)

Parrot, André. *Sumer.* New York: Golden Press, 1961.

Steele, Francis R. *The Code of Lipit-Ishtar.* Philadelphia: University Museum, 1949.

Woolley, C. Leonard. *The Art of the Middle East.* New York: Crown Publishers, 1961.

IV RELIGION

Dhorme, E. *Les religions de Babylonie et Assyrie.* Paris: Presses Universitaires de France, 1945.

Falkenstein, Adam, and Soden, W. von. *Sumerische und akkadische Hymnen und Gebete.* Zurich: Artemis Verlag, 1953.

Gadd, Cyril J. *Ideas of Divine Rule in the Ancient Near East.* London: Oxford University Press, 1948.

Jean, Ch.-F. *La religion sumérienne.* Paris: Paul Geuthner, 1931.

Labat, René. *Le caractère religieux de la royauté assyro-babylonienne.* Paris: Librairie d'Amérique et d'Orient, 1939.

Moortgat, A. *Tammuz.* Berlin: W. de Gruyter, 1949.

Sjöberg, Ake. *Der Mondgott Nanna-Suen.* Vol. I. Stockholm: Almquist and Wiksell, 1960.

V LITERATURE

Falkenstein, Adam. *Sumerische Goetterlieder.* Vol. I. Heidelberg: Carl Winter, 1959.

Gordon, Edmund I. *Sumerian Proverbs.* Philadelphia: University Museum, 1960.

Kramer, Samuel N. *Sumerian Mythology.* New York: Harper & Bros., 1961.

Van Dijk, J. J. A. *La sagesse suméro-accadienne.* Leiden: Brill, 1953.

VI EDUCATION

Falkenstein, Adam. "Der Sohn des 'Tafelhauses,'" in *Die Welt des Orients,* III (1948), 172–86.

Gadd, Cyril J. *Teachers and Students in the Oldest Schools.* London: School of Oriental and African Studies, University of London, 1956.

Kramer, Samuel N. *Schooldays.* Philadelphia: University Museum, 1949.

Landsberger, B. *Die Fauna des alten Mesopotamiens.* Leipzig: S. Hirgel, 1934.

VII CHARACTER

Kramer, Samuel N. "Love, Hate and Fear: Psychological Aspects of Sumerian Culture," in *Eretz-Israel,* V (1958), 66–74.

———. "Rivalry and Superiority: Two Dominant Features of the Sumerian Cultural Pattern," in *Selected Papers of the Proceedings of the Fifth International Congress of Anthropological and Ethnological Sciences* (1956), 287–91.

VIII LEGACY OF SUMER

Baltrushaitis, M. *Art sumérien, art roman.* 1934.

Kramer, Samuel N. "Sumerian Literature and the Bible," in *Analecta Biblica,* XII (1959), 185–204.

INDEX

347